MARGARET FULTON
My
Very Special
Cookbook

MARGARET FULTON

My
Very Special
Cookbook

OCTOPUS
AUSTRALIA

CONTENTS

First published 1980 by Octopus Books Pty Limited
55 Lavender Street, Milsons Point, NSW 2061

© 1980 Octopus Books Pty Limited

ISBN 0 7064 1291 5

Produced by Mandarin Publishers Limited
22a Westlands Road, Quarry Bay, Hong Kong

Printed in Hong Kong

Acknowledgments

I have received stimulus, encouragement and help from many directions in making 'my very special book' a reality.

Julie Gorrick, a friend and journalist colleague of many years, has contributed imagination, research skills and an earthy sense of humour to the job. They say laughter is a tonic and with Julie around the hard work does seem to slide down more easily!

Meg Thomason, a Cordon Bleu graduate and home economist, has a perfectionist approach to food that was invaluable in writing and testing recipes, and shares my belief that we eat with our eyes as well as our stomachs. Thank you for everything, Meg.

My niece Paula Fulton helped to type the manuscript and kept us going with tea and coffee and Pauline Robertson restored peace and order to my home after a hectic day's photography in the kitchen.

It has been a pleasure working with Lewis Morley, who took most of the photographs in the book. He is not only a craftsman but an artist in his own field, and his great interest in food encouraged me in many ways – a quality shared by Rodney Weidland, who took other photographs. I also thank *Woman's Day* for allowing me to use some of the food photographs that I first prepared for their pages.

In all the photographs you will see my own favourite china, glassware and silver, collected over many years and used from day to day in my home. If you love good food you want to enhance it with beautiful settings and I particularly want to acknowledge Christofle of France, Georg Jensen of Denmark, Lauffer of the USA, Arabia of Finland and Pillivuyt of France.

I am grateful to the food suppliers in my village of Balmain, and to these specialty cookware shops – The Balmain Scullery, Eloise Thunderpuss Parlour and The Village Store, Balmain.

The recipes themselves include many of my own favourites, old and new. I appreciate that I have been able to include a few special recipes that have appeared in the pages of *New Idea*, with the permission of my editor and friend Dulcie Boling. The book wouldn't have been the same without them.

Many of my friends will recognise some of their recipes and I thank them all for cooking beautiful meals.

To my own family, you know how much I owe you for supporting and encouraging me. Your love and interest adds a dimension of pleasure to my work that could come in no other way. You are all very special to me. Having you and the work I love makes my whole world a very special place.

INTRODUCTION

Writing this book has been a very special event for me in several ways. It is the first time I have combined the two sides of cooking in one book. There is all the basic information (from boiling an egg to roasting a chicken) plus a wealth of recipes for those looking for a different dish to prepare for family meals or something special for entertaining. Both of these sections go hand in hand for that ever growing band of people who love to cook.

It is also cooking brought completely up to date for the way we live today. New techniques, products, equipment and changing attitudes towards cooking and eating have all been considered. You will find much of the 'New Wave' approach included, as well as timeless classics and innovative ideas from around the world.

I have included an introduction to most recipes, which is useful in giving the 'feel' of the finished dish and have added notes where they will be helpful.

I am repeating the system which proved such a success in my first book, *The Margaret Fulton Cookbook*. The recipes have been given a one, two or three spot rating.

- A simple and quick recipe that a beginner could accomplish with ease.
- ● ● Dishes for the average cook with a knowledge of basic techniques but requiring a little more time.
- ● ● ● A special dish, requiring more skill and probably taking some time to prepare.

Beginners should not be discouraged from trying three spot recipes, just be prepared to give them more time and concentration.

The commonsense approach to cooking has been combined with the fun of learning and the joy of creating . . . not to say the satisfaction of eating. It has to be a special art form that combines all those magic ingredients.

Here's to all of us who love to cook!

NOTES

In some parts of the world cooks are already at ease with metric measures. In other countries the changeover to metrics is recent or still going on. I have included both metric and imperial measures to make the recipes as easy as possible. It is advisable to buy the equipment approved by the Standards Association of Australia. For more information on the cups and spoons, see page 11.

All spoon measurements are level
All cup measurements are level
Use a measuring cup or jug for liquids
All ovens should be preheated to the specified temperature, particularly for cakes, biscuits and pastry recipes
Unless otherwise specified, use a standard egg of 55 g weight
Use granulated sugar unless otherwise specified

THE COMMONSENSE WAY TO GOOD COOKING

Is cooking worth the trouble? Very definitely yes! Is it worth the trouble to learn the fine points of cooking? Again a definite yes!

You have to learn the basic information about cooking any food to get it right, but the learning soon becomes a part of the pleasure, fascination and challenge of this creative art. And it's one art you can practise any time to give great pleasure to others, as well as yourself.

Even if you are strictly a 'survival' cook, this section is for you. I have written it for the new single, who really doesn't know how to boil an egg; for those bored with the few things they can already cook, but uncertain how to branch out; for the harried worker who doesn't want to get involved in 'fancy' cooking but does want to manage the necessary buying and cooking efficiently and to eat enjoyably. And of course, for the housewife who may still feel a little uncertain about one or two basic processes. What is the temperature for roasting a leg of lamb and how long does it take to cook? How much meat should you buy per serving? How do you make gravy? Can you grill a pork chop? How do you get potato chips really crisp?

Last but not least, this section is also for the keen cook who needs a quick checkpoint for an occasional detail – the quantity of raw rice to give 2 cups of cooked or the proportion of butter to flour in a béchamel sauce. It is all here, and to set you off on the right track I have also given a list of the kind of cookware I use, the kind of knives, and a few of the gadgets that have become basics in my own kitchen.

However, if you're the kind of adventurous cook who likes to plunge straight into a recipe, don't think you have to linger over this chapter before getting started. The recipes are complete in themselves and set out in a way I am sure you will find easy to follow.

This chapter is here when you need it for ready reference, but use it to suit your own needs and experience.

This is a chapter to make learning what it should be – half the fun of cooking!

UTENSILS

It is not necessary to have great numbers of fancy utensils or machines to cook well. It is important, however much or little you cook, to have good, dependable equipment that does the job. Some basics such as good knives and saucepans are expensive – in that case, put all your money into one or two excellent pieces that you can put to many uses and add to them as you are able, rather than buy a set of second-raters. Look for equipment in shops that supply the professionals, or in specialist cook shops.

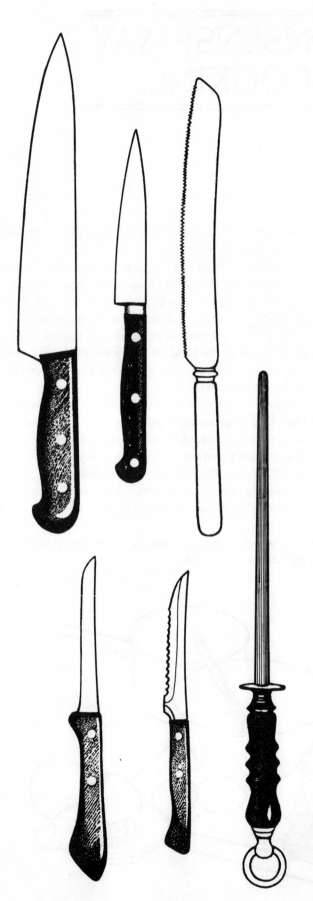

Knives

Top quality knives are all-important. If you are a serious cook, take a deep breath and pay what you must for, at least, the chef's knife listed here first. Try to also buy the paring knife. All the others are desirable, but you can survive with just these two and a stone or steel for keeping them with a good edge.

French-style Chef's Knife (large and heavy). A 25 cm (10 inch) blade is a good size. Most professional chefs still use carbon-steel blades, which take a fine edge and resharpen easily, but they can be a nuisance to keep clean and rust free. You will probably be better served by stainless steel, which can still have an edge like a razor if you look after it as I advise below.

Paring Knife This is a much smaller version of the chef's knife, with an 8–10 cm (3–4 inch) blade. It fits the hand for peeling and close work.

Serrated Knife Buy this knife with a blade at least 20 cm (8 inch) long. A serrated knife is the best tool for cutting bread and pies and cakes without squashing them.

Boning and Filleting Knife Also useful for slicing meats. It has a narrow, flexible blade as opposed to the rigid blade of the chef's knife. Usual length of blade is about 15 cm (6 inch).

Fruit and Vegetable Knife This has a smaller, serrated, pointed blade, usually about 10 cm (4 inch) in length. It should be stainless to prevent staining or marking by the acids in fruit.

A Stone or a Steel This is a must. No knife, however razorsharp, will hold its edge for long without attention. Pick up the steel nearly every time you pick up your knife, and just draw the edge, from heel to tip, down the front and then the back of the steel several times, almost flat. Have your knives resharpened, professionally, three or four times a year.

Keep your knives sharp at any cost, drawing the blade over an oilstone or even using one of those handy sharpening wheels if you can't conquer a steel.

Care of your knives Knives must be stored separately to preserve their edge. You can buy a special rack or block for the purpose or simply fasten a strap, nailed on at intervals to fit your knives, across the inside of a cupboard door. Slip the knives into the slots for easy storage. Knives should be washed separately, and by hand, as soon as you have used them. Rub them with salt on a cloth wrung out in cold water after using for onion or garlic.

Measuring Cups and Spoons

These *are* necessary to ensure success with recipes. To help you with the changeover to the metric system, I have included both metric and imperial measures in this book. The exact conversions between metric and imperial units are quite complicated, but my recipes preserve the correct balance of ingredients.

I have used cup and spoon measurements wherever possible to simplify things and I advise you to have the following in your kitchen.

Nest of 4 Graduated Measuring Cups These come in ¼, ½, ⅓ and 1 cup sizes. Use for measuring dry ingredients.

Measuring Cup The standard 250 ml metric cup should be used for measuring liquids.

Litre Measuring Jug For measuring larger quantities of liquid. This shows both cup and metric measures and is marked every 100 ml up to 1 litre and every metric cup (250 ml) up to 1 litre.

Set of Graduated Measuring Spoons The Australian standard tablespoon of 20 ml and teaspoon of 5 ml. The set includes a tablespoon, teaspoon, half-teaspoon and quarter-teaspoon.

Scales are an enormous asset, and nowadays are usually marked in both metric and imperial measures. Scales are needed for weighing meat, vegetables and bulky items.

The Chopping Board

This should be thick and flat so as to resist warping after many washings. Unless the board is absolutely flat, the slicing knife misses a through cut of the food. It should be large enough to hold the food that falls away from the knife and perhaps scatters a bit. Scour it with a handful of salt and cold water after using it for onion or garlic. Wood is better than hard plastic because it is kinder to knives.

Bowls

A graduated set of three is ideal. Buy pottery or heatproof glass, not plastic. Pottery or heatproof glass will clean more satisfactorily and also serve as pudding basins or sit over a saucepan to become a double boiler. A few good quality melamine mixing bowls are a useful addition.

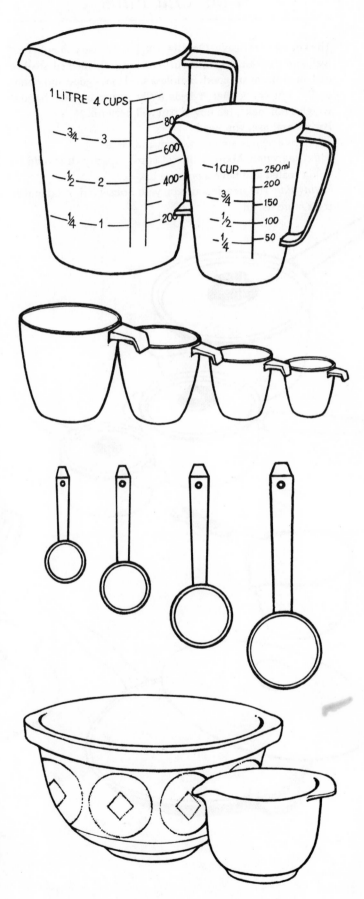

Pots and Pans

The key word is heavy. Only a thick, heavy base will hold heat well and distribute it without scorching. Enamelled steel or cast aluminium are good. Stainless steel looks good and cleans easily, but check that it feels really heavy in your hand – weight, not looks, tell how a pan will perform.

For general use, you need:

Three Saucepans small, medium and large.

Milk Saucepan About 1 litre (4 cups) capacity. It should be teflon coated and have a pouring lip.

Frying Pan The size depends on your household. A lid makes it far more useful.

Ovenproof Dishes and Casseroles

You will probably build up a collection of these as the shops are full of temptations. The basics to aim for are:

Gratin Dishes One or more, in varying sizes. These are shallow and open and are designed so that food can be browned on the top either in the oven or under the grill. Gratin dishes are even more useful if they are flameproof (can be used on top of the stove) as well as ovenproof.

Casseroles Choose sizes appropriate to your needs, but be sure they are thick based and have well-fitting lids. A casserole is far more useful if it is flameproof, so it can be used on top of the stove for preliminary browning of meat, etc. The best all-purpose material, in my opinion, is heavy, enamelled cast-iron. Flameproof pottery can also be very good, and in recent years the Finns have developed some excellent flameproof pottery. Pyroceram is spectacular in its ability to withstand extreme changes from cold to heat. It performs well in the oven, but, being a poor conductor, tends to develop hot spots which can scorch the food when used on top of the stove.

Roasting Pan Buy two pans if possible, so one can act as a lid when called for. If no roasting pan is available, a large gratin dish or a shallow casserole without its lid can double for the job.

Rack Should fit into the roasting pan to hold roasts, and may double as a cake or biscuit cooler.

Good quality basic equipment makes cooking easier and is a sound investment. Start with essentials then add as you can.

Above: A food processor chops, slices and blends all manner of foods in a few seconds. Spanish teacake is prepared in just a few minutes (see page 307).

Right: Eggs are among the most versatile of foods and the French omelette is one of the world's great classic egg dishes (see page 21).

14

This cheese basket offers a selection of blue cheese, green peppercorn, Brie and Gouda cheeses. Fresh dates and Quince Cheese (see page 342) make a good contrast.

Spoons, Whisks and Spatulas

Wooden Spoons Have one or more. Keep one spoon especially for highly flavoured foods such as garlic, onions and curries. This stops the flavour transferring and avoids curry flavoured custards.

Wooden Spatulas Like a wooden spoon without the bowl. They are used for stirring sauces, where a spoon would collect a lump of thicker paste in its bowl.

Rubber Spatula For getting all the food out of bowls and pans and for folding and spreading.

Wire Whisks Wonderful for beating egg whites and for blending ingredients smoothly into sauces and soups.

Rotary Beater Buy a strong, good quality one with smooth action.

Other Basic Essentials

Sieves Nylon for fruit purées, metal for sifting flour and straining vegetables.

Grater A square stainless steel one is the best buy.

Lemon Squeezer

Potato Peeler Peels potatoes, carrots, apples and cucumbers. Will also string beans and flake almonds; a swivel blade is best.

Egg/Fish Slice With slots to drain fat or liquid.

Rolling Pin A plain, heavy cylindrical one is best.

These are the basic essentials which you will get out and use again and again. There are, of course, dozens of more specialized items that you may want for particular operations – piping bag, poultry shears, skewers, ladles, potato masher, dredgers, rotary grater, pastry brush, cake tins, soufflé dishes and so on.

Add slowly to your basic collection, after considering whether a special item will really earn its keep and storage in your kitchen.

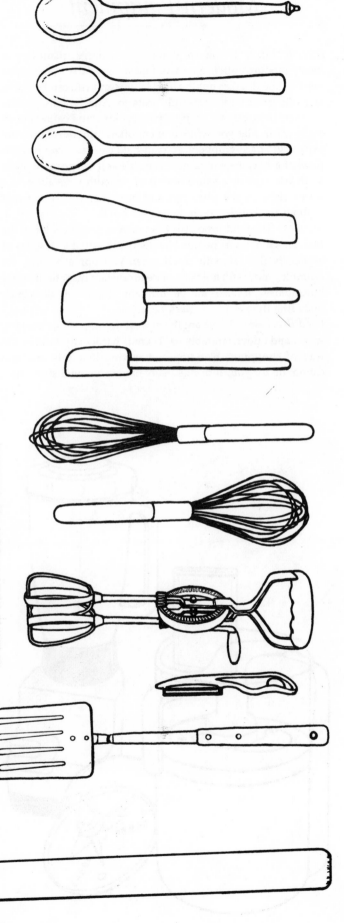

Modern Equipment

Electric Mixer If you are going to beat large quantities or heavy mixtures often, you will find a large mixer on a stand worthwhile. It takes out the hard labour and you can be doing something else while it steadily beats on. Attachments, such as a mincer or juicer, are useful if your cooking and eating habits really mean that you will use them often, otherwise they are expensive space-grabbers. A hand-held electric mixer has less power for big jobs, but is more versatile as it can go to the stove to whisk eggs or a sauce over heat, smooth vegetables to a purée right in the saucepan and beat ingredients together without transferring them to another bowl.

Blenders The food processor has taken over quite a lot of the blender's functions, but the blender is still valuable. It gives an especially fine, smooth result when you purée a soup, for example, and it still holds its place for instant mayonnaise and hollandaise. It also makes brilliant drinks of all kinds, including the meal-in-a-glass variety.

Food Processors These are the newest darlings of the cooking world and understandably so. There is hardly anything in the way of chopping, blending and mixing that this machine cannot do for you. It brings many haute cuisine dishes, once forbiddingly difficult, within your reach.

Freezers It is hard to imagine cooking today without any recourse to a freezer. It is useful for storing ingredients such as fresh breadcrumbs, tomato purée and stocks in convenient quantities and for holding leftovers until they can return in a fresh guise. A freezer enables us to make good bulk buys in meat and poultry and means we can have at hand the inevitable, but so useful, frozen vegetables and sliced bread for toast!

How much freezer is right for you? It depends on what you want from it and on how organised you are prepared to be about using it to advantage. A big freezer full of good food can be blissful security, and a money saver too, but you do have to be reasonably systematic about planning, purchasing, storing and using those goodies, in order to make the cost of the freezer and of running it worthwhile. You will find advice in this chapter on freezing different foods.

Microwave Ovens This innovation is not likely to replace the conventional oven but it does perform so many small miracles that it seems to have a place in a busy household that can afford the luxury of this most modern of cooking aids. In my own household I use the microwave many times a day, not for complete cooking of dishes but for all the little jobs it does along the way. It is a luxury but used wisely it is an asset.

EGGS

If you have eggs, you have a meal. Eggs are nutritious, economical and quick to prepare. While eggs are one of the quickest things in the world to cook and probably one of the easiest, there are a few pitfalls – as anyone who has cooked a poached egg for the first time or curdled a custard will tell you. Eggs are sensitive to high heat and to overcooking, so as with many things don't be lulled into carelessness by the apparent simplicity of cooking an egg.

Buying Eggs

Buy the freshest eggs you can find (for a town-dweller, the best you can do is to buy at a busy shop, where the eggs are sold quickly).

To check freshness, break an egg on to a plate. The yolk should dome up well and the white should be thick and translucent. A stale egg spreads out thinly and weakly.

Eggs are marketed in several sizes. Recipes in this book, unless otherwise stated, assume that you are using 55 g (2 oz) eggs.

To Store Eggs

Never wash eggs before storing. Keep them in the refrigerator, away from strong tasting foods. An egg will stay fresh for a week or two if kept cold, but for a much shorter time if kept in a warm place.

It is a good idea to remove eggs from the refrigerator the day they are to be used. Eggs at room temperature are less likely to break in hot water than very cold eggs, the yolks and whites mix more readily and the whites will beat to greater volume.

To store egg whites, put in an airtight container in the refrigerator. To use them, measure 1½ metric tablespoons for each egg white. To store egg yolks, cover with water (which is drained off before using) and refrigerate.

To Freeze Eggs Eggs can be frozen, but the yolks become gummy unless they are stabilized with salt or sugar. To freeze whole eggs, break and stir gently, then mix in ½ teaspoon of salt or 2 teaspoons of sugar for every six eggs; label accordingly and use for savoury or sweet dishes, as appropriate.

To freeze egg yolks, stir and add ½ teaspoon of salt or 2 teaspoons of sugar for every 6 yolks. Label and use for sweet or savoury dishes as appropriate. Egg whites can be frozen just as they are, and, when thawed, will whip up like fresh ones.

Thaw eggs quickly and use promptly. *Never refreeze.*

Basic Ways of Cooking Eggs

Always cook eggs over a gentle heat. Even boiled eggs should only be simmered or they become tough. The exception is an omelette, which should be cooked fast, but very briefly.

Boiled Eggs

•

Have eggs at room temperature, or, if they are straight from the refrigerator, warm for a few minutes in hot water. Heat enough water in a saucepan to cover the eggs. When the water boils, place the eggs one at a time in a spoon and lower gently into the water. Keep the heat high until the water reboils. Lower the heat or draw the pan aside a little so that it only simmers. Time the eggs *from the time the water reboils*, as follows:

Size of Egg	Soft	Medium	Hard
45 g (1½ oz)	2 min. 40 sec.	3 min. 20 sec.	7 min.
55 g (2 oz)	3 min.	3 min. 50 sec.	8 min.
60 g	3 min. 20 sec.	4 min. 15 sec.	10 min.

To prevent unsightly darkening of the yolk surface of a hard-boiled egg, take care not to overcook it. As soon as it is done cool it rapidly under cold running water, tapping it gently all over to crack the shell. Shelled hard-boiled eggs should be stored in cold water.

Poached Eggs

•

Use very fresh eggs, straight from the refrigerator as they hold their shape better.

Take a shallow pan with a lid, half-fill it with water, add a dash of vinegar and bring just to the boil. Break each egg into a cup and slip it gently into the water. As soon as the last egg is in, place the lid on, take the pan off the heat and time 3½ minutes for soft eggs or 4 minutes if you like them firmer.

Lift the eggs out with an egg slice, rest for a few moments on a clean cloth or kitchen paper to drain, then slide off and serve at once.

Poached eggs are usually served on hot buttered toast for breakfast, but there are other ways. Serve the eggs on spinach, with poached haddock or coat with mornay sauce and a little grated cheese and place under the grill for a moment, they make a delicate meal for any time of the day.

Scrambled Eggs
•

Break the eggs into a bowl allowing at least two per person. Add salt, freshly ground pepper and one tablespoon of milk or cream per egg. Beat with a fork until thoroughly mixed.

Melt a nut of butter in a small saucepan, preferably a non-stick one, and let it just melt and foam slightly. Keep the heat low, pour the eggs in and immediately begin to stir with a wooden spoon or spatula, making sure to reach into the curves and keeping the bottom well scraped. When the eggs are set but still very creamy, serve at once. Take the eggs off the heat when they are just a little softer than you want them, as they will firm up from their own heat by the time you have dished them up.

Variations

With Bacon Fry the bacon first and use the bacon fat, instead of butter, for scrambling the eggs. Alternatively, pour the eggs in on top of the fried bacon and stir together.

With Cheese Add 1 tablespoon of grated cheese, for every two eggs, to the raw mixture.

With Herbs Add chopped parsley, snipped chives or any other herb, to taste, to the raw mixture.

Cold Scrambled Egg Sounds strange? It makes a beautiful topping for asparagus, prawns, salami or smoked salmon, placed on a slice of buttered bread for a Danish open sandwich.

Fried Eggs
•

Melt enough bacon fat or butter in a frying pan to cover the bottom. Break the eggs, one at a time, into a cup and slide them into the pan. If the fat splutters too strongly turn the heat down or draw the pan aside a little. If the eggs cook too quickly the whites will be tough. If there is no sizzling at all, the fat is not hot enough to set the whites. Turn the heat up, and when the whites are setting, turn it down again. As the eggs gently fry, baste by spooning the fat from the pan over the yolks to set the 'veil' of white over them. When the whites are set but the yolks are still wobbly, the eggs are fried as most people like them. Lift out with an egg slice and serve at once.

Some people like a 'turned' egg, and this also helps to cook the yolk on the top; flip the egg over, leave for a few seconds, and serve.

Bacon and Eggs • Remove rind from bacon with scissors or hold a straight knife blade against the rind and tear it off towards you. Place the bacon in a cold pan and cook slowly over a gentle heat for 4–6 minutes, turning with tongs two or three times.

If you like crisp bacon, keep pouring off the fat as it runs out (this can be kept for frying the eggs). Remove the bacon to a warm plate and keep hot. Add a little extra fat or butter to the pan, if needed, and fry the eggs as above.

Baked Eggs
•

Preheat oven to moderate (180°C/350°F). Butter small ramekins and carefully break an egg into each one. Season with salt and freshly ground pepper and cover with a teaspoon of warm cream or melted butter. Place in the oven and bake for 8 to 10 minutes or until the white is set and the yolk still runny. Serve in the ramekins.

Variations

Place a spoonful of cooked, diced bacon, ham, chicken liver or salami or cooked chopped spinach, in the bottom of each ramekin before breaking in the egg. Alternatively, sprinkle the egg with grated cheese before adding the cream, or use a spoonful of cheese or tomato sauce instead of the butter or cream to cover the egg.

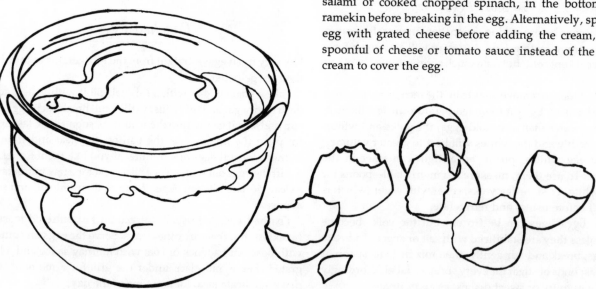

Omelettes

Be sure that you have everything ready that you will need before you start to cook an omelette – the filling, omelette pan heated and at hand, the serving plate hot and the eater waiting.

Basic French Omelette

• •

3 eggs
1 tablespoon water
½ teaspoon salt
freshly ground pepper
15 g (½ oz) butter

Have the eggs at room temperature. Break the eggs into a bowl, add the water and beat lightly with a fork to just combine the whites with the yolks. It is important not to overbeat as it makes the omelette tough. Add the salt and a grinding of pepper.

Melt half the butter in a frying pan and when the foam has subsided pour in the beaten eggs. Using a fork or a metal spatula pull the egg mixture from the edge towards the centre, allowing the uncooked mixture to run to the outside. Do this until the eggs have set underneath but the top is still quite moist.

Flip over one third of the omelette towards the centre, then turn over again so that it is folded into three. Roll out on to a heated plate.

Melt the remaining butter in the same pan and when it is sizzling pour it over the omelette. Serve at once. *Serves one*

Variations

If you are going to fill the omelette, spoon the heated filling across the centre just before it is rolled up and turned out. You will need about 3 tablespoons of filling for each individual omelette.

Asparagus Use only the tips of cooked fresh or canned asparagus. Season with salt and pepper and heat in a little butter.

Mushroom Chop some mushrooms and cook lightly in a little butter, season to taste. For an elegant finish, trim the stem of one mushroom level with the cap, slice downward and just colour the slices in butter, then lay them, neatly overlapping, along the top of the finished omelette.

Crab or Salmon Flake some canned crab or salmon and heat in a little cream, with a chopped shallot and a grating of cheese.

Cheese Mix 60 g (2 oz) grated Cheddar cheese with 1 tablespoon chopped parsley and a grinding of pepper. Sprinkle half the mixture over the omelette before folding and the rest over the top.

Fine Herbs The official fine herbs are parsley, chervil, tarragon and chives. Add any two, three or all of the herbs, finely chopped, to the uncooked mixture before making the omelette.

Onion Cook 1 sliced onion in butter for 10 to 15 minutes or until soft. Stir in ½ cup grated cheese and season to taste.

CHEESE

Cheese means a world of flavours. It can appear in every course on the menu; it combines magnificently with other foods; makes the perfect companion to wine or stands alone as an ever-ready snack. Nutritionally, it is one of your best buys, giving a wide range of vitamins and minerals and more protein, weight for weight, than any other food.

Buying Cheese

Cheeses are classified by texture.

Fresh unripened cheeses such as cottage cheese, ricotta and cream cheese are used for salads and savouries and for cooking, especially in sweet dishes.

Soft cheeses include Camembert, Brie and blue vein. Serve them on the cheese board or for dessert with fruit. Mozzarella is another soft cheese that melts lusciously for pizzas or other Italian dishes.

Firm cheeses are the all-rounders, splendid as cocktail food, sandwich fillings, on the cheese board or with fruits or grated into sauces, soups, fondues or vegetable dishes. Cheddar, Gruyère, Emmenthal, Edam and Gouda are some of the most famous.

Hard cheeses such as Parmesan and Romano have undergone long maturing and develop a sharp flavour. These are grating cheeses to sprinkle over pasta or rice or to hand at the table as a garnish for soups.

To Store Cheese

Cheese keeps best if it has some air circulation. In general, store it in a loosely covered container in the refrigerator. Delicately flavoured dessert cheese is best stored on a plate and covered with just damp cheesecloth or muslin in the refrigerator. Hard cheese may be hung on a hook in the kitchen, as the cheese-sellers hang it.

Remove cheese from the refrigerator at least an hour before serving it. It cannot release its full flavour when cold and a very soft cheese will be rubbery instead of richly flowing.

The firmer the cheese the longer it will keep. Fresh unripened cheeses stay at their best for only a few days; soft cheeses for a week or more and firm cheeses up to a month or so. Hard cheese will keep for a very long time if it has good air circulation around it.

You need never waste a scrap of cheese. Dried up or mouldy pieces can have the mouldy surface cut off and be grated and frozen for use in cooking. Make your own good potted cheese by grating all the little leftover bits (or whiz them in a food processor) and add softened butter and sherry, port or brandy to give a creamy texture, with herbs, nuts, spices, mustard or cayenne pepper for extra flavour.

To Freeze Cheese Freezing affects the texture of most cheese, making it crumbly and unsuitable for table use. Flavour is not affected, so cheese may be frozen and later used for cooking. Wrap it well in moisture-proof wrapping.

It is a good idea to freeze cheese in small separate quantities that will be right for a single dish. Flavour is not fully restored until the cheese is completely thawed, but you can add it frozen to dishes that are going to be heated.

Serving and Cooking Cheese

A cheese board should offer a choice from cheeses of distinctly different flavours and textures. You may select just one soft and one firm cheese to serve at the dinner table, or a wider choice to accompany drinks or for a wine and cheese party. Remember, that generous wedges of just a few cheeses look far more tempting than lots of little pieces! Soft flowing cheeses such as Camembert should be placed on the cheese board uncut and may be served on a grape or lettuce leaf.

The French say that unbuttered French bread is the proper thing to serve with cheese but water biscuits or other crisp thin crackers are also an excellent accompaniment. For variety, oat cakes (Scottish or Irish) are another idea.

Cheese is usually listed after dessert on printed menus and is often served at the very end of the meal, but I prefer to do as the French do and put the cheese board on the table after the main course so that diners can finish their red wine with some cheese.

When you are using cheese in cooking remember that overcooking makes it tough, so always heat it very gently and for no longer than it takes to melt. Hard cheese must be finely grated so that it will melt readily. Firm or soft cheese should be shredded rather than grated and very soft cheese need only be sliced before adding to a dish.

FISH

Fish is a delicate food and must be cooked carefully to preserve its moisture and fine flavour. Once you understand the few simple principles of handling and cooking fish, it can be one of your most versatile and useful stand-bys.

Fish is the basis of some of the most exquisite dishes in the world, and it is also the hurried cook's friend. A few minutes on the grill, in the pan or poaching dish, a little garnish, and you have a meal to serve proudly to anyone.

Buying Fish

Freshness is everything. Buy fish where it comes in and goes out quickly, from a fish shop with a good source of supply. The fish market of course is ideal.

Learn to recognise freshness. A fresh fish has a bright, clear eye, flat gills which are red underneath, a clenched mouth and feels slippery, not tacky.

If you are buying fillets, the flesh should be firm and resilient and the skin should again be slippery but not tacky. Above all, your nose tells you. All fish should 'smell of the sea', fishy but fresh. If there's the slightest hint of ammonia, don't buy, the 'off' smell will persist through cooking.

How much to Buy If you are buying whole fish, allow 500 g (1 lb) per person; if buying fillets, you will get 2 large or 3 average servings from 500 g (1 lb).

To Store Fish

Don't store fish for long, unless you are freezing it. Buy on the day of use, if possible. Store fish in the coldest part of the refrigerator, loosely covered in foil.

To Freeze Fish Prepare the fish as for cooking. Cut the fish into steaks or fillets and skin them, if preferred. Several fillets may be packed together to suit the family's needs. Each piece should be separated by a sheet of freezer paper.

If freezing fish whole, remove the scales, head and fins. Gut the fish, then wash and dry with absorbent paper. Wrap each fish separately in freezer paper and overwrap in a freezer or polythene bag. Use within a month or two for the best results.

Shellfish such as oysters and scallops should be removed from the shell and frozen in containers, covered with their own juices, and with the addition of a brine, made by adding two teaspoons of salt to 500 ml (2 cups) of water, if necessary.

Crab and lobster should be cooked, the meat removed from the shell and packed in containers.

To Prepare Fish

If you are buying fish, ask the fishmonger to clean and scale it for you. If the fish has been given to you or you have caught it yourself, you can do the scaling and cleaning at home. Spread out several thicknesses of newspaper under a chopping board making sure a large area is covered, as the scales fly everywhere. Wash the fish briefly in cold water, scales are more easily removed from a wet fish. Grasp the fish firmly with a cloth, by the tail. Beginning at the tail, scrape firmly towards the head with a small rigid knife, a sharp old spoon or a serrated fish scaling knife. Hold the knife at a slight angle, towards the tail, from the upright. Repeat on the other side.

Next, gut the fish. With a small, sharp knife, cut the entire length of the belly and pull out the entrails with your hand. It's not really messy or difficult, as they are all enclosed in a thin pouch which should come out easily. Wash the fish inside and out under cold running water. With a small knife remove the dark vein, which is inside the fish, under the backbone. Wash again and dry the fish well.

Filleting and Skinning Fish

To Fillet Round Fish With a sharp, flexible knife make a clean cut along the backbone of the fish from the back of the head to the tail. Cut round behind the head. Place the knife flat along the backbone and cut, with a sliding action, until the fillet is freed all the way to the tail. Turn the fish over and cut away the second fillet in the same way. (See below.)

To Fillet Flat Fish For fish such as flounder, lay the fish on a board with the tail towards you. Make a cut down the back-bone from the head to the tail. Flat fish, such as flounder, have the backbone in the centre, not at the edge.

Starting from the head, on the left hand fillet, cut round behind the head, and using a sharp flexible knife, slide the blade down along the bones to the tail. Remove the fillet, then turn the fish round and remove the second fillet in the same way, but work from tail to head. Turn the fish over and repeat with the two fillets on the other side. (See right.)

To Skin Fish Fillets Place the fillet, skin side down, on a board with the tail towards you. Make a small cut through the flesh at the tail end. Dip your left fingers in salt and hold the skin firmly, if right-handed. Pull the skin towards you, while with the right hand you ease a knife between the flesh and skin. Reverse if left-handed. To remove any fishy odour from the board, knife and your hands, rinse in cold water then rub with salt and vinegar. (See below right.)

Basic Ways of Cooking Fish

Fish is easy to cook, but it is also easy to spoil. The one great rule is, don't overcook. Fish usually cooks in minutes only, so watch it carefully. When the flesh turns white, it is cooked. For a whole fish, insert a toothpick into the thickest part, near the bone. If it slides in easily and you can flake the flesh a little away from the bone, the fish is cooked.

Shallow-fried Fish

•

For small whole fish, steaks or fillets coat the fish with seasoned flour, with flour, beaten egg and breadcrumbs, or with flour and batter.

Heat 5 mm (¼ inch) of oil in a frying pan. When the oil is hot enough to brown a small cube of bread in less than 60 seconds, it is ready. Place the fish in the oil and cook on both sides until golden brown and the flesh is white.

Cooking time depends on the thickness – a fillet 1 cm (½ inch) thick takes only 2 or 3 minutes on each side. Drain on crumpled kitchen paper and serve immediately.

Fillets Sauté Meunière • Skin the fillets as described left. Put a little clarified butter, or half oil and half unsalted butter, in a frying pan, using just enough to cover the base. Dip the fish into milk then dust lightly with seasoned flour and place into the hot butter mixture. Cook the first side for 2 to 4 minutes or until a delicate brown, then turn and cook the other side. Remove to a hot plate.

Add a little more butter to the frying pan and while foaming, add the strained juice of a lemon, chopped parsley, and salt and pepper. Pour over the fish, garnish with sliced lemon and serve at once.

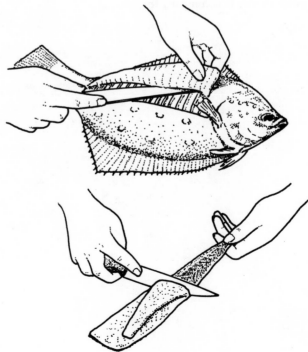

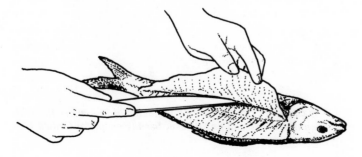

Deep-fried Fish
••

This is fish in the traditional Fish and Chips style.

Batter for Fish • Sift one cup plain flour and a pinch of salt into a bowl. Make a well in the centre. Lightly beat one egg and one egg yolk (reserve the white for later) and stir into the well with 2 tablespoons melted butter. Gradually stir in 1 cup beer or soda water. Stir until the mixture is smooth, then cover and stand in a warm place for 1 hour. Just before using, fold in the stiffly beaten egg white. This quantity of batter is sufficient for 6 thick fillets.

To Fry Fish Dry the fish on paper towels. Flour lightly and dip in the batter. Heat 1 cm (½ inch) of oil in a large frying pan. When the oil is ready place the fish in and allow 2 to 4 minutes each side, according to thickness. Drain on crumpled kitchen paper. Serve as soon as possible with lemon wedges.

Note: Do not crowd the fillets together in the pan. If necessary, cook them in batches, keeping the cooked pieces hot in a warm oven with the door open. It is also better that the diner waits for the fish, not the fish wait for the diner.

Poached Fish
•

This method is suitable for fillets, steaks or small whole fish.

Prepare a court bouillon. Place 1 cup water, ½ cup white wine or 1 tablespoon white wine vinegar, 1 bay leaf, 1 small sliced onion, 2 parsley stalks and 1 teaspoon salt in a pan. Bring to the boil then simmer for 5 minutes; strain. Pour into a flameproof dish, add the fish, then cover with foil or buttered kitchen paper. Poach very gently over a slow heat, or in a moderately slow oven (160°C/325°F) until the fish is white and flakes easily.

Note: Fish must poach and *never* boil (see Words You Should Know, page 346). Poaching liquor should just cover the fish – increase this recipe if necessary. The liquor can be used to make a sauce to accompany the fish.

Grilled Fish
•

The secret of success with grilling fish is to use thick, skinned fillets or steaks and to cook on one side only on a preheated grilling pan, metal tray or grilling rack covered with foil (the edges turned up to make a tray).

Heat the foil-covered pan and melt 15 g (½ oz) butter per piece of fish. Wipe the fish with damp kitchen or paper towels, sprinkle with a little flour and season with salt and pepper. Turn in the melted butter to coat. Grill for about 8 minutes for a 2 cm (1 inch) thick steak, and 4 to 5 minutes for a fillet. During grilling, baste once or twice with the pan juices.

Small whole flat fish (sole or flounder), can be grilled in the same way. Other fish are grilled on both sides – if thick, slash two or three times through the thickest part. A small whole fish takes about 15 minutes to grill.

Baked Fish
••

This method is suitable for whole fish and thick fish steaks. Generously butter an ovenproof dish. Place the fish in, brush with melted butter or oil, season with salt and pepper and add a little lemon juice or white wine. Cover with well-buttered foil or greaseproof paper. Bake in a hot oven (200°C/400°F), allowing 6 to 10 minutes for every 500 g (1 lb), plus 6 to 10 minutes over. Cooking time depends on the thickness of the fish; a stuffed fish will take a little longer to cook. Baste several times with the pan juices during cooking. It is easiest to serve baked fish if you choose a cooking dish that can go straight to the table. Alternatively, line a baking dish with a double thickness of aluminium foil, allowing it to overlap at each end and form 'handles'. Then you can easily transfer the cooked fish to a heated serving platter.

Fish cooks to perfection with a minimum of fuss under the grill. Even new cooks will find it easy. See the recipe for Grilled Fish (above).

Right: First quality lamb has light, reddish-pink meat with an even edge of firm white fat. Fresh herbs are a natural partner.

Below: Stir-fried vegetables are bright and crisp (page 34). With them are Stuffed Zucchini (page 221) and Artichokes à la Grecque (page 196).

Trussing a chicken before roasting, helps it to keep a good shape. The chicken is also easier to carve after cooking. Add different herbs for your own special touch (see right).

POULTRY

Chicken is full of possibilities. Will you have it roasted, poached, fried or grilled? Curried? In a creamy sauce, in red wine, hot or cold? It is the most versatile of all meats, excellent value for money and just as ready to provide a simple meal for one as to star at a dinner party.

Mass marketing has brought the other great table birds, duck and turkey and goose, into our kitchens more often than before, but they still have an air of glamour which pays a compliment to guests. Game birds such as quail and pheasant are also a superb choice for a very special occasion.

Buying Poultry

You can be reasonably confident that any prepackaged bird labelled as a roaster will be quite young and tender. In chicken pieces, look for soft white skin as a sign of young birds. If you are buying unpackaged chicken, the classic test for a young, and therefore tender bird, is that the end of the breastbone is flexible and bends readily when pressed. A good duck or goose should have a plump breast with a pliable breastbone and a creamy colour. A turkey should have bluish-white skin and a broad plump breast.

How Much to Buy

Chicken
For each serving, allow approximately:
375 g (12 oz) for roast or fried chicken;
500 g (1 lb) for grilling or barbecuing and 250–500 g (8 oz – 1 lb) for casseroles, depending on whether there are other ingredients, such as vegetables, to extend each serving.
500 g (1 lb) of raw chicken will give 1 cup cooked chicken for salads etc. Chicken pieces, such as breast, yield a little more.
Duck
Duck has a larger carcass and less meat than chicken.
1.4 kg (3 lb) duck, roasted, will serve 2 to 3 people
1.6 kg (3 lb 2 oz) will serve 3 to 4
2 kg (4 lb) will serve 4
2.5 kg (5 lb) will serve 5 to 6
Turkey
A 3–4 kg (6–8 lb) turkey, unstuffed weight, will serve 8 to 10 people
A 4–6 kg (8–12 lb) bird will serve 10 to 14
A 6–8 kg (12–16 lb) bird will serve 14 to 16
Goose
Allow 750 g (1½ lb) goose per serving

To Store Poultry

Use fresh poultry within two or three days of purchasing. If it is prepackaged, take it out of its package. Store in the coldest part of the refrigerator, loosely covered with foil, muslin or Chux cloth wrung out in water.
To Freeze Poultry Poultry to be frozen must first be dressed. Giblets should be wrapped and frozen separately, not inside the bird, because their recommended storage time is less. Birds may be halved or jointed ready for cooking, then wrapped well in freezer paper or foil. Several pieces may be packed together, separated by sheets of freezer paper.

Never stuff a bird before freezing. The stuffing slows the rate of freezing, will become moist and may develop off flavours.

Thaw frozen birds slowly, preferably in the refrigerator. This will take from 24 to 48 hours depending on size. Pieces of poultry can be cooked without thawing, but will need to be done at a moderate heat and for longer than usual. Test to make sure the pieces are completely cooked.

Basic Ways of Cooking Poultry

Follow recipes carefully for poultry dishes, paying special attention to the suggested cooking times. Overdone poultry becomes dry and stringy. To check a roast bird, pierce the thickest part of the thigh with a skewer. The juices should run clear. Test with a skewer, too, to see whether fried, sautéed or grilled pieces are cooked through. Clear juice shows that they are done.

Roast Chicken

Set the oven at hot (200°C/400°F). Put a little salt and pepper, 30 g (1 oz) butter and a little tarragon, rosemary or other herbs inside the chicken.
Truss the chicken Shape the bird with both hands, tucking the neck flap underneath the folded wing tips at the back. Take a piece of string and place the middle of the string below the breast and bring it down over the wings to cross underneath. Bring the ends of the string up to tie the legs and the parson's nose together. Rub all over with 30 g (1 oz) of butter.

Lay the chicken on its side on a rack set in a roasting pan. Place in the oven for 10 minutes then turn on to the other side. Reduce the heat to moderately hot (190°C/375°F) and continue to cook, turning and basting every 15 minutes. Turn on its back for the last 20 minutes to brown the breast. Allow about 25 minutes cooking time for every 500 g (1 lb). Very small birds will take a little more and very large birds a little less time per 500 g (1 lb).
Gravy Pour off all but 2 tablespoons of juice from the pan. Add 1 scant tablespoon flour and stir well over moderate heat until lightly browned. Pour in the remaining juice or juices and water to make 1½ cups, stir until thickened, and season with salt and pepper.

Fried Chicken
● ●

Only young chicken should be fried. Dust serving pieces with flour and coat with beaten egg and fine breadcrumbs. In a heavy frying pan heat enough butter and oil to come halfway up the chicken pieces. When the foam subsides, arrange the chicken in one layer. Don't crowd the pan, and fry in batches if necessary. Cook over a moderate heat until golden on one side then turn and cook the other side. Cooking time will be from 15 minutes for breasts to 25 minutes or so for thicker pieces. Drain the chicken on crumpled kitchen paper and serve immediately.

Poached Chicken
●

This method is especially suitable for birds whose tenderness is doubtful and also to make juicy, flavourful meat for salads, sandwiches and dishes calling for cooked chicken.

Take a heavy saucepan, put in the chicken and cover with water for pieces, or add water to come to the top of the thighs (with the bird lying on its back) for a whole chicken. Add salt and pepper and a little chopped carrot, celery and onion and a few herbs. Cover and cook very gently, just simmering, for 30 minutes or more if the bird is a boiler. Test with a skewer in the thickest part of the thigh. When the meat feels tender and does not resist the skewer it is done. Cool in the liquid where it will continue to 'cook' then store in a covered bowl with some of the liquid which has now become chicken stock to use in soups or sauces.

Braised Chicken
● ●

This is the method that gives chicken casserole with the chicken brown but moist and served in its thickened juices. You can use pieces or a whole bird (which should be trussed before cooking).

Choose a heavy casserole, heat a little butter in it and when the foam subsides place the chicken in and brown all over. Remove the chicken and add a little sliced carrot, celery and onion to the casserole. Fry until golden then place the chicken on top of the vegetables. Add a few herbs and salt and pepper and pour over 2 cups of chicken stock or water, with a

little dry red or white wine if liked. Cover the casserole and cook slowly, just simmering, for at least an hour for a whole bird and about 30 minutes for pieces. Test with a skewer, the meat should feel very tender and the juices should run clear. When cooked, remove the chicken and keep warm, thicken the liquid slightly with beurre manié, (see Words You Should Know, page 346), whisked in a little at a time, then return the chicken to the casserole and serve.

Note: You can add small potatoes or other vegetables to the casserole to serve with the chicken. Time the additions so that the vegetables will have their usual cooking time in the liquid.

Sautéed Chicken
● ●

Heat a little butter and oil in a heavy frying pan. When the foam has subsided, place well-dried chicken pieces in, skin side down in one layer. Don't crowd the pan; cook in batches if necessary. Cook briskly, shaking the pan a few times, for 2 or 3 minutes until golden, then turn and sauté the other side. As the chicken browns, remove to a warm plate and season with salt and pepper. Replace the leg and thigh pieces in the pan, add a little more butter if necessary and cook slowly for 8 or 9 minutes. Add the breast and wing pieces, cover and continue cooking for about 15 minutes, turning and basting several times during cooking. When the chicken is cooked, remove from the pan and keep warm. If liked, add spring onions, chopped parsley, mushrooms, tomatoes or wine or a combination of these, to the pan and cook for a few minutes to make a sauce for the chicken.

Grilled Chicken
● ●

This is ideal for smaller chickens or tender pieces. For a whole bird, split in half and cut away the back and rib bones. Arrange the pieces, skin side down, on the preheated and greased rack of a grilling pan. Melt a little butter and brush the chicken with it. Grill under a moderate heat, turning once and basting with butter often. Grilled chicken halves take from 30 to 50 minutes to cook; test with a skewer to tell when they are done. Pieces take 15 to 20 minutes depending on size; cook as for halved chickens, turning once during cooking.

MEAT

Meat is probably considered the finest food we have at our command. It represents hearty eating and well-being and it is the basis of a vast range of good dishes. As meat has become more expensive, it becomes a greater challenge to get the very best from it and to widen our repertoire to include interesting treatments of the lesser known cuts and variety meats.

Buying Meat

You can judge meat to some degree by its appearance, but you must rely largely on the skill and integrity of your butcher for first class meat. Shop around until you find the right butcher and treasure him. Eating is the final test, but here are some points to help you appraise quality.

Beef should be bright cherry red when freshly cut, and finely grained. There should be flecks of fat (marbling) through it. The fat should be firm, smooth and creamy white.

Lamb should have light reddish-pink flesh and an even edging of firm white fat.

Pork should have pale pink, finely grained flesh, pearly white fat and thin, smooth skin.

Veal should be very pale, pinkish, finely grained and smooth. There should be only a thin edge of white satiny fat. The bones are large in proportion to the size and should be bluish white.

How Much to Buy

The amount of meat for each serving varies, of course, with appetites and the type of dish. As a general guide, allow:

125–250 g (4–8 oz) per serving of boneless cuts such as stewing meat, roasts and steaks and minced meat.

155–250 g (5–8 oz) of meat with some bone, such as chops, T-bone steaks and rib roast on the bone.

375–500 g (12 oz–1 lb) of bony cuts such as spare ribs, lamb shanks and bone-in shoulder.

To Store Meat

As a general rule, the larger the piece of meat, the longer it will store. Minced meat, sausage and variety meats should be cooked within 24 hours of purchase.

Diced meats should be used within about 48 hours. Steaks and chops will keep for 2 to 4 days and roasts for 3 to 5 days. Store meat in the coldest part of the refrigerator, loosely covered with foil.

To freeze meat It is practical to prepare meat ready for cooking by trimming or cutting it up before freezing. Wrap meat well in foil or freezer wrap. You may wish to pack several pieces such as steaks or chops etc. together in the right quantity for one dish or one meal. Separate each with sheets of freezer paper.

Cooking Meat

Tenderness in meat depends partly on the age of the animal and also on the cut. Tender cuts come from those parts of the animal where the least body movement occurs, such as the loin and rump. These cuts respond to dry-heat cooking: so roast, grill, fry and sauté them.

Tougher cuts have more connective tissue and need slow cooking with moisture: braise, stew, pot-roast or poach these cuts. In these slow cooking processes, the liquid should never go above simmering point. (See Words You Should Know, page 346.) Some meat dishes are traditionally called 'boiled' but this is a misnomer – meat that is cooked at full boiling point loses its juices and becomes tasteless and dry. Boiled meat is in fact simmered or poached in the liquid.

Always remove meat from the refrigerator in time for it to reach room temperature right through before cooking it. Cooking times are based on meat at room temperature.

When is meat done? Cooking times given with recipes may be used as a guide, but the shape of the piece, the quality of the meat or the efficiency of your stove can cause variation.

To test large pieces of meat, a meat thermometer is ideal as it is marked at the correct internal temperature for different meats. Insert the thermometer into the thickest part of the meat away from fat and bone, leave for a minute then read it.

Failing a thermometer, or for small cuts, press the meat with your finger. If it is soft and spongy it is not cooked through. If it is soft but quite springy, it is medium-rare. If it is firm with little resilience, it is well-done.

You can also test by inserting a skewer into the thickest part of the meat and checking the juice that comes out. If it is red, the meat is rare; if pink, medium; if clear, well-done.

Basic ways of Cooking Meat

To Roast Meat

There are two styles of roasting.

For quick roasting, the meat is put into a hot oven (220°C/425°F) for the first 20 minutes then the heat is lowered to moderate (180°C/350°F) for the rest of the cooking time. If you love that crispy brown outside to the meat, this is the method you will probably prefer.

For slow roasting, the meat is cooked in a moderately slow oven (160°C/325°F) for the whole cooking time. This gives moister meat with less shrinkage, but it does not have a crisp outside.

To roast meat Preheat the oven and place the meat on a rack in a roasting pan. If the meat is placed straight into the pan the bottom part will fry as the fat collects. A roast is cooked uncovered.

Except for pork, meat should be basted every 15 to 20 minutes with fat or pan juices. Pork is not basted as this prevents the crackling from becoming crisp. Lamb and beef will usually provide their own fatty juices, but veal should be spread with butter or covered with bacon as it has little natural fat of its own.

Always allow meat to rest in a warm place for 15 minutes before carving. This is imperative. It allows the juices to settle into the tissue so that when it is carved the meat holds its juices.

Guide to Roasting times

(For medium done roasts)

Type of meat	Quick roasting	Slow roasting
	(220°C/425°F) for 20 minutes then (180°C/350°F)	(160°C/325°F)
Beef	20 minutes per 500 g (1 lb) plus 20 minutes	30 minutes per 500 g (1 lb) plus 30 minutes
Lamb	25 minutes per 500 g (1 lb) plus 25 minutes	40 minutes per 500 g (1 lb) plus 40 minutes
Veal	Not suitable	45 minutes per 500 g (1 lb) plus 45 minutes
Pork	35 minutes per 500 g (1 lb) plus 35 minutes	Not suitable

To Grill Meat

Because grilling is a quick and dry method of cooking the most tender cuts are the most suitable, though it is possible to grill some of the cheaper cuts successfully after marinating or tenderizing.

Preheating the grill is most important. It should be as hot as possible for red meats and moderately hot for white meats. Allow up to 20 minutes heating before starting to cook. When you are ready to start, brush the food with oil or melted butter and the grill rack with oil, then place the food on the rack. Turn the meat with tongs or two spoons *not* with a fork as this will prick the meat and allow the juices to escape.

To grill red meat It is best to have steak cut thick, about 3.5 cm (1½ inch). Cook a thick cut under very high heat for a minute or two on both sides to seal in the juices, then lower the heat to moderate. Better still lower the meat from the heat and continue to cook, turning once, until the meat is cooked as desired.

Thinner pieces such as lamb chops are grilled quickly for the whole cooking time; if the source of heat seems too hot lower meat from grill rather than reduce heat. Most modern grills can be elevated and lowered.

A thick steak will take about 15 minutes for medium-rare, 20 minutes for medium. Lamb chops and cutlets, cut 2 cm (¾ inch) thick, will take 8 to 10 minutes.

To grill white meat Pork and veal should be cut 2 cm (¾ inch) thick and grilled under moderate heat, basting or brushing often with oil or butter and turning once.

Pork or veal should be cooked until well-done with juice that runs clear. Pork of this thickness takes about 14 to 16 minutes, veal about 12 to 14 minutes. Veal may be dusted with a little flour after brushing with oil or butter to give a golden finish.

To Fry Meat

To shallow fry meat This is the cooking method used for meat in a coating, usually egg and breadcrumbs. Breaded lamb cutlets and Wiener Schnitzel are examples.

In a heavy frying pan heat enough butter and oil to come halfway up the pieces. When the foam subsides arrange the pieces in one layer without crowding the pan. Cook in batches, if necessary. Cook over a moderate heat until golden then turn and cook the other side. If cooking the meat in batches, keep each batch warm in the oven until ready to serve.

Drain on crumpled kitchen paper and serve immediately.

To Sauté Meat

Meat to be sautéed should be a tender, quick cooking cut. Tournedos and filet mignon, liver, lamb cutlets and noisettes come to mind. Have the meat at room temperature.

Heat a little butter and oil in a heavy frying pan and when the foam subsides put the pieces in, in one layer. Don't crowd the pan, as steam will form if there is no space between the pieces. Keep the heat high and shake the pan to stop the food from sticking. When beads of blood appear on the surface of the meat, turn and brown the other side. If the pieces of meat are thick, turn the heat down or draw the pan aside a little and cook until done as you like it.

To Braise Meat

Braising is the cooking method that gives us casseroles of tender brown meat in its own rich sauce. It is used for meat that is cut into small pieces, serving size pieces or for joints, and is a good treatment for some of the less tender cuts.

Heat a little fat in a heavy flameproof casserole and brown the meat all over. Cook in batches if necessary. Remove the meat and add sliced vegetables to the casserole; these are usually a selection from carrots, celery, onion and garlic. Fry the vegetables until golden, place the meat on top of them and add about 2 cups of stock, water, wine or a mixture of these. Season to taste with salt and freshly ground pepper. Bring to simmering point on top of the stove and then simmer very gently either on top of the stove or in the oven.

You can thicken the sauce at the end of the cooking with a beurre manié (equal quantities of butter and flour blended together). Beat the beurre manié in, a small piece at a time, until well blended then simmer for a few minutes.

VEGETABLES

A well cooked vegetable is a delight, a badly cooked one is a crime. Remember that most vegetables are beautiful to look at and reasonably edible before they are cooked, so that they require only a modicum of sympathetic treatment to bring them to perfection for the table.

Buying Vegetables

Try to buy on the day that supplies come into the shop, in quantities that you will use within a day or two for greens and salad vegetables, a week or two for root vegetables.

When buying root vegetables, look for those that are clean, firm, unmarked and well-shaped. Green vegetables should be crisp and brightly coloured. Brussels sprouts, cabbage, cauliflower and broccoli should be firm and tightly grown. Most really fresh vegetables have a sheen, while beans have a velvety look.

Storing Vegetables

Do not wash vegetables until you are ready to use them.

Store leaf vegetables, peas and beans in plastic bags or a covered crisper, in the refrigerator. The exception is watercress, which should have the stem ends trimmed and then stand in 2.5 cm (1 inch) of water in a covered container in the refrigerator.

Cut any leaves away from root vegetables before storing in a cool, dry, dark place on racks or in baskets raised from the floor to ensure adequate ventilation.

Freezing vegetables All vegetables *except* those which have a high water content and are eaten raw, such as lettuce and cucumber, can be frozen. These will be limp and mushy when thawed. Tomatoes and celery will also be soft and collapsed, but they can be used in cooking.

Vegetables to be frozen should first be blanched in boiling water or steam to arrest the working of enzymes that would affect colour, flavour and nutritive value during storage. Preparation for freezing and blanching times vary with different vegetables and you should consult a freezer book for detailed instructions.

Most vegetables should be cooked frozen, check a freezer book for details.

Basic Ways to Cook Vegetables

To Boil Vegetables

The rule of thumb is that vegetables that grow under the ground, 'in the cold and dark', should be cooked 'in the cold and dark', that is they should be placed in cold salted water just to cover and cooked with the lid on.

Vegetables that grow above the ground, 'in heat and light', should be cooked 'in heat and light', that is in boiling salted water with the lid off. The exception to this general rule are small, new root vegetables which are placed into boiling salted water.

The watchword for all vegetables is, do not overcook. Cook greens and other, above-ground vegetables, only until they are tender but still slightly crunchy. Drain thoroughly and either toss with a little butter and serve at once or place immediately under cold running water to refresh (stop cooking and set the colour). When ready to serve, reheat the vegetable by tossing with butter over a fairly low heat.

Cook root vegetables until just tender when tested with a fine skewer; further cooking will make them soggy. Drain well and return to the saucepan for a minute or so, shaking once or twice over a low heat to dry off.

To Bake Vegetables

Root vegetables and pumpkin can be baked unpeeled. Scrub well and brush with oil or wrap in foil if you want a soft skin. If you want crisp skin on potatoes or sweet potatoes, rub with a little salt instead of oil. Bake unpeeled vegetables on a flat oven tray or directly on the bars of the oven rack at 220°C (425°F) until they are soft all the way through when tested with a fine skewer. An average potato takes about 50 minutes.

Vegetables to accompany a roast should first be peeled and parboiled (for about 5 minutes) then drained and dried well and the surfaces lightly scored with a fork. About 30 minutes before the meat will be done, either place the vegetables in the roasting pan or in a separate pan with some of the fat from the roast, plus extra hot dripping or butter if needed. Turn the vegetables so they are coated all over with the fat and bake, uncovered, until browned and tender.

To Shallow Fry Vegetables

Vegetables which cook quickly, such as onions, mushrooms, tomatoes, eggplant and zucchini can be sliced and sautéed in a little butter and oil, turning once. If liked, dredge a little seasoned flour on the slices before they are sautéed to give a crusty finish.

Sautéed potatoes, one of the great potato dishes, is made by boiling unpeeled old potatoes. Peel the potatoes and slice thickly then cook briskly in a little butter and oil, turning constantly, to give the desired crumbly outside of potatoes cooked in this way.

Chinese stir-fried vegetables This is the wonderful Chinese way with vegetables that leaves them crisp-tender and bright in colour. They are traditionally cooked in a wok but can be done in a frying pan.

Use a mixture of leafy vegetables, such as spinach and cabbage, tender vegetables such as mushrooms, zucchini and bean sprouts and firmer ones such as broccoli, beans and root vegetables.

Cut each vegetable into uniform pieces, slices or shreds, and the broccoli into little branches. Parboil the tougher vegetables in a little water or stock, drain and dry well.

Heat until very hot, about 2 teaspoons of oil for each 500 g (1 lb) of vegetables. If liked, add a slice or two of fresh ginger or garlic for a minute then discard before adding the vegetables.

Place those vegetables that take the longest to cook into the pan first. Add the more tender vegetables about a minute or two later and the leafy vegetables last. Keep the heat high and stir and toss the vegetables constantly so that they are all coated with oil. Cook until just tender but still crisp, usually about 3 or 4 minutes.

Sometimes a little water or stock is added, the wok or pan is covered and the vegetables are steamed for a minute or two.

Turn immediately on to a hot serving dish and be sure that the diners are ready – stir-fried foods should be eaten at once.

To Deep Fry Vegetables

French fries and potato chips ● ● This is the method that produces the classic French-fries or potato chips.

Cut potatoes into uniform thick slices or sticks, and wash and dry well.

Half-fill a deep fryer or large saucepan with oil and heat to 170°C (360°F). Failing a thermometer, test with a cube of bread; the oil is ready when the bread browns in 60 seconds.

Place the potatoes, about a cup at a time, into the oil and fry until they are soft but not coloured. If possible, use a frying basket.

Lift out the potatoes, drain and place on absorbent paper. Repeat with the remaining raw potatoes. You can do this stage

hours ahead of serving time but in any case, cool at least 5 minutes before starting the second stage.

Heat the oil to 190°C (390°F) (when a bread cube browns in 30 seconds) and fry the potatoes again for a few minutes until crisp and golden brown. Drain on absorbent paper and salt lightly. Serve at once.

Vegetable fritters ● ● Vegetables such as onion, eggplant, green pepper, zucchini and mushrooms are coated with flour, egg and breadcrumbs or dipped into batter or into seasoned flour, then milk and flour again, then deep-fried at 190°C (390°F) until golden. Cauliflower or broccoli pieces, artichoke hearts and other vegetables may also be deep-fried in this way but are cooked first.

To Steam Vegetables

Steaming gives excellent flavour and texture, though green vegetables lose some of their bright colour because they must be cooked covered. Bring an inch or two of water to the boil in a saucepan and then set a steaming basket or colander containing the prepared, salted vegetables in the saucepan (the water must not touch the bottom). Cover tightly and steam for 3 to 5 minutes longer than the vegetable usually takes when boiled.

To Braise Vegetables

Celery, leeks, Brussels sprouts, broccoli, lettuce and endive can be braised to make a first course or an interesting accompaniment.

Blanch the vegetables by cooking, uncovered, in boiling salted water until half-done. Drain and place in a shallow baking dish with melted butter. Turn to coat in the butter then add stock, to come half-way up the vegetables. Cover and cook slowly on top of the stove or in the oven until the vegetable is very tender and the liquid has reduced to make a sauce in which the vegetable is served.

Vegetables cooked à la grecque are examples of braised vegetables (see page 58).

RICE AND PASTA

Learn to cook these two great staples perfectly and use them to make splendid one-dish dinners, fast economical lunches, interesting first courses and hearty puddings, or as the indispensable accompaniments to many meat and seafood dishes.

Buying Rice and Pasta

There are reputedly over 7,000 varieties of rice, but most cooks are only concerned with the main differences. Rice may be short, medium or long grain.

Short plump grain is best for puddings because it clings together more when cooked to give a creamy texture. The short grains are favoured for risottos, rice rings and moulds. Italian grocers sell plump, almost round rice which is ideal for risottos.

Medium and long-grain rice are used for plain boiled rice and savoury rice dishes. They cook to give separate, well-defined grains so that the dish is not sticky or lumpy. Basmati rice from Pakistan is wonderful in pilaus and birianis.

Brown rice has the brown husk still on it, giving a nutty flavour. Since the husk is bran, using brown rice is an excellent way to add roughage to the diet. It is washed then soaked in cold water for 30 minutes before cooking, and takes much longer to cook than polished (white) rice, about 30–45 minutes.

Wild rice is a type of grass, grown in North America. It is very expensive but has an intriguing flavour which goes well with poultry. You should find it at continental delicatessens.
How much to cook Rice cooks to approximately 3 times its raw volume. One cup raw rice weighs 200 g (7 oz) and will make 6 to 7 servings of plain boiled rice as an accompaniment.

Pasta comes in over 500 different kinds and shapes. Substitute one kind for another or use an unusual shape.
How much to cook 500 g (1 lb) raw weight of pasta serves 4 as a main course, 6 as a first course or accompaniment.

To Store Rice and Pasta

Buy only as much rice or pasta as you expect to use within about a month. If they are held for long periods they may develop weevils. Store airtight in a dry, cool place.
To freeze rice and pasta Plain boiled rice and pasta can be frozen but this is seldom worthwhile as they need no more effort and time to cook freshly. Made-up rice and pasta dishes can be frozen for a short time – one month maximum is recommended. Pack them in lidded containers. Do not freeze rice or pasta in liquid, e.g. in a soup, as they go mushy.

Cooking Rice and Pasta

Boiled Rice

•

This is one method for rice as a hot accompaniment, or for rice salad. Depending on the type of rice, wash if necessary.

In a large saucepan bring 12 cups of water with 3 teaspoons of salt and 2 lemon slices to a rapid boil. Slowly sprinkle in 1½ cups of rice through your fingers. Stir once then cook, uncovered, for 12 to 15 minutes; keep the water at a brisk boil.

Test by lifting out a grain or two and testing between your teeth. The rice is cooked when it is soft but still slightly resistant to the teeth; this is called al dente.

Drain the rice in a colander and run hot water through it to separate the grains and wash out any clinging starch.

Rice may be kept hot in a colander standing over a saucepan of boiling water, and covered with a kitchen towel. This method is virtually foolproof in producing fluffy rice with the grains separate, and is a good one to begin with.

Steamed Rice

•

Use hot as an accompaniment or cold for salads, or cook a day ahead and chill overnight then fry for Chinese dishes.

Add ½ teaspoon salt to 2 cups of water in a saucepan and bring to the boil. Slowly sprinkle 1 cup of rice, keeping the heat high so that the water does not come off the boil. Stir once, then cover with a well-fitting lid and turn the heat to very low (if necessary use an asbestos mat). Avoid lifting the lid until the last few minutes of cooking. Cook very gently for 17 to 20 minutes until a test grain is tender but firm when bitten. Remove from the heat, uncover and fluff up with a fork.

To Cook Pasta

All pastas are cooked initially in the same way. Depending on the dish, the pasta may then simply have a sauce added or it may be combined with other ingredients and baked.

Take a pan that will hold a large quantity of water. You will need at least 12 cups for 250 g (8 oz) of pasta. Bring the water to a rapid boil, add 3 teaspoons of salt and a teaspoon of oil and drop the pasta in, keeping the pieces separate. Stir well and boil rapidly until it is tender but firm when tested.

Spaghetti will take about 12 minutes; tagliatelle (long ribbon strips) about 8 minutes; vermicelli (long thin threads) 8 to 10 minutes; ravioli (squares of pasta) about 15 minutes and cannelloni (large pipes or squares) about 12 minutes.

When placing long spaghetti in the water, hold a handful at one end and put the other end in. As the spaghetti softens, curl it round until it is all submerged, pushing in the last ends.

When pasta is cooked, remove from heat, pour 2½ cups of cold water into the pan to stop boiling, then drain well. For best results, pasta should be served immediately.

35

Grains and Pulses

These are some of man's oldest basic foods. Use them as your mother did to stretch the more expensive ingredients in a hearty soup or stew, but don't miss their potential as stars in their own right for today's stylish, health-conscious way of eating.

Whole grains and pulses (dried peas, lentils and beans of all kinds) are rich sources of vitamins and minerals. They also contain proteins which, though incomplete in themselves, need only be served with a small quantity of eggs, milk, cheese or meat to contribute handsomely to your protein needs.

Feature traditional dishes of grains and pulses from other cultures. The Middle Eastern Hummus bi Tahina (savoury chick pea dip) and Tabbouli (tomato, cracked wheat and herb salad) are now favourites with Western food enthusiasts.

Besan (chick pea flour) gives distinctive flavour to Indian-style vegetable fritters and atta (fine wholemeal flour) makes flat breads to accompany a curry.

Serve a purée of dried beans or peas, smothered with butter and flavoured with bacon or garlic and black pepper, instead of an ordinary cooked vegetable with sausages, pork or poultry.

Make your own muesli with toasted oats, wheatgerm and dried fruits for a top-nourishment breakfast or whiz a tablespoon of wheatgerm with a tablespoon each of lemon juice and honey, an egg and a cup of orange juice in the blender for an instant meal in a glass.

Buying Grains and Pulses

The dried form is the traditional and most economical way to buy grains and pulses, but you can now find some already cooked in cans. If you are buying them dried, get only the amount that you are likely to use in a month or so. These foods lose flavour and may be subject to infestation if kept for long periods. For the same reason, buy where they are sold fairly fast so that you are getting fresh stock. You will find a reasonable variety at good groceries and supermarkets but a visit to a health food store or better still a shop specializing in ethnic foods will offer a wider choice of interesting possibilities.

One cup of peas, beans or lentils weighs about 220 g (7 oz) and will expand to 2 to 2½ cups after cooking. This will equal two 300 g (9½ oz) cans.

To store grains and pulses

Store in airtight containers in a cool place and, as noted before, try to use them within a month of purchase.

To freeze grains and pulses

Cooked grains and pulses freeze well. Pack them in covered containers. Thaw in the refrigerator before using or use them straight from the frozen state by heating over simmering water or adding to a casserole or soup for heating.

To Cook Grains and Pulses

Grains and pulses are usually soaked in cold water overnight before cooking but beware of soaking them for too long as they may ferment. A quick and good way to tenderize them for cooking is to cover with cold water, bring to the boil and simmer for 2 minutes. Remove from the heat and let stand, tightly covered, for 1 hour. This is almost equivalent to 8 hours soaking. Cook in the same water unless it is bitter – if so, drain and cover with fresh water to cook, adding salt. You can also add flavourings such as an onion, carrot, celery, bouquet garni, garlic or bacon bones or trimmings according to the dish.

Pulses vary in cooking time according to the variety and age. Bring to the boil and skim well then cover the saucepan and simmer over a low heat. Cook lentils, which seldom need soaking for about 30 minutes; peas and beans for about an hour, then try one from time to time until they are tender to the bite.

Cooking with dried peas and beans can be tricky as the minerals in the water and the degree of heat used can affect different types of beans in different ways. It is difficult to determine the age of a dried bean, but the older it gets the drier it becomes, so this will have a bearing on cooking time.

Sugar and acid foods such as tomatoes tend to have a hardening effect on beans, therefore always soften beans thoroughly before using them in baked beans, chilli and similar recipes.

To cook barley, cover with salted cold water then simmer until tender. Cracked wheat for tabbouli is not cooked but soaked in cold water for about 2 hours then drained, squeezed as dry as possible and spread on a tea-towel to dry further.

Perfectly grilled steak needs a preheated grill (see page 32 for directions). Serve steak with a choice of mustards, crusty bread and a salad.

Above: Toasted oats, wheatgerm and dried fruits combine to make a nourishing muesli. Add orange juice or meal in a glass (see page 36) for a well-rounded breakfast.

Right: Rice can be simple or exotic. In this dish the rice is coloured and flavoured with saffron (see page 246) then teamed with Spiced Chicken Breasts (see page 144).

SAUCES AND SALAD DRESSINGS

The world of fine sauces rests on just a few techniques. You don't have to 'learn' dozens of sauces; become proficient at three or four ways of putting one together and you will find that every new sauce you meet is only a variation of one you already know.

All good sauces have one thing in common: they complement the food they accompany but do not overwhelm it. A good sauce is made from the best possible ingredients so that it has a delicate, natural flavour and character in its own right. Remember, it is the actual flavour of the ingredients that makes the finished sauce, and nothing less can give the same taste and appearance.

A sauce should have body but must never be so thick that it sits heavily on the food.

A pouring or flowing sauce should run freely off a spoon, a coating sauce should be just dense enough to cling to the food but not to blanket it thickly. Be ready to add a little more milk, cream, stock or hot water if your sauce is too heavy.

A white or light-coloured sauce should ideally be seasoned with white pepper. Black pepper will show as dark specks in the sauce.

The classic sauces are one of the glories of cooking and they will always be used. However, we must admit that the cream, butter and eggs which make them so beautiful also conflict with today's health-conscious light eating style. To help you balance your diet while still eating well, I have included in this section some clever sauces from the Cuisine Nouvelle or New Wave Cooking which depend on purées of vegetables or fruit or on light non-starch thickeners, such as Crème Fraiche and Fromage Blanc for thickening.

Storing Sauces

Sauces should be stored in the refrigerator. Cover with plastic wrap placed directly on to the surface of the sauce, and then with a lid. Most sauces can be reheated. Place the bowl or pan containing the sauce in a pan of hot water and stir over very gentle heat until it reaches the desired temperature. Emulsion sauces such as Hollandaise and Béarnaise must not be heated beyond lukewarm; place the sauce container into a pan of warm water off the heat and stir.

Freezing Sauces

Sauces thickened with flour or a purée can be frozen. To serve, thaw and heat in a bowl over gently simmering water or in the top of a double boiler, stirring often. Hollandaise-type sauces may also be frozen. Thaw and warm by standing the container in warm water, stirring the sauce often.

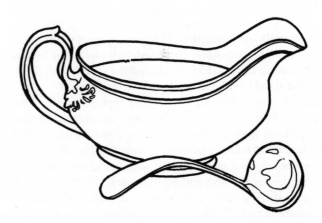

Making your own sauces is enjoyable and worth it for the end result and taste. From the rear: Béchamel (page 42), Vinaigrette (page 46), Mayonnaise (page 45) and Mint Chutney (page 63).

Sauces Based on a Roux

A roux is a cooked mixture of fat and flour which thickens a liquid to make a sauce. The fat used for white sauces is generally butter and for brown sauces, oil or clarified butter.

A roux may be white, blond (straw-coloured) or brown; the different colours are used for specific sauces. The colour of a roux depends on how long it is cooked but it must always be cooked over a low heat and stirred constantly. Cooking the roux over a high heat would make the sauce grainy in texture instead of smooth.

The thickness of a roux-based sauce depends on the proportion of flour to liquid. Brown sauces should not have more flour added than the recipe states, but

Béchamel and Velouté (and their variations) may be made thicker or thinner depending on their use.

For a flowing sauce to use as an accompaniment in a separate sauce boat or as the basis of a cream soup, the basic proportion is 30 g (1 oz) of butter and 1 tablespoon of flour to 1 cup of liquid.

For a coating consistency to cover food in the dish in which it is to be served, the basic proportion is 60 g (2 oz) of butter and 2 tablespoons of flour to 1 cup of liquid. If you are going to finish the sauce with a liaison of egg yolk and cream (which thickens a little more) you will need a slightly higher proportion of liquid. A thicker consistency still, with 90 g (3 oz) of butter and 3 tablespoons of flour to 1 cup of liquid, is called a panada and is used as a base for binding croquettes or for soufflés.

Béchamel Sauce

•

This is the basic white sauce to serve on vegetables or fish. It has its own delicate flavour or can be developed with flavourful additions into other well-known sauces.

2 cups milk
1 slice onion
8 peppercorns
1 bay leaf
1 small celery stalk
blade of mace
60 g (2 oz) butter
2 tablespoons flour
salt
white pepper
nutmeg

Place the milk in a saucepan with the onion, peppercorns, bay leaf, celery and mace. Heat gently until it is just below boiling point (when a few bubbles form round the edge). Take off the heat and stand for 20 minutes to infuse; strain.

Melt the butter in a heavy saucepan then stir in the flour. Lower the heat and cook gently for 1 minute, stirring. Remove the pan from the heat, allow to cool for a minute or two then add the milk all at once and stir until smoothly blended. Return the saucepan to a medium heat and stir continually until boiling. Lower the heat and allow to cook very gently for 15 minutes, stirring frequently. Season with salt, and pepper to taste and add just a hint of nutmeg. *Makes approximately 2 cups*

Variations

Mornay Sauce To 2 cups of Béchamel Sauce, gradually add 45 g (1½ oz) grated Parmesan, Gruyère or sharp Cheddar cheese and a pinch of dry mustard.

Use to coat fish, vegetables, chicken or eggs. To make the dish into a gratin, place under a hot grill or in a hot oven until the top is golden.

Cream Sauce To 2 cups of Béchamel Sauce, add ¼ cup of cream. Bring to the boil then add a few drops of lemon juice.

Use for food that is served creamed – eggs, chicken, vegetables, veal. Add a tablespoon of capers and a teaspoon of chopped parsley to serve with grilled or poached fish.

Mushroom Sauce To 2 cups of Béchamel Sauce, add 125 g (4 oz) diced, sautéed mushrooms.

Serve with grilled lamb or with poultry, eggs or fish.

Mustard Sauce To 2 cups of Béchamel Sauce, add 1 tablespoon of dry English mustard blended with a little water.

Serve with boiled meats such as corned beef or with poached fish.

Parsley Sauce To 2 cups of Béchamel Sauce, add 4 tablespoons finely chopped parsley and a few drops of lemon juice.

Serve with corned beef, tripe, poached chicken or fish.

Horseradish Sauce To 2 cups of Béchamel Sauce, add 2 tablespoons of prepared horseradish.

Serve with boiled meats such as fresh beef or tongue.

Brown Sauce

••

Brown Sauce (or one of its variations) is used with roasts, grills and sautées of red meat and also with browned poultry. It is an essential ingredient in French cooking for some of the great savoury meat dishes.

2½ cups brown stock
3 tablespoons clarified butter or olive oil
1 small carrot, finely diced
1 small onion, finely diced
1 small stick celery, finely diced
1 tablespoon flour
1 tablespoon tomato paste
bouquet garni
5 peppercorns
few mushroom trimmings (optional)
salt
freshly ground black pepper

Warm the stock and set aside. Heat the clarified butter or oil in a heavy saucepan, add the vegetables and cook over a low heat until the vegetables are golden, stirring occasionally. Stir in the flour and continue to cook very slowly, stirring all the time until the roux is hazelnut brown. Remove from the heat and cool a little. Add 1½ cups of the stock all at once and stir until smoothly blended. Stir in the tomato paste and add the bouquet garni, peppercorns and mushroom trimmings, if using. Return to a medium heat and stir until boiling. Half-cover with a lid and simmer for 25 minutes. Skim off any scum that rises to the surface during this time. Add half the reserved stock, bring to the boil again and skim. Simmer for 5 minutes. Add the rest of the stock, boil up and skim again. The addition of cool stock accelerates the rising of fat and scum and helps to clear the sauce. If the pan is tilted slightly the scum and fat will rise on one side only and can be easily removed. Simmer for 5 minutes more, taste and adjust the seasoning as necessary and strain, pressing the vegetables to extract the juice. *Makes approximately 2 cups*

Variations

Madeira Sauce Simmer 2 cups Brown Sauce until reduced by half then stir in ¼ cup of Madeira. Reheat but do not allow to boil.

Serve with fine cuts of beef such as tournedos or Beef Wellington or the best cuts of ham, veal or poultry.

Sauce Chasseur Cook 1 chopped shallot until soft but not coloured in 15 g (½ oz) butter. Add 60 g (2 oz) finely sliced mushrooms and cook until golden. Pour on ½ cup dry white wine and boil to reduce by half. Stir in 1¼ cups Brown Sauce and 2 teaspoons tomato paste, and simmer for 2 minutes.

Serve with grills and sautés of meat and poultry.

Bordelaise Sauce Put 2 finely chopped shallots and ½ cup red wine in a saucepan and reduce to half the original volume by boiling. Add 1 cup Brown Sauce and simmer for 10 minutes.

Meantime cut some beef marrow into small dice, poach in a small amount of water for a few minutes and drain. Add to the sauce just before serving with ½ teaspoon chopped parsley.

Serve with grilled or sautéed steaks.

Note: Beef marrow is the fat in the centre of marrow bones. Ask the butcher to split them or cut into short lengths so that you may easily remove the marrow.

Velouté Sauce

•

An elegant accompaniment to vegetables and meats, and an integral part of many classic fish, chicken and veal dishes and the basis for other sauces.

2½ cups light stock (chicken, veal or fish according to the dish the sauce will accompany)
60 g (2 oz) butter
2 tablespoons flour
salt
white pepper
few drops lemon juice (optional)
2 egg yolks
2 tablespoons cream

Warm the stock and set aside.

In a heavy saucepan melt the butter. Stir in the flour and cook over a low heat, stirring constantly until the roux is straw-coloured. Remove from the heat, cool for a minute or two then add the stock all at once and stir until smoothly blended.

Return the saucepan to a medium heat and stir continually until boiling. Lower the heat and cook very gently for 15 minutes, stirring frequently.

Season with salt and pepper and a little lemon juice. Stir the egg yolks into the cream in a small bowl. Stir in a little of the hot sauce then add the mixture to the sauce, stirring over a low heat. Cook, stirring, until the sauce is glossy and a little thicker, but do not allow it to boil. *Makes approximately 2 cups*

Variations

Sauce Aurore To 2 cups of Chicken Velouté, add 1½ tablespoons tomato paste and 1 tablespoon butter.

Serve with eggs, fish, chicken or vegetables.

Sauce Bercy Boil 1 finely chopped spring onion in ¼ cup white wine until the liquid has almost evaporated. Stir in 2 cups Velouté, 2 teaspoons lemon juice and 1 tablespoon chopped parsley. Serve with fish or chicken.

Curry Sauce Cook 60 g (2 oz) chopped onion and 2 to 3 table-spoons of curry powder in the butter before adding the flour for the roux. Omit the egg yolk and cream liaison and finish the sauce with 4 tablespoons cream and 1 tablespoon lemon juice. Serve over fish, veal, lamb, chicken or eggs.

Sauce Poulette Add an extra squeeze of lemon juice and 2 tablespoons chopped parsley to 2 cups of Velouté sauce.

Serve with chicken, also delicious with vegetables.

EGG AND BUTTER SAUCES

These rich and luscious sauces are thickened by the emulsifying action of egg yolk on butter and an acid ingredient which is lemon juice for Hollandaise Sauce and a reduction of vinegar or dry vermouth with aromatics for Béarnaise sauce. Note that these are warm, not hot sauces. If they have to be held for a time before serving, place in a container standing in a pan of warm water and cover with a piece of plastic wrap placed directly on the surface of the sauce. They may be refrigerated and reheated very gently over some warm water – this is what is often done in restaurants.

Hollandaise Sauce

• • •

Sublime with asparagus, vegetables, fish and eggs.

2 egg yolks
1 tablespoon water
125 g (4 oz) unsalted butter
small pinch salt
few drops lemon juice

Heat about 2.5 cm (1 inch) of water in the bottom of a double boiler or a saucepan over which a mixing bowl will fit. Bring just to simmering and have some cold water ready to add from time to time so that this water never boils. Place the egg yolks and the tablespoon of water in the top of the double boiler or the bowl and whisk over the bottom saucepan until the yolks thicken slightly.

This stage is called a sabayon and is reached when you begin to see the bottom of the pan between strokes and the mixture clings to the whisk when it is raised from the pan.

Now add the butter, small piece by piece, by slipping it through your fingers to soften it slightly. Whisk constantly all the time, incorporating each piece of butter well before adding the next piece. When all the butter has been added and the sauce is creamy, add salt and just a little lemon juice.

If the sauce refuses to thicken or if it curdles, don't worry, there is a remedy. Rinse out a mixing bowl with hot water then put in a teaspoon of lemon juice and a tablespoon of the sauce. Beat with a wire whisk until they thicken together then beat in the rest of the sauce a little at a time, whisking each addition well until quite smooth before adding the next. *Makes approximately ½ cup*

Blender Hollandaise

•

Marvellous to be able to make this luxury sauce so quickly and easily! The blender version is perhaps a shade less delicate than the hand-made version but is still very good. You can also make Hollandaise in a food processor, following these instructions.

3 egg yolks
1 tablespoon lemon juice
1 tablespoon water
125 g (4 oz) unsalted butter
salt
white pepper

Place the egg yolks, lemon juice and water into the blender. Cover and blend at high speed for a few seconds. Cut the butter into pieces and melt in a small saucepan until foaming hot but not browning. Remove the stopper from the middle of the blender lid, turn on to top speed and pour the butter in very slowly. The sauce will thicken almost immediately. Season to taste with salt and pepper. *Makes approximately ½ cup*

Variations

Hollandaise with Egg Whites Fold 2 stiffly beaten egg whites into one quantity of Hollandaise sauce just before serving. This makes a lighter sauce and gives more servings.

Serve with fish, asparagus or eggs.

Sauce Mousseline Fold ½ cup of cream, lightly whipped, into one quantity of Hollandaise sauce just before serving.

Serve with fish, asparagus or other vegetables.

Sauce Vin Blanc Place ½ cup fish stock and ¼ cup dry white wine in a saucepan and boil until reduced to 2 tablespoons. Using this reduction in place of the lemon juice and water and proceed as for making Hollandaise sauce.

Serve on poached fish.

Mayonnaise

••

Homemade mayonnaise with its sumptuous texture and fresh, subtle flavour is a world away from most bottled products. It takes only about 10 minutes to make by hand once you have mastered the technique and is faster still with an electric beater, blender or food processor. Mayonnaise has dozens of uses, can be varied endlessly and will transform such simple ingredients as canned fish and hard-boiled eggs into an elegant dish.

2 egg yolks
½ teaspoon salt
pinch white pepper
½ teaspoon dry mustard
2 teaspoons vinegar or lemon juice
1 cup olive oil, salad oil or a mixture of both

Have all the ingredients at room temperature. Warm the eggs and oil in hot water if they are cold. Rinse out a mixing bowl with hot water and wrap a damp cloth round the base to keep it steady.

Place the egg yolks, seasonings and 1 teaspoon of the vinegar or lemon juice in the bowl and beat with a wire whisk to combine. When they are thick, begin to add the oil, drop by drop from a teaspoon, whisking constantly and incorporating each addition thoroughly before adding the next. As the mixture thickens, the oil flow can be increased to a steady thin stream but you must keep beating constantly. Stop pouring every now and then to check that the oil is well blended. If the mayonnaise should show signs of breaking or curdling beat in a teaspoon or two of boiling water before adding more oil. When all the oil is incorporated, beat in the remaining vinegar or lemon juice. *Makes approximately 1 cup.*

If either hand-made or machine-made mayonnaise refuses to thicken or if it curdles, take a clean warmed bowl and beat an egg yolk with ½ teaspoon vinegar, then gradually beat in the curdled mayonnaise very slowly at first and then more quickly.

Variations

Garlic Mayonnaise or Aïoli Crush 2 or 3 cloves of garlic to a paste with salt in a bowl. Add the egg yolks and seasonings and mix until thick then add the oil as for the basic recipe. Do not add too much vinegar.

Serve with boiled meats, fish and cold cooked or raw vegetables.

Sauce Tartare Mix 2 teaspoons chopped capers, 1 tablespoon chopped gherkin, the chopped whites of 2 hard-boiled eggs, 2 teaspoons chopped mixed fresh herbs and seasonings to taste into 1 cup Mayonnaise. A little cream may be added to lighten the consistency. Serve with fried or grilled fish.

Green Herb Mayonnaise Stir a little cream and 1–2 tablespoons of finely chopped mixed fresh herbs with some chopped watercress or blanched spinach leaves into 1 cup Mayonnaise.

Serve with cold fish or eggs.

Mayonnaise made in the Food Processor or Blender

•

Place the egg yolks, seasonings and 1 teaspoon of the vinegar or lemon juice in the bowl and blend for a few seconds. With the motor running, pour the oil in very gradually, ensuring that each addition has been absorbed before adding more. When all the oil has been incorporated, add the remaining vinegar or lemon juice.

Béarnaise Sauce

•••

Serve with grilled steak, tournedos or roast beef, also with shellfish and some vegetables. Any leftover sauce should be kept for serving on cold roast beef or chicken sandwiches.

¼ cup white wine vinegar or dry vermouth
1 spring onion, finely chopped
4 peppercorns, crushed
1 bay leaf
¼ teaspoon dried tarragon
1 sprig thyme or ¼ teaspoon dried thyme
2 egg yolks
125 g (4 oz) unsalted butter, at room temperature
salt
white pepper
1 teaspoon finely chopped tarragon or parsley
(optional)

Place the vinegar, spring onion, peppercorns, bay leaf, tarragon and thyme in a small saucepan and boil until reduced to 1 tablespoon of liquid. Strain, pressing to extract all the flavour.

Place the reduced flavoured vinegar and egg yolks in the top of a double boiler or in a mixing bowl that fits over a saucepan of hot water kept just on simmering point. Whisk the egg yolks over the water until they thicken slightly.

Add the butter by slipping it through your fingers to soften it slightly or cut it into small pieces and drop it in a piece at a time. Whisk all the time, incorporating each piece of butter before you add the next. When all the butter has been added the sauce should be smooth and creamy. Taste and adjust the seasoning with the salt and pepper and add the tarragon or parsley, if liked. *Makes approximately ½ cup*

Vinaigrette

•

*Vinaigrette or French dressing as it is often called,
is essential for a classic green salad and is used with other
vegetables and salads
Salad greens must be washed and dried well so that
the dressing will cling to the leaves. When dressing rice,
potato or cooked vegetable salads, pour vinaigrette
over and toss gently while still warm so that the flavour is
absorbed. Even if a potato salad, for instance, is to
have mayonnaise or sour cream as its final dressing, it is often
moistened first with vinaigrette while warm to give
added depth of flavour.
The usual proportion of oil to vinegar or lemon juice is three
parts to one, but this can be varied to suit your
taste. If you find this proportion too oily, try adding salt
rather than more vinegar to cut the oiliness. Look
for good vinegars and interesting oils for your vinaigrette.
Cider vinegar, red or white wine vinegars or
flavoured vinegars such as tarragon or herb are excellent.
Olive oil is traditional and superb but walnut oil will
give a subtle flavour variation. Buy only as much oil as you
will use within a month or so and keep it well
stoppered in a cool place, the refrigerator
if necessary.*

2 tablespoons good vinegar
½ teaspoon dry mustard
¼ teaspoon salt
freshly ground black pepper
½ cup oil

Put the vinegar into a small bowl with the mustard, salt and
pepper. Mix well with a fork or birch whisk and slowly add the
oil, beating well. Taste as you go to get the proportion you like.
Makes approximately ½ cup

Variations

Garlic Dressing For a delicate garlic flavour, peel and bruise 1
or 2 cloves of garlic and steep in the vinegar for an hour or two
before making the dressing. For a pungent flavour, crush 1 or 2
peeled cloves of garlic to a paste with the salt, add the vinegar
and other seasonings then the oil.
Fresh Herb Chop 1 to 2 tablespoons of fresh parsley, chives,
tarragon or basil, or a mixture of herbs, add half of them to one
quantity of Vinaigrette and sprinkle the other half over the
salad. Alternatively, you can chop ¼ teaspoon of dried herbs
together with a tablespoon of parsley and use in the same way.

SAUCES OF THE CUISINE NOUVELLE

Cuisine Nouvelle or New Wave Cooking is an alternative approach which allows you to eat lovely dishes without jeopardizing your shape or your health. It replaces fattening and over-rich ingredients with others that provide flavours and textures as tempting as before but do not add lots of kilojoules (calories) and saturated fats. Butter, cream and eggs appear occasionally but in greatly reduced amounts. Starch and sugar have almost disappeared.

Sauces of the Cuisine Nouvelle are thickened by reduction, by puréeing fruit or vegetables or by non-starch thickeners. Crème Fraîche and Fromage Blanc are two non-starch thickeners that are important. Crème Fraîche can be used to make sauces, as a topping for desserts or as an ingredient in sweet dishes. Fromage Blanc is particularly good in sauces for vegetables.

Cuisine Nouvelle is characterized by lightness and delicacy. Cooks all over the world are turning to it as a refreshing change from rich and heavy food and it is featured more and more in the most stylish restaurants.

Crème Fraîche

•

*Crème Fraîche is sold everywhere in France where its slight
tang is greatly appreciated. This recipe keeps well,
for as long as fresh cream, and can be used in many recipes
calling for fresh cream.*

1 tablespoon buttermilk
2 cups whipping cream

Stir the buttermilk and cream together in a small saucepan and heat gradually until tepid; the cream should feel slightly cool on the back of your finger. Remove pan from the heat, pour the mixture into a bowl, cover with plastic wrap and cover with a towel or blanket. Stand in a warm place for 8 hours, then store in the refrigerator. *Makes 2 cups*

To whip Crème Fraîche, add one-third of its volume (approximately ⅔ cup) of very cold milk, water or crushed ice, with a little sugar to taste, and whisk.
Note: Whipping cream has a butterfat content of 30–37 per cent. Cream with a higher butterfat content will work but cream with a lower butterfat content will not.

Fromage Blanc

•

This white cheese features in many Cuisine Nouvelle recipes and is often mixed with puréed vegetables as a sauce for meat, poultry or fish.

100 g (3½ oz) low fat cottage cheese
125 g (4 oz) natural yogurt
3 teaspoons lemon juice

Place all the ingredients in a blender or food processor and blend thoroughly. Fromage Blanc should be smooth, shiny and as thick as lightly whipped cream. Cover and store in the refrigerator for 12 hours before using. *Makes approximately 1 cup*

Creamy Sauce for Meat or Vegetables

•

1 cup chopped, cooked vegetables
¼ cup Fromage Blanc
salt
freshly ground pepper

Blend the vegetables and Fromage Blanc in a blender or food processor until smooth. Taste and adjust the seasoning.
Note: For the vegetables, choose one or a mixture of the following – mushrooms, cauliflower, spinach, onions, carrots, celery and tomatoes (these can be canned). Simmer until soft in a little stock, or water and a stock cube, with a few fresh herbs or a pinch of dried herbs, then drain well. Use a selection of these vegetables, sieved or puréed in a blender or food processor, whenever a recipe calls for vegetable purée as a thickener.

Gravy Cuisine Nouvelle

•

To make gravy without flour for roast meat, pour off all the fat from the pan then add 1 cup of stock, or vegetable water with a stock cube. Heat, stirring to incorporate all the good brown bits in the pan. Stir in 3 tablespoons of vegetable purée (see the Note above) and a few drops of brown colouring if needed. Taste and adjust the seasoning.

Garlic Sauce

• •

Serve with fish, boiled meats or vegetables.

2 slices white bread
½ cup skim milk
2 egg whites
⅛ teaspoon salt
2 cloves garlic, crushed
½ cup oil
1 teaspoon fresh lemon juice

Trim the crusts from the bread and soak in the skim milk. Mash the bread with a fork in a bowl. In a separate bowl, beat the egg whites with the salt for 1 minute or until foamy. Add the egg whites and garlic to the bread then gradually add the oil, beating constantly until the sauce begins to thicken. Add the lemon juice and the skim milk remaining from the soaked bread; continue to beat until thickened. *Makes approximately 1 cup*

Fresh Tomato Sauce

•

Serve with vegetables, sautéed veal, steak or pasta.

4 medium tomatoes
1 teaspoon olive oil
1 clove garlic, crushed
1 spring onion, chopped
1 teaspoon tomato paste
bouquet garni
⅔ cup chicken stock

Peel the tomatoes by covering with boiling water, and counting to 10. Drop the tomatoes into cold water then slip the skins off with your fingers. Cut in half and squeeze gently to flip out the seeds and excess juice; chop.

Heat the olive oil in a saucepan, add the garlic and spring onion and cook over a low heat for 2–3 minutes. Add the chopped tomatoes, tomato paste, bouquet garni and stock and cook for 15 minutes. Remove the bouquet garni and purée the sauce in a blender or food processor. If the sauce is too thin, return it to the pan and reduce it by boiling. *Makes approximately 1 cup*

Green Sauce

• •

A herby sauce to serve over new potatoes, rice or pasta.

1 tablespoon chopped capers
1 tablespoon chopped parsley
1 tablespoon chopped basil or watercress
1 clove garlic, chopped
¼ teaspoon salt
freshly ground pepper
½ cup olive oil
2 tablespoons lemon juice

In a small bowl mash the capers, parsley, watercress, garlic and salt together until they form a smooth paste. If preferred, the unchopped food may be processed in a food processor or blender until smooth. Add the oil, a tablespoon at a time, beating or processing after each addition, until the oil is absorbed. Add the lemon juice gradually while beating or processing. *Makes approximately ¾ cup*

Mushroom Sauce

• •

This is a lovely 'New Wave' sauce for almost any meat or poultry. It is also good with freshly cooked pasta. Thickened with the mushroom purée and Fromage Blanc, it typifies the new approach to sauce making.

1 teaspoon butter
125 g (4 oz) mushrooms, chopped
2 tablespoons port
2 cups light stock
1 tablespoon Mushroom Purée (see below)
1 tablespoon Fromage Blanc
juice of half a lemon
salt
freshly ground pepper

Melt the butter in a heavy-based saucepan and add the mushrooms. Cook uncovered, very slowly, stir from time to time until all the moisture from the mushrooms has evaporated. Add the port and stock. Simmer uncovered for 20 minutes, the volume should be reduced by one-third. Strain, reserving the liquid in the pan.

Place the Mushroom Purée and Fromage Blanc in a blender or food processor. Add the lemon juice and a little of the liquid from the saucepan and blend until smooth. Stir into the contents of the pan, season and reheat. *Makes approximately 1½ cups*

Mushroom Purée Chop 60 g (2 oz) button mushrooms and toss in a little lemon juice. Place in a pan with 1 cup skim milk, a pinch of salt, pepper and a hint of nutmeg, Simmer, uncovered, until the liquid is reduced to 1 tablespoon. Purée in a blender or food processor. This is a useful thickening ingredient that may be made in larger quantities and stored frozen or kept covered in the refrigerator for up to a week.

Sweet Sabayon Sauce

• • •

This is a version of the popular zabaglione and is a lighter topping for desserts and fruit than the traditional custard or cream.

⅔ cup sweet white wine with flavourings of your choice (see below)
2 egg yolks
½ cup cold water

Simmer the wine and flavourings together, uncovered, until reduced by half. Put the egg yolks and water into a bowl and whisk until thick and creamy. Away from the heat, pour the egg yolks slowly into the hot wine, whisking all the time. The egg yolks will thicken and give volume and lightness to the sauce. Serve warm or cold. *Makes approximately 1 cup*
Flavourings: Add any of the following to the wine: a strip of orange or lemon peel, a small piece of cinnamon stick and two cloves or a vanilla bean.

Fruit Purée Sauces

•

These are made from any fresh or poached soft fruit puréed in a blender or food processor. Strawberries, raspberries, melon, stone fruits such as apricots and peaches, ripe pears, cooked apples and tropical fruits such as mango, pawpaw and pineapple are all superb. Sharpen the flavour with a little grated lemon or orange rind and add one tablespoon of Crème Fraiche per cup, if you want a creamy effect. Serve a sauce of one fruit over another fruit for an easy dessert with panache – raspberry sauce over strawberries, strawberry sauce over peaches or melon, or pineapple sauce over sliced oranges.

Roquefort Puffs (page 62) are crisp little hot pastries made from puff pastry. Add black olives, radishes and quail eggs (available from the delicatessen) for a tasty first course.

THE FIRST COURSE

All over the world, we find people serving first courses of great originality, colour and flavour. The marvellous Italian antipasti is one version, and in Spain the custom is personified in the array of delicious snacks or 'Tapas' that appear on every bar counter. 'Tapa hopping' is as popular in Spain as the pub crawl in England!

In a French home, it would be unthinkable to begin the main meal of the day without a first course, and often it is a simple plate of hors d'oeuvre – perhaps just one plump sardine, a couple of olives, a crisp red radish and a slice of fresh tomato sprinkled with herbs; or cold meat, fish or vegetables dressed with a delectable sauce or vinaigrette.

There is good sense behind this happy custom. A first course stimulates the appetite without taking the edge off it, which means the main course can be a moderate one . . . but as well, by serving a mixture of things you are able to use leftover foods imaginatively. You can also stretch luxury items such as a small tin of crab, a piece of Roquefort cheese or a little jar of caviar so everyone has a taste.

A first course may also be soup, the time-honoured favourite, little hot pastries, savoury tarts and pancakes, or fruits and vegetables in many guises – the possibilities are literally endless. Once you get into the first course habit, you will enjoy the challenge and fun of creating your own special combinations.

You will find first course recipes for soups, tarts and pancakes, quiches and pâtés elsewhere in the book. Here, I am concentrating on the lighter side of the story – hors d'oeuvre, small pastries, oysters, eggs, avocados, fruits and vegetables – delicious things that will whet the appetite without satiating it.

I recommend the first course to you, not just for a special-occasion dinner party but as an everyday pleasure at family meals.

For a cold starter consider Oriental Salad, which combines crisp bean sprouts, prawns and ham in an interesting dressing (see page 52).

51

Potted Kippers

••

Something for the busy hostess. Serve individual pots with hot toast as a first course or this spread is good to serve with drinks, accompanied by crisp biscuits or Melba toast and pickled cucumbers.

3 kippers
2 tablespoons lemon juice
250 g (8 oz) butter
¼ teaspoon cayenne pepper
anchovy essence to taste
extra 60 g (2 oz) butter, melted

Cover the kippers with boiling water and leave to stand for 5 minutes. Drain and pat dry with kitchen towels. Flake the fish, removing the skin and bones and place half, with the lemon juice, in an electric blender or food processor fitted with the double edged steel blade. Cream 125 g (4 oz) of the butter until soft and add to the fish in the blender, blending until smooth. Place in a bowl. Repeat the process with the remaining fish and butter. Beat the two mixtures together in a bowl until smooth and well combined. Season to taste with cayenne pepper and anchovy essence. Pack into small pots and cover with a film of the melted butter, which has been skimmed of the residue of white salts. *Serves 6*

Potted Shrimps

••

Shrimps do not appear in southern waters, but the larger prawns may be used for this delectable first course.

500 g (1 lb) cooked prawns, shelled
125 g (4 oz) butter
¼ teaspoon each ground mace and nutmeg
pinch cayenne pepper
1 teaspoon mixed spice
freshly ground pepper

Cut the prawns into small pieces. Melt two-thirds of the butter in a large frying pan. When the foam subsides, add the prawns and the mace, nutmeg, cayenne pepper, mixed spice and pepper. Toss in the butter for a few minutes. Spoon into a small pot and pack down lightly. Melt the remaining butter, skim it quickly and pour over the prawns; there should be enough to cover the 'shrimps'. Cover with a round of foil and chill in the refrigerator. Serve with Melba toast. *Serves 4*

Potted Crab

•

Prepare as for Potted Shrimps but use 2 × 185 g cans crabmeat, drained and picked over for any cartilage or use about 1½ cups fresh crabmeat.

Scallops Madras

•

Coquilles (scallops) St. Jacques are one of the classic first courses. In this version, it is not necessary to make a separate sauce, and the little curry powder adds an intriguing flavour.

3 onions
1 clove garlic
90 g (3 oz) butter
500 g (1 lb) scallops
½ cup soft breadcrumbs
1 tablespoon chopped parsley
1 teaspoon curry powder
salt
freshly ground pepper
½ cup cream
breadcrumbs and butter

Chop the onions finely and crush the garlic. Sauté in the butter until translucent and soft, but not brown. Blanch the scallops in water to cover for about 3 minutes. Drain. Add the scallops to the onions with the breadcrumbs, parsley, curry powder and cream and season to taste with salt and pepper. Spoon into 4 scallop shells or small ovenproof dishes. Sprinkle with the additional breadcrumbs and dot with butter.

Bake in a hot oven (200°C/400°F) for 10 minutes to brown the tops. *Serves 4*

Oriental Salad

•

The Chinese love chilled foods and serve many delicious salads as a starter – you will often find the combination of ham and seafood. Serve this salad as a first course in individual Chinese Bowls and offer chopsticks – an ice-breaker to any party!

250 g (8 oz) cooked prawns
125 g (4 oz) sliced ham
1 small green pepper
4–6 spring onions
1 cup fresh bean sprouts

Oriental Dressing

3 tablespoons peanut or light sesame oil
1 tablespoon vinegar
2 teaspoons soy sauce
1 teaspoon grated fresh ginger
1 small clove garlic, chopped
½ teaspoon chilli oil (optional)

Shell and devein the prawns and cut the ham into ribbons. Halve the pepper, remove the ribs and seeds and shred finely. Cut the spring onions into diagonal slices. Rinse the bean

sprouts and nip the ends. Combine the prawns and ham with the vegetables in a bowl and chill until ready to serve.
Make the dressing: Place all the dressing ingredients in a bowl and beat with a fork or whisk until it thickens a little.

Just before serving, pour the dressing over the salad and toss through to coat. *Serves 6 as a first course, 4 as a light salad*

Chicken Sate with Peanut Sauce

• • •

*In Indonesia and Singapore, little sates are often cooked over charcoal burners at roadside stalls while you wait.
If you have a hibachi, you may like to cook them outdoors for your own guests – or let them cook their own.
Peanut sauce is the traditional accompaniment, and may be mild or hot to suit your own taste. The amount of sambal oelek given here produces a medium to hot sauce.*

20 wooden sate skewers
(obtainable from
Chinese grocery shops or specialty food and
hardware shops and delicatessens)
¼ cup lemon juice
2 tablespoons soy sauce
2 cloves garlic, crushed
1 teaspoon sugar
1 teaspoon salt
375 g (12 oz) boneless chicken
6 spring onions to garnish

Soak the skewers in water to cover for 2 hours (this stops them from charring during cooking) and drain on paper towels. Meanwhile, combine the lemon juice, soy sauce, crushed garlic, sugar and salt in a bowl. Cut the chicken into bite-sized cubes and add to the marinade. Let it stand, covered, for 2 to 4 hours then drain, reserving the marinade.

Thread the chicken on to the skewers, using about 4 or 5 pieces on each. Grill under a medium heat for about 4 minutes on each side, basting once or twice with the reserved marinade. Or cook on the hibachi, turning once and brushing each side with the marinade. Arrange on a platter to serve and garnish with the shredded spring onions. Serve the sauce separately for dipping. *Serves 4–5*

Peanut Sauce

2 tablespoons crunchy peanut butter
30 g (1 oz) butter
1 tablespoon soy sauce
1 teaspoon lemon juice
½ teaspoon sugar

¼–½ teaspoon sambal oelek
¼ cup cream
reserved marinade

In a saucepan combine the peanut butter, butter, soy sauce, lemon juice, sugar and ¼ teaspoon of the sambal oelek. Stir in the cream. Taste and add more sambal oelek, if liked. Heat over a moderate heat, stirring until smooth. Add any remaining marinade and heat again, but do not boil.

Serve in a bowl surrounded by the chicken sates.
Note: Sambal oelek is a preparation made from dried, hot red peppers and is available from most delicatessens and food markets. If it is not available, substitute dried chilli powder – add just a pinch at first, then taste, adding more if necessary.

Boneless chicken is now also widely available from poultry shops, or you can buy 3 chicken breasts and carefully cut the meat away from the bone with a small, sharp knife.

Paillards of Raw Beef with Green Peppercorn Sauce

• •

*For those fans of steak tartare here's another appetizing way of serving raw beef. It makes a great starter for a luncheon or dinner followed by a light egg dish such as an omelette or quiche Lorraine, or a savoury soufflé.
The cornichons (tiny green gherkins) and green peppercorns are available at specialty food shops.*

500 g (1 lb) boneless sirloin

Green Peppercorn Sauce
¾ cup olive oil
½ cup chopped parsley
3 tablespoons capers
3 tablespoons chopped green olives
2 tablespoons Dijon style mustard
12 cornichons
2 tablespoons green peppercorns
2 cloves garlic, crushed
2 tablespoons vinegar

Trim the steak of all fat then partially freeze until it is firm. With a sharp knife, slice the meat very thinly and arrange the slices on 6 chilled plates. Spoon some of the sauce over each portion or transfer the sauce to a dish and serve separately. *Serves 6*

Green Peppercorn Sauce

To make the sauce blend all the sauce ingredients in a blender or a food processor fitted with the double-edged steel blade for 5 to 10 seconds or until the mixture is well combined but not smooth. If using a food processor, this is best done in short, sharp bursts.

Mixed Hors D'Oeuvre

With a little imagination, your kitchen cupboard and refrigerator will always be ready to supply enough items for a colourful hors d'oeuvre selection. Serve on one large platter for people to help themselves, or on individual small plates, and pass crusty bread and butter or little hot rolls if you want to make it more substantial before a light main dish.

No need for lavish preparation, though one or two special touches like whipped butter with radishes or a piquant Rémoulade sauce will add extra interest to your basic ingredients. Here is a selection of ideas to start you off:

Artichoke Hearts These come in two forms, packed in oil or brine. If using artichokes in oil, drain well and season with freshly ground black pepper. The artichokes in brine should be drained, then washed well and marinated in vinaigrette dressing. Drain before serving.

Tomato Slices Cut firm, medium-size tomatoes into thick slices. Sprinkle with vinaigrette dressing and chopped, fresh herbs (basil is delicious) or chopped chives. Or garnish with a spoonful of thick sour cream and add a little red or black lumpfish roe.

Stuffed Celery Choose tender celery stalks. Wash and peel off any strings. Fill the hollow of each stalk with cheese spread or mashed sardines flavoured with lemon juice and a little pepper. Cut in finger lengths to serve.

Beetroot Boats Tiny whole beetroot are available in jars from continental delicatessens and are very useful to have on hand. Carefully scoop out a little hollow in the top of each beetroot (use a melon baller or a sharp spoon) and fill the hollow with Formosa Butter. Sprinkle with chopped herbs or chives.

Formosa Butter Cream 60 g (2 oz) butter with a wooden spoon. Push the yolks of 2 hard-boiled eggs through a sieve, and blend into the butter. Season with ½ teaspoon mustard, salt and freshly ground pepper. Half a teaspoon of curry powder may be used instead of mustard for a change.

Radishes with Butter This is a favourite way of eating radishes in France. Cut each radish into half lengthwise and garnish each half with a dab of whipped butter, or a little pat of plain, unsalted butter.

Asparagus Spears Choose the slim, white variety. These are tender and delicious, but don't break up. Drain, then sprinkle with a little vinaigrette dressing and finely chopped parsley.

Marinated Mushrooms Baby mushrooms are obtainable in jars, packed in brine. Drain well, then marinate in vinaigrette, flavoured with a crushed garlic clove and a sprinkle of dried herbs or chopped fresh herbs. Drain before serving.

Cucumber with Sour Cream Peel the cucumber, leaving a little green on the surface, and score it horizontally with the tines of a fork. (This gives an interesting fluted edge when you cut it into vertical slices.) Cut in thick slices, salt lightly, and leave for 15 minutes or so. Wash under cold running water, pat dry with paper towels, and garnish each slice with a spoonful of sour cream and a little lumpfish roe, chopped chives or a sprinkle of paprika. Danish lumpfish roe is available in small jars in either the red or black variety, and is a useful standby.

Pickled or Canned Fish With the great variety of delicious fish and shellfish now readily available, it's easy to keep a few jars or tins on hand. Choose from plump pickled mussels, sardines large or small, salmon, herrings in various sauces, prawns, mackerel or crab. Mussels should be drained, then marinated in vinaigrette dressing and drained again before serving, or can be sprinkled with lemon juice and freshly ground black pepper. Prawns should be drained and rinsed in cold running water, then seasoned with lemon juice, salt and pepper and served with a good mayonnaise. Herrings and sardines may be served as is, salmon and crab should be picked over for any skin, bones or cartilage, and served with mayonnaise or sour cream or a seasoning of lemon juice, salt and pepper. Arrange in crisp lettuce cups and sprinkle with finely chopped parsley or snipped chives.

Sliced Cold Meats As with the Italian antipasti, cold meats are often served as part of an hors d'oeuvre selection. You might consider thin slices of rare roast beef or corned beef moistened with vinaigrette dressing, thin slices of salami, chunks of pepperoni or cabonassi, slices of pastrami, smoked beef, ham deluxe or prosciutto. Thinly sliced meats can be rolled, folded loosely into triangles, or arranged in overlapping slices.

Cheese Cubes of cheese will add colour and flavour to your platter. You might have Edam, Gruyère or Danish blue, or Cheddar, or the salty white Feta, which seems to go so well with olives.

A nice idea is to serve two or three cheeses that give contrast in flavour and texture – for instance, the firm, nut-sweet Gruyère with the softer-textured Ambrosia, or crumbly Feta, which is specially good with tiny dolmades or rice-stuffed baby eggplant.

Pepper slices An easy way to prepare peppers for a quick first course is simply to slice off the tops, remove the seeds, cut into rings and season with salt and pepper. You may use green, yellow or red peppers or a colourful mixture of the three. Drizzle over a little vinaigrette if liked. The red pepper, by the way, is simply the ripe green pepper, while the yellow pepper is the half-ripe stage. Red peppers are milder and sweeter than green, and four times richer in vitamin C, so make full use of them while they are in season.

Olives and Pickles There is a special section on olives in this chapter, but it's worth mentioning them again as part of your mixed hors d'oeuvre. Don't forget the many interesting pickles, either – large dill pickles, gherkins, the tiny dill midgets, sweet and sour gherkins, and the Continental-type mixed vegetable pickles.

Delicatessen Specialties Watch out for other interesting items on the shelf of your food market or delicatessen. In fact, it adds a little fillip to your ordinary food shopping to watch out for things that will fit into an antipasti or hors d'oeuvre selection. Just a little can here, a bottle there, and over the months you will be able to build up your reserve supplies, so there are always a few different things on hand to add to crisp fresh vegetables, meats and cheese.

Note: When arranging your hors d'oeuvre selection (either on one large platter or individual plates) consider the balance of colour, texture and flavour. For example, contrast the sweetness and colour of a ripe tomato with the crispness of green pepper and the salty tang of black olives. Red radishes look and taste marvellous against a background of wafer-thin ham slices and pale green cucumber boats. Just let your artistic eye be your guide and your first course will look as good as it tastes.

ANTIPASTI

One of the most colourful, appetizing and versatile of dishes is antipasti, the splendid Italian version of hors d'oeuvre. Antipasti may be hot or cold, may be passed around as an accompaniment to drinks (in which case they should be easy to manage with the fingers), served at the table as a first course, or appear on their own as a satisfying, light luncheon or supper.

When serving antipasti as a first course, they should not be so copious that they dull the appetite for the dishes to follow. You should also be careful not to duplicate flavours – if meat is to be the main course, be sparing with the meat in the antipasti, and the same with fish and shellfish.

Apart from these simple rules, let your imagination and your budget be your guide. For a special dinner, you might include caviar, pâté, smoked salmon, oysters, prawns or lobster in your antipasti display. But the most commonly used ingredients are not expensive ones. They include crisp salad greens, cold cuts of meat, stuffed, hard-boiled eggs, olives, tuna, anchovies, sardines, smoked or marinated herrings, marinated artichokes and mushrooms and pickled vegetables,

served with crusty bread and butter. It is the unexpected which is half the charm of the antipasti.

Most of these ingredients are easy to find in your local supermarket or delicatessen. Use unsalted butter for its delicate, fresh flavour; choose raw vegetables carefully for colour and freshness, and make sure you use the finest, virgin olive oil when a recipe calls for oil, it can transform simple foods into a meal anyone would appreciate. The proportions of all recipes for antipasti may of course be adjusted to suit the number of people you wish to serve.

Antipasti Freddi

•

Here's a basic antipasti tray, served cold.

1 small can tuna in oil, drained
1 small can mixed antipasto, drained
8 thin slices Italian salami
8 thin slices prosciutto
8 anchovy fillets
1 small can artichoke hearts, drained
12 large green olives
2 teaspoons capers in oil
1 small can pimientos, drained
4 slices tomato
4 pickled peppers, drained
8 large black olives

Use a large oval platter. Place the tuna and antipasto in the centre of the dish, and arrange all other ingredients around them in an attractive pattern (cut the artichokes, pimientos and peppers into quarters). Serve with crusty bread and butter.
Serves 8
Note: Cans of antipasto are imported, and may be found in good delicatessens and food departments.

FRUITS AND VEGETABLES MAKE A GOOD BEGINNING

When you are planning a rich or substantial main course, you want a first course that is lighter in character. I frequently find the answer in fruits or vegetables. Ripe melons and figs are traditional partners to prosciutto. Take advantage of the lovely ripe fresh dates now appearing in our fruit shops, they can be used in many ways, or use the big, preserved dates. Fresh vegetables achieve a totally new glamour and flavour when they are marinated in a piquant vinaigrette or dressed with a good olive oil or served with a light creamy dressing.

Pears Japonaise

••

Fresh pears give a most refreshing and unusual start to a meal. Rings or wedges of ripe pineapple may be used instead of pears if you wish.

4 large, ripe pears
caster sugar
lemon juice
finely chopped mint, to serve

Dressing

1 large egg
3 tablespoons tarragon vinegar
2 tablespoons caster sugar
pinch of salt
3 tablespoons lightly whipped cream

Peel the pears, cut into quarters and remove the cores. Arrange 4 quarters on each of 4 small dishes and sprinkle well with the lemon juice and a little caster sugar, turning to coat on all sides with the juice. Allow to stand while making the dressing.

To make the dressing, beat the egg and add the vinegar and sugar with a pinch of salt. Cook in a double boiler, over gently simmering water, and stir continually until thick. Remove, and allow to cool. When quite cold fold in the whipped cream, then taste and adjust the seasoning. Just before serving, spoon the dressing over the pears and sprinkle with a little finely chopped mint. *Serves 4*

Sizzling Grapefruit

•

Don't save grapefruit only for breakfast, they make a simple but elegant first course grilled with brown sugar and rum. Choose fruit which is heavy and as thin skinned as possible.

Allow half a grapefruit per person, and chill grapefruit to make it easier to cut into segments.

Cut each grapefruit in half, then cut around the outside, between the flesh and the skin, slipping the knife under the central core and removing any pips. (A curved, serrated-edge grapefruit knife is especially made for this purpose.)

Cut in between the grapefruit segments, loosening them completely, then remove the membrane between each segment and the core. Sprinkle each grapefruit half with 1 tablespoon dark rum and 1 tablespoon brown sugar. Place under a pre-heated grill and leave until the top is bubbling and the grapefruit is beginning to be flecked with brown. Serve hot.

Prosciutto and Melon

•

Prosciutto, a raw, cured ham, is readily available under various names at delicatessens and Italian shops. Parma ham is the classic for this dish, but is not so easy to find outside Italy.

2 small melons (rockmelon or honeydew)
250 g (8 oz) prosciutto, thinly sliced
black pepper

Chill the melons, cut each into wedges and remove the seeds. The melon may be detached from the skin, if preferred. Serve with the very thinly sliced prosciutto, either arranged over the melon wedges or rolled into neat cigarette shapes and served alongside.

The only seasoning is coarsely ground black pepper straight from the pepper mill. *Serves 6*
Variation: When fresh figs are in season, serve them peeled with prosciutto on the side.

Grilled Pineapple

•

Cut a whole unpeeled pineapple into 6 wedges, cut away the core and the flesh from the skin, leaving a small piece at the end of the flesh attached to the skin. Place the wedges, skin side down, directly on a grilling rack.

Sprinkle the pineapple with a little dark rum and some brown sugar. Cook them under a moderate heat until they are heated through and the sugar sizzles. *Serves 6*

Dates, Prunes and Figs

These three fruits make light, interesting hot appetizers to serve with drinks when you add a savoury stuffing, wrap them in bacon and grill. Fresh dates or the large, preserved dates may be used in any of the recipes given. Choose large, soft dessert prunes and they won't need to be soaked before using, but the firmer variety may need to be soaked in hot tea or fruit juice to plump them.
The firm type of dried fig will also need to be soaked before stuffing, but the new preserved figs (which come in plastic packets) are already plump and soft and ready to use.

Grilled Stuffed Figs ● Soak dried figs in sherry or port for 36 hours. Split and fill with nuts or cream cheese, or a combination of the two, or Cheddar cheese. Wrap with thinly sliced bacon strips and secure with a toothpick. Grill until the bacon is crisp and the figs are heated through.

Grilled Stuffed Dates ● Fill dates with an almond, a piece of walnut, a cashew nut or a little peanut butter. Wrap with thinly sliced bacon, secure with a toothpick and grill until the bacon is crisp.

Savoury Stuffed Dates ● Fill dates with whole or chopped nuts, cream cheese, peanut butter, or a stuffing made by combining cream cheese with a little mayonnaise, finely chopped celery and onion, pepper and salt to taste.

Grilled Stuffed Prunes ● Drain soaked and stoned prunes on absorbent paper. Stuff each with a lightly salted walnut half. Wrap with half a thinly sliced bacon rasher and secure with a toothpick. Grill until bacon is crisp and the prunes are heated through. Cream cheese may be added with the walnut as a stuffing.

Devils on Horseback ● Soak 12 dessert prunes in hot water to cover for 30 minutes. Simmer in liquid with ½ bay leaf until tender, then drain and stone. Halve 6 anchovy fillets and wrap each around an almond half. Fill the prunes with the anchovy almonds. Wrap half a thinly sliced bacon rasher around each prune and secure with toothpicks. Place on a baking tray and grill until crisp.

Golden Wine Frappe

●●

For a refreshing start on a hot day, serve a chilled frappe in your prettiest glass bowls or cups.

2 envelopes (6 teaspoons) gelatine
½ cup water
1 cup orange juice
¼ cup lemon juice
¼ cup raspberry topping (optional)
1½ cups sauterne
pinch of salt
grated nutmeg to taste
3 oranges

Sprinkle the gelatine over the water and leave to soften. Dissolve the gelatine over hot water then pour into a large container, suitable for the freezer. Strain in the orange and lemon juices and add the raspberry topping, if using. Stir in the sauterne, salt and nutmeg. Peel 2 of the oranges, remove the pith and cut the segments free from the membranes. Remove the pips then add the segments to the juices. Chill then freeze for at least 2 hours.

When ready to serve, break up the jelly and place in chilled serving bowls or cups. Cut the remaining orange into thin slices, dip in sugar and garnish each dish with an orange slice. *Serves 6–8*

Buttermilk fruit sorbet

●●

This makes a light first course. Surround with sliced fresh fruits such as peaches, apricots, or strawberries; canned fruit may be used in place of fresh.

1 cup puréed fruit
sugar to taste, approximately ¼ cup
2 tablespoons lemon juice
pinch of salt
1½ cups buttermilk
2 teaspoons gelatine
1 tablespoon water
fresh fruits in season

Turn the freezer to the coldest setting. Place the fruit purée, sugar, lemon juice, salt and buttermilk in a bowl. Stir well until the sugar is dissolved. (Alternatively, this can be done in a blender or food processor fitted with the double edged steel blade. In this case, the fruit does not need to be puréed first.) Taste the mixture and add more sugar if necessary. The flavour should be sharp, not sweet.

Sprinkle the gelatine over the water and leave to soften, then dissolve over hot water. Fold gelatine into the buttermilk mixture and pour into a freezer tray. Freeze until firm then turn into a chilled bowl and beat briskly with chilled beaters until fluffy. Return to the freezer until firm again.

Serve in scoops surrounded by fruits in season. *Serves 6*

VEGETABLES À LA GRECQUE

VEGETABLES VINAIGRETTE

The Greek way of cooking vegetables is to simmer them in an aromatic liquid flavoured with garlic, tomato, herbs and olive oil. Chilled in the cooking liquid, they make a wonderful first course. For a special dinner, you might like to offer a variety of vegetables cooked separately this way. Or you can cook two or three vegetables together when they take the same cooking time.

This is another good way of serving vegetables chilled. They are very lightly cooked until tender but still firm then allowed to marinate in a vinaigrette dressing. Fresh vegetables are preferred, but canned vegetables such as artichokes, broad beans, wax beans or champignons, may be prepared in this way also. They should be drained well and rinsed under cold, running water before marinating.

Leeks à la Grecque

••

One of my favourite vegetables, I enjoy leeks this way
Serve as a starter or as a vegetable with grilled meat

6 young leeks
1 tablespoon chopped, fresh tarragon or
1 teaspoon dried tarragon
1 tablespoon lemon juice
1 clove garlic, crushed
1 tablespoon chopped parsley
1 tomato, peeled and seeded
pinch dried thyme
salt
freshly ground pepper
1 bay leaf
¼ cup olive oil
1 cup water

Trim the root ends and remove any coarse outer leaves, only the white part and a little of the green of leeks is edible. Slit the leeks right down one side and wash thoroughly under cold running water to remove any grit. Place the trimmed leeks in a heavy saucepan large enough to take them whole. Add the remaining ingredients. Cover the pan and bring to the boil. Reduce heat and simmer for 8 to 10 minutes. Allow to cool, then chill if to be eaten cold. *Serves 6*

Variations

Leeks in Red Wine Prepare leeks as above but use 1 cup of red or white wine instead of the tomato and water.
Green Beans à la Grecque Substitute 750 g (1½ lb) young green beans for the leeks. Wash, top and tail, but leave whole. Cook as above.
Zucchini Use 500 g (1 lb) zucchini cut into diagonal chunks.
Mushrooms à la Grecque Choose 500 g (1 lb) button mushrooms. Carefully wash then trim and cook as above.

Cauliflower Vinaigrette

•

1 small head cauliflower

Dressing

3 tablespoons olive oil
1 tablespoon wine vinegar
1 garlic clove, crushed with ½ teaspoon salt
freshly ground black pepper
½ teaspoon French mustard
1 tablespoon finely chopped herbs mixed together
(parsley, chives, tarragon, oregano)

Break the cauliflower into small florets and cook in boiling, salted water until just tender, about 4 minutes. Drain and refresh under cold running water. Place in a serving dish.

To make the dressing, combine the oil, vinegar, garlic, pepper and mustard. Stir in the chopped herbs and spoon the dressing over the cauliflower. Allow to marinate for at least 2 hours before serving and serve chilled. *Serves 6*

Different vegetables Many vegetables can be prepared this way. They are lightly cooked until firm but still tender, drained and refreshed under cold running water, then steeped in the vinaigrette.

★ 500 g (1 lb) small onions
★ 500 g (1 lb) carrots. Leave whole if very small, otherwise cut into small sticks.
★ 500 g (1 lb) button mushrooms. Wipe with a cloth dipped in lemon juice and cook for 5 minutes.
★ 500 g (1 lb) snow peas (mange-tout). Wash, remove strings and ends. Cook for 1 minute only.
★ 500 g (1 lb) French beans. Top and tail and if small, cook whole. Otherwise, cut in half.

LET'S PRAISE THE AVOCADO

References to the avocado have been found in records kept by Spanish explorers as far back as 1519. As avocado farms flourish in California, Israel and Australia and many sub-tropical climates the whole world has become enchanted by the delicate nutty flavour and velvety, buttery texture of the avocado.

Avocados make a splendid first course for special occasions. They are perfect served quite simply, just cut in half with a little vinaigrette poured into the hollow left by the stone, or may be stuffed with crab or tiny prawns and topped with mayonnaise.

The fruit may vary from the large variety with a smooth green skin, a smaller type with a knobbly dark skin through to the small, seedless ones. All have the same delicious texture and flavour, just the outsides are different.

When buying avocados, it is a good idea to choose them already ripe on the day you wish to serve them. A hard avocado may not ripen in time for your dinner party and you and your guests will be disappointed.

If firm or hard, keep at room temperature for two or three days until soft to the touch. An hour or two before serving put in the refrigerator, but never store avocados in the refrigerator unless they are ripe.

Here are some special ways to serve this delectable fruit.

Avocado Stuffed with Crabmeat and Lime Mayonnaise

••

The lime mayonnaise is made in a flash in your blender. If you don't have a blender, see page 45 for an alternative method of making mayonnaise.

1 × 185 g can crabmeat
2 celery stalks, finely sliced
1 tablespoon lime juice
salt
freshly ground pepper
²⁄₃ cup lime mayonnaise
2 avocados, chilled
watercress, parsley or lettuce leaves to garnish

Pick over the crabmeat and remove any tissue. Flake in a bowl. Add the celery to the crabmeat with the lime juice and salt and

pepper to taste; fold in enough mayonnaise to moisten. Halve the avocados and remove the seeds. Place the avocado on a plate and spoon the crab mixture evenly between the four halves. Top with the remaining lime mayonnaise. *Serves 4*

Lime Mayonnaise

••

1 egg
2 tablespoons lime juice
½ teaspoon dry English mustard
½ teaspoon grated lime rind
½ teaspoon grated onion
½ teaspoon salt
1 cup olive oil, salad oil or a combination of both
1 tablespoon warm water (if required)

Place all the ingredients, except the olive oil and water in a blender. With the motor at high speed, blend the mixture, adding the oil in a steady flowing stream. Taste and adjust the seasoning and add the warm water, if necessary, to thin the mayonnaise. *Makes 1 cup*

Avocado Salad Suzette

••

A most luxurious yet hearty salad which would be a perfect first course before a light main dish, or could be a meal in itself for luncheon or supper. The lime juice adds a special touch, but if fresh limes are not available from your greengrocer you may substitute lemon juice. Strange as it may sound, a delicious accompaniment is crispbread spread with guava jelly or quince paste.

2 potatoes
6 rashers bacon
2 hard-boiled eggs, chopped
¼ cup minced onion
3 spring onions, chopped
1 canned pimiento, cut into strips
salt
freshly ground pepper
½ cup mayonnaise
2 tablespoons lime juice
2 avocados

Cook the potatoes in boiling salted water until tender, then peel and cut into dice. Sauté the bacon rashers in a frying pan until crisp. Drain on paper towels and crumble into a salad bowl. Add potatoes, eggs, onion, spring onions, pimiento and salt and pepper to taste. Toss lightly, cover and chill the mixture for 1 hour. In a small bowl, combine the mayonnaise and lime juice. Fold the dressing lightly into the potato mixture with the avocados which have been peeled, seeded and cut into cubes. *Serves 6*

Avocados Jamaican

••

Here is a hot dressing for avocados, with the extra intrigue of a dash of dark rum. It is easy to make in double quantities and will keep well in the refrigerator in a covered jar.

2 avocados, chilled

Sauce

2 tablespoons butter
1 tablespoon warm water
1 tablespoon red wine vinegar
1 tablespoon sugar
1 tablespoon Worcestershire sauce
1½ teaspoons tomato sauce
½ teaspoon dry mustard
4 cloves
¼ teaspoon salt
dash Tabasco sauce
1 tablespoon dark rum

To make the sauce combine all the ingredients, except the rum, in a saucepan and bring to a boil, stirring, over a moderate heat. Reduce the heat to low, cover, and simmer the mixture for 5 minutes, stirring occasionally.

Remove from the heat and discard the cloves. Add the rum, and cook the sauce for another 2 minutes.

Halve and seed the avocados. Score the cut sides of the avocados lightly and spoon the hot sauce among them. The combination of a hot sauce with chilled avocados is delicious.
Serves 4 as a first course

Avocado Rolls

••

Make this distinctive hors d'oeuvre well ahead of time to allow for proper chilling and mellowing of the flavours.

2 large avocados
1 cup finely chopped cashew or pistachio nuts
500 g Philadelphia cream cheese, softened
½ cup grated Cheddar cheese
2 teaspoons lime or lemon juice
1 clove garlic, crushed
½ teaspoon Worcestershire sauce
½ teaspoon salt
few drops Tabasco sauce
paprika
½ cup finely chopped nuts

Peel and stone the avocados and mash with a fork. In a bowl combine the avocados with the remaining ingredients except the paprika and nuts. Cover and chill for 30 minutes. Halve the

mixture and shape each half into a thick cylinder, about 4 cm (1½ inch) in diameter. Roll the cylinders in the paprika then the nuts and wrap in foil. Chill for at least two hours before serving. Cut into slices and serve on crisp croûtons of fried bread or crackers.

THE VERSATILE OLIVE

The olive is a native of the Mediterranean where so many people depend on its oil for a living. The fruit of the olive is black or green. The black olives are picked ripe and are full-flavoured and mellow while the green are picked immature and are firm and tangy. They are often pickled and stuffed with pimiento, anchovy or almonds.

Olives have an interesting salty flavour which seems to complement aperitifs better than anything else. Stop at any little café or bar around the Mediterranean and you are likely to be offered a plate of olives, both black and green, along with salami, cheese and some crisp vegetables.

While olives are an excellent appetizer served au naturel, there are interesting ways in which you can treat them to make them a specialty of your house. All of the olive ideas, given below, will keep for several months.

Mixed Italian Olives

••

250 g (8 oz) green olives
250 g (8 oz) black olives
3 stalks celery, chopped
1 green pepper, chopped
1 red pepper, chopped
1 clove garlic, crushed
½ cup olive oil
¼ cup vinegar
freshly ground black pepper
oregano to taste

Lightly crack the olives with a kitchen mallet or flat part of a kitchen knife until the pits show or make a deep cut into the flesh with a sharp pointed knife. Combine the olives with the remaining ingredients in a bowl. Cover and stand at room temperature for 2 days. Ladle into sterilized jars with firm fitting lids and store in the refrigerator. Use as part of an antipasti tray or in salads, rice salads etc.

Olives with Dill

••

1 kg (2 lb) large green olives
3 cloves garlic, crushed
2 red chilli peppers
3 sprigs fresh dill, or 1 teaspoon dried dill
1 bay leaf
½ cup olive oil
¼ cup vinegar

Drain the olives and lightly crack to break the surface or until the pits show. Combine with the remaining ingredients, cover and stand for a day or so in a cool place. Put in sterilized jars, seal, and store in the refrigerator.

Olive ideas

Herbed Olives • Put 500 g (1 lb) olives in a large glass jar which has a tight-fitting lid. Add 1 small red chilli, 2 cloves garlic, lightly smashed and 1 sprig fresh dill or thyme. Pour over sufficient olive oil to cover the olives. Cover the jar and marinate for at least 2 days before serving. For a stronger flavour, each olive may be slit with a sharp pointed knife before they are marinated, then the garlic and herb oil penetrates the flesh of the olives.
Note: Oil used to marinate olives acquires a delicious added flavour and may be used in cooking or it may be used over again, so is never wasted.
Grecian-style Olives • Put 500 g (1 lb) Calamata olives (these are the black, shiny olives with sharp pointed ends) in a jar, cover with vinegar and allow to stand for 2 days. Drain (keeping the vinegar for further use) and pack into the jar alternately with thin slices of lemon and finely sliced celery. Cover with olive oil and keep in a cool place for at least a week before serving.
Olive and Rice Salad • Toss cooked rice with cubes of ham, freshly chopped parsley and black olives and moisten with vinaigrette dressing. This gives a good contrast of colours, textures and flavours, and may be served as an appetizer on its own or as a part of an antipasti.

HOT PASTRIES

Nothing sets a meal off to a brighter start or gives such a boost to a party that's beginning to flag than the appearance of a tray of hot savouries. Nowadays you don't have to be a dab hand at making pastry. Excellent puff pastry can be bought from most frozen food shelves, so too can that crisp, light as air filo pastry that is really best made by the experts.

Most of these little savouries can be prepared ahead, and left on their baking trays until they are ready to be cooked, so they can emerge from the oven light, crispy golden and very tantalizing.

Pakoras (Savoury Fritters)

••

At the sunset hour many homes in India take on a radiant glow when interesting savouries are served with a brisk cup of tea or a refreshing drink. It is a pleasant time of the day. Pakoras are just one of the snacks served. Mint chutney or tomato sauce are popular accompaniments for Pakoras and other finger foods.

1 onion
1 large eggplant
red or green peppers
cauliflower florets
oil or ghee for deep frying

Batter

1 cup besan or plain flour
1 small red chilli, chopped
½ teaspoon salt
½ teaspoon Garam Masala
⅔ cup water

Peel and slice the onion and separate into rings. Slice eggplant into medium slices. Halve the peppers and remove the seeds and membrane, quarter if small or cut into eighths if large.

To make the batter, sift the flour into a bowl and add the chopped chilli, salt and Garam Masala. Make a well in the centre and pour in the water, beating with a wooden spoon and gradually drawing in the flour from the sides. Beat until smooth. Add more liquid if necessary to make a thin batter.

Dip the prepared vegetables in the batter to coat. Heat ghee or oil in a deep, heavy pan and quickly fry battered vegetables a few at a time until golden and crisp. Drain on crumpled kitchen paper and serve warm.
Note: Besan flour is chick pea flour and is available at Asian food stores. It has a distinctive taste that ordinary wheat flour cannot really match for this dish.

Roquefort Puffs

• •

*When you're having guests, little hot, savoury pastries are
lovely to pass around with pre-dinner drinks. This
recipe is especially useful, because you can prepare the
puffs ahead of time and store them on baking
trays in the refrigerator. Then, as guests arrive, it's just a
matter of popping a tray into a hot oven to cook.
It's a versatile recipe too, because almost any well-flavoured
cheese may substitute for the Roquefort. You can
use blue cheese as a second choice, or may like to try
Emmenthal, or a robust Cheddar.*

250 g (8 oz) puff pastry
250 g (8 oz) Roquefort or blue cheese
1 egg, beaten

Roll out the pastry on a lightly floured board to a rectangle
about 30 × 25 cm (12 × 10 inch). Cut in half lengthwise, so you
have two pieces of pastry 30 × 12.5 cm (12 × 5 inch). Cut the
cheese into 16 thin fingers, about 5 cm (2 inch) long. Lay two
rows of cheese, consisting of eight sticks, along the length of
the pastry leaving an equal space between each. Brush around
each stick of cheese with a little water. Lay the second sheet of
pastry over the top and press down well between each piece of
cheese. Cut between the cheese into fingers about 4 cm
(1½ inch) wide and 6 cm (2½ inch) long. Place on a baking tray
and brush with beaten egg. Chill.

Bake in a preheated, hot oven (200°C/400°F) for 15–20
minutes or until golden brown and puffed.

Serve hot. *Makes 16*

A friendly word: Don't be put off by all the figures. The
transition to metrics can make things seem more complicated,
but it does help to know the exact size to roll the pastry the first
time you make it. This is simply a rectangle, cut in half. The
little sticks of cheese are placed on one half of the pastry,
topped with the other half and cut in between.

Parmesan Sticks

•

If you have puff pastry left over from a dish or only use half a
package, it can be used to make Parmesan sticks. Roll the
pastry out thinly on a lightly floured board sprinkled, about
2 mm (⅛ inch) thick, with grated Parmesan or other sharp
cheese. Prick pastry all over with a fork and brush it with
slightly beaten egg white. Sprinkle with more cheese and a
little paprika, and press the cheese into the pastry with the
rolling pin. Cut into strips about 2 cm (¾ inch) wide and
12–15 cm (5–6 inch) long. Dampen the baking tray and place
the pastry strips on it, twisting them if desired. Chill. Bake in a
preheated hot oven (200°C/400°F) for about 10 minutes.

Samoosas

• • •

*These Indian savouries are semi-circular pastries filled with
minced lamb, subtly flavoured with spices and
herbs. They are deep fried until golden and crisp and are
wonderful with pre-dinner drinks.*

Pastry
1 cup plain flour
½ teaspoon salt
1 tablespoon ghee or butter
3–4 tablespoons lukewarm water
oil for deep frying
Filling
1 tablespoon ghee
2 cm (1 inch) piece green ginger, grated
2 onions, chopped
2 tablespoons chopped mint
2 teaspoons curry paste or powder
1 teaspoon salt
250 g (8 oz) minced lamb
½ teaspoon saffron threads
1 cup hot water
1 tomato, peeled and chopped
juice ½ lemon
½ teaspoon Garam Masala

To make the pastry, sift the flour and salt into a bowl. Rub in
ghee or butter with fingertips. Add the water and knead the
pastry in bowl to form a stiff dough. Cover the bowl with a
cloth and allow to stand while preparing the filling.

Heat the ghee and gently fry the grated ginger, half the
chopped onions and the mint until the onions are soft and
golden. Stir in the curry paste or powder and salt and fry for 2–3
minutes. Add the minced lamb and cook for 5 minutes,
stirring. Meanwhile, soak the saffron threads in hot water and
stir into meat mixture with the tomato. Bring to the boil, turn
the heat very low and cook, uncovered, for 30–40 minutes,
stirring occasionally. The meat should be tender and the
moisture evaporated. Add the lemon juice and Garam Masala.
Allow to cool and mix in the remaining onions.

Divide the pastry into 14–16 even-size pieces. Shape each
into a ball and roll out on a lightly floured board as thinly as
possible, keeping the shape round. Cut each circle in half and
moisten the edges with milk. Place a small spoonful of filling on
one side of the pastry and fold the other side over. Press the
edges together and trim with a fluted cutter if liked.

Heat oil in a heavy pan and fry the Samoosas, a few at a time,
until golden brown. Drain on crumpled kitchen paper.

Serve hot. A bowl of mint or coriander chutney may be
offered for dipping. *Makes approximately 30*

Piroshki

• • •

It just wouldn't be a party or celebration at my house if these hot savoury yeast breads were not served. I'm always being asked for the recipe, so now you can share it.

Yeast Dough

60 g (2 oz) fresh compressed yeast
2½ tablespoons sugar
3 cups plain flour
1¼ cups milk
125 g (4 oz) butter
2 teaspoons salt
1 egg yolk
beaten egg to glaze

Filling

3 large onions
60 g (2 oz) butter
250 g (8 oz) speck
1 teaspoon white pepper

In a small bowl combine the yeast and ½ tablespoon of the sugar. Stir until the yeast becomes liquid. Sprinkle with 1 teaspoon of the flour and leave in a warm place. Place the milk, butter, salt and remaining sugar in a saucepan. Heat gently until lukewarm, stirring occasionally. Sift the remaining flour into a large mixing bowl. Make a well in the centre and pour in the milk mixture, yeast mixture and lightly beaten egg yolk. Stir with a wooden spoon, gradually incorporating the flour. Beat the dough with a wooden spoon, or your hand, for 3 minutes until smooth and elastic. Sprinkle a little flour on top, cover and place in a warm place until double in bulk, about 1 hour.

To make the filling, chop the onions and fry in the butter until golden. Cool. Chop the speck very finely and mix with the onion and pepper. Turn the dough out on to a floured board, knead lightly and take a large tablespoon-size piece of dough for larger Piroshki, or a walnut-sized piece of dough for the tiny appetizer Piroshki. Place a teaspoon of filling on the dough, a little more for the larger ones, and fold edge over to enclose the filling. Mould into little balls.

Place on lightly greased baking trays and leave in a warm place to prove for 15 minutes. Brush with beaten egg and bake in a very hot oven (230°C/450°F) for 10–15 minutes until golden and cooked.

This quantity makes 45 to 50 tiny appetizer size Piroshki for pre-luncheon or dinner drinks or to serve with soups. For picnics, barbecues or family eating count on 30 larger Piroshki.
To freeze: Piroshki freeze well, for up to 4 weeks. Pack in small batches (the amount you would be likely to serve at one time) in oven bags. It is a simple matter to lift them out of the freezer and pop them straight into a moderate oven for about 10 minutes to reheat.
Note: Speck, the specially cured and smoked bacon, is available from most good delicatessens; if you cannot get this then smoked streaky bacon is a good substitute.

Mint Chutney

• •

Serve with little meatballs or fried fish or the spicy and delectable Samoosas and Pakoras of India.

6 spring onions
1 cup mint leaves
2 teaspoons grated fresh ginger
1 clove garlic, crushed
1 teaspoon salt
1 teaspoon sugar
1 tablespoon lemon juice
½ cup yogurt

Roughly chop the spring onions and pack all the ingredients, except the yogurt, into a blender or food processor fitted with a steel blade. Blend until finely chopped. If you don't have a blender then everything has to be finely chopped by hand. Add the yogurt and whirl in the blender only until mixed through. Spoon into a small bowl, smooth the surface, cover and chill until serving time.

Coriander Chutney

Prepare as for mint chutney, but replace mint with an equal quantity of fresh coriander leaves. (Fresh coriander is sold at Chinese greengroceries as Chinese parsley – it's one and the same thing.)

Mushroom Turnovers

• • •

A savoury mushroom filling combines with melting cream cheese pastry in these little turnovers, which make ideal finger food at a cocktail party or may be served as a first course at dinner.

Pastry

125 g (4 oz) packaged cream cheese
125 g (4 oz) butter
1½ cups plain flour
beaten egg to glaze
sesame seeds

Filling

60 g (2 oz) butter
4 spring onions, chopped
250 g (8 oz) mushrooms
60 g (2 oz) ham
1 tablespoon lemon juice
salt
freshly ground black pepper
¼ cup sour cream

To make the pastry, beat the cream cheese and butter in a mixing bowl, add the sifted flour and mix to a dough. Wrap in greaseproof paper and chill overnight or for several hours. (If left overnight, allow to stand at room temperature for an hour or so before rolling out; it is soft and light so handle with care.) Roll the pastry out thinly and cut into rounds with a 6 cm (2½ inch) fluted cutter, or the rim of a glass, dipped in flour each time so it won't stick to the pastry.

Put a teaspoonful of filling on each round, moisten edges with a little beaten egg, and fold over to form a turnover. Seal well, pressing round the edges with the tines of a fork. Glaze with egg and sprinkle with sesame seeds. Bake in a hot oven (200°C/400°F) for 10 minutes, or until golden brown.

Filling: Melt the butter and cook the onions until soft. Finely chop the mushrooms, including the stalks, and add to the pan with the lemon juice. Cook over a moderately high heat, stirring often, for 5 minutes. Remove from the heat and stir in the chopped ham, salt and pepper to taste and the sour cream.

Allow to cool before using. *Makes about 36*

Note: These turnovers may also be made in a larger size and served as a luncheon dish, with a crisp green salad.

FILO PASTRY

For those who like pies but dislike making pastry, filo is the answer to your prayers. All you do is separate the thin sheets, brush them with melted butter or oil and layer them in a tin. Add the filling and top with more filo layers. Mark into shapes. Bake in a hot oven (230°C/450°F) and serve. Nothing could be simpler.

Delicate filo pastry, which bakes into light crisp flakes is known to most of us in Greek dishes, but its popularity doesn't stop there. Filo is known in the Middle East under a variety of names. To the Turks it is Yufka, to the Tunisians Brik and sometimes it is spelt Phyllo. Whatever name you know it as, filo is a joy to use and has many uses.

Although filo is easy to use there are a number of points to remember for successful cooking. Filo dries very quickly once unwrapped. Remove from the packet and open on to a dry teatowel. Do not separate sheets. Cover with another teatowel, with a lightly dampened one. Remove each sheet as you require it, keeping the remainder covered.

Butter each sheet of pastry lightly before using or brush with olive oil for savoury pies.

Filo pastries freeze well so they are ideal for entertaining. A good tip is to sprinkle the top layer of filo with water before baking to make the top crisp.

Besides its traditional uses, filo also lends its crispness to first courses, main dishes and desserts of your own choice.

Here are some recipes that make a perfect first course or hot pastry for the savoury tray.

Indian Beef Triangles

• • •

125 g (4 oz) butter
1 large onion, chopped
2 cloves garlic, crushed
2 tablespoons curry powder
1½ teaspoons grated fresh ginger
1½ teaspoons salt
1 teaspoon sugar
¼ teaspoon cayenne pepper
750 g (1½ lb) minced beef
500 g (1 lb) filo pastry

Melt 30 g (1 oz) of the butter in a large heavy based frying pan. Add the onion and garlic and cook until the onion has softened. Stir in the curry powder, ginger, salt, sugar and cayenne pepper and cook for 1 minute. Add the minced beef and cook until browned and crumbly. Set aside.

Melt the remaining butter and cool slightly. Stack 24 sheets of filo between 2 dry teatowels with another dampened one on top. Brush 1 sheet of filo with butter, cut in half lengthwise, and fold each half in half lengthwise. Brush the halves with butter. Place 1½ teaspoons of the meat mixture in the corner of one end of each half. Fold the filo over the filling, enclosing to form a triangle. Continue to fold the pastry over in triangles until you come to the end of the strip. Make triangles with the remaining filo and meat. Place on a buttered baking tray and brush with melted butter. Bake in a moderately hot oven (190°C/375°F) for 20–25 minutes or until they are golden. *Makes 48 triangles*

Tiropetes

• • •

Anyone who has been to Greece will have enjoyed these little hot, savoury pastries with a glass of ouzo. Now they can be duplicated at home, for frozen filo pastry and Feta cheese are available in most food markets and good delicatessens.

375 g (12 oz) filo pastry
1 bunch spinach
2 onions
30 g (1 oz) butter
3 eggs, beaten
½ cup finely chopped spring onions, including some green ends
250 g (8 oz) Feta cheese, chopped
1 teaspoon nutmeg
½ cup finely chopped parsley
salt
freshly ground black pepper
90 g (3 oz) unsalted butter

Wash the spinach well and remove the white stalks. Place the leaves in a saucepan, cover, and steam until tender, about 5 minutes. Drain spinach and chop very finely or whirl in a food processor fitted with a steel blade. Remove excess liquid by placing in a sieve and pressing with a wooden spoon.

Chop the onions finely and fry in the butter until golden brown. Mix in a large bowl with the eggs, spring onions, Feta cheese, nutmeg, parsley, spinach and salt and pepper to taste.

Lay the filo pastry flat on a dry teatowel and cover with a second dry teatowel and then a damp teatowel, so pastry will not dry out as you work. Cut each sheet of filo pastry in half lengthwise. Fold each piece in half lengthwise. Brush with melted butter.

Place a teaspoonful of the spinach filling in one corner of the pastry strip. Fold the corner of the pastry over the filling until it meets the folded edge of the pastry, forming a triangle. Continue to fold the pastry over in triangles until you come to the end of the strip. Brush top with melted butter and place on an ungreased baking tray. Repeat until pastry and filling are used up. Bake in a moderately hot oven (190°C/375°F) for 45 minutes until puffed and golden brown. *Makes approximately 36* **Note:** A packet of frozen spinach (315 g/10 oz) may be used in place of the fresh spinach. Cook according to packet directions and drain thoroughly before using.

Variation

Bourekaki are made from exactly the same ingredients as Tiropetes, except that the pastry is spread in layers in a cake tin, with melted butter brushed on each pastry layer, the filling placed in the middle, and more buttered pastry layers placed on top. It is marked into squares then baked in a moderately hot oven (190°C/375°F) for 45 minutes or until golden.

Cheese Puff Triangles

• • •

500 g (1 lb) Feta cheese
375 g (12 oz) ricotta cheese
3 eggs
½ cup finely chopped parsley or mint
375 g (12 oz) filo pastry
250 g (8 oz) melted butter

Crumble the Feta cheese, add the ricotta and mix together well. Add the eggs, beat thoroughly and fold in the parsley or mint. Cut the filo, folded as it is in the packet, into 3 equal portions. Place one strip at a time on a flat surface and brush with melted butter. Fold in half lengthwise, making a strip about 5 cm (2 inch) wide. Brush with butter.

Place 1 tablespoon of cheese mixture in the bottom right hand corner of the strip and fold the corner over into a triangle. Continue folding to the end of the strip making sure that you retain a triangle shape with each fold. Lightly butter the finished triangles and place on a baking tray. Bake in a hot oven (200°C/400°F) for 20 minutes or until golden, turning after 10 minutes to brown evenly. Serve hot. *Makes approximately 36*

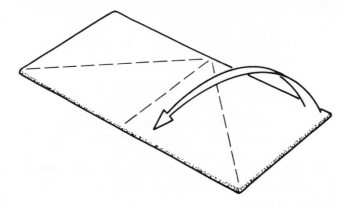

SPREADS AND DIPS

With a little dish of savoury spread or dip and some crisp crackers or toast on hand, you're prepared for any emergency.

Eggplant Caviar

••

This dip doesn't taste like the genuine, expensive caviar, but looks like it — which is why it is often referred to as the 'poor man's caviar'. Serve piled in a bowl with rounds of Lebanese bread for dipping. Guests break the bread as they dip. It may also be used to top hot toast or fried croûtons as an hors d'oeuvre.

2 medium eggplants
salt
freshly ground pepper
olive oil
2 cloves garlic
¼ teaspoon cinnamon
2 tablespoons vinegar
1 tablespoon lemon juice
½ cup chopped parsley

Wash the eggplant and cut in half lengthwise. Score cut surfaces diagonally several times. Sprinkle generously with salt and place upside down on a plate. Place a spoon under the plate to tilt it on one side so the juice will drain away; leave for 1 hour. Rinse in water to remove the excess salt, then wipe eggplant dry and arrange cut-side up on a baking tray. Season with salt and pepper and drizzle with a little olive oil. Bake in a moderate oven (180°C/350°F) for 1 hour, or until soft.

Remove from the oven, cool slightly, then scoop the flesh from the skin. Finely chop the flesh, then mash with a fork or purée in an electric blender. Add crushed garlic and beat until smooth. Gradually beat 2 tablespoons olive oil into the purée until it is like a thick mayonnaise, adding more oil if necessary. Stir in remaining ingredients. Mix well, cover and chill.

Liver Sausage Canapés

•

125 g (4 oz) liver sausage
1–2 tablespoons cream
2 tablespoons chopped parsley
rye bread or hot buttered toast

Combine the liver sausage with the cream and parsley and mix to a paste. Serve on buttered rye bread or toast, cut into triangles or fingers.

Walnut Spread

•

With a blender or food processor in your kitchen, many delicious appetizers can be made in seconds. Serve this nut spread on hot, wholegrain toast, on croûtons or crisp savoury biscuits. No butter is required as the oil in the nuts gives a smooth, buttery texture.

1 cup shelled walnuts
2 garlic cloves, crushed
2 slices of bread, crusts removed
2 teaspoons vinegar
2 teaspoons olive oil
¼ teaspoon salt

Soak the bread in water then squeeze the water out. Place all the ingredients in a blender or a food processor fitted with a steel blade and whirl for 5–10 seconds until well mixed. *Makes about 1 cup*
Note: Pine nuts make an interesting variation instead of walnuts.

Piquant Salmon Spread

•

Here's an appetizer for a busy day — it's made in minutes from ingredients usually found in the pantry. If lime juice is not available, substitute lemon juice or white vinegar. Use a good quality pink or red salmon.

1 × 440 g can salmon
⅓ cup mayonnaise
¼ cup finely chopped onion
1 tablespoon dry sherry
1 tablespoon finely chopped parsley
1 teaspoon Dijon style mustard
1 clove garlic, crushed
freshly ground pepper
2 teaspoons soy sauce
1 tablespoon lime juice
salt

Drain the salmon and remove all the skin and bones. Mash in a bowl with the remaining ingredients, adding salt to taste. Chill until ready to serve. Serve in a bowl with black bread, Melba toast or Lebanese bread as an appetizer with drinks or as a first course at the table.

An antipasti platter is colourful and looks inviting. See the recipe for Antipasti Freddi on page 55 and the ideas on page 54 and go on to create your own antipasti display.

The inventive cook might offer Indian Beef Triangles, Samoosas, Coriander Chutney and Herbed Black Olives. The recipes can be found in the First Course Chapter.

ALL THE WORLD LOVES AN OYSTER

Like avocados and olives, oysters are a classic beginning to a meal almost everywhere you go in the world – and many places claim the 'world's greatest oysters' as their own! Living as I do in Sydney, I think our rock oyster is incomparable for delicacy of flavour and firm, just-right texture – but I admit there is also much to be said for the oysters of New Zealand, Ireland, the USA and other homes of this marvellous little mollusc.

Oysters may be enjoyed in a great many ways. Eaten fresh on the half shell, with a sprinkling of lemon juice, a grind of black pepper, and some brown bread and butter to accompany them, they are perfect in their own right, but there are other good ways to serve them cold – and numberless ways to serve them hot. Traditionally they are baked or served on rock salt, but this is an optional refinement.

Here is a selection of ideas for you.

Oysters with Caviar

•

When you're in the mood for absolute luxury, try this superb – yet simply prepared – combination of flavours and textures.

2 dozen oysters, on the half shell
rock salt or crushed ice
1 carton sour light cream
1 teaspoon onion juice
cayenne pepper
1 small jar black or red caviar or lumpfish roe

Make a bed of rock salt or crushed ice on 4 plates, and arrange the chilled oysters in their shells on the salt.

Mix the cream with the onion juice and a pinch of cayenne pepper. Spoon a little cream over each oyster to cover it, then carefully spoon a strip of caviar on top of the cream. Serve immediately.
Note: To obtain onion juice, grate ½ peeled onion over a bowl until you have collected the required amount of juice. *Serves 4*

Oysters Served on Rock Salt

•

Oysters are delicious and always popular served with this cocktail sauce.

2 dozen oysters on the half shell
rock salt (available from butchers, health food or specialty shops)
2 lemons, quartered
thinly sliced brown bread
butter

Cocktail Sauce

½ cup tomato paste
dash Tabasco sauce
squeeze lemon juice
2 tablespoons cream
½ teaspoon prepared horseradish
salt
freshly ground black pepper

Chill the oysters. Place some rock salt on 4 plates, with a small bowl in the centre of each for the sauce. Cut the crusts from 4 slices brown bread, butter lightly, and cut each slice into four. Fill the bowls with the cocktail sauce, arrange oysters on the bed of rock salt, and pass the bread and butter separately. If rock salt is difficult to find, use a bed of crushed ice instead.
Serves 4 as a first course
Cocktail Sauce: Combine the tomato paste, Tabasco sauce, lemon juice, cream and horseradish; season with salt and pepper to taste.
Note: The rock salt is re-usable. Store in a covered container, and use as a base for all your cold oyster dishes and for holding the shells firm when baking oysters.

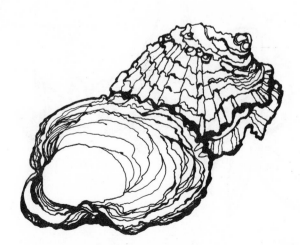

Oysters à L'Américaine

•

There are many versions of 'American' oysters. In this one, no sauce is added, but a topping of buttered breadcrumbs gives crispness.

2 dozen oysters, on the half shell
rock salt
cayenne pepper
1 cup fine, soft white breadcrumbs
6 tablespoons butter
salt
pepper

Line a baking sheet with rock salt, and arrange the oysters on it. Squeeze a few drops of lemon juice over each oyster and season with just a touch of cayenne pepper.

Melt 3 tablespoons of the butter in a small pan, and toss the breadcrumbs in it. Cook, stirring often, until the breadcrumbs are golden.

Melt the remaining butter in a saucepan and season well with lemon juice and salt and pepper.

Sprinkle the breadcrumbs over the oysters, top each with a little of the seasoned butter, and brown under a grill until the breadcrumbs are crisp and the oysters are heated through.

Serve at once, garnished with parsley. *Serves 4*

Oysters Florentine

• •

When you see 'Florentine' in a recipe you know there is spinach in the dish, and this most versatile vegetable teams particularly well with oysters.

2 dozen oysters, on the half shell
1½ cups spinach purée (or very finely chopped cooked spinach)
Mornay sauce, see below
freshly grated Parmesan cheese

Remove the oysters from their shells, carefully reserving any liquor. Make the Mornay sauce. Put a small spoonful of spinach in each shell, top with an oyster, and cover with the Mornay sauce. Sprinkle lightly with Parmesan cheese and brown in a hot oven (200°C/425°F) until the tops are brown and bubbly. *Serves 4 as a first course*

Mornay Sauce

oyster liquor plus enough milk to make 1 cup
1 slice onion
4 peppercorns
small bay leaf
30 g (1 oz) butter
1 tablespoon flour
2 tablespoons grated Parmesan cheese
salt
freshly ground black pepper
nutmeg

Put the oyster liquor and milk in a saucepan with the onion, peppercorns and bay leaf. Place on a low heat to infuse, but do not allow to boil. Remove from heat, strain and cool.

Melt the butter in a small saucepan and when it is sizzling stir in the flour. Lower the heat and cook gently for 1 minute, stirring all the time. Remove the pan from the heat and stir in the liquid almost all at once, stirring until smooth. Place the sauce back on the heat and stir constantly until it boils. Stir in the grated cheese. Season to taste with salt, pepper and a hint of nutmeg.

Note: If making this sauce for dishes that do not contain seafood, simply use a cup of milk in place of the oyster liquor and milk. You may enrich the sauce further by adding an egg yolk (lightly beaten and folded into the hot sauce) and/or 1 to 2 tablespoons cream.

Fried Oysters

••

*This is a delicious way of using fresh, bottled oysters when
oysters on the shell aren't available. It also seems
very popular with people who normally 'don't like oysters'
(and there are a few!). Just be sure to fry the oysters
at the last moment – they should be served immediately.*

2 bottles oysters (about 2 dozen)
1 egg
fine breadcrumbs
oil for frying
2 lemons
fried parsley to garnish
freshly ground black pepper

Strain the oysters over a saucepan, reserving the liquid. Bring
the liquid to the boil, add the oysters and cook for 30 seconds
only, just until the oysters are plump. Cool the oysters in the
liquid, then drain and remove the beards. Beat the egg lightly
in a bowl and dip each oyster in the egg then in the
breadcrumbs, coating well.

Heat enough oil to cover the oysters in a deep fryer or
saucepan. Place the oysters in a frying basket and fry until crisp
and golden. This will only take a few minutes and this is best
done in two or three batches.

Drain, and arrange in a bowl on a napkin, garnishing with
lemon quarters and fried parsley. Or arrange 5 to 6 oysters per
person on a slice of hot, buttered toast and garnish the
individual plates with lemon and parsley. Grind a little black
pepper over before serving. *Serves 4*

Fried Parsley: This makes an interesting and decorative
garnish for many dishes. Wash 6–8 stalks of parsley, dry well,
then pick off in little sprigs. Place in a frying basket and lower
into hot oil to cover. Leave in the oil for a few moments to crisp,
then remove and drain well on paper towels.

Oyster Fritters

••

*Crisp batter surrounds each plump oyster for delectable
flavour and texture contrast.*

oysters
Batter

½ cup flour
pinch of salt
⅓ cup warm water
1 tablespoon oil
1 egg white, stiffly beaten

Poach some oysters for 30 seconds in their own liquor. Cool,
drain and remove the beards.

Make the batter by sifting the flour with the salt into a bowl.
Make a well in the centre, add the water and oil and gradually
combine with the flour. Beat with a whisk until the mixture is
smooth. When ready to use, fold in the stiffly beaten egg white.

Dip each oyster in batter and deep fry, a few at a time, in
sizzling oil until crisp and golden.

Garnish with lemon quarters and serve with Tartare Sauce
(see below).

Tartare Sauce Many good commercial tartare sauces are now
available. To make your own, take 1 cup of mayonnaise and
add 1 teaspoon each of chopped capers, chopped gherkins,
chopped spring onions, chopped green olives and chopped
parsley. Taste for seasoning, and add a little salt or pepper or
vinegar as desired.

EGGS

Stuffed Eggs

••

Stuffed eggs served on a bed of shredded lettuce are one of the great standbys for a first course, but they are also enjoyed as finger food on the hors d'oeuvre tray or on a platter with other delectable nibbles. Stuffed eggs are simple, quick and delicious. The egg whites can be kept fresh in a bowl of cold water and the yolks made into various stuffings to be filled into the whites at the last moment.

6 eggs
3 tablespoons mayonnaise
2 teaspoons French mustard
salt to taste
pinch cayenne pepper
strips of red pimiento

Lower the eggs into a saucepan of gently boiling water to which a good pinch of salt has been added. Cook gently for 10–12 minutes. Stir the eggs for the first 8 minutes so that the yolks will be centred. Remove from the heat and plunge immediately into cold water.

When the eggs are completely cold shell them and cut in half lengthwise, using a stainless steel knife (other metals will discolour the eggs). Remove the yolks carefully and push through a sieve.

Mix in the remaining ingredients. If the mixture is too thick for piping add a little more mayonnaise. Using a 1 cm (½ inch) plain rosette tube, pipe the mixture into the egg whites and decorate with strips of red pimiento.

Variations

Small jars of chopped ham, chicken, smoked ham or one of the good pastes can be worked into the yolks, or use any of the suggested variations:

Chicken and Ham Boil 6 eggs, shell, and cut in half lengthwise. Remove yolks carefully and push through a sieve. Add 60 g (2 oz) finely chopped chicken, 60 g (2 oz) finely chopped ham, 60 g (2 oz) butter and salt and pepper to taste to the yolks. Pipe or spoon into the whites and garnish each half with a tiny sprig of parsley.

Anchovy Soak 4 anchovy fillets in milk for 20 minutes, drain and pound very finely. Stir into the sieved yolks of 6 eggs with 60 g (2 oz) butter, and pipe or spoon into the egg whites. Garnish with anchovy fillets to serve. (A little cayenne pepper may be added to the yolk mixture if desired.)

Caviar Mash the yolks of 6 eggs with 60 g (2 oz) butter or 3 tablespoons mayonnaise, 1 teaspoon lemon juice and 2 tablespoons caviar. Fill into the egg whites and garnish with red or black caviar or lumpfish roe.

Smoked Salmon Pound 3 slices of smoked salmon in a mortar, or mash with a fork, and stir into the mashed yolks of 6 eggs with 3 tablespoons mayonnaise. Pipe or spoon into the whites and garnish with a small strip of smoked salmon.

Prawns Finely chop 60 g (2 oz) cooked prawns. Stir into the mashed yolks of 6 eggs with 3 tablespoons mayonnaise, a pinch of cayenne pepper and a pinch of nutmeg. Pipe or spoon into the whites and garnish each half with a small whole prawn.

BEAUTIFUL SOUPS

Beautiful soup so rich and green,
Waiting in a hot tureen.

Most of us would agree with these immortal words from *Alice in Wonderland*. Soup *is* beautiful, especially homemade soup. There is something reassuring about soup that seems to attach itself to the cook as well. In Central Europe they even have a saying, 'If you meet a girl who cooks good soup, marry her!'

Soup can be a meal in itself or a tempting first course. A bowl of piping hot homemade soup is one of the nicest ways to start a meal, whether it's a simple family occasion or a special meal for guests. A hearty soup, thick with vegetables, is one of the most welcome and warming winter meals you can have.

In cold weather we make hot, hearty soups from winter vegetables, pasta, rice, dried beans and peas, and often add ham, meat or sausage. In summer, cooling vegetables such as beetroot, celery, cucumber and tomato add a delicious flavour to light stocks, while cream soups are lovely all year round. There are thick vegetable purées; soups enriched with cream and egg yolks; soups with big chunks of meat or chicken; soups thickened with rice or barley – an endless variety. Some soups require a well-flavoured stock, others are made with just water. Good brands of stock or bouillon cubes or canned consommé can be used.

As well as being nourishing, soups are economical, especially those using winter vegetables such as carrot or pumpkin, or the cheaper meats like oxtail or tripe. Many soups are just as good, if not better, reheated.

Canned and dried soups also have their place in busy lives, and may be combined for interesting flavours, or enlivened with finely chopped herbs, a little sherry, a swirl of cream or grated cheese.

Don't forget the little garnishes which add so much to the appeal of a soup. You can have croûtons, just lightly salted or garlic flavoured, a sprinkling of parsley, little pastry shapes, julienne vegetables, crackers or just crusty bread and butter.

It's easy to make good soup. Once you've discovered the pleasures of soup making, you'll want to include soup in almost all your meals.

STOCK

The importance of stock

We must give credit where credit is due and it is the French who have taught us the importance of good stock in flavouring sauces, casseroles and soups. Not that stock is hard to make, it is simply the flavourful liquid obtained from simmering together the bones, trimmings and flesh of meat, chicken or fish with vegetables, seasonings and water. The liquid is then strained through a fine strainer or cheesecloth and chilled, so that the fat which rises to the top can be easily removed.

The success of good stock depends on its distinctive flavour. Whether beef, chicken or fish, it should taste of that food; only few vegetables should be cooked with the meat and bones so that their flavour does not intrude. Make sure the butcher gives you beef bones for beef stock, lamb does not give the same richness. Lamb or mutton has its place, and excellent Scottish soups are made from them, but the two (beef and lamb) don't combine well.

Veal is used for white stock and the Chinese make a light stock with pork bones or a combination of pork and chicken. Each meat with its bones has a use.

Slow cooking and skimming the surface of the stock when it first comes to the boil is important, as it helps give a clear stock. Strain the stock carefully and refrigerate if possible. Surface fat on the stock is more easily removed when the stock is completely cold.

Stock will keep in the refrigerator for a 1 week, protected by the layer of fat, or 6 months in a freezer. Particles of meat or vegetables in the stock will reduce the storage time, so care should be taken when straining. It is a good idea, especially if you make a lot of soup, to make a large pot of stock and refrigerate or freeze it for later use.

Although not all soups are made from stock, carefully made stock is so essential to good cooking that it's well worth making. The ingredients are cheap and easily obtainable. Consider the pressure cooker and Crock-Pot (electric slow cooker) as modern aids to stock making.

Some basic stocks are referred to in the recipes in this chapter, and throughout this book and here is how to make them:

Beef Stock

•

1 kg (2 lb) beef bones (shank, marrow bone or
rib bones or a combination)
500 g (1 lb) chopped shin of beef
1 carrot, thickly sliced
1 onion, thickly sliced
2 teaspoons salt
about 3 litres (5 pints) cold water or enough to
cover the bones
1 teaspoon black peppercorns

Bouquet garni

2 celery stalks
4 sprigs parsley
1 sprig thyme
1 bay leaf

Put the bones into a large saucepan, then add the other ingredients and the bouquet garni, tied together and cover with cold water. Bring slowly to the boil, skim the surface well, then simmer very gently, half-covered, for 4 to 5 hours, (very slow simmering for a long time is the secret of well-flavoured stock). Strain through a fine sieve, cool, then chill in the refrigerator. Remove the surface fat before using.

This stock is used in brown sauces and soups. Clarified, it is also used in clear soups, and the method follows below.

Brown Stock

•

This uses the same ingredients and method as for beef stock but the bones and vegetables are first browned to give a richer colour to the stock.

Place the bones in a roasting pan with the carrot and onion, and roast in a hot oven (200°C/400°F) until a good, rich brown colour, place in a large saucepan.

Rinse out the roasting pan with a little water, scraping any brown sediment from the bottom, add to the bones and proceed with the recipe for beef stock.

To Clarify Stock

Remove all fat from the cold stock and place in a saucepan with 2 egg whites, lightly beaten, and the 2 egg shells. Bring slowly to the boil, whisking occasionally with an egg whisk. Allow the liquid to rise in the pan as it reaches boiling point, then lower the heat, and simmer very gently for 20 minutes.

You will find that as the egg whites cook they attract and hold any remaining particles of fat and residue that might cloud the stock. Strain through a colander lined with butter muslin, and you have a clear liquid which is the basis of many delicious soups.

Chicken Stock

•

500 g (1 lb) chicken bones
(carcass, backs or wings)
about 6 cups cold water (enough to cover bones)
1 teaspoon salt
1 carrot, halved
1 teaspoon black peppercorns

Bouquet garni

1 celery stalk
3 sprigs parsley
1 sprig thyme
1 bay leaf

Place the bones in a large, heavy saucepan. Cover with cold water and add the remaining ingredients and the bouquet garni, tied together. Bring to the boil and carefully skim the surface. Cover pan and simmer very slowly for 3 to 4 hours. Strain through a fine sieve and cool. Refrigerate until needed, then remove the fat which has risen to the top of the stock, leaving the flavoured jelly underneath.

This stock keeps for a week in the refrigerator, and is used for white sauce as well as soups.

Note: Use fresh bones for clear, well-flavoured stock. Your poultry supplier often has a bag of bone pieces (carcasses, wing tips etc.) at a very reasonable price, or you may use necks and backs. Giblets if available may also be added to the stock, except the chicken liver, which is inclined to give a bitter taste.

Fish Stock

•

This stock is used in many fish sauces and soups, and can be frozen or will keep well in the refrigerator for a week.

1 fish head and bones (a snapper head is ideal)
5 cups cold water
1 cup white wine, or the juice of a lemon plus
water to make a cup
1 teaspoon white peppercorns

Bouquet garni

1 celery stalk
3 sprigs parsley
1 sprig thyme
1 bay leaf

Place all the ingredients and the bouquet garni, tied together, in a large saucepan and bring to the boil. Skim the surface, and simmer very gently for 20 minutes.

Strain through a fine sieve or cheesecloth.

Note: For the best flavour, stock must be simmered, never boiled. Instead of a snapper head, you can use two or three heads of smaller fish, or bones and trimmings left after filleting fish. You will need about 500 g (1 lb) altogether.

White Stock

•

This is made as for chicken stock but veal bones (knuckle is ideal) are used in place of the chicken, or half veal and half chicken.

If using veal bones, save the bone from a shoulder or ask the butcher for a veal knuckle which he will saw in two to fit your saucepan.

Chinese Style Stock

•

A stock which combines chicken with pork bones gives a very delicate flavour which is characteristic of Chinese soups. To make this stock, use approximately 500 g (1 lb) chicken bones to 500 g (1 lb) pork bones.

Pork rib bones are good ones to use, and your butcher will save these for you if you give a little notice.

Put the bones into a deep saucepan and add 1 carrot and 1 onion, halved, a slice of fresh, green ginger, two spring onions cut into pieces, 1 teaspoon salt and 1 teaspoon white peppercorns. Add 5 cups of water (or enough to cover the bones) bring to the boil, skim the surface, then simmer very gently for 2 to 3 hours. Strain and cool, then refrigerate until needed. Use for Chinese soups.

ACCOMPANIMENTS FOR SOUP

An interesting accompaniment and garnish can make all the difference to a soup, adding flavour, colour and texture. Crusty fresh bread or rolls, hot herbed, cheese or garlic bread, little cracker biscuits, or crisp toast, are all quick to serve and go well with most soups, or you might like to try any of the following:

Crisp Accompaniments

Melba Toast Lightly toast slices of bread. Using a very sharp knife, cut each slice of toast through the middle producing two extremely thin slices. Place on a baking tray, and brown in a hot oven (200°C/400°F) until crisp and golden. Serve in a small basket. Melba toast should be stored in an airtight tin. It is a good idea to keep a supply on hand as it goes with so many things.

Croûtons Remove the crusts from thick slices of bread (use toast bread if possible). Cut the bread into 1 cm (½ inch) dice. Heat some oil, or a mixture of butter and oil, in a frying pan, making sure it is deep enough to cover the bread cubes. When hot, add bread and fry until golden, watch it carefully, because this will take only a short while. Remove the croûtons with a slotted spoon, and drain on absorbent paper. Sprinkle with a little salt before serving.

Croûtons can be made ahead of time, and reheated for 2 or 3 minutes on a baking tray in a hot oven. They are delicious with cream soups, and are the classic accompaniment to split pea soup.

Cheese croûtes Toast slices of bread on one side only. Spread the untoasted side with equal quantities of butter or margarine and grated cheese, mixed together. Brown under the grill, cut into triangles or squares and serve immediately.

Fleurons When making puff or flaky pastry, roll out the trimmings and cut into tiny crescent shapes with a fluted cookie cutter. Bake in a hot oven (200°C/400°F) for 10 minutes, and store in an airtight tin. Fleurons may be served cold or reheated for a few minutes in a hot oven. To vary the flavour, they may be brushed with milk or beaten egg and sprinkled with sesame or poppy seeds before baking.

Tiny Puffs (profiteroles) When making choux pastry (see recipe page 296), save a few tablespoons of the paste. Make a cone of greaseproof paper, fill with the paste, and snip off the end. Press out very small portions, about the size of a hazelnut, on to a lightly greased tray, and bake in a moderate oven (180°C/350°F) for 10 minutes, until puffed and golden. These are delicious with clear soups, and may be served in a separate bowl or floated on the soup.

Garnishes for Soup

As well as accompaniments, interesting and colourful additions may be made to the soup itself.

For Clear Soups

Float very thin slices of orange, lemon or lime on top. Add julienne (match-size) strips of vegetables like celery, carrots, parsnips and leeks, which have been cooked for a minute or two in a little salted water, until tender but crisp.

Add finely chopped parsley, chives, mint or other fresh herbs (not too much, or the flavour will overpower the soup).

To Cook in the Soup

Fine noodles, small pasta or macaroni shapes may be cooked in the soup to add body and texture. Brown or white rice and barley are good additions to hearty vegetable soups, and should be added for the appropriate cooking time towards the end of the cooking.

For Cream Soups Sprinkle with finely chopped parsley or snipped chives.

Just before serving, add a spoonful of salted, whipped cream and a dash of paprika or a sprig of parsley for colour. Spoon a little fresh cream over in a swirl shape just before serving.

Top with cubes of avocado dipped in a little lemon juice to prevent browning, or a teaspoon of finely shredded ham.

For Cold Soups Garnish with whipped, salted cream, finely chopped parsley, or finely chopped fresh vegetables (the type used in the soup) or snipped chives.

For Thick Soups When you are planning to serve a soup as the main course, extra nourishment and flavour comes from the addition of thickly sliced sausage such as cabanossi, clobassi, ham sausage or frankfurts. Chopped or match stick shapes of cooked meats, tongue, ham or chicken are also delicious garnishes. Add them in the last minute of cooking, so they just heat through. Chopped, hard-boiled egg makes a colourful and nutritious topping, and grated cheese may be sprinkled on top of individual bowls or served separately.

For an informal buffet party, it is a nice idea to serve a tureen of soup surrounded by various accompaniments and garnishes, so guests may help themselves. You might offer various breads and rolls, crackers, croûtons, grated cheese, Melba toast, and perhaps a choice of savoury butters.

Savoury Butter Work some herbs, a dash of lemon juice and salt and pepper into some unsalted butter. Chill, and cut into pats to serve. For anchovy butter mix butter with a little anchovy paste. Mustard butter and curry butter are made in the same way, and garlic butter is made with a crushed garlic clove, salt and pepper.

Vegetables à la Grecque are lightly cooked vegetables marinated in an aromatic sauce. Leeks, beans and mushrooms are ideal (see page 58).

Above: For a dinner party, serve a splendid first course of Avocados stuffed with crabmeat and accompany with Lime Mayonnaise (see page 59).

Right: Vegetables Vinaigrette and Stuffed Eggs topped with red and black caviar are as inviting as a still-life painting. See recipes on pages 58 and 72.

A Few Words on Soup

A blender is invaluable if you wish to make cream soups with a velvety texture and good flavour. If you don't have a blender, the soup may be pushed through a fine sieve to purée it. The food processor may also be used, but the texture will be just a little coarser.

Stock cubes are a great standby in place of homemade stock, but lack the jellied quality and delicacy of homemade stock, and tend to give a sameness of flavour. Good brands are available and are well worth the extra cost. Better still, make a batch of stock in double or triple quantities and freeze it for future use.

Do serve hot soup in hot soup plates, and chilled soups in chilled plates. If serving chilled soups from a tureen at the table, it looks spectacular set in a bed of crushed ice. A tureen of hot soup may be kept over a candle warmer at the table, ready for second helpings.

Hunt around for interesting bowls and cups in which to serve your homemade soups. Hearty soups look appetizing in earthenware or pottery bowls in rich colours. Iced soups need something more delicate looking, perhaps on a stem or in crystal, or those inexpensive Japanese lotus shaped bowls. Cream soups are often served in traditional porcelain soup cups with double handles.

You will find an interesting and inexpensive variety of bowls in shops that stock Chinese ware, and second-hand shops often yield treasures. Bowls don't have to match, as long as they are linked together by shape or colour.

Enjoy your beautiful soup!

HEARTY SOUPS

'Like most Frenchmen, I was raised on soup.' It was the famous chef, Louis Diat, talking. 'In our country home,' he went on, 'we had soup for luncheon, soup for dinner and always soup for breakfast. For us, a steaming bowl of thick, hearty leek and potato soup was a far better way to begin the day than the porridge of the British or the American's strange meal of orange juice and ham and eggs.'

Louis Diat of the Ritz-Carlton was a legend in his own lifetime, and though he lived in a world of luxury cuisine never overlooked the importance of good, homely soup. Soup for breakfast may be a bit hard for the average person to accept, but soup for luncheon and dinner is a very good idea, especially in the chilly days of winter. As a beginning to a meal it can seldom be bettered, and if it is a thick, hearty, stick-to-the-ribs kind of soup, it can be the meal itself. Many countries have these soup-meals and consider them a treat with accompaniments such as crisp croûtons, crusty bread, grated cheese or chopped, raw vegetables.

In a pot of well made soup you have an economical meal which retains every bit of the goodness and flavour of the ingredients used. Follow with a green salad, fresh fruit and cheese for a well-rounded meal.

The quantities for some of the soups may seem large, but they keep and reheat so well and everyone enjoys them so much, it makes good sense to make a generous quantity while you're at it.

Leek and Potato Soup

(Potage Bonne Femme)

••

Some soups are extraordinarily versatile – they can turn up again and again, looking and tasting quite different. Potage Bonne Femme is a good example. After it is puréed, it becomes Potage Parmentier and when chilled, and with cream added it becomes Vichyssoise.

4 leeks or onions
60 g (2 oz) butter
salt
white pepper
4 medium-sized potatoes, peeled and diced
6 cups chicken stock or water and stock cubes
2 cups hot milk
a little extra butter
croûtons or chopped parsley to garnish

Halve the leeks lengthwise, wash thoroughly to remove all the grit, then finely slice. Melt the butter in a heavy saucepan, add the leeks or sliced onions and cook over a low heat until soft but not brown. Season with a little salt and pepper, and add the potatoes. Stir in the chicken stock or water and stock cubes. Cover and simmer gently for about 30 minutes, or until the potato is tender. Blend in the hot milk and a little butter. Taste, and if necessary, add more salt and pepper. Serve hot in a tureen and garnish the soup with fried croûtons (see page 76) or chopped parsley. Serves 6–8 or 4 with enough leftover to serve a different way.

A light touch of curry powder adds interest to the onion sauce in Scallops Madras (see page 52). Add fresh lime slices, chopped parsley and coriander sprigs for colour.

Potage Parmentier

••

Prepare Leek and Potato Soup or use any leftover. Purée in an electric blender or in a food processor fitted with the double sided steel blade – this should be done a few cupfuls at a time – or push through a sieve. Reheat and lighten the soup with 4 tablespoons cream and 60 g (2 oz) butter. Serve hot, sprinkling with parsley or croûtons.

Vichyssoise

••

Make Leek and Potato Soup, omitting the butter added at the end of the cooking time. Allow the soup to cool, then purée in a blender or food processor, or push through a fine sieve. Stir in 1 cup cream and chill. To serve, top with a spoonful whipped cream or sour cream and sprinkle with finely snipped chives or parsley. Vichyssoise may also be served hot.

Pasta and Chick Pea Soup

••

A hearty soup-stew from Rome which easily serves 8 to 10 hungry people. Accompany with crusty bread and cheese.

250 g (8 oz) chick peas
salt
¾ cup olive oil
1 large clove garlic, crushed
8 anchovy fillets, finely chopped
3 tablespoons chopped parsley
4 large tomatoes, peeled and chopped
3 teaspoons dried rosemary
6–8 cups water
250 g (8 oz) elbow macaroni
grated Parmesan cheese

Place the peas in a large saucepan with cold water to cover. Bring to the boil, then remove from the heat and leave overnight. Next day, drain the peas, cover with fresh water, add a little salt and simmer until tender, about 1½ hours.

Heat the oil and slowly cook the garlic, anchovies and parsley for 5 minutes, stirring constantly. Do not allow to brown. Add the chick peas and liquid, tomatoes, rosemary and water. Bring to the boil, cover and simmer for 30 minutes.

Cook the macaroni in a large saucepan of boiling salted water until almost tender, about 8 minutes. Drain and add to the soup. Simmer the soup for a further 5 minutes to completely cook the macaroni, stirring occasionally. Season to taste with salt and serve with plenty of grated cheese. *Serves 8–10*

Tomato and Sweet Pepper Soup

••

Beaten eggs, flavoured with cheese, are stirred into this famous soup from Tuscany. The toasted bread should be thick slices of crusty French.

⅓ cup olive oil
2 onions, sliced
2 red peppers
1 cup diced celery
500 g (1 lb) tomatoes, peeled and chopped
salt
freshly ground pepper
2 litres (8 cups) boiling water
3 eggs
¾ cup grated Parmesan cheese
6 crusty bread slices, toasted

Heat the oil in a large heavy pan and gently cook the onions until soft and transparent. Remove the seeds and ribs from the peppers, then cut the flesh into strips. Add the peppers to the pan with the celery and tomatoes. Season to taste with salt and pepper and cook over a high heat for 5 minutes. Add the boiling water and cook for 30 minutes, taste and adjust the seasoning if necessary. Beat the eggs until smooth with a pinch of salt and stir in the cheese. Remove soup from heat and quickly stir in the egg mixture. Ladle into soup bowls over the slices of toasted bread. *Serves 6*

Goulash Soup

••

As the name implies this is a hearty soup and it tastes better when made the day before eating. It is often served in the crowded beer halls in Munich, Germany.

500 g (1 lb) shin of beef
60 g (2 oz) speck or bacon
1 large onion, finely chopped
1½ tablespoons paprika
salt
freshly ground pepper
2 tablespoons vinegar
1 tablespoon tomato paste
1 tablespoon caraway seeds (optional)
1 clove garlic
½ teaspoon marjoram
2 litres (8 cups) Beef Stock (page 74) or water
and stock cubes
3 medium potatoes

Cut the meat into small squares. Slice the speck or bacon, cut into strips and heat gently in a large pan until the fat runs. If speck is very lean add a little oil. Add the onion and cook with the speck until it is golden. Sprinkle with paprika and stir for 1 minute, then add the meat and brown very lightly. Sprinkle with a good pinch of salt and grinding of pepper and stir in the vinegar and tomato paste.

Simmer for 3–4 minutes, then add the caraway seeds, if using, crushed garlic, marjoram and stock or water and stock cubes.

Bring to the boil, cover and simmer over a very low heat for 45 minutes or until the meat is almost tender.

Peel the potatoes and dice. Add to the soup and cook for a further 20 minutes or until the potato is tender. Taste, and adjust the seasoning before serving. *Serves 6*

Lentil Soup

•

Slices of smoked sausage turn this hearty inexpensive soup into a meal. Check with your local delicatessen and be sure to choose a sausage that tastes best when heated.

2 cups lentils
3 litres (12 cups) Beef Stock (page 74)
1 ham bone or 8 bacon bones
1 pickled pig's trotter
2 medium potatoes
3 stalks celery, diced
2 teaspoons plain flour
½ cup sour cream
salt
freshly ground pepper
pinch grated nutmeg
smoked sausage, like Kransky

Wash and drain the lentils. Put into a bowl with plenty of water to cover and allow to soak for at least 2 hours. Drain and put into a large saucepan with fresh water to cover. Bring slowly to the boil and allow to cook for 10 minutes, then drain.

Return the lentils to the pan and add the beef stock, ham bone and pig's trotter. Bring to the boil and simmer for 2½–3 hours.

Lift the bone and trotter out and strain the soup, rubbing the lentils through the sieve, or cool the mixture and blend until smooth in an electric blender.

Return the soup to the saucepan and add the peeled and diced potatoes and celery. Bring to the boil and simmer for 30 minutes or until the potatoes are cooked. Blend the flour with the sour cream. Stir in a little of the soup and then stir back into the soup and simmer, stirring occasionally, for 10 minutes. Season with salt, pepper and nutmeg.

About 20 minutes before serving the soup, put the sausage into a saucepan of cold water, bring to the boil and simmer very gently for 10 minutes. Drain and slice. Place a few slices in each bowl and ladle the soup over. *Serves 6–8*

Scotch Broth

•

1 kg (2 lb) scrag neck of mutton
2.5 litres (10 cups) water
¼ cup pearl barley, soaked overnight
1 teaspoon salt
½ cup chopped celery
1 carrot, leek, turnip and onion, diced
freshly ground pepper
chopped parsley

Remove as much fat as possible from the mutton, then cut into small pieces. Put the meat and bones in a large saucepan, cover with the cold water and bring slowly to the boil. Remove the scum and add the drained barley and salt and simmer for 20–30 minutes. Add the prepared vegetables and freshly ground pepper. Cover and continue cooking gently for about 1½ hours. Remove the bones, cut any pieces of meat off them and return the meat to the soup. Skim fat from the surface of the soup. Adjust seasoning and sprinkle with parsley. *Serves 8*

Heat the oil in a large pan and gently cook the chopped ingredients with a small piece of the red chilli, until soft and beginning to colour. Add the drained beans and ham bone, cover with the water, season lightly with salt and pepper and simmer very gently for 2 hours, or until the beans are tender. Remove the ham bone and discard. Scoop out half the beans and purée in a blender or push through a sieve. Return the bean purée to the soup.

To make the cheese garnish: heat the oil and sauté the bruised garlic cloves and thyme until the garlic is golden. Strain half the oil into the soup, discarding garlic and thyme and stir the soup vigorously. Arrange the sliced bread in the base of a large ovenproof casserole or soup tureen and sprinkle with half of each grated cheese. Pour the soup over the bread, then cover the floating bread with wafer thin slices of onion, the remaining oil and grated cheese. Bake in a moderately hot oven (190°C/375°F) for about 30 minutes. *Serves 6*

Cheese-topped Bean Soup

••

From Italy, a bean soup in which half the haricot beans are puréed to thicken the soup while the rest are left whole. It is served with a topping of toast covered with sliced onions and grated cheese, then baked in the oven in the same way as French onion soup.

2½ cups (1 lb) haricot beans
1 clove garlic
1 onion
1 carrot
1 stalk celery
1 bunch spring onions, well washed
1 sprig rosemary
2 tablespoons olive oil
1 fresh red chilli
1 ham bone
2 litres (8 cups) water
salt
freshly ground pepper
Cheese Garnish
¾ cup olive oil
2 cloves garlic
pinch thyme
8 slices crusty bread
⅓ cup grated Parmesan cheese
½ cup grated Gruyère cheese
1 onion, very finely sliced

Cover the beans with cold water and set aside to soak for 12 hours or overnight; drain. Finely chop the garlic, onion, carrot, celery, spring onions and rosemary.

Chick Pea and Ham Soup

••

An adaptation of a Spanish soup recipe, this flavourful meal-in-a-bowl combines chick peas and veal in a stock made rich with a veal knuckle and ham bone. For extra sustenance, there's rice and vermicelli.

1 cup dried chick peas
250 g (8 oz) veal shoulder, boned
1 veal knuckle
1 ham bone
1 bay leaf
¼ teaspoon cayenne pepper
¼ teaspoon dried thyme
125 g (4 oz) speck, diced
1 onion, finely chopped
1 large potato
1 cup sliced cabbage
¼ cup rice
¼ cup broken vermicelli

Put chick peas into a bowl, cover with water and leave to soak overnight. Next day, drain the peas, put into a large saucepan with 2.5 litres (10 cups) of water. Add the veal shoulder and knuckle, the ham bone, bay leaf, cayenne pepper and thyme. Bring the soup to the boil, cover and simmer for 2 hours.

Heat the speck in a saucepan until the fat runs. Add the onion and cook until transparent. Peel the potato and cut into 1 cm (½ inch) cubes. Add to the soup with the onion mixture and cabbage. Simmer, covered for 30 minutes.

Add the rice and vermicelli and cook for 20 minutes or until the rice is cooked. Remove the ham bone. Cut the veal into large cubes and remove any meat from the veal knuckle. Return the meat to the soup, and reheat if necessary before serving. *Serves 6–8*

Peasant Soup

••

You can use any combination of vegetables for this soup, whatever is on hand. It is one of the simplest and quickest soups to make, as it doesn't require stock. It is ready as soon as the vegetables, which have been sliced finely, are tender.

2 cloves garlic
500 g (1 lb) onions
1 leek
250 g (8 oz) carrots
250 g (8 oz) white turnips
500 g (1 lb) potatoes
½ small savoy cabbage (the curly, bright green one)
250 g (8 oz) green beans
250 g (8 oz) streaky bacon, diced
½ cup olive oil
9 cups hot water
salt
freshly ground pepper

Crush or finely chop the garlic. Peel and roughly chop the onions; wash and slice the leek; peel and dice the carrots, turnips and potatoes; shred the cabbage, and cut the beans in 2.5 cm (1 inch) diagonal pieces.

Heat the oil in a large saucepan, add the garlic, onions, leek, and bacon and cook very gently until the onion is soft but not brown. Add the remaining vegetables and cook, stirring vigorously, for 2 minutes. Add the hot water, bring to the boil, then season with salt and pepper and simmer until the vegetables are tender. Serve with crusty bread. *Serves 6–8*

Soupe aux Choux

(Cabbage Soup)

••

Soup is very often the basis of the evening meal in France, as the main meal is eaten in the middle of the day. Cabbage soup is a typical soup of Auvergne, the central mountainous province renowned for its hearty meals.

¼ cabbage, about 500 g (1 lb)
1 tablespoon bacon fat or butter
125 g (4 oz) streaky bacon, chopped
1 large onion, finely sliced
1–2 cloves garlic, crushed
6 cups well-flavoured stock
salt
freshly ground pepper
1 large potato (optional)

Remove core from the cabbage, and shred finely. Drop into boiling, salted water, bring to the boil then drain well. Melt the fat or butter in a heavy pan, add the bacon, onion and garlic and cook over a low heat for about 10 minutes, until the fat begins to run out of the bacon. Add the well-drained cabbage, and stock, and bring slowly to the boil. Season with salt and pepper to taste and simmer gently for about 1 hour. Peel and slice the potato, if using, and add to the soup for the last 30 minutes. Dilute the soup with more stock if it becomes too thick. Serve very hot. *Serves 6–8*

Haricot Bean Soup

••

This soup is basically a thick bean purée. Haricot beans are cooked to the stage where they are soft but not disintegrated. The celery, leeks and tomato should also be very soft so that they can easily be pushed through a sieve. An egg yolk liaison binds the soup.

1 cup haricot beans
6 cups water
bouquet garni
1 medium onion, peeled
1 clove garlic, peeled
4–5 stalks celery, finely chopped
2 leeks (white part only) or 2 onions, finely chopped
60 g (2 oz) butter
4 large tomatoes, peeled
salt
2 egg yolks

Soak the beans in water to cover overnight. Place the beans and water in a saucepan with the bouquet garni and the whole or halved onion and garlic. Cook for about 1 hour or until tender. Cook the celery and leeks or onions in 30 g (1 oz) of butter until soft, but not coloured. Chop the tomatoes roughly, add to the pan and sauté gently for about 10 minutes. Discard the onion, garlic and bouquet garni from the beans. Combine the beans and liquid with the sautéed vegetables and rub through a sieve or purée in an electric blender or food processor. Return to the pan, season with salt and bring to the boil, stirring.

Just before serving, remove from the heat and mix in the egg yolks which have been combined with 2 tablespoons of hot soup. Stir in the remaining butter. Reheat, but do not allow to boil. Serve with croûtons of bread, fried in garlic flavoured oil. *Serves 6*

Tourin Bordelais

(Onion Soup)

••

*The mention of French onion soup conjures up
visions of a rich beef stock to which has been added very
thin onion rings, cooked in butter until they almost
melt away. But there's more then one French onion soup!
This one, thickened with egg yolks, is a speciality
of Bordeaux.*

60 g (2 oz) fatty bacon
3 large onions
salt
5 cups water
2 egg yolks
vinegar
6 thick slices French bread

Finely chop the bacon, put in a heavy pan and cook gently until
it renders out the fat. Peel and slice the onions as finely as
possible and cook slowly in the bacon fat, stirring until they
begin to soften. Season with salt, cover and cook slowly for
30 minutes, stirring as necessary, when they should be reduced
almost to a pulp. Pour over the cold water, bring slowly to the
boil and simmer for 10 minutes.

Beat the egg yolks with a few drops of vinegar and a few
spoons of the hot soup, then pour back into the soup, stirring
constantly. Do not allow the soup to boil. Serve very hot over
slices of bread baked in the oven until dry. *Serves 6*

Liver Dumplings in Broth

••

*Old fashioned dumplings are even more delicious when
they are flavoured with liver and served
in a nourishing soup.*

125 g (4 oz) liver (beef, calf, lamb, pork or chicken)
½ small onion
1 egg yolk
¼ teaspoon salt
pinch freshly ground black pepper
pinch of dried thyme
pinch grated nutmeg
1½ tablespoons chopped parsley
1½ slices bread, crusts removed
milk or water
approximately ½ cup sifted flour
5–6 cups stock

Trim the liver and mince with the onion, this can be done in a
blender or food processor. Remove to a bowl. Add the egg yolk,
salt, pepper, thyme, nutmeg and parsley. Soak the bread in
milk or water to moisten and squeeze out excess liquid. Add to
the liver. Add enough flour to make a soft dough.

Bring the stock to the boil. Dip a teaspoon in the stock then
fill with liver dough and drop the dough into the simmering
soup. Dip the spoon into the soup each time, before shaping
another dumpling. Cover the pot and simmer for 10 to 15
minutes, depending on the size of the dumplings. *Serve 6–8*

Italian Fish Soup

• • •

A superb fish soup which can be made simply with fish such as whiting, jewfish, bream, morwong or with a rich mixture of fish and shellfish. The fish should be scaled, then cut into small cutlets, steaks or thick fillets. As for Bouillabaisse, the pieces should not be too small.

3 tablespoons olive oil
1 small onion, chopped
2 tablespoons chopped celery leaves
1–2 cloves garlic, crushed
good pinch saffron
4 tomatoes, peeled and chopped
2 cups water
¾ cup dry white wine
salt
freshly ground pepper
dash cayenne pepper
1.5 kg (3 lb) mixed seafood
lemon juice (optional)
chopped parsley
8 slices crusty bread

Gently heat the oil in a heavy pan, add the onion and cook very slowly until transparent, but not coloured. Add the celery leaves, garlic and saffron, then the tomatoes. Cook, stirring occasionally, until reduced to a pulp. Add the water and wine. Season with salt to taste, plenty of freshly ground pepper and a dash of cayenne pepper. Simmer for 5 minutes. If the broth is too thick add a little more water. Add the prepared seafood and cook gently. Fish steaks take only 5–8 minutes, until the flesh flakes. If using mussels, cook only until they open. Cooked lobster and prawns require heating only. Taste and, if necessary, add more seasoning. If liked, a little lemon juice can be squeezed over. Serve garnished with chopped parsley. Accompany with sliced bread, which has been baked in a slow oven until golden. *Serves 4–6*

Note: The fish soup may be served with Rouille, a pepper and garlic sauce.

Rouille Place 4 cloves garlic in a mortar, food processor or blender with 1 or 2 canned pimientos, 3 egg yolks and a pinch of powdered saffron. Add 1 cup olive oil drop by drop, stirring with a pestle or processing or blending as you would for mayonnaise. Continue until the sauce is thick and smooth.

Osso Buco Soup with Burghul

• •

When buying the veal knuckle ask your butcher to slice it for you. If the veal is not available buy sliced shin of beef, instead.

This soup is sometimes made with crushed wheat instead of burghul. Soak wheat overnight and then cook with the meat until very tender. The cooking time varies, depending on the quality and age of the grain, but it generally takes about 2 hours.

2 knuckles of veal, sliced into 3 or 4 pieces
2 litres (8 cups) cold water
1 carrot, scraped
1 onion, peeled
1 teaspoon ground cinnamon
salt
freshly ground black pepper
1 cup burghul or crushed wheat
3 tablespoons finely chopped parsley

Wash the meat and bones, and put into a large saucepan with the water. Bring to the boil then remove the scum. Add the crushed wheat (if using), the carrot and onion, both whole, and flavour with the cinnamon. Season with salt and pepper and simmer gently, covered, for about 2 hours or until the meat is tender. Remove the vegetables and bones, leaving the meat in the pan.

If using burghul, add at this stage and simmer for about 15 minutes or until it is well cooked. Add more water if the mixture becomes too thick. The burghul will absorb a lot of liquid and expand considerably. Adjust the seasoning and serve garnished with the chopped parsley. *Serves 6*

SIMPLE SOUPS AND CHOWDERS

Vegetables can be cooked quickly in stock or water to make delicious soups. More hearty combinations of starchy vegetables like potatoes, cooked with fish, produce wonderful chowders.

Learn a few basic tricks to produce soups with great appetite appeal:

Cook chopped or sliced vegetables first in butter, or a mixture of butter and good oil, just to the point where they are soft and translucent. This brings out the distinctive flavour of the vegetables.

Vegetables for unstrained soups should be cut into convenient sizes for eating.

Add a little flour to the vegetables and butter, and cook for a minute before adding the stock, if a thicker soup is required. This also gives the soup a little 'body'.

Bring the soup to the boil, reduce the heat, and simmer only long enough to cook the vegetables and make a good blend of flavours

Salt only lightly at the beginning; taste and adjust the seasoning, if necessary, before the soup is served.

Fresh Tomato Soup

• •

In this soup, the lovely fresh flavour of tomatoes is retained by quick cooking, and enhanced with a pinch of sugar. Enjoy it hot or chilled, as is or puréed in a blender. Use basil when in season or parsley and a touch of marjoram or lemon thyme.

4 ripe tomatoes
1 tablespoon olive oil
1 clove garlic, crushed
2 tablespoons fresh herbs (parsley, basil
or combination)
pinch of sugar
2½ cups Chicken Stock (see page 75)
salt
freshly ground pepper

Peel the tomatoes by holding over a gas flame for 30 seconds, then the skins will easily slip off, or cover with boiling water, count to 10 then plunge into cold water and skin. Cut the blossom end from the tomatoes, halve and flip out the seeds, then chop.

Heat the oil and add the tomatoes, garlic and 1 tablespoon of the chopped herbs. Add a pinch of sugar and cook gently for 5 minutes, then add the stock and cook for a further 5 minutes. Taste and adjust the seasoning.

Serve immediately, sprinkled with the remaining herbs to garnish and croûtons or crostini (slim bread sticks). Or cool, place in the refrigerator and serve chilled. *Serves 6*

Pea and Egg Drop Soup

• •

6 dried Chinese mushrooms
1 cup fresh or frozen peas
4 cups chicken stock
2 eggs, lightly beaten
sesame or chilli oil (optional)

Soak the mushrooms in hot water for 15 minutes. Remove the stalks and cut into thin slices. Place the peas, mushrooms and stock in a large saucepan. Bring to the boil and simmer for 5 minutes. Remove from the heat and add the eggs, stirring until they separate into strands. Add a few drops of either sesame or chilli oil for a distinctive Chinese taste. Serve immediately. *Serves 6*

Rice Soup with Lemon

•

For a true Italian taste, more rice would be added to this soup, but I like this lighter consistency. You can vary it to your own taste by adjusting the amount of stock used.

⅓ cup raw rice
5 cups chicken or beef stock
2 egg yolks
juice of 1 lemon, strained
½ cup grated Parmesan cheese
2 tablespoons water

Wash the rice, and pour into the rapidly boiling stock. Boil for 15 to 20 minutes, or until the rice is cooked to your taste. Beat the egg yolks, lemon juice, Parmesan cheese and water together. Pour this mixture into a warm soup tureen and gradually pour in the boiling rice soup, stirring continuously. *Serves 6*

Pumpkin makes a golden, creamy, delicately flavoured soup. Add croûtons for a crunchy texture (see pages 96 and 76).

Five Minute Lettuce Soup

• •

For four people, heat four cups of chicken stock to simmering point (use homemade stock or water and stock cubes). When it starts to simmer, toss in about half a small lettuce or the outside leaves of a lettuce very finely shredded, and simmer for 3–5 minutes. Just before serving, beat two eggs with a few drops of soy sauce, add a little of the hot soup to blend, then pour into the soup. Serve immediately.

Crème à la Markova

•

This was a favourite of the great ballerina Alicia Markova. Add a good dash of Vermouth to a can of tomato juice, and just bring to the boil. Serve immediately, and float a spoonful of sour cream in the centre of each bowl.

Spanish Fish Chowder

• •

Capers and black olives add piquant flavour to this easily made chowder, which is a meal in itself served with warm, crusty bread and butter. For a true Spanish flavour try to get the fresh coriander, sometimes sold as Chinese parsley.

2 large potatoes
1.5 kg (3 lb) white fish fillets (flounder, leather jacket, haddock or whiting)
¼ cup olive oil
2 onions finely chopped
2 cloves garlic, chopped
3 tablespoons tomato paste
¼ cup pitted, small black olives, halved
2 tablespoons capers, drained and chopped
6 cups Fish Stock (see page 75)
finely chopped parsley or coriander

Bouquet garni

6 sprigs parsley
3 sprigs thyme
1 bay leaf

Peel and cook the potatoes then cut into 1 cm (½ inch) cubes. While the potatoes are cooking, check the fish fillets to make sure there are no bones then cut into 4 cm (1½ inch) pieces. In a deep saucepan, heat the oil and sauté the onions until soft and lightly coloured but not brown. Add the garlic and cook for

1 minute, then add the tomato paste and the bouquet garni, tied together.

Add the fish to the pan with the potatoes, olives and capers then pour in the fish stock. Stir gently to combine. Simmer the chowder over a moderately low heat for 6 to 8 minutes, or until the fish flakes easily when tested with a fork. Remove and discard the bouquet garni, ladle the chowder into heated soup bowls and sprinkle with chopped parsley or coriander. *Serves 6*

Smoked Haddock Chowder

•

I first tasted this fish in the home of a friend who always proclaimed she 'couldn't cook', and indeed, on a few occasions I had tended to agree with her! But she had created this short-cut recipe for herself, using packet soup and the result is truly delicious. For ravenous appetites, it would make a hearty first course before the main dish, but for luncheon or a light supper it is a satisfying meal in itself, served with crusty rolls.

250 g (8 oz) smoked haddock or other smoked fish
1 packet spring vegetable soup
2 potatoes, peeled and diced
1 cup frozen peas (optional)
½ cup cream or evaporated milk
salt
freshly ground pepper
chopped parsley

Cover the haddock with unsalted cold water and bring slowly to the boil. Poach gently for 2 minutes, drain, cool and flake. Prepare the soup according to the packet directions, using 1 litre (4 cups) of water. When boiling add the potatoes. Simmer for 10 minutes, then add flaked fish and peas, if using, and cook for a further 5 minutes. Stir in the cream or milk and remove from the heat. Check for seasoning, adding salt and pepper if necessary, ladle into bowls and sprinkle with the chopped parsley. *Serves 4*
Note: This is a wonderful week-end soup so it's worth making a double quantity.

Italian Fish soup is topped with a peppery mayonnaise called Rouille (see page 87). The combination of hot and cold is intriguing.

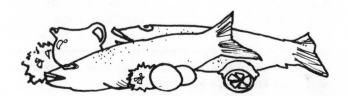

Clam Chowder

••

In the United States, fresh clams are used for this traditional chowder, but a delicious result may be obtained with canned clams. This is a hearty, but quickly made soup.

1 × 290 g can clams
1 thickly cut bacon rasher
oil for frying
1 onion, finely chopped
2½ cups water
2 medium potatoes, diced
salt
freshly ground pepper
1½ cups milk
½ cup cream
finely chopped parsley

Drain the clams, reserving the liquid and chop into small pieces. Finely dice the bacon and fry in a little oil in a deep saucepan until crisp. Add the onion and cook slowly until the onion starts turning golden. Add the clams, the reserved liquid and the 2½ cups of water. Bring to the boil and add the potatoes. Season well with salt and pepper and cook until the potatoes are tender. Remove the mixture from the heat and slowly add the milk and cream, which have been heated together. Serve immediately, sprinkling each bowl with a little finely chopped parsley. *Serves 6*

Borsch

•

Flavoured and coloured ruby red with beetroot, Borsch is the best known of all Russian soups. It is wonderful served hot or cold, and lends itself to many variations.

5 cups chicken stock
1 carrot, roughly chopped
1 turnip, roughly chopped
2 medium raw beetroots, chopped
salt
freshly ground pepper
vinegar to taste

Bring the chicken stock to the boil. Add the carrot, turnip and beetroot. Season with salt and pepper and simmer for 5 minutes, when the soup should be a good, red colour. Remove 1 cup of the liquid, return the soup to the heat and simmer for a further 15 minutes. Strain and add the reserved soup. Add a few drops of vinegar to taste.

Serve hot or cold in any of the following ways: Offer a small jug of vinegar, a dash gives the soup piquancy. Cut 1 medium beetroot into julienne strips and add raw to the soup. If serving hot, heat through gently. Stir 1 tablespoon of sour cream into each bowl of soup before serving, or top with a dollop of sour cream and sprinkle with snipped chives. *Serves 6*
Note: Borsch should be a good, clear red colour. When raw beetroot is added to the stock it bleeds, giving a rich colour which soon fades to a muddy brown. By removing and reserving a cupful of brightly coloured stock at the beginning, it is then added to the soup just before serving to give the soup its traditional rosy glow.

Variations

Orange Borsch • Strain the borsch before adding the seasoning. Stir in 1½ cups of fresh or canned orange juice with seasoning to taste. Chill. Blend a tablespoon of cream into each serving.
Jellied Orange Borsch • • Dissolve 2 teaspoons gelatine in a little hot borsch before the orange juice is added. Finish as for orange borsch, stirring the dissolved gelatine into the cooled soup. Chill until firm. To serve, chop the jellied soup roughly. Pile into chilled soup dishes and garnish with a spoonful of sour cream and a sprinkling of snipped chives.

Bouillon with Pastina

•

Pastina or pastine are the very tiny pasta so perfect for soups. Choose from several shapes, including tiny bows, small rings, stars and little beads of pasta the size of barley.

6 cups chicken stock
¾ cup pastina
1 tablespoon chopped parsley
¾ cup freshly grated Parmesan cheese

Bring the stock to the boil and add the pastina. When stock returns to the boil, lower the heat and cook for 10–15 minutes or until the pastina is tender, stir occasionally. Season the soup if necessary with salt and pepper, add the parsley and serve piping hot with grated Parmesan on the side. *Serves 6*

CREAM SOUPS

Thick, velvety cream soups can be made from all sorts of vegetables, poultry and seafoods. They are mainly made with a basic soup thickened with a roux of butter and flour, or the vegetables are pushed through a sieve to make a thick purée. Often, they are finished off with a liaison of egg yolks and cream, which 'binds' the soup, preventing it from separating and the solids from settling on the bottom.

At the same time, this gives the soup an indescribably rich and smooth texture.

Cream of Chicken Soup

• • •

This is one of the great classics and most delicate of cream soups.

60 g (2 oz) butter
⅓ cup rice flour
2 teaspoons salt
5 cups hot chicken stock
1 onion, halved
2 stalks celery, sliced
2 leeks, sliced
1–2 egg yolks
½ cup cream
white pepper
1 cup diced, cooked chicken

Melt the butter in a heavy saucepan, add the rice flour and blend well. Cook gently, stirring, until the roux turns a pale golden colour. Add the salt and hot chicken stock, stirring constantly. Add the onion, celery and leeks (use the white part of the leeks with just a little of the green, making sure it is washed free of grit). Bring the soup to the boil, skim if necessary, and simmer covered for 1 hour. Stir occasionally to make sure the vegetables do not stick. Force the soup through a fine sieve or mouli, or purée in a blender or food processor in several batches.

Wash out the saucepan, return the soup and reheat. Beat the egg yolks with ¼ cup of the cream, mix with a little of the hot soup, and add to the soup to heat, stirring constantly. Add the remaining cream, and correct the seasoning with a little salt and white pepper. Add the chicken and heat through. *Serves 6*

Note: The cooked chicken can be some of the chicken cut from a boiling fowl, if this was used to make the stock. Failing this, buy 2 boned, half chicken breasts, and gently poach in 1 cup chicken stock for about 10 minutes. Keep aside. When required, remove from stock and cut into dice. Or dice the cooked chicken and store until needed, moistened with a little stock to prevent drying out.

Cream of Cauliflower Soup

• •

Egg yolk and cream enrich this delicately flavoured soup. Add a sprinkling of snipped chives for colour when serving, and accompany with crunchy croûtons or bread sticks.

1 medium cauliflower
4 cups chicken stock
⅓ cup milk
30 g (1 oz) butter
salt
white pepper
pinch grated nutmeg
2 egg yolks
¼ cup cream

Remove the outside leaves from the cauliflower and break into florets. Drop the cauliflower into a pan of boiling, salted water and cook until tender, about 10 minutes. Drain and press through a sieve or purée in an electric blender. Place in a pan, add the stock, and bring slowly to the boil. Add the milk, butter, salt, pepper and nutmeg. Combine the egg yolks with the cream, add a little of the hot soup, blend well, and return to the pan. Cook gently without boiling until the soup thickens. Serve immediately. *Serves 4–6*

Cream of Green Pea Soup

•

When you have to serve something delicious in a hurry, remember this soup – it's made in minutes from simple ingredients that are usually on hand.

1½ cups frozen peas
2 cups water
1 bay leaf
sprig fresh thyme or pinch dried thyme
pinch sugar
2 teaspoons arrowroot
½ cup milk
½ cup cream or evaporated milk
salt
freshly ground pepper

Do not thaw the peas. Bring the water to the boil with the bay leaf, thyme and sugar. Add the peas and cook for 5 minutes. Remove the bay leaf and purée the peas in an electric blender until smooth, or push through a sieve. Blend the arrowroot with a little milk and add the remaining milk and cream. Bring to the boil, stirring gently, and season to taste with salt and pepper. Garnish with sliced frankfurts, crisp bacon pieces or a spoonful of sour cream sprinkled with paprika. *Serves 4–6*

Zucchini Soup

•

Fresh vegetables are cooked briefly in a little butter and oil to bring out the flavour, then stock is added. Only a little more cooking is required and the vegetables are tender enough to purée, retaining all their flavour and goodness and providing their own thickening.

2 teaspoons butter
2 teaspoons oil
1 small onion, peeled and chopped
6 zucchini, thickly sliced
1 medium potato, peeled and sliced
salt
freshly ground pepper
½ teaspoon dried tarragon (optional)
3 cups Chicken or Beef Stock (see pages 74 or 75)

Heat the butter and oil in a pan, add the prepared vegetables, and sprinkle with salt, pepper and tarragon. Cover and cook over a low heat for 10 minutes, shaking the pan occasionally and checking that the vegetables do not colour. Add the stock and simmer, covered, for 10 minutes until the vegetables are soft. Cool, then push through a sieve or purée in a blender in several batches. Reheat the soup, adding more seasoning if necessary. For extra richness, 1 tablespoon of cream may be added to each serving. *Serves 4*

Cream of Pimiento Soup

•

This is a colourful soup, with bright red flecks of pimiento through it and nourishing, as well, with the addition of grated cheese and milk to the chicken broth.

1 small onion, chopped
30 g (1 oz) butter
2 canned pimientos, chopped
3 tablespoons flour
1½ cups chicken broth
1½ cups milk (or half milk and half cream)
¾ cup grated cheese
salt
freshly ground black pepper

Sauté the onion in the butter until the onion is tender, but not brown (take care not to burn). Add the pimentos. Blend in the flour, then gradually add the chicken broth and milk, or milk and cream. Stir over a low heat until thickened. Add the cheese, and stir until melted. Season with salt and pepper and serve. *Serves 4*

Cream of Curried Pea Soup

•

Here's a soup that is delicious served hot or chilled. Fresh green peas are the basis of many excellent soups although frozen peas can be substituted if you cannot find really tender, fresh ones. With an electric blender or food processor to help, this delicately flavoured soup takes only 20 minutes from start to finish.

1 cup shelled, fresh peas
1 medium onion, sliced
1 stalk celery with leaves, sliced
1 medium potato, sliced
1 clove garlic, peeled
1 teaspoon salt
1 teaspoon curry powder
2 cups chicken stock
1 cup cream

Place the prepared vegetables, garlic, salt, curry powder and 1 cup of the stock in a saucepan and bring to the boil. Cover, and simmer for 15 minutes. Place the vegetables and liquid in a blender, removing the garlic if preferred. Cover and blend the mixture. Remove the cover, and with the motor running, add the remaining stock and cream. Alternatively, push the peas through a fine sieve and return the purée to the pan with the stock and cream. Stir to combine and reheat gently. Serve hot with croûtons.

This soup can also be served chilled, top with whipped cream and snipped chives or parsley. *Serves 6*

Cream of Oyster Soup

••

For a gala finish to this soup the additional oysters can be rolled in flour, dipped in beaten egg then coated in dry, fine breadcrumbs. Fry in hot oil until golden, drain on kitchen towels and thread quickly on to skewers, allowing 3 to 4 oysters per person. An unusual garnish for a special occasion.

45 g (1½ oz) butter
3 tablespoons flour
4 cups Fish Stock
salt
ground white pepper
squeeze lemon juice
½ cup cream
2 egg yolks
2 dozen oysters
additional 2 dozen oysters for garnish (optional)

Melt the butter in a large saucepan, remove from heat and blend in the flour. Return to the heat and cook, stirring, for a few minutes until a pale straw colour. Add the stock and bring slowly to the boil, stirring constantly. Lower the heat and simmer gently for 10 minutes. Season to taste with salt, white pepper and lemon juice. Combine the cream with the egg yolks, add a little of the hot soup then pour slowly into the pan. Do not allow to boil after this addition. Place the oysters into a soup tureen and pour in the hot soup. Serve with the extra oysters, prepared as above, if liked. *Serves 6*

Fish Stock: Wash 750 g (1½ lb) fish bones, preferably a snapper head, and place in a large pan with enough water to barely cover. Add 1 large onion, peeled and sliced, 1 stalk celery and 1 carrot, sliced, a piece of bay leaf the size of a 10 cent coin, a piece of thyme, ½ teaspoon salt and 6 peppercorns. Add ½ cup dry white wine and a slice of lemon. Cover and simmer very gently for 25 minutes. Strain and use.

Cream of Lettuce Soup

••

If you haven't tasted lettuce soup, be prepared for a delicious surprise. Lightly cook the lettuce and the soup will have a lovely green colour. This is a rich soup, so the rest of the meal can be light and simple.

60 g (2 oz) butter
1 small onion, chopped
1 large lettuce, chopped
salt
freshly ground pepper
3 cups chicken stock
2 egg yolks or 2 teaspoons arrowroot
½ cup cream
fried croûtons and chopped mint

Melt the butter in a large saucepan, add the onion, and cook until soft but not brown. Add the lettuce to the pan, season with salt and pepper and cook over a low heat for 5 minutes, or until the lettuce is soft. Rub through a sieve or purée in an electric blender with a little of the stock.

Heat the remaining stock and add the lettuce purée. Beat together the egg yolks or arrowroot and cream. Stir into the soup mixture and cook over a low heat, stirring all the time, until the soup begins to thicken. Do not let the soup reach boiling point. When beginning to thicken, remove from the heat, taste and adjust the seasoning if necessary, and serve with fried croûtons and freshly chopped mint. *Serves 6–8*

Pumpkin Soup

••

A little nutmeg enhances the delicate, nutty flavour of this golden soup, which is best eaten the day it is made.

1.5 kg (3 lb) pumpkin
90 g (3 oz) butter
1 large onion, finely chopped
2 cups water or chicken stock
3 tablespoons flour
1 cup hot milk
1 egg yolk
salt
freshly ground pepper
cream and ground nutmeg or croûtons to serve

Peel and chop the pumpkin into chunks. Melt 60 g (2 oz) of the butter in a heavy pan and add the onion and pumpkin. Cook gently for about 10 minutes, stirring frequently. Add the water or stock, cover and simmer until the pumpkin is tender. Cool slightly and push through a sieve or purée in an electric blender with a little of the milk.

Melt the remaining butter in the rinsed-out pan and blend in the flour. Cook for 1 minute without colouring, and add the pumpkin purée. Gradually stir in the milk and simmer gently for about 10 minutes. Add salt and pepper to taste. Just before serving, combine the egg yolk with a little of the hot soup and return to the pan without allowing to boil.

Taste and adjust the seasoning, if necessary. Serve in heated bowls with a spoonful of fresh cream on top and a sprinkle of nutmeg or crisp croûtons. *Serves 6*

SOUPS WITH A TOUCH OF CLASS

These are soups that are just a little bit different, with that touch of class which can start a meal off in a very special way. These are 'show-off' soups.

It's not that other soups are not every bit as enjoyable, but I'm talking about the ones you don't see all that often, mainly because of their cost, or the scarcity of one of the ingredients. It's well worth while hunting for that can of turtle soup, bunch of watercress, oysters or fresh mussels, or peeled walnuts that are used to give distinction to these special soups.

Then there are chilled soups, which are finding more of a place in our lives and with very good reason. They are delicious in the summer months when appetites flag, they take on an important air when served in a bed of crushed ice, and they're practical – for if there's a change in the weather, most of them take kindly to being heated gently and served hot.

Oyster Soup Rockefeller

•••

In some countries you'd need to be as rich as Rockefeller to make this soup – don't let the price of fresh oysters put you off, substitute with a can of oysters (not smoked) and sit back and enjoy the feeling of wealth.

1 bunch spinach
60 g (2 oz) butter
1 small onion
1 tablespoon flour
1 cup fish or chicken stock
2 cups milk
1–2 egg yolks
1 cup cream
24 fresh, bottled or canned oysters
salt
freshly ground pepper

Wash the spinach leaves carefully to remove any grit. Remove the white stalks, make a stack of the spinach leaves, roll up and slice. Put the leaves in a large saucepan, cover, and steam gently for 3–4 minutes. Drain off any water. Chop the spinach finely, or chop in a food processor fitted with the double-edged steel blade.

Melt the butter in a large saucepan, add the chopped onion and cook gently until the onion is soft. Add the flour and blend

in, cook for 1 minute. Add the spinach, stock and milk and bring slowly to the boil, stirring. Reduce the heat, cover and simmer gently for about 10 minutes.

Mix the egg yolks with ½ cup of the cream, add a little of the hot soup, and use to thicken the soup by stirring over a gentle heat. Add remaining ½ cup of cream and the oysters, which have been halved (do this over the soup, as you don't want to lose any of the precious oyster juice). Taste and adjust the seasoning and serve hot. *Serves 6*

Potage au Cresson

(Cream of Watercress Soup)

● ● ●

Sprigs of watercress are a popular garnish in French restaurants. Small bouquets are prepared and kept in iced water ready to finish a special dish. The leftover stalks are used to make this classic soup. Watercress is often seen growing wild by a river, but for those in the city some greengrocers and most Chinese stores sell it in large bunches.

1 bunch watercress
30 g (1 oz) butter
1 onion, finely chopped
1 tablespoon plain flour
3¾ cups milk
salt
freshly ground pepper
2 egg yolks
½ cup cream
extra watercress sprigs to garnish
croûtons

Pick off the sprigs of watercress and reserve about 2 cups. Wash the watercress, remove any fine hairs and shred finely, including the stalks.

Melt the butter in a large saucepan, add the onion and watercress, cover and cook gently for about 5 minutes or until soft. Draw aside and blend in the flour. Bring the milk to a boil, pour on to the watercress and season well with salt and pepper. Simmer gently for about 15 minutes. Rub the mixture through a sieve or purée in an electric blender, then strain through a sieve. Return the soup to the pan and reheat slowly. Combine the egg yolks and cream. Stir a little of the hot soup into the egg yolks then stir back into the pan. Heat the soup only until it thickens slightly – do not boil.

Finely chop sprigs of watercress and stir into the soup. Taste and adjust the seasoning, and decorate with watercress sprigs. Serve croûtons separately for sprinkling on the soup. *Serves 4–6*
Note: If using a blender, don't neglect to rub the purée through a sieve after blending as this removes any remaining fine hairs.

Lady Curzon Soup

●

A soup with a legend! Lady Curzon, wife of the great Viceroy of India was ordered by her physician and husband to refrain from tippling. She fooled both of them when she introduced this delicious soup at dinner one evening – they sipped away oblivious of what they and she were enjoying, thanks to the spicy flavour of curry powder. Never underestimate a woman!

2 × 300 g cans concentrated clear turtle soup
¾ cup cream
¾ cup brandy
2–3 teaspoons curry powder

Heat the soup with 2 soup cans of water, according to the directions on the can. Mix the cream, brandy and curry powder together in a small saucepan and warm over a gentle heat. Add to the soup and reheat but do not allow to boil. Serve immediately in small soup cups and accompany with Cheese Sables. *Serves 6*
Note: If turtle soup is not the concentrated variety, it will be necessary to make up the quantity (5 cups) with an extra 2 cans of soup.

Boula

••

*Green turtle soup is becoming a rarity. A good rich beef
consommé may be substituted and makes a good
stand-in but made in its original way this really is one of the
world's most elegant soups.*

500 g (1 lb) fresh green peas or 300 g (10 oz)
frozen peas
2 × 300 g cans clear turtle soup
½ cup sherry
salt
freshly ground pepper
½ cup cream

Shell the peas, or use frozen ones, and cook until tender in a
little boiling salted water. Drain and press the peas through a
fine sieve. Add the turtle soup to the pea purée and heat to
boiling point. Add the sherry and season to taste with salt and
pepper. Ladle the soup into individual earthenware casseroles.
Whip the cream and put a generous spoonful on each serving.
Put the casseroles under a grill for 2–3 minutes or until the
cream is lightly browned. Serve immediately. This soup may
also be served in small china bowls with the cream stirred
through. *Serves 4–6*

Creamy Pot Herb Soup

•••

*Fresh herbs and fresh green peas add a flavour of spring to
this creamy soup. If fresh peas are not available,
you may substitute frozen peas, but for the wonderful
flavour you do need fresh herbs – although
carefully micro-dried fresh herbs are fine.*

1 leek, washed and sliced
1 cup shelled fresh green peas
4 cups chicken stock
3 spring onions
2 tablespoons snipped chives
small bunch fresh chervil
6 sprigs parsley
30 g (1 oz) butter
1 tablespoon flour
½ cup milk
salt
freshly ground black pepper
2 egg yolks
¼ cup cream

Cook the leek and peas in 3 cups of the stock in a covered
saucepan until tender. Meanwhile, chop very finely the spring
onions, chives, chervil and parsley. Melt the butter in a

saucepan, add the flour and stir until well blended. Bring the
milk and remaining cup of stock to the boil and add all at once
to the roux mixture, stirring vigorously with a whisk. Season to
taste with salt and pepper.

Blend the sauce with the leek and peas and the stock in which
they were cooked. Add the chopped spring onion and herbs
and mix well.

Beat the egg yolks with the cream, blend with a little of the
hot soup and add to the soup.

Reheat stirring over a gentle heat, but do not boil. Serve hot.
Serves 6

Cold Senegalese Soup

••

*This creamy soup, with its subtle curry flavour,
would be perfect for a luncheon party. You might like to
serve it with traditional curry accompaniments
such as coconut, peanuts, sultanas, poppadums, sliced
banana with lemon juice, so guests can add their
own garnishes.*

60 g (2 oz) butter
1 medium onion, coarsely chopped
1 stalk celery, sliced
1 tablespoon flour
2 teaspoons curry powder
1 apple, peeled and chopped
1 cup diced, cooked chicken
5 cups Chicken Stock
1 bay leaf
½ cup cream, chilled

Melt the butter in a frying pan, add the onion and celery and
cook until the vegetables are soft but not coloured. Add the
flour and curry powder and cook, stirring, for several minutes.

Transfer the mixture to an electric blender. Add the apple,
chicken and about 1 cup of the chicken stock and blend until
smooth.

In a saucepan combine the puréed mixture with the
remaining stock, add the bayleaf and bring to the boil. Remove
and discard the bayleaf and chill the soup. Just before serving,
stir in the chilled cream. *Serves 6–8*

*Soup accompaniments include Melba toast, croûtons, fleurons,
whipped cream and profiteroles. See page 76 for the accompaniments
and 88 for the recipe for Fresh Tomato Soup.*

Right: Smoked Haddock Chowder (see page 91) is a substantial soup. Add crisp rolls and butter and lunch is ready.

Below: One of the world's great soups, Vichyssoise combines leeks, potatoes, chicken stock and cream (see page 82). It is served cold.

Avocado Soup

(Sopa de Aguacate)

• •

A delicious summer soup, served chilled. A few crunchy corn chips or tostadas (crisp fried tortillas) may be munched with this soup to give a Mexican flavour.

3 medium avocados
1–2 tablespoons lemon juice
1 cup milk
1½ cups chicken stock or water
1 teaspoon salt
dash Tabasco sauce

Halve the avocados, remove the stones and peel. Cut the avocados lengthwise into wafers, set half aside and sprinkle with some of the lemon juice. Place the first batch of avocados with the milk and stock in a blender. Blend until smooth – this should be done in several batches. Add salt, Tabasco sauce and the remaining lemon juice. Combine thoroughly. Coarsely chop the remaining avocado. Add to the soup and combine gently. Chill thoroughly. If too thick, thin down with a little stock or cream. This should make about 4 cups *Serves 4–6*

Walnut Soup

• •

Shelled walnuts are the secret of this beautiful soup. Shelled walnuts can be bought in cans or at a good Chinese grocer. If you have to prepare them yourself, cover the walnuts with water, bring slowly to the boil, simmer for a few minutes, then drain and start peeling. A few extra hands make the job simpler.

125 g (4 oz) walnuts, chopped
1 clove garlic, crushed
4 cups beef or chicken stock
¾ cup cream
salt
freshly ground pepper

Using a pestle and mortar, food processor or electric blender, pound the walnuts with the garlic and a little of the stock until quite smooth. Add to the remaining stock.

In a large saucepan, heat the cream to boiling point then stir in the walnut mixture. Heat gently and season with salt and pepper. Serve hot or chilled. If serving hot out-of-doors, take to the table in a previously heated, covered tureen and serve in warm soup cups. *Serves 6*

Chopped green olives and olive oil add a touch of the Mediterranean to whole baked fish. This is an easy recipe, see page 107.

Iced Tomato Dill Soup

• •

Fresh dill is available from many greengrocers, or you may be lucky enough to have it in your own herb garden. If the fresh is not available, use a good quality dried dill.

3 large tomatoes, peeled and sliced
1 medium onion, sliced
1 small clove garlic, crushed
1 teaspoon salt
¼ teaspoon freshly ground black pepper
3 sprigs fresh dill or 1 teaspoon dried dill
1 tablespoon tomato paste
¼ cup cold water
½ cup cooked macaroni, any type
1 cup chicken stock
¾ cup cream

To garnish

fresh dill sprigs, chopped
1 peeled chopped tomato

Put the tomatoes into a saucepan with the onion, garlic, salt, pepper, dill, tomato paste and water. Cover and simmer for 15 minutes. Transfer to an electric blender or food processor fitted with the double-edged steel blade. Add the macaroni, cover, and turn the motor on to high. Uncover, and with the motor running add the stock and cream. Chill, and serve garnished with the chopped dill and tomato.

Chopped parsley or finely snipped chives can be substituted if fresh dill is not available. *Serves 4*

Iced Pepper Soup

•

A nutritious refreshing soup that can be made in a few seconds. Use red or green peppers.

2 large peppers
2 cups chicken stock
2 tablespoons lemon juice
¼ teaspoon Worcestershire sauce
2 cloves garlic, chopped
salt
freshly ground pepper
sour cream to garnish

Remove the seeds and membrane from the peppers and dice. Place the peppers in a blender container with 1 cup of the stock, the lemon juice, Worcestershire sauce, garlic and salt and pepper to taste. Blend at high speed until fairly smooth, then add the remaining stock. Taste and adjust the seasoning and chill. Serve with a dollop of sour cream. *Serves 4*

Iced Spinach Soup

•

Here is just about the easiest chilled soup you can make — yet it is deliciously creamy and lovely to look at.

30 g (1 oz) butter
1 onion, finely chopped
1 clove garlic, crushed
1 can spinach
4 cups chicken stock
salt
freshly ground black pepper
1 cup cream
snipped chives

Melt the butter and sauté the onion and garlic until transparent. Add the spinach, chicken stock and salt and pepper to taste. Simmer for about 8 minutes, then chill. Just before serving taste and adjust the seasoning and add the cream. Serve cold, sprinkled with snipped chives. *Serves 4–8*
Note: When fresh spinach is available use instead of the canned to make into a very fine soup. Wash the leaves of 1 bunch of spinach, remove the white stalks and roughly chop the leaves. Place in a large saucepan, cover, and steam for about 5 minutes shaking the pan to prevent burning. Drain and chop the spinach or run through a food processor or blender then proceed with the recipe, replacing the canned spinach with fresh.

Lebanese Cucumber Soup

• •

A refreshing soup for hot weather, it becomes a light meal when a few extra hard-boiled eggs are chopped to sprinkle over each serving.

1 cucumber
salt
2 cups cold chicken stock
²⁄₃ cup tomato juice
2 small cartons natural yogurt
½ cup buttermilk
freshly ground pepper
1 cup coarsely chopped, shelled and
cooked prawns
1 clove garlic
1 tablespoon chopped mint
1 hard-boiled egg, chopped

Peel the cucumber, leaving a little of the dark green skin on for colour. Dice finely, put on to a plate and sprinkle lightly with salt. Tilt the plate and leave to drain for 30 minutes. Drain the cucumber thoroughly after 30 minutes. Meanwhile combine the cold chicken stock, tomato juice and yogurt, and mix until very smooth. Add the cucumber, buttermilk, salt, pepper and prawns. Chill for a few hours.

Rub a soup tureen or small bowls with the cut clove of garlic. Pour in the soup, sprinkle with the chopped mint and hard-boiled egg just before serving. *Serves 6*

Iced Tomato Cucumber Soup

• •

Many iced soups are simply a salad in a well-flavoured liquid, such as the Spanish Gazpacho. This refreshing tomato and cucumber soup has diced raw cucumber and a combination of chopped herbs blended into a rich tomato stock. A little sugar added in the beginning brings out the best flavour of the tomatoes.

1 kg (2 lb) ripe tomatoes
4 cups chicken stock
1 teaspoon sugar
pinch grated nutmeg
salt
freshly ground pepper
30 g (1 oz) butter
1 tablespoon plain flour
2 cups peeled, diced cucumber
2 tablespoons chopped parsley
2 teaspoons chopped fresh basil or dill or
½ teaspoon dried
1 cup light sour cream
extra dill to decorate

Chop the tomatoes roughly and place in a pan with 2 cups of the stock and sugar. Bring to the boil and simmer gently for 15 minutes. Push through a sieve and return to the pan. Bring to the boil again and add the nutmeg and salt and pepper to taste. Work the butter and flour together to a smooth paste and whisk into the tomato mixture in small pieces, until boiling. Simmer for 5 minutes and pour into a bowl. Stir in the remaining stock and allow to cool. Add the cucumber, parsley, dill and sour cream. Taste and adjust the seasoning.

Chill well before serving and garnish with dill or parsley. *Serves 6*

FRESH FROM THE SEA

If there are no fairies at the bottom of my garden there is no feeling of loss, for I know the joy of sinking into a peaceful sleep to the gentle calls of the fishermen who ply their boats in the water that laps my garden wall.

Indeed there can be no sound or sight more reassuring than their calls and the brave little lights bobbing up and down in the cold of the night – for I know that tomorrow will be a good day at the local fish market.

Fish markets are fascinating: it would be a poor creature whose heart did not respond to the atmosphere, the strong smells notwithstanding. I regret that I have never visited The Fulton, the fish market that has become a legend in its lifetime and has kept New York city supplied with all manner of seafoods. Fisherman's Wharf in San Francisco, Puerto Mont in Chile, Helsinki's harbourside market square, the north of Scotland as the herring boats return from the North Sea, Dublin Bay . . . waves of nostalgia sweep over me as I think of them.

No Aladdin's cave could hold more promise, with fish heaped like treasure in chests overflowing with silver, gold, ruby and sapphire hues. There are boxes of rosy snappers, silvery smelts and sardines, gleaming metallic tuna, mackerel and jewfish, flat fish, round fish, big and small fish, ten thousand whitebait to a kilo (want to count them!), crates of crabs, crayfish and yabbies alive and wriggling, and the vivid pink and coral mounds of those that have already hit the pot, plus bags of oysters all smelling of the sea.

I have always loved fish and shellfish. Perhaps it is no coincidence that I now live close to the sea and a fresh fish market, where every kind of fresh fish and shellfish is available – even delicacies like tiny sardines, octopus and skate. I am thankful for my excellent delicatessen, where there is a supply of such treats as caviar from Russia, smoked salmon from Nova Scotia, herrings from the Baltic, glistening red salmon roe from Canada. The infinite variety of good food from the sea makes shopping an adventure in itself.

There are also occasions when frozen, canned, dried and the less glamorous smoked fish comes into its own. If you can't always depend on fresh fish you can still enjoy it in these convenient forms, and the nutritive value is the same. Fish is not only a good source of protein, but also of calcium, iron, iodine and niacin, and contains useful amounts of vitamins B_1 and B_2. With potatoes, rice or pasta and a crisp green salad or green vegetables it makes a complete and well-balanced meal.

Fish should be cooked with care, and it helps to love fish. I feel sorry for those whose sense of smell is almost too acute for easy living, and aren't really keen on preparing bought fish. My advice is to get the fishmonger to scale, clean, fillet – whatever is necessary. Most good fish shops understand and are most obliging about this.

In the chapter on the basics of cooking (see page 22) you will find information on choosing, cleaning and storing fish, and the basic ways to cook it – frying, grilling, poaching and baking. But you needn't always be basic with fish. In the Middle East, the Orient, the Pacific and in many parts of Europe and the Americas, fish is cooked in dozens of different ways and I hope you will try some of them.

Just one warning – fish must never be overcooked, and the rest is plain sailing!

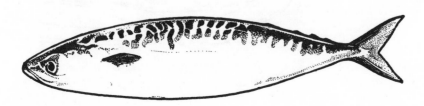

BAKED FISH AND VARIATIONS

An excellent way to prepare a whole fish is to bake it, and there are infinite variations. Fish can be baked either stuffed or plain, basted with a sauce or just a little butter, wrapped in foil or left uncovered, served in its own juices or with a separate sauce, and so on.

When buying a whole fish for baking, ask the fishmonger to scale and clean it for you, but to leave the head and tail intact. If you're lucky enough to catch your own, do the same thing – you will find instructions on cleaning fish in the beginning of the book, on page 23.

Always wipe the fish dry with paper towels, sprinkle with a little lemon juice and rub the inside cavity with salt as a basic step before baking.

To Serve Whole Baked Fish

A whole fish looks spectacular on the table, and you will want your family or guests to see it. Don't be frightened of serving it at the table – it's not difficult if you take a few simple steps beforehand. There's no harm in practising once or twice in the kitchen before giving your first public performance.

If the fish is large or very thick, it will be easier to serve, and cooking time will be reduced, if you make three or four diagonal slashes through the skin and half-way into the flesh on each side before baking. Have the slashes far enough apart to give you serving-size portions of fish. When the fish is cooked, transfer it to a heated platter.

At the table, lift the top portions of fish from the backbone with a fish server or a flat palette knife, and serve them. Then remove the backbone, which should now come away easily, and serve the bottom portions of fish. Some people are adept at handling fish and turn it over, but this takes practice.

An alternative method is used by the Chinese. The fish is not slashed before baking, but at the table a cut is made through the skin and flesh with a sharp knife right down the centre of the fish, and the skin and flesh loosened on the edges and behind the head. For a large fish, each long fillet may need to be cut through into smaller portions, as the diagram shows. When the top portions of fish are removed the fish is quickly flipped over on its other side, and the bottom pieces are cut and served.

It may sound tricky, but it's not! Practice helps. If you go to a Chinese restaurant and order a whole fish, you will be able to see a practical demonstration of this serving method. Otherwise, just take your whole fish and your sharp knife and off you go!

For large or thick fish make four diagonal slashes half-way through the flesh before baking, cooking time will be reduced and the fish is easier to serve

The Chinese are adept at serving fish at the table, a cut is made through the centre of the fish and the skin and flesh loosened on the edges. For a large fish cut through into smaller portions, the flesh lifts easily off the bones.

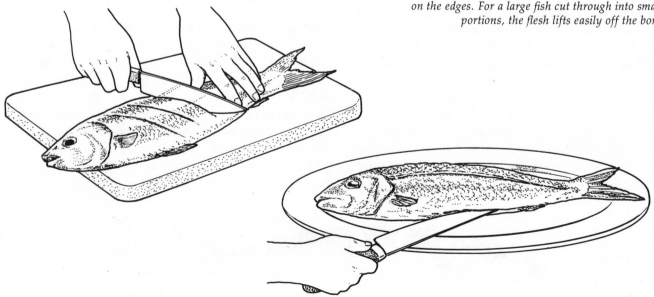

Baked Fish with Olives

•

This dish is generally made with red mullet, which are available for short periods of the year, usually around June, in Australian waters. If you can purchase red mullet, do try them. You'll recognise them from other red fish by the goatee-type beard! Other small fish may be used.

6 small fish (red mullet, whiting,
small bream etc.)
salt
²⁄₃ cup olive oil
½ cup white wine vinegar
½ cup green olives, pitted and chopped

Make sure the fish are cleaned and well scaled. Wipe with paper towels and sprinkle inside and out with a little salt. Place the fish in a baking dish. Drizzle with the oil and vinegar. Bake in a moderate oven (180°C/350°F) for 15 minutes, turning carefully with an egg slice half-way through. Remove the fish from the pan and keep warm. Add the olives to the pan and place over a low heat. Stir well, and spoon the olives over the fish, with a little of the pan juices. *Serves 6*

Baked Snapper with Herbs and Oyster Sauce

•

1.5–2 kg (3–4 lb) snapper
lemon juice
salt
freshly ground black pepper
60 g (2 oz) butter, melted
2 cups soft white breadcrumbs
1 sprig marjoram, chopped or pinch dried marjoram
2 tablespoons chopped parsley
cayenne pepper to taste
2 rashers bacon, cut in two

Have the fish cleaned, but leave the head and tail intact. Rub with lemon juice and sprinkle the cavity with salt. Preheat the oven to hot (200°C/400°F). Heat the butter in a frying pan and lightly brown the crumbs in it. Add the marjoram, parsley, salt, pepper and cayenne pepper and mix together. Stuff the fish loosely with the mixture and close the cavity with skewers and string.

Line a baking dish with foil by using a double thickness and allowing it to overlap at both ends. This will make handles, so it is easy to lift out the cooked fish without breaking it.

Grease the foil, place the fish on it and arrange the bacon on top. Bake, uncovered, for 30 to 40 minutes or until the fish

flakes easily when tested with a fork. While the fish is cooking, make the Oyster Sauce. Using the foil as handles, transfer the fish to a heated platter. Pour over the Oyster Sauce and serve. *Serves 4–6*

Oyster Sauce

1 dozen oysters (bottled are ideal)
30 g (1 oz) butter
1 tablespoon flour
½ cup cream
salt
white pepper

Melt the butter in a small saucepan. Blend in the flour with a whisk and add the oyster liquor. Lightly whisk over a gentle heat until thickened. Add the cream gradually until a shiny, smooth sauce results. Add the oysters and heat through (do not allow to boil). Taste and adjust the seasoning and serve over the baked fish.

Baked Fish Fillets

Fillets also lend themselves to oven baking, and are especially convenient prepared this way when you are in a hurry – just pop them in the oven and they cook without watching while you are getting the vegetables or salad ready. However, there are just a few things to keep in mind if you want perfectly cooked baked fillets, moist and flavourful.

First, remember that fillets will cook quickly, so the timing must be right or they could dry out and lose flavour. (See the section on basic fish cooking in the beginning of the book for advice on timing, page 23.)

Second, use a high oven temperature for best results – about 200°C/400°F.

To retain moisture, bake the fillets in buttered foil, or in a sauce, or in a coating of buttered egg and breadcrumbs (in which case they become oven-fried fillets as the recipe on page 108 shows).

Quick Baked Fillets of Fish

•

Preheat the oven to hot (200°C/400°F). Butter an ovenproof dish and arrange 500 g (1 lb) of fish fillets in it. In a small saucepan place ²⁄₃ cup undiluted canned soup (tomato, celery, mushroom or asparagus) with 2 tablespoons milk or dry white wine. Bring to the boil, add a few grains of cayenne pepper, and pour over the fish. Bake uncovered for 10 minutes and serve with buttered rice and a crisp green salad.

Note: There are also some interesting sauce mixtures available. Lawrys White Wine Sauce would be excellent, made according to the directions and poured over the fish as above.

Baked Fish with Sour Cream and Anchovies

•

500 g (1 lb) fish fillets
1 onion, sliced
rind of ½ lemon
1 parsley sprig
1 bay leaf
4 peppercorns
salt to taste
1 cup water
1 cup dry white wine

Sauce

30 g (1 oz) butter
1 tablespoon flour
1¼ cups reserved court bouillon
¾ cup sour cream
6 anchovy fillets, chopped
butter

Wipe the fish with damp paper towels, skin if necessary and check for bones.

Prepare a court bouillon by combining the onion, lemon rind, parsley, bay leaf, peppercorns, salt to taste, water and wine in a deep-sided frying pan large enough to hold the fish. Bring to the boil, add the fish fillets, and poach for five minutes.

With a slotted spoon or spatula, carefully transfer the fillets to a buttered baking dish just large enough to hold them. Strain the court bouillon and reserve 1¼ cups.

To make the sauce: Melt the butter in a small saucepan, sprinkle in the flour and cook for one minute, stirring to blend thoroughly. Gradually add the reserved court bouillon, stirring continuously, and continue stirring over a gentle heat until the sauce is thickened. Blend in the sour cream, mixing well.

Sprinkle the chopped anchovies over the fish, then spoon the sauce over. Dot the top with butter and bake in a hot oven (200°C/400°F) for 15 minutes to heat through and brown the top, or you can brown the dish under a medium grill. *Serves 4*

Oven-fried Fish Steaks

•

4 fish steaks or fillets
1 teaspoon salt
¾ cup evaporated milk
¾ cup fine dry breadcrumbs
¼ cup grated Parmesan cheese
¼ teaspoon thyme
60 g (2 oz) butter, melted
paprika
lemon wedges

Dry the fish steaks thoroughly with paper towels. If using fillets cut into serving pieces. Preheat the oven to very hot (230°C/450°F). Add the salt to the milk and combine the breadcrumbs with the cheese and thyme. First dip the fish into the milk and then into the crumbs. Arrange the fish in a well-greased baking dish and spoon the butter evenly over. Bake in the hottest part of the oven for about 20 minutes for thick steaks or 12 minutes for fillets. Garnish with paprika and lemon wedges and serve hot. *Serves 4*

Baked Kippered Herrings

•

This would make an elegant Sunday brunch, served with creamy scrambled eggs and accompanied by hot bread rolls or hot buttered rice.

6 plain smoked kippered herrings (canned or packaged)
butter
juice of ½ lemon
few drops of Tabasco sauce
Worcestershire sauce (optional)
chopped parsley

Scrambled Eggs

4 eggs
¼ cup cream
30 g (1 oz) butter

Preheat the oven to hot (200°C/400°F). Lightly butter a baking dish and arrange the herrings in it. Dot with butter and bake until the butter melts and the fish is heated through, about 15 minutes. In a small saucepan or butter warmer, combine 3 tablespoons butter, the lemon juice, Tabasco and Worcestershire sauces. Pour over the hot herrings and serve sprinkled with chopped parsley. Serve with the scrambled eggs and hot buttered rolls or rice.

While the kippers are cooking, make the scrambled eggs. Beat the eggs with the cream. Melt the butter in a small pan (preferably Teflon-lined) and add the eggs. Cook gently, stirring now and again, until set. *Serves 6*

TROUT . . . A VERY SPECIAL FISH

What is the best way to enjoy trout?

Many fishermen who eat the trout they catch on the scene feel the ideal way is to dip them in flour and sauté each side quickly in butter or bacon fat, or a mixture of the two.

A classic method in Switzerland and France is to poach the trout until just cooked in a well-flavoured court bouillon, then serve them hot with little buttered potatoes – or cold, with a good mayonnaise or interesting sauce. For small fresh trout there's nothing nicer than to grill them whole, basting with butter and a squeeze of lemon juice.

Then we have the all-time favourites Trout Meunière and Trout Almandine – pan-fried trout with a topping of golden almonds, butter and lemon juice.

I confess I like trout all these ways, and hope you will like to try them as well! If fresh trout aren't available, look for the excellent frozen trout now available in the freezer section of many supermarkets.

Trout Meunière

•

Fish cooked meunière style is simply fish dusted lightly with seasoned flour then cooked quickly in butter until golden brown. It is a quick, practical method of cooking thick fish fillets or any small, whole fish – yet the results are as delicious as the most complicated recipe. There is a story that the Emperor Napoleon christened this method of cooking fish. He stopped at a small inn, called La Belle Meunière (The Beautiful Miller) because it was the miller's pretty wife who did the cooking, and found the pan-fried trout so delicious he decreed that the fish cooked this way should always be known as 'la belle meunière'.

Today we have shortened the title to simply Meunière but the method hasn't changed. The fish are cleaned and the fins trimmed close to the body. The head may be left on if desired (small fish are often cooked and served with both heads and tails intact). If the fish is thick, it is often slashed diagonally on both sides a couple of times. This keeps the fish from curling up as it cooks, and also allows the heat to reach the centre of the fish.

If you don't have a lovely fresh trout for this dish, frozen trout may be used (allow to thaw first at room temperature) or any small whole fish or fish fillets.

2 whole trout
milk
seasoned flour
60 g (2 oz) butter
2 tablespoons oil
extra 30 g (1 oz) butter
1 lemon
chopped parsley

Dry the trout. Dip in milk, then dust lightly with the seasoned flour, patting it lightly on the surface to dust off any excess. Melt the butter and oil in a frying pan, large enough to hold the trout without crowding.

When the butter is foaming, add the trout and cook until golden brown on the bottom, about 6 minutes. Turn carefully with a spatula and brown the other side. The trout is cooked when the flesh flakes easily when tested. Test by lifting up the flesh around the centre backbone with the tip of a sharp-pointed knife.

When the trout is cooked, transfer to a hot serving dish and place a few slices of lemon on each fish. Heat the extra butter in the pan and when it foams add a good squeeze of lemon juice. Season with salt and pepper to taste and pour the sizzling butter over the fish. Garnish the platter with chopped parsley, or parsley mixed with snipped chives.

Fish cooked meunière style may also be served with a delicious almond butter, and then it becomes Trout Almandine. *Serves 2*

Trout Almandine

•

Cook 3 or 4 trout in the meunière style, see page 109. Remove to a serving platter and keep warm. Make the Almond Butter sauce and pour over, serve immediately.

Almond Butter Sauce

60 g (2 oz) butter
¼ cup blanched, sliced almonds
1 tablespoon lemon juice
salt
freshly ground pepper

Heat the butter and gently fry the almonds until golden brown, do not allow to burn. Add the lemon juice, salt and freshly ground pepper to taste. Pour over the hot fish and serve at once. This sauce is also perfect with grilled or sautéed fish and goes well with vegetables such as broccoli, asparagus or green beans.
Note: The dedicated fish cook may want to splurge on one of the beautiful oval copper pans with stainless steel lining – perfect for pan frying fish, and lovely enough to go straight to the table. The French also make a cheaper version in cast iron, not as glamorous to look at, but just as effective to cook in.

Trout Poached in Court Bouillon

•

3–4 whole trout, fresh or frozen
1½ cups water
1½ cups dry white wine
1 bay leaf
2 sprigs parsley
6 peppercorns
½ onion, sliced
1 stalk celery
1 teaspoon salt

Have the trout cleaned and gutted but leave the heads and tails intact. If the trout is frozen, do not allow to thaw. Trim the fins close to the body. Place all the remaining ingredients in a pan, large enough to hold the trout placed side by side, and bring to the boil. Lower the trout into the boiling court bouillon and then start to count the cooking time: cook for exactly 5 minutes for fresh trout, or 8 minutes for frozen trout.

If serving hot, carefully remove the trout to a heated platter and pour over a little melted butter. Garnish the platter with lemon wedges and serve with tiny buttered new potatoes and a crisp green salad. *Serves 3–4*

If trout is to be served cold, allow to cool in the court bouillon. Remove the skin from the trout just before serving, and serve with a bowl of mayonnaise.

Trout with Pink Mayonnaise

•

Prepare the trout as directed left and cool in the court bouillon. Drain carefully and place on a flat working surface. Remove a strip of skin from the top middle section of each trout, for a decorative finish, but leave the heads and tails. Make the mayonnaise.

Pink Mayonnaise

1 cup Mayonnaise (see page 45)
1 tablespoon tomato paste
grated rind and juice of ½ lemon
salt
freshly ground black pepper

Combine all the ingredients, tasting for seasoning. Spoon the mayonnaise on the bottom of an attractive serving platter. Arrange the cold trout on the mayonnaise, and garnish with lemon slices and wedges of lime. *Serves 3–4*

Cold Poached Trout with Cucumber Sauce

•

This cool, beautiful green and white sauce has a base of Fromage Blanc, so even dieters may enjoy it without a guilty conscience!

poached trout
lemon wedges and parsley sprigs to garnish

Cucumber Sauce

1 small cucumber
½ cup Fromage Blanc (see page 47)
1 tablespoon lemon juice
pinch paprika
1 tablespoon snipped chives
½ teaspoon chopped dill

Poach the trout in court bouillon and allow to cool in the liquid (see left). Drain carefully and arrange on a platter with lemon wedges and sprigs of parsley. Serve the sauce separately.
Make the sauce: Peel the cucumber, cut in half lengthways and scoop out the seeds. Chop very finely. Combine the cucumber with the other ingredients, mix well, and spoon into a pretty bowl to serve.
Note: Sour cream, the light sour cream is ideal, may replace the Fromage Blanc in this recipe.

*Cold poached trout looks inviting served with pink mayonnaise and
a decorative lime and lemon garnish (see left).*

THE DELIGHTS OF COLD FISH

In many countries, cold fish plays almost as big a role as hot fish in family meals and special occasions. The Japanese have their delectable and beautiful-to-look-at Sushi and Sashimi, the Spanish their Escabeche, the Scandinavians their myriad versions of cold herrings and mackerel and the South Americans their Ceviche. In Scotland, fish is cooked and cooled in an aromatic liquid to become 'soused fish' and in the South Pacific raw fish is 'cooked' in lime or lemon juice and served with coconut cream, salads or toppings.

If you are feeling in an adventurous mood towards cooking, or want to serve something unusual and special for a dinner party, don't overlook the many possibilities of fish served cold. There's more to it than just splurging on smoked salmon or opening a can of sardines, as you'll see from the following recipes.

Soused Fish

•

Fish like herring and mullet take well to gentle cooking in acidulated water, as the vinegar cuts back the oiliness of the fish. It's also a good way of turning an inexpensive fish into a dish that's quite glamorous! Serve it as a first course, as part of a light lunch, or with any alfresco meal.

6 small mullet or herring
1 onion, sliced
2 bay leaves
1 clove
4 allspice berries or peppercorns
1 teaspoon salt
½ cup vinegar
water to cover

Ceviche (see above) is a version of cold fish salad often served in Mexico. Add a bowl of puréed avocado if you like.

Clean, scale and remove the fish heads. Lay the fish on a working surface, cut off the fillets and remove any bones. Place slices of onion on the centre of each fillet and roll up, skin side out, from head to tail, securing with a toothpick if necessary.

Place the rolled fish in a heavy flameproof casserole or pot with the bay leaves, clove, allspice or peppercorns and salt. Pour over the vinegar and just cover with water. Cover and cook over a low heat for 1–1½ hours or until the fish flakes easily when tested with a fork.

Transfer the fish to a serving dish, deep enough so the fish can be covered with liquid. Strain over sufficient cooking liquid to cover the fish. Cool, then chill in the refrigerator, where the liquor will set into a soft jelly. Serve with cucumber salad. *Serves 6*

Note: As this dish will keep well for up to 2 weeks in the refrigerator it's a great way of making the most of fish when they're running!

Ceviche

••

This version of cold fish salad is found in much of South America and in Mexico. The combination of textures is particularly interesting. If you wish, a separate bowl of finely-chopped chilli peppers can be offered with the Ceviche, so guests may help themselves.

500 g (1 lb) white, firm-fleshed fish fillets
2 lemons or limes
2 tomatoes, peeled and seeded
1 small green pepper, diced (or a mixture of red and green pepper)
4 tablespoons olive oil
4 tablespoons finely chopped parsley
1–2 tablespoons wine vinegar
dash Tabasco sauce
½ teaspoon oregano
salt
freshly ground black pepper
lettuce cups
1 avocado
6 pimiento-stuffed olives, sliced

Remove the skin and any bones and cut the raw fish into small dice. Place in a glass or china bowl and cover with lemon or lime juice. Cover and leave for at least 3 hours, turning the fish with a wooden spoon from time to time. Drain off the juice. Dice the tomatoes and add to the fish with the pepper, olive oil, parsley, vinegar, Tabasco sauce, oregano and salt and pepper to taste, stir to mix and spoon the Ceviche into individual bowls lined with chilled lettuce cups. Serve garnished with the diced avocado and sliced olives. *Serves 4*

Note: Diced avocado may be added to the Ceviche or make a purée of avocado, season with salt and pepper and a touch of Tabasco sauce and use as a sauce to spoon over the salad.

Tahitian Fish Salad with Coconut Cream

••

Any firm, white fish fillets are suitable for this dish. Limes are becoming more readily available now – or you might be lucky enough to have your own lime tree!

1 kg (2 lb) firm-fleshed fish fillets
juice of 4 or 5 lemons or limes (limes for
preference)
1 green pepper, diced
1 red pepper, diced
3 stalks celery, sliced into strips
4 spring onions including green parts, chopped
3 hard-boiled eggs
½–¾ cup Coconut Cream
salt
freshly ground black pepper

Carefully remove the skin and bones from the fish and cut into thin strips. Place the fish in a china or glass container. Pour the lemon or lime juice over the fish, cover and chill for at least 3 hours. Turn with a wooden spoon from time to time. Do not use a metal spoon. The juice will turn the fish white and opaque, so it looks cooked. Squeeze the juice from the fish by placing it in a plastic colander and pressing with a wooden spoon. Put into a bowl and add most of the peppers, reserving some for garnish, the celery, spring onions and chopped, hard-boiled eggs. Stir in the Coconut Cream and toss well. Season to taste with salt and pepper.

Place the fish salad in a large serving dish or shell, and chill. Or serve in individual bowls or shells. Garnish with the reserved chopped peppers to serve. *Serves 6–8*

Coconut Cream

•

Put 2 cups desiccated coconut into a saucepan with 1 cup of milk. Bring slowly to the boil. Cool, then put in an electric blender for a few seconds at high speed. Strain through a sieve lined with muslin, then squeeze the muslin to extract all the cream.

If you don't have a blender, pour the coconut mixture through a fine strainer, then push down with a wooden spoon to extract as much liquid as possible.

Keep the liquid in the refrigerator until ready to use, then skim off the creamy top for the salad. The remaining Coconut Cream can be used in a curry.

Cold Fish Italian Style

•

The centre of many a good restaurant buffet table can often be a cold fish, elaborately decorated and always absolutely delicious. A cold fish can star at a family meal, too. Just cook the fish with the same care as the professional chef, add a simple garnish and provide a bowl of good, homemade mayonnaise or vinaigrette. A green side salad and some crusty bread is all you need to make a memorable meal.

1.5 kg (3 lb) fish (snapper, cod or jewfish)
salt
1 cup water or Fish Stock (see page 75)
½ cup wine

To garnish and serve

parsley sprigs
2 lemons, quartered
1 cup Vinaigrette Dressing (see page 46) mixed
with 1 tablespoon chopped parsley or 1½ cups
Mayonnaise (see page 45)

Scale, clean and wash the fish thoroughly. Butter a large baking dish and line with buttered aluminium foil, allowing the ends to overlap and form handles; this makes the fish easy to remove when cooked. Lay the fish on the foil.

Bring the water or fish stock and wine to the boil and pour over the fish. Cover with foil and cook on top of the stove for 15–20 minutes, or until fish flakes easily when tested with a fork, or bake in a hot oven (200°C/400°F) for about 30 minutes. Add 2 cups of cold water to stop the cooking process and allow the fish to cool completely in the liquid. Drain, and carefully remove the skin. Place on a serving platter and garnish with the parsley sprigs and lemon quarters. Serve the vinaigrette or mayonnaise separately. A cold potato salad is nice with this. *Serves 6*

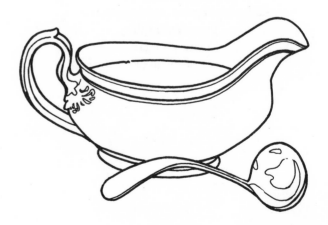

Cold Stuffed Baby Squid (Calamaretti)

• • •

An Italian recipe rich in flavour. There are many kinds of squid available. Some have a very white backbone called a cuttle, hence the name cuttlefish. Though not quite as tender as the squid with a transparent membrane, they are still excellent. Fresh squid are becoming available in more and more fish shops, and are always to be found at fish markets.

12 small squid
1 can anchovy fillets
2 cups fresh breadcrumbs
2 cloves garlic, crushed
2 tablespoons chopped parsley
½ cup dry white wine
1 tablespoon capers, drained
salt
freshly ground black pepper
½ cup olive oil
½ cup water

Gently pull away the tentacles from the hood (pocket-like) part of the squid, then hold under cold running water to rinse away the ink. Use a little salt to remove any stubborn traces of black ink.

Pull out the hard material which forms the skeleton. Peel the skin from the squid body and tentacles. Chop the heads and tentacles very finely with a sharp knife. Leave the squid bodies whole.

Soak the anchovy fillets in milk to remove the strong taste. Drain, chop and place in a bowl with the finely chopped squid, the breadcrumbs, garlic, parsley and wine. Season lightly with salt and generously with pepper. Mix thoroughly and stuff each of the squid bodies with a little of the mixture. Arrange the squid in a large, flameproof casserole and add the oil and water. Cover tightly and bring to the boil on top of the stove. Reduce heat and simmer gently until tender, about 30 minutes, or place in a moderate oven (180°C/350°F) and bake for 1 hour. Cool in the liquid, then chill in the refrigerator and serve cold. *Serves 6*
Note: The squid may also be served hot as a superb winter first course.

EASY AND DELICIOUS

Because fish should be cooked lightly but quickly to maintain texture and flavour, most fish recipes are a joy for busy cooks.

Here are some that produce marvellous results with the minimum of attention.

Fish in Citrus Sauce

•

The combination of fish and citrus juice is a very popular one, full of protein and vitamin C. The chopped olives and red pepper add considerably to the flavour of the dish as well as giving it a colourful appearance.

4 small whole fish, 250–375 g (8–12 oz) each
2 tablespoons oil
1 large onion, finely chopped
½ cup black olives, pitted and quartered
½ cup chopped red pepper
1 teaspoon ground coriander
½ teaspoon salt
freshly ground black pepper
4 tablespoons orange juice
2 tablespoons lemon juice
15 g (½ oz) butter
1 hard-boiled egg, finely chopped

Clean and wash the fish. Heat the oil in a heavy pan, and sauté the onion until soft and golden, add the olives, red pepper, coriander, salt, pepper and orange and lemon juices. Melt the butter in a large ovenproof casserole, add the fish and pour over the citrus sauce. Cover with buttered paper and bake in a moderate oven (180°C/350°F) for 25 minutes or until the fish is cooked, basting with the sauce several times during cooking. Arrange the fish on a serving dish and pour over the sauce, sprinkle with the chopped egg and serve at once. *Serves 4*

Crisp Fried Garfish

•

Don't worry about the bones in garfish. After you remove the main backbone the remaining tiny bones are eaten up along with the deliciously sweet, fine-textured flesh.

12 whole garfish
1 egg, beaten
seasoned flour
30 g (1 oz) butter
2 tablespoons oil
2 tablespoons chopped parsley
lemon wedges

Scale, clean and remove the heads and backbones of the fish. Dry on kitchen towels. Dip the fish in the beaten egg then coat with seasoned flour.

Heat the butter and oil in a heavy frying pan, when hot add the fish and cook for 4 minutes on each side or until browned and crisp. Sprinkle with chopped parsley and serve with lemon wedges. *Serves 4*
Note: To remove the backbone of the fish, lay fish as flat as possible on a board and press with a rolling pin or milk bottle. Grasp the tail and pull out the backbone, which should come out easily.

Fish with Fennel

•

When the lovely Florence fennel is in season you will want to use it in many ways. Here, the subtle aniseed flavour blends with fish in a creamy wine sauce, a simple-to-make dish that's special enough for gourmet guests.

6 white fish fillets
salt
freshly ground black pepper
60 g (2 oz) butter
2 tablespoons flour
¾ cup dry white wine
¾ cup cream
nutmeg
1 bulb fresh fennel
2 tablespoons sherry
chopped parsley

Skin the fish fillets if necessary, and check carefully for bones. Season with salt and arrange in a buttered gratin or baking dish just wide enough to hold them comfortably.

Heat the butter in a saucepan, sprinkle in the flour, and stir with a wire whisk until slightly coloured. Add the wine and stir over a moderate heat until smooth. Gradually add the cream and continue stirring until smooth and a good, flowing consistency. Cook gently for a few minutes and season to taste with salt, pepper and nutmeg.

Prepare the fennel: trim, halve, and chop finely, then blanch by dropping into a saucepan of boiling salted water and bringing the water back to the boil. Drain through a colander and cool under running water.

Add the fennel and sherry to the cream sauce, and carefully spoon over the fish fillets. Bake uncovered in a moderate oven (180°C/350°F) for 30 minutes. Sprinkle liberally with chopped parsley, and serve directly from the baking dish. *Serves 6*
Note: When fennel is out of season, celery can be substituted in this recipe. Use 3–4 stalks, remove any coarse ribs and strings before chopping and blanching. For that fennel taste add 1 teaspoon ground fennel seeds. As with fennel, celery adds texture as well as flavour to the dish.

Flounder Fillets Veronique

• •

We would all love to have a steady supply of fish fresh from the sea, but frozen fish can still taste wonderful — especially if you take the time to dress it up a little. This dish is special enough for a party.

350 g pkt frozen flounder fillets, thawed
¾ cup white wine
½ cup water
1 tablespoon lemon juice
salt
freshly ground black pepper

Sauce
45 g (1½ oz) butter
1 tablespoon flour
½ cup cream
pinch grated nutmeg
1 cup green grapes, peeled and seeded

Fold the flounder fillets and arrange in a buttered ovenproof dish. Add the wine, water, lemon juice, salt and freshly ground pepper. Cover with a sheet of buttered greaseproof paper or foil, crimping the edges around the dish, and bake in a moderate oven (180°C/350°F) for 20 minutes. Carefully remove flounder fillets from fish liquor, place on a warm serving dish. Cover and keep warm. Reserve the fish liquor.
To make the sauce Melt the butter in a heavy saucepan and remove from the heat. Blend in the flour then the reserved fish liquor. Return to heat, bring to the boil, stirring, and simmer for 2 minutes. Remove from the heat, stir in the cream and season with salt, freshly ground pepper and nutmeg. Add the grapes. Spoon the sauce over the fish and serve. *Serves 6*
Note: To remove seeds easily from grapes, peel first then use the bent end of a new hair-clip to extract the pips from the grapes. If peeling seems too much of a job then just leave the skins on.

Fish Curry with Tomato

•

Some of the best curries I have tasted in India and the South Pacific have had fish as a main ingredient. An extra bonus for the busy cook is that fish curries are quickly made – this one takes about 20 minutes from start to finish. The fresh coriander (Chinese parsley) gives a distinctive taste, failing this use mint which goes surprisingly well in a fish curry.

500 g (1 lb) fish fillets
2 tablespoons ghee or oil
1 onion, chopped
2 cloves garlic, chopped
2 tablespoons chopped fresh coriander or mint
1 teaspoon ground cumin
1 teaspoon ground turmeric
½–1 teaspoon chilli powder
2 ripe tomatoes
1 teaspoon salt
1½ teaspoons garam masala
lemon juice to taste

Wash the fish and cut into serving pieces. Heat the ghee or oil in a heavy frying pan, add the onion, garlic and coriander and cook gently until golden. Add the cumin, turmeric and chilli powder and stir until the spices are cooked.

Peel and halve the tomatoes, flip out the seeds and chop the flesh. Add to the pan with the salt and garam masala and stir until the tomato is cooked to a pulp. Stir in the lemon juice and taste and adjust the seasoning.

Put the fish into the tomato sauce, spooning it over the the fillets. Cover and simmer for 10 minutes, or until fish is cooked. Serve with rice. *Serves 4*

Sweet and Sour Fish with Ginger Sauce

• •

This sauce is excellent and suitable for most of the fish available at our markets, either whole or filleted. It may be served with poached, baked or fried fish.

1.5 kg (3 lb) whole fish (bream or snapper)
flour
salt
oil for frying
parsley or fresh coriander sprigs

Scale and clean the fish, rub generously with oil and dust with the flour seasoned with salt. Heat enough oil to cover the base of a frying pan and fry the fish until golden brown on both sides, about 10 minutes. Test gently with the point of a sharp

knife to see if it is cooked. Drain on crumpled kitchen paper. Serve with the Ginger Sauce spooned over, and garnish with parsley or coriander sprigs. *Serves 6*

Ginger Sauce

1–2 tablespoons finely slivered fresh ginger
¼ cup sugar
¼ cup vinegar
1 tablespoon soy sauce
1 cup water
salt
¼ cup chopped mushrooms (see note)
¼ cup chopped spring onions
1 teaspoon cornflour
1 tablespoon water

Combine the ginger (left in the thinnest slivers or cut into julienne shreds), sugar, vinegar, soy sauce, water and salt and simmer for 5 minutes. Add the mushrooms and spring onions and cook for another few minutes, until the mushrooms are tender. Mix the cornflour and water to a smooth paste and stir into the sauce. Simmer for a few minutes until the sauce thickens. Serve immediately over the fish.
Note: Chinese dried mushrooms are best for this dish. Soak them in hot water for 10 minutes and drain well before using.

Squid with Garlic and Parsley

• •

For those who enjoy squid, this recipe from Tuscany is a must. Choose very small squid for best results.

750 g (1½ lb) small squid
salt
freshly ground black pepper
½ cup olive oil
1 clove garlic, bruised
1 tablespoon chopped parsley
½ lemon
triangles of fried bread

Wash the squid and gently pull the tentacles from the hood or body of the squid, then hold under running water and rub away the ink. Cut off the 'beak' (a hard portion in the centre of the tentacles) leaving the tentacles in a flower shape. If the squid are large, cut the hood into thick slices. Season with salt and pepper.

Heat the oil, add the garlic, and when it starts to turn golden, discard. Add the squid, and cook over a medium high heat for about 5 minutes, turning. Add the tentacles and fry for 1 minute longer. Drain and serve very hot, sprinkled with parsley and a squeeze of lemon juice. Accompany with triangles of fried bread. *Serves 4*

Fried Squid (Calamari)

• •

*This is a dish often found in Italian restaurants,
and is one of the simplest but most delicious ways of serving
squid.*

500 g (1 lb) squid
1 egg
½ cup milk
flour
salt
freshly ground pepper
1 cup fine, dry breadcrumbs
oil for deep-frying

Clean and skin the squid. Rinse thoroughly and discard the ink
sacs. Cut the squid into 2 cm (¾ inch) rings and pat dry.

In a shallow dish beat the egg with the milk. Dredge the
squid in the flour, seasoned with salt and pepper, dip in the
egg mixture, and then roll in the breadcrumbs. Heat 8–10 cm
(3–4 inch) of oil in a deep-fryer to 200°C/400°F. Fry the squid
rings in the oil until golden, about 2 minutes. This should be
done in several batches, do not overcrowd the pan. Drain on
paper towels, sprinkle with salt and serve with Tartare Sauce
(see page 45 or 71). *Serves 6 as a first course*

Sesame Fish Steaks

•

3 large fish steaks or fillets
salt
30 g (1 oz) butter
2 cups soft breadcrumbs
⅛ teaspoon freshly ground pepper
3 tablespoons toasted sesame seeds
½ teaspoon whole thyme leaves, crumbled
extra 60 g (2 oz) butter, melted

Set oven temperature to moderate (180°C/350°F). Dry the fish
steaks with paper towels and place in a buttered baking dish.
Sprinkle the steaks with a pinch of salt and top each with
2 teaspoons of the butter.

Combine the remaining ingredients, adding 1 teaspoon of
salt, and sprinkle the breadcrumb mixture thickly over the
steaks. Bake, uncovered, in a moderate oven for 15 to 20 minutes
or until the fish flakes easily when tested with a fork. *Serves 6*

Fish Yucatan Style

(Mero en Mac-cum)

•

*If you like full-flavoured dishes you will want to try
this fish recipe from Mexico, with chilli adding the traditional
touch of fire. Instead of cooking the chillies with the
fish, they may be offered separately so each diner can add just
enough for his own taste – a good idea if you're not
sure of your guests' preference for hot foods.*

4 large fish fillets (gemfish, jewfish or snapper)
4 cloves garlic, crushed
1 teaspoon oregano
½ teaspoon ground cumin
salt
freshly ground pepper
¼ cup orange juice
½ cup olive oil
2 tomatoes
1 onion, thinly sliced
½ small hot chilli, seeded and chopped
chopped parsley or fresh coriander
(Chinese parsley)

Wipe over the fish fillets, skin and cut into serving-sized
pieces. Arrange on a large plate or glass dish. Combine the
garlic, oregano, cumin, salt, pepper and orange juice and pour
over the fish pieces. Allow to marinate for 30 minutes.

Choose a flameproof baking dish just big enough to hold the
fillets comfortably. Coat the bottom of the dish with ¼ cup of
the olive oil. Arrange the fillets in the dish and pour the
marinade over. Peel and halve the tomatoes, flip out the seeds
and roughly chop. Combine the tomatoes with the sliced onion
and chopped chilli and spoon over the fish. Sprinkle with the
remaining olive oil.

Cover the dish with aluminium foil and simmer over a gentle
heat for 15 minutes, or until the fish flakes easily when tested
with a fork. Sprinkle the fish with chopped parsley or coriander
and serve. *Serves 4–6*

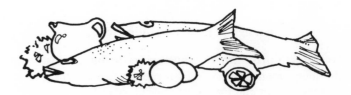

SKATE (RAY)

The wings of the ray are incredibly cheap in southern waters in comparison with England and France, where they are considered a delicacy. You will find pieces and wings at the markets or some fish shops – don't pass them by. They are delicious.

Skate must first of all be scrubbed and washed in plenty of water so as to remove stickiness. The 'wings', if very large, are cut into pieces weighing from 155–250 g (5–8 oz). They should be cooked in water which has been fairly strongly salted and acidulated with lemon juice or vinegar. The pieces are then drained and skinned (the latter operation being accomplished by scraping each side), and the extremity is cut off as it consists only of bone. The pieces are then put back into the cooking liquor and kept warm for their final preparation.

Skate with Black Butter

••

Skate is most often served in this way. Drain the hot cooked pieces, pat dry with paper towels and arrange on a serving dish, keep hot. Season with salt and pepper and sprinkle with capers and chopped parsley. Pour over plenty of black butter. *Black Butter* Allow 15 g (½ oz) butter per serving and cook in a frying pan until it just turns brown. Add a few drops of vinegar in the pan then pour over the skate.

CANNED AND SMOKED FISH

One of the greatest stand-bys a cook can have is a supply of canned fish, and the variety seems endless.

Sardines in all sizes, mussels, kippers, herrings, salmon, oysters, tuna, mackerel, sprats, squid, shrimp, whitebait – you find them all in most food markets, and all of excellent quality.

Canned fish is a natural part of an antipasti platter or hors d'oeuvre tray, features in delicious snacks and sandwiches, makes an appetizing lunch with crisp salads, and lends itself to a variety of main course recipes. Smoked fish is also available in many forms and keeps well in the refrigerator.

Smoked Haddock Delmonico

••

Here's a very special version of old-fashioned fish pie, with eggs and cheese for extra protein and flavour.

750 g (1½ lb) smoked haddock
¼ cup butter
3 tablespoons flour
1 cup cream
1 cup milk
1 small onion
1 bay leaf
salt
freshly ground black pepper
4 hard-boiled eggs, quartered
creamy mashed potatoes, about 2 cups
grated Parmesan cheese
additional butter

Place the fish in a shallow pan, barely cover with water, and simmer covered for 15 minutes. Drain and cool the fish. Remove the bones and flake into good-sized pieces.

Melt the butter in a saucepan, add the flour and stir with a wire whisk until blended. Meanwhile, bring the cream, milk, onion and bay leaf slowly to a boil, allowing time for the onion and bay leaf to flavour the milk. Strain. Add all at once to the roux mixture, stirring vigorously with the whisk until thickened and smooth. Season the sauce with salt and pepper.

Combine the fish and eggs with the sauce and mix carefully to avoid mashing the fish. Spoon into a buttered casserole dish and pile the creamy mashed potatoes over the dish, or pipe, using a star tube if desired. Sprinkle the Parmesan cheese over the top, dot with a little butter and bake in a preheated hot oven (200°C/400°F) until the top is golden brown. *Serves 6*

Smoked Haddock with Egg Sauce

•

Smoked haddock with egg sauce is a traditional British dish. The creamy sauce and eggs complement the full-flavoured taste of the fish. Serve surrounded with new potatoes in Parsley Butter.

1.25–1.5 kg (2½–3 lb) smoked haddock fillets
milk and water to cover (half and half)
1 onion, studded with 3 cloves
1 bay leaf
freshly ground black pepper
30 g (1 oz) butter
1 tablespoon flour
4 tablespoons cream
1 tablespoon chopped parsley
3 hard-boiled eggs
750 g (1½ lb) boiled new potatoes
Parsley Butter

Cover the fish with the milk and water. Add the onion, bay leaf and freshly ground pepper. Bring to the boil, turn down to simmer and poach for 10 minutes or until cooked. Remove the fish, drain and keep warm.

Melt the butter in a saucepan, stir in the flour and strain in enough of the haddock liquor to make a sauce the consistency of pouring cream. Simmer the sauce for 15 minutes, then stir in the cream and parsley. Finely chop the eggs and add to the sauce. Coat the potatoes in Parsley Butter and arrange around the fish. Spoon over a little of the sauce and pass the rest in a sauceboat.

Parsley Butter To 60 g (2 oz) softened butter, beat in 1½ tablespoons finely chopped parsley.

Tuna with Peas

•

An Italian way of serving tuna which combines so well with fresh green peas. Frozen peas may be substituted but like many good dishes there is a subtle difference.

3 tablespoons oil (drained from tuna – make up
with olive oil if necessary)
2 × 425 g cans tuna in oil
1 onion, finely chopped
2 tablespoons tomato paste
1 tablespoon chopped parsley
500 g (1 lb) green peas
salt
freshly ground black pepper
pinch sugar

Heat the oil in a large saucepan and sauté the onion over a medium heat until soft. Add the tomato paste, parsley, peas and sufficient water to barely cover the peas. Season with salt, pepper and a pinch of sugar. Cook, covered, for 10 minutes. Add the tuna, broken into chunks, and simmer for three minutes longer. Serve over freshly-cooked spaghetti tossed with butter and Parmesan cheese, or with rice or noodles or crusty bread and butter. *Serves 6*

Salmon Kedgeree

•

Kedgeree can be one of those unfortunate dishes reminiscent of nursery or lean days, or it can be one of the best dishes in the world when properly made. Fresh salmon is the first choice, but for most of us a good red canned salmon is more than acceptable. Serve as a light supper or luncheon dish, or if you enjoy inviting guests to brunch this is just the thing.
Poached, smoked cod may be substituted for the salmon.

1 cup raw rice
2 × 220 g cans salmon
60 g (2 oz) butter
2 hard-boiled eggs, finely chopped
2–3 tablespoons cream
salt
freshly ground pepper
pinch of cayenne pepper
chopped parsley

Cook the rice in boiling salted water until tender, drain well. Keep hot over boiling water or in a slow oven. Remove all the skin and bones from the salmon and flake gently. Melt the butter in a saucepan, add the salmon, eggs, cream, salt, pepper and cayenne pepper and stir until hot. Combine the fish mixture with the hot rice, and add the parsley, turn on to a hot serving dish and shape into a pyramid with a fork. *Serves 5–6*

For an authentic Chinese touch, leave the heads and shells intact for King Prawns in Shell with Tomato sauce (see page 128). Serve with bowls of boiled rice.

Right: With geese becoming more available, you can plan a roast goose Christmas dinner. See page 154 for directions on how to carve a goose and page 159 for stuffings.

Below: Breast of Chicken Normandy with Walnut Sauce is a beautiful dish for a special occasion. The recipe and details for preparing the tomato garnish are on page 143.

For Quail Borghese, the birds are first roasted then finished off on a bed of puréed green peas and garnished with ham and watercress. (See recipe page 157.)

LOBSTERS

In southern waters we catch magnificent crayfish which find their way on to menus as lobster. These 'crays' as they are called are in fact the spiny lobster which is not really a lobster at all but a marine crawfish. So much for that! Most of us accept them as lobsters.

In all lobster cookery, one should start with a live lobster, but only the truly dedicated will or can do this. When local but freshly-cooked lobsters are available (avoid the frozen ones), one of the best ways of treating them is to simply serve cold, dressed with a good, homemade mayonnaise. Sometimes it is practical to extend lobsters with a beautiful salad.

Lobster Parisienne makes a superb dish, and its success depends on tender lobster flesh and very young, impeccably fresh vegetables carefully cooked – plus a good mayonnaise.

Lobster Mayonnaise

• • •

A famous dish, and one of the first to go from any buffet table.
The mayonnaise includes a little tomato paste,
which adds a delicate pink colour. Garnish, if liked, with
parsley sprigs and the small lobster claws.

2 cups raw rice
3 ripe tomatoes, skinned, seeded and diced
2 tablespoons chopped parsley
approx. ¾ cup Vinaigrette (see page 46)
1 cold cooked lobster

Mayonnaise

2 egg yolks
freshly ground black pepper
pinch of dry mustard
1 tablespoon vinegar or lemon juice
1½ cups oil
2 tablespoons cream
2 teaspoons tomato paste

Cook the rice in plenty of boiling, salted water, drain and rinse in cold water. Drain well. Place in a bowl and add the tomatoes, and parsley. Mix with sufficient vinaigrette to moisten and give a good flavour – about ¾ of a cup.

Arrange the seasoned rice in a long shape on a serving dish, mounding it up to roughly resemble the shape of a lobster. Split the lobster in half, remove the tail flesh and cut into slices. Crack the main claws and carefully pick out the meat. Arrange the pieces of lobster on top of the rice. Cover with plastic wrap

and put in a cool place until ready to serve. Meanwhile, make the mayonnaise.

To make Mayonnaise: Place the egg yolks, a grinding of pepper, the mustard and vinegar or lemon juice in a bowl. Beat with a wire whisk until well blended, then gradually blend in the oil. Add it drop by drop at first until the mixture begins to thicken, then it may be added in a gentle stream, while you continue beating with the whisk. When thick and smooth, carefully mix in the cream and tomato paste. Spoon over the lobster and serve. *Serves 6*

Lobster Parisienne

• • •

2 small, freshly-cooked lobsters
2 cups cooked, diced, mixed, carrots,
beans and peas
2 tomatoes, skinned, seeded and diced
4 tablespoons mayonnaise (see page 45)
extra mayonnaise
2 hard-boiled eggs, chopped
paprika

Split the lobsters in half and carefully remove the meat from the tails and claws. Combine the cooked vegetables, tomatoes and mayonnaise and use to fill the shells, dividing evenly between them. Cut the lobster meat in slices and arrange on top of the vegetable mixture. Spoon a little more mayonnaise over, sprinkle with the eggs and paprika, and serve. *Serves 4*

SCALLOPS

We normally buy scallops already removed from their pretty shells (which are the classic shell shape seen in Botticelli's painting of Venus rising from the sea). However, scallops seem to retain their subtle flavour and firm texture remarkably well in their journey from the sea to the fishmonger's window or the freezer, and although expensive are excellent value for money, as there is virtually no waste. Don't discard the coral, the little orange 'tongue' on the scallops. They add flavour as well as colour to your finished dish.

Coquilles St Jacques à L'ail

(Scallops with Garlic Butter Sauce)

••

Because of the increasing number of Spanish restaurants, the dish of garlic-flavoured prawns has become well-known and liked. The French way of cooking scallops with garlic is, I think, even better.

500 g (1 lb) scallops
seasoned flour
75 g (2½ oz) butter
1 tablespoon olive oil
1 small clove garlic
2 tablespoons finely chopped parsley
lemon wedges

Wash the scallops and dry with kitchen towels, removing the dark beard, but keeping the coral. Dust in seasoned flour, shaking well to remove any excess. Melt 15 g (½ oz) of the butter with the oil in a sauté pan and when the foam subsides, sauté the scallops until light golden. Transfer to a heated dish and keep warm.

Clarify the remaining butter by melting it slowly, and skimming off the foam. Spoon the clear butter into a container and discard the milky solids left at the bottom. Return the clarified butter to the pan and heat until it sizzles without colouring. Remove from the heat and stir in the finely chopped garlic. Pour over the scallops and serve at once sprinkled with chopped parsley and garnished with lemon wedges. *Serves 4*

Curried Scallops

••

A curry flavour seems to go particularly well with scallops, and adds a golden colour to the creamy sauce.

1 kg (2 lb) scallops
90 g (3 oz) butter
3–4 spring onions, chopped
2 teaspoons curry powder
2 cups dry white wine
bouquet garni (2 sprigs parsley, 1 bay leaf and
2 sprigs thyme, tied together)
2 teaspoons butter
2 teaspoons flour
½ cup cream
salt
freshly ground black pepper

Wash the scallops and dry on kitchen towels, remove any dark beard but keep the coral.

Melt the butter in a heavy saucepan over a medium heat and add the spring onions and curry powder. Stir for 1 minute. Add the wine, scallops and bouquet garni and bring to the boil. Reduce the heat and poach for 5 minutes. Transfer the scallops to a serving dish or 6 individual scallop shells or dishes with a slotted spoon, and keep warm.

Reduce the cooking liquid to 1½ cups by rapid boiling and discard the bouquet garni. Make a beurre manié by blending the butter and flour together. Gradually stir into stock in small pieces, and bring to boiling point. Add the cream, season to taste with salt and pepper and cook gently, stirring for a few minutes, but do not allow to boil.

Pour the sauce over the scallops and sprinkle with finely chopped parsley to serve. *Serves 6*

Scallops Sauce Verte

••

This is a lovely dish in which the scallops are lightly poached in vermouth then coated with a green mayonnaise sauce.

500 g (1 lb) scallops
½ cup dry vermouth
½ onion, chopped
parsley sprig
1 bay leaf
salt
freshly ground pepper

Sauce Verte

3–4 spinach leaves
1 cup Mayonnaise (see page 45)
¼ cup finely chopped parsley
3 tablespoons snipped chives
1 tablespoon finely chopped fresh dill or
½ teaspoon dried dill
extra mayonnaise (optional)

To Serve

lettuce leaves
chopped parsley

Wash and dry the scallops. Remove any brown parts but retain the coral. In a saucepan, heat the vermouth with the onion, parsley sprig, bay leaf, salt and pepper. Add the scallops and simmer gently for about 3–4 minutes or until tender, shaking occasionally. Drain and cool.

To make the Sauce Verte: Trim the white stalks from the spinach leaves. Steam the washed leaves in a covered saucepan for 1 minute only, then rinse in cold water. Press out the water and chop finely.

Blend the homemade mayonnaise with the parsley, spinach, chives and dill. Add extra mayonnaise to taste, if necessary.

To serve, place the scallops in a bowl lined with the lettuce leaves, cover with the Sauce Verte and garnish with a sprinkling of parsley. Alternatively, set the lettuce leaves in 4 individual dishes (scallop shells look nice). Divide the scallops between the shells and top with green mayonnaise and sprinkle with parsley. *Serves 4*

THE ART OF DRESSING A CRAB

If you live close to waters where crabs are found no doubt you have had the excitement of catching your own. At fish markets they are usually available both live and cooked, and many fish shops also keep a regular supply. In some lucky areas fresh-picked crabmeat is available, and lends itself to many delectable dishes.

Crabs are cooked in salted water or court bouillon only until they change colour. Few people will face up to killing them first, so most buy crabs already cooked. There still remains the question of tackling the armour to get at the sweet flesh. This preparation of the crab for eating, with perhaps the addition of extra flavours, is quaintly called 'dressing' the crab – though really, it is more in the nature of undressing it.

Anyway, here is how to make the crab fashionable, both in appearance and flavour.

To Dress Cooked Crab

First remove the big claws and set aside. **(1)** Twist off the small claws and remove the undershell body of the crab. **(2)** Cut the undershell body of the crab in two – the main flesh lies between the cartilages, close to the legs. Now the tedious job begins: with a skewer, pick out all the white meat into a bowl – it helps to break the undershell where naturally marked. Crack the claws then remove the meat and shred. **(3)** Spoon out the creamy yellow meat from the top shell. **(4)**

The meat is now dressed with a little vinaigrette, or seasoned simply with salt and pepper and a bowl of good mayonnaise served separately. Or the body meat may be mixed with seasonings and replaced in the shell for interesting variations of flavour and texture.

A favourite seasoning is to combine any of the 'mustard' from the crab with salt and pepper, a few spoonfuls of dry breadcrumbs and a spoonful of cream. You will recognise the mustard easily by its creamy yellow colour, it is found in the body of the crab. A plentiful amount of creamy mustard is also your assurance that the crab is fresh.

Here are some other ideas for seasoning. Combine any one of the following mixtures with the flaked body meat of the crab, then pile the mixture back into the shell.

★1 teaspoon horseradish, 1 teaspoon snipped chives, a squeeze of lemon juice, salt and freshly ground pepper and a little cream.

★2 small anchovy fillets, rinsed and pounded, with 1 tablespoon of finely chopped parsley and a little cream.

★2 teaspoons of finely chopped capers, a squeeze of lemon juice and a drop or two of Tabasco sauce.

★ 1 small clove of crushed garlic, 3 soft green olives, finely chopped, and a grinding of black pepper.

If the claws are to be cracked at the table, don't forget nutcrackers to make the job easier. Finger bowls are also a helpful idea, and of course, a plentiful supply of napkins, paper or cotton.

1

2

3

4
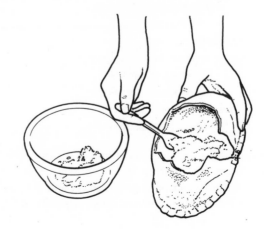

PRAWNS

Prawns, shrimp, scampi – they all belong to the same family, and all share the same sweet, tender, succulent flesh that makes them a favourite everywhere in the world.

Some people can never get enough of them! I remember a birthday party once, where the guest of honour asked us all to bring (instead of a present) a bowl of cooked prawns. He provided the fresh bread and butter and the cold beer that goes so well with seafood, and peeling the prawns provided entertainment and supper all in one. It was a memorable night.

However, there are other good ways to eat prawns besides plain boiled or the ubiquitous sizzling garlic and I hope you will try some of them.

Chinese Prawn Balls

• • •

The gift of taste is something to treasure. By learning to make this dish correctly you will soon recognise the delicacy and intricacy of a good dish. The prawn flesh should be finely chopped, the water and cornflour provides lightness, and the pork fat makes the texture gliding and tender. Water chestnuts are an optional addition for those who want a crispy contrast.
Serve these as part of a Chinese meal, as a first course on a bed of shredded lettuce, or as part of a special hors d'oeuvre tray.

500 g (1 lb) raw green prawns
125 g (4 oz) pork fat
2 tablespoons chopped water chestnuts
(optional)
3–4 tablespoons water
½ teaspoon salt
½ teaspoon fresh ginger juice
(grate a piece of green ginger)
3 egg whites
4 tablespoons cornflour
peanut oil for deep-frying
Fried Pepper Mix

Shell the prawns, wash and pat dry. Chop the pork fat very finely, then add to the prawns and chop them together, gradually adding the water, salt, ginger juice, and chopped water chestnuts if desired. Continue to chop, gradually adding

the 3 egg whites and the cornflour. This is best done on a chopping board, using a broad-bladed Chinese chopper. With care it can be done in a food processor fitted with a steel blade. Heat a wok, and add enough oil to allow the prawn balls to fry freely, about 5 cm (2 inch) in deepest part, or use a saucepan. Take a handful of the prawn paste and squeeze it through the index finger and thumb into the hot oil, tipping the ball into the oil with the aid of a spoon. (With a little practice you will soon make perfect balls. If this method seems difficult, lightly wet the hands and roll the balls, the size of a small walnut, between your two palms.)

Fry the balls for about 3 minutes, until a pale golden colour. Because of the high moisture and fat content, these balls take longer to cook than plain prawns. When fried to a golden colour outside, the inside is still moist and tender. Serve them immediately with a dish of Fried Pepper Mix for dipping.
Serves 6

Fried Pepper Mix

5 tablespoons salt
4 teaspoons black pepper
½ teaspoon five-spice powder (optional)

Stir the salt, pepper and spice together in a small pan over a low heat until very dry and aromatic. Cool and store in a tightly closed container. Use for dipping crisp skin chicken, prawn balls, duck etc.
Note: 5-spice powder is available at Chinese grocery shops and many delicatessens.

King Prawns in Shell with Tomato Sauce

• •

If you are serving this dish the authentic Chinese way, with the heads and shells intact, don't forget finger bowls and plenty of paper napkins, or set each diner's place with a rolled, moist hot towel in its own little bamboo basket.

1 kg (2 lb) green king prawns
2 tablespoons oil
2 tablespoons Chinese wine or sherry
1 teaspoon sesame oil
Gravy
1½ tablespoons tomato sauce
1 tablespoon chilli sauce (Linghams)
pinch salt
¼ teaspoon sugar
2 tablespoons chicken stock
½ teaspoon monosodium glutamate
1 tablespoon shredded green ginger
½ teaspoon cornflour
2 teaspoons water

Shell the prawns, removing the head but leaving the tail shell intact, remove the dark veins. If the prawns are very large, cut each in half. Wash lightly and dry thoroughly. Heat a wok or frying pan, add the oil and stir-fry the prawns until a good red colour, about 2 minutes. Sprinkle with the Chinese wine or sherry. Combine Gravy ingredients in a bowl, add to prawns, cover and bring to the boil. Reduce heat and simmer gently for 3–4 minutes. To serve, add a teaspoon of sesame oil for a final touch and serve hot.

Note: Although I have said to remove the heads and shell from the prawns in this recipe, the authentic recipe doesn't call for it. The Chinese like to nibble at the shells of the prawns, it's all a matter of taste. Garnish if liked with shredded spring onion.

Prawn Soufflé de Luxe

● ● ●

Here's a double delight – cheese soufflé top and bottom, with a buttery, whisky-flavoured prawn filling. If you are nervous about the timing and serving of a soufflé, I've included a do-ahead guide.

Cheese Soufflé Mixture:

45 g (1½ oz) butter
¼ cup flour
1 cup milk
salt
pinch cayenne pepper
pinch paprika
45 g (1½ oz) each grated Parmesan and Cheddar cheese
4 egg yolks
5 egg whites

Filling

30 g (1 oz) butter
2 tablespoons whisky
250 g (8 oz) prawns, shelled

Do ahead

Cheese soufflé mixture: Melt the butter in a saucepan and stir in the flour to form a roux. Cook over a gentle heat for a minute, stirring all the time, then remove from the heat and gradually stir in milk, making sure the sauce is smooth. Return to the heat and bring to the boil, stirring the sauce constantly until it thickens. Cook over a low heat for 3–5 minutes. Remove from the heat and allow to cool slightly.

Season with salt, cayenne pepper and paprika and then add the cheeses gradually. Set aside and cover with damp greaseproof paper pressed on to mixture to prevent a skin forming.

Lightly grease a 5-cup soufflé dish and tie a collar of greased paper around the outside so it stands about 8 cm (3 inch) higher than the rim of the dish or use 4–6 individual soufflé dishes.

40 minutes before serving

Prepare the filling: Melt the butter in a small frying pan, add the prawns for a minute to heat through. Warm the whisky, set alight and pour flaming over the prawns. Shake the pan until the flames die out then remove from the heat.

Heat cheese mixture over a low heat until tepid. Beat the egg yolks into the mixture, one at a time. Whisk the egg whites stiffly. Using a metal spoon, stir 1 tablespoon of egg white into the cheese mixture and then fold in remaining egg white.

Pour half the mixture into the prepared soufflé dish, carefully add the prepared prawns and cover with the remaining mixture. Bake in a preheated moderately hot oven (190°C/375°F) for 25–35 minutes, or until the soufflé is well risen and a crisp, golden brown crust has formed on top. Remove from the oven, take off the paper collar and place on a hot dish (this helps to stop the soufflé from sinking so rapidly). Serve immediately. *Serves 4–6*

Note: If using individual soufflé dishes, cook for 10–12 minutes.

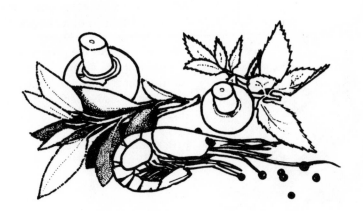

Grilled Prawns

••

Sage is a popular herb with veal and pork and teams amazingly well with seafoods. Use the large green prawns which many fish shops or Chinese groceries sell. Scallops, which are readily available, are also excellent prepared in this way.

16 large green prawns, shelled and deveined
½ cup brandy
16 thin slices prosciutto or ham
16 fresh sage leaves or 8 halved bay leaves
¼ cup fresh breadcrumbs
salt
freshly ground pepper
2 teaspoons lemon juice

Marinate the prawns in the brandy for 1 hour. Drain and wrap each prawn in a slice of prosciutto or ham. Thread on skewers alternately with the sage or halved bay leaves. Place under a preheated grill and cook until the ham begins to sizzle. Roll skewers in the breadcrumbs, season with salt and pepper and cook under the grill until golden brown, turning to brown all sides. Sprinkle with lemon juice and serve immediately. *Serves 4*

Chinese Fried Prawns

•••

Spanish style garlic prawns became a craze that found its way on to just about every restaurant menu throughout the world. The Chinese have a version that is every bit as good, and in fact more interesting. This is the original Tientsin way of frying prawns.

12 large green prawns
1 cup peanut oil
2 tablespoons sesame oil
½ cup spring onions, cut into match-stick strips
1 teaspoon finely chopped green ginger
1½ tablespoons soy sauce
½ teaspoon garlic, chopped finely
1 tablespoon dry sherry or Chinese wine
½ teaspoon monosodium glutamate

Shell, devein and wash the prawns. Heat the peanut oil in a frying pan or wok, add the prawns and fry for 1 minute. Remove the prawns and pour off all the oil except 1 tablespoon. Add the sesame oil to the pan and heat, then add the spring onions and ginger. Stir-fry for a minute, and add the soy sauce, prawns, garlic, wine and monosodium glutamate. Fry for two more minutes over a high heat, stirring briskly. Serve hot. *Serves 3–4*

Note: Prawns fried this way may be served European-style with crusty French bread to mop up the juices, or with individual small bowls of rice.

Prawns with Rémoulade Sauce

••

A delightfully piquant dressing makes prawns a special treat.

1 kg (2 lb) cooked prawns
2 tablespoons chopped dill pickle or gherkin
1 tablespoon chopped capers
1 cup Mayonnaise (see page 45)
1½ teaspoons prepared mustard
1 tablespoon chopped chives or parsley

Shell and devein the prawns and arrange on a chilled plate. Combine the remaining ingredients and pile in a bowl. Chill until serving time. Serve the prawns and Rémoulade Sauce with crisp salad greens and thin brown bread and butter if liked. *Serves 4*

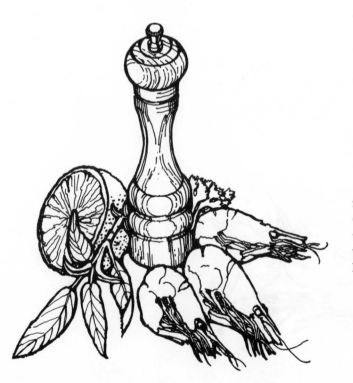

MUSSELS

To Prepare Fresh Mussels for Cooking

This prolific blue-black bivalve falls into the shellfish category and supplies lovely flavour and versatility for a reasonable outlay – hence its nickname of 'the poor man's oyster'.

The rule for all mussels (whether gathered by you or bought from the fish market) is that they *must* be alive when cooked. Live mussels hold their shells so tightly together it is hard to prise them open, so discard any mussels with open shells – they're definitely not fresh and mustn't be eaten.

And a word of warning to the amateur mussel hunter – in major cities it is best to buy them from the market, as the waters surrounding cities are likely to be polluted. The delicate flavour and firm texture of the mussel can be appreciated in simple ways. For example, they may be steamed open in wine flavoured with some aromatics then served on the half shell. The mussel is eaten with a fork, the juice is drunk from the shell, and any remaining liquor mopped up with crusty bread. With a glass of chilled white wine, it's a simple but perfect meal.

Fresh mussels may also be combined with other ingredients to make dishes of greater complexity, in which the sweet, delicate flavour is still allowed to predominate. And there is a place for the bottled variety in soups, chowders, and in fillings for vol-au-vents or pasta sauces.

Buy at least 500 g (1 lb) of mussels for each person. When you get home, rinse the mussels several times in running water, then thoroughly scrub each mussel with a clean, stiff brush or pot scourer to remove mud, seaweed or any dirt that may cling to them.

Pull away the beard that clings around the edge of the shell and discard any mussel which is not tightly closed. Soak in cold water for 10 minutes (they should disgorge any sand) then rinse again in running water, and they are ready to cook. All this preparation may sound a little finicky, but the time spent is well repaid in the final, delicious results.

To Open Mussels in the Oven Arrange the cleaned mussels in a single layer in a baking pan and place the pan in a preheated very hot oven (230°C/450°F) for 7 to 8 minutes, or until the shells have opened. Throw away any unopened mussels. (This method is used in the recipe for Mussel and Eggplant Salad, which follows.)

Mussel and Eggplant Salad

●●

This is in the manner of the 'New Wave' cooking, in which flavours are blended in interesting and unexpected combinations. The dish is light but elegant – a talking point for gourmet friends

1 kg (2 lb) fresh mussels
1 medium eggplant
⅓ cup oil
1 teaspoon salt
freshly ground black pepper
½ teaspoon thyme

Dressing

2 tablespoons lemon juice
1 teaspoon anchovy paste
1 clove garlic, crushed
⅓ cup finely chopped onion
¼ cup toasted pine nuts

To serve

lettuce leaves
finely chopped parsley

Open the prepared mussels in the oven, as described on page 131. Remove the mussels from their shells, discard the black rims, and chill in a covered bowl in the refrigerator.

Peel the eggplant and cut into dice. Combine in a baking dish with the oil, salt, freshly ground pepper to taste, and the thyme. Bake in a preheated hot oven (200°C/400°F) for 30 minutes, or until the eggplant is tender. Cool. Combine the Dressing ingredients in a salad bowl. Add the chilled mussels and eggplant mixture and toss lightly with a fork until well combined. Chill, covered, for several hours.

To serve, place crisp lettuce leaves on a platter and arrange the salad on top. Garnish with the finely chopped parsley. *Serves 2 as a main course, or 4–6 as part of a meal*

Barbecued Mussels

●●

If you can buy dried fennel stalks (often available from Continental fruit shops and some delicatessens) or gather them from the roadside, you will be able to enjoy this spectacular way of cooking mussels in the open.

Make a fire on the barbecue in your favourite way. Arrange cleaned mussels on a metal tray and strew a thick layer of dried fennel stalks over the top. Place the tray over the glowing coals, and then set fire to the fennel stalks. As they burn, the aromatic fennel flavour permeates the opening mussels, a marvellous combination. Remove the tray as soon as the mussels have opened, pick off any remaining stalks, and serve on the shell with crusty bread and butter to mop up the juices.

Mussels Steamed in Wine

(Moules Marinière)

●●

This is the classic dish served so often in fine restaurants – but easy to make at home, and every bit as delicious.

1 kg (2 lb) mussels
4 spring onions, finely chopped
4 parsley stalks
1 bay leaf
sprig thyme
freshly ground black pepper
60 g (2 oz) butter
2 cups dry white wine
1 teaspoon flour
little chopped parsley

Clean the mussels as described above. Place in a wide pan with the spring onions, herbs, pepper, half the butter and the wine. Cover the pan and cook over a high heat for 5 minutes, shaking the pan occasionally. Remove the mussels as soon as they open, discarding the top half of each shell. Arrange the mussels in warm soup plates. Strain the cooking liquid and return to the pan. Mix the remaining butter with the flour, and add to the liquid. Boil rapidly, stirring, until slightly thickened. Pour over the mussels in each soup bowl and sprinkle with chopped parsley. Serve at once with crusty bread, creamy butter and dry white wine. *Serves 2 as a main course or 4 as a starter*

Variations

Mussels with Cream: Replace the butter and flour used for thickening with ¾ cup of cream. Reduce the cooking liquid from the mussels by about one third by rapid boiling, then stir in the cream and cook gently to thicken a little. Pour over the mussels and serve.

Mussels with Pernod: Prepare as for Mussels with Cream, adding 2 tablespoons of Pernod along with the wine.

Right: Today, there is a turkey size for every family. Use two different stuffings for interest. Roasting instructions are on page 153.

Economical chicken wings are used to make Chicken Wings Chasseur (page 148) and can be served with Saffron Rice (page 246).

FISH SOUPS AND STEWS

Hearty fish soups can be a meal in themselves, with crusty rolls and a salad, while the lighter soups make an imaginative first course for a dinner party or a family meal. If Fish Stock is required, see the recipe on page 75.

Crab Bisque

●

This is an easy version of bisque, using canned crab. If fish stock is not convenient to make, substitute a can of cream of oyster soup, diluted according to the directions on the can.

1 × 185 g can crabmeat
60 g (2 oz) butter
2 tablespoons chopped parsley
2 tablespoons chopped celery
2 tablespoons chopped spring onions
1 tablespoon flour
3 cups Fish Stock
1 teaspoon prepared horseradish
½ cup dry white wine
juice ½ small lemon
salt
freshly ground black pepper
pinch cayenne pepper
½ cup cream
snipped chives or chopped parsley

Pick over the crabmeat and discard any cartilage. Melt the butter in a heavy saucepan and add the parsley, celery and spring onions. Cook gently for 5 minutes, stirring occasionally, until the vegetables are soft. Sprinkle the flour into the pan and stir over a moderate heat until well blended. Add the Fish Stock and horseradish and simmer for 10 minutes, then add the wine, lemon juice and crabmeat. Bring to the boil again and taste for seasoning, adding salt, freshly ground pepper and a pinch of cayenne pepper to taste.

Stir in the cream. Heat gently, but do not boil. Serve in soup bowls, garnished with snipped chives or chopped parsley. *Serves 4*

Note: The flesh from 2 small, or 1 large cooked crab can be used instead of canned crabmeat. In this case, the Fish Stock called for in the recipe can be made from the shells instead, following the general instructions on page 75.

Spanish Fish Stew

● ● ●

For this versatile recipe, you may use any combination of seafood which adds up to 1.5 kg (3 lb). A medium-size (425 g) can of tomatoes may also be used instead of fresh tomatoes – include the juice as well. The saffron is optional; it is an expensive ingredient used for special occasions by the Spanish, who love and appreciate its wonderful flavour and the gorgeous colour it gives to food.

500 g (1 lb) snapper fillets
500 g (1 lb) flounder fillets
250 g (8 oz) prawns, green for preference
250 g (8 oz) scallops
1 cup dry white wine
2 large ripe tomatoes
¼ cup olive oil
a good pinch of saffron threads (optional)
2 cloves garlic, crushed
1 onion, finely chopped
1 tablespoon chopped parsley
1 cup water
salt
freshly ground black pepper
2 bread slices

Skin the fish fillets and check for any remaining bones, cut into serving pieces. Shell and de-vein the prawns. Wash and dry the scallops, trim off any dark parts but retain the coral. Put all the fish in a deep bowl and cover with the wine. Peel the tomatoes, halve and remove the seeds, then roughly chop.

Heat the oil in a large, heavy frying pan, with a lid, and add the saffron threads, garlic and onion. Sauté for about 5 minutes, until the onion is soft but not brown, stirring well. Add the chopped tomatoes, parsley and water and stir to blend. With a slotted spoon, carefully lift the fish, prawns and scallops from the wine and arrange on top of the vegetables. Pour the wine over the fish, cover with a lid and simmer for 5 minutes. Taste, and season well with salt and freshly ground black pepper. Break or cut the bread slices into small pieces, and stir into the stew with a fork, being careful not to break the fish. Ladle gently into bowls, and serve with lots of crusty bread and butter. *Serves 6*

EVERYONE LIKES POULTRY

Mrs. Beeton and Lord Byron should have been around today; they would be happy with what is going on in the modern poultry shop. 'The wings, the breast and merry thought are esteemed the prime part of a fowl, and are usually served to the ladies of the company, to whom the legs, except as a matter of paramount necessity, should not be given' stated Mrs. Beeton. Byron gave it as one reason why he did not like dining with ladies. They always had the wings of fowls which he himself preferred.

Everyone has a favourite part of the chicken and today it is a simple matter to provide 100 merry thoughts (parsons' noses) or chicken wings, to say nothing of those great all-time favourites, drumsticks and chicken breasts. We are cooking chicken in different ways too. Chicken roasted in buttery stock the French way has become *the* way to roast a bird, steamed chicken is something we've learnt from the Chinese – to steep rather than simmer, so that the chicken emerges tender, moist and succulent. Tandoori chicken is no longer reserved for those visiting northern India, it's being prepared in modern ovens throughout the Western world.

Everything is edible in the chicken, including the neck, liver and giblets. Finally, the carcass will make excellent soup, stock and gravy. Chicken is one of the easiest of foods to prepare; you can poach, grill, fry or roast it; curry it; cook and serve it with red or white wine or add flavour with herbs and vegetables. Chicken just has to be one of the most versatile foods on earth.

For those who lament modern mass marketing of poultry, claiming loss of flavour (chickens not tasting like chickens any more) then you just pay extra and go where specially bred free-range table birds are on sale. An unfrozen, fresh fowl certainly has the edge on its mass-market cousin. The good thing about it all is that poultry is there at prices to suit most pockets and every need.

It's a great step forward that you can buy what you want in poultry, including ducks, drakes, geese, pheasants, guinea hens and quail.

To begin with, it's a sensible idea to master the basic ways of cooking poultry to perfection, and you will find these in the first chapter, on pages 29–30. From then on, the world of innovative poultry cooking is waiting to welcome you – so it's time to fly!

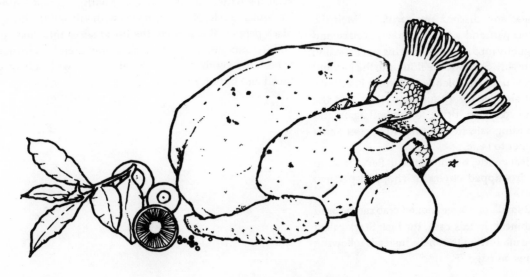

Roast Chicken (French Style)

••

If you like roast chicken that is plump, tender and moist, yet still has that crisp skin, cook it the French way. Basting with stock keeps the chicken juicy, and yet the skin will crisp to a golden brown during the last 15–20 minutes.

1 roasting chicken, about 1.75 kg (3½ lb)
90 g (3 oz) butter
salt
freshly ground pepper
a few tarragon or parsley stalks
3 strips orange rind
⅔ cup chicken stock

Wipe the chicken inside and out with damp paper towels. Put 30 g (1 oz) of the butter, a little salt and pepper, the tarragon or parsley stalks and the orange rind inside the chicken.

Truss the chicken: Put the chicken on its back and cut a small hole in the skin at the base of the breast to push the tail through and close the vent. Pull skin over neck and secure by folding wing tips back over skin. Run string around the wings, cross over the back, turn chicken and tie legs together, keeping them close to the body.

Rub the bird all over with the remaining butter and place on its back in a baking dish with ¼ cup of the stock. Roast in a hot oven (200°C/400°F) for 20 minutes, then turn the chicken on its side and baste with stock. Reduce the heat to moderately hot (190°C/375°F) and continue to cook, turning and basting the chicken every 15 minutes and adding more stock as necessary.

Throughout the cooking, there should be just enough liquid in the pan to keep the juices from scorching. Cook for 1–1½ hours until chicken is done, turning the bird on its back for the last 15 minutes to brown the breast. To test if it is cooked, run a fine skewer into the thigh joint of the chicken. If the juice that runs out is pink, the chicken is not quite cooked; if it is clear, with no tinge of pink, the chicken is ready.

Take the chicken from the pan and remove the string, keep in a warm place while making the gravy.

To make the gravy, pour off all but 4 tablespoons of juices from the pan. Add 1 scant tablespoon of flour, and stir well over a medium heat until lightly browned. Add the remaining stock or stock and water to make 1½ cups. Stir until thickened then season with salt and freshly ground pepper.

Carve the chicken, following the instructions on the right. Serve with the gravy. *Serves 6*

Cream gravy: Make the gravy as above and just before serving, stir in 3 tablespoons cream. Heat but do not boil.

To Carve a Chicken

Place the chicken on a chopping board. Hold the chicken firm with a carving fork through to the back, and cut the skin between the leg and carcass. Press the leg gently outwards, with the flat blade of the knife to expose the joint. Cut through between the ball and socket joint and remove the leg. With a large chicken divide the leg in two, for a good portion of thigh meat with drumstick.

With the knife at the top end of the breastbone opposite where the breast and wishbone meet, cut down parallel to one side of the wishbone for a good slice of breast and the wing. **(1–2)**.

Repeat the first two steps on the other side of the bird.

Cut off the wishbone by carving behind it, down in front of the carcass. **(3)** Carve the remaining breast in good slices. **(4)**

To serve The white meat can be arranged in overlapping slices at one end of the heated platter, with slices of dark meat at the other. Stuffing can be served on the platter or separately.

1–2

3

4

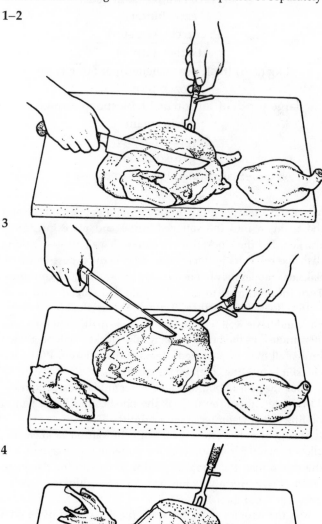

Alsatian Chicken

••

Alsace must seem like the promised land, its borders embrace Germany and Switzerland and it is rich in the earth's bounties. Not the least of its treasures are its Cordon Bleu chefs and master cooks who cannot help but cook well. The chefs and cooks produce imaginative dishes like Alsatian chicken, which is richly hued saffron noodles and green peas, topped with a crispy golden skinned chicken.

Roast Chicken

1.5 kg (3 lb) plump roasting chicken
salt
freshly ground pepper
a little chopped fresh or dried tarragon
60 g (2 oz) butter, softened
extra butter
½ cup chicken stock

Alsatian garnish

1 kg (2 lb) fresh peas (shelled), or 500 g (1 lb)
frozen peas
large pinch of saffron or 1 tablespoon turmeric
½ cup cream
60 g (2 oz) butter
185 g (6 oz) noodles
½ cup grated Parmesan cheese

Mix about 1 teaspoon salt, freshly ground pepper to taste and the tarragon into the softened butter and place inside the chicken. Put the chicken on its side in a well greased baking dish and rub extra butter generously over the exposed surface. Bake in a moderately hot oven (190°C/375°F) for 20–25 minutes. Turn the bird over to the other side and spread with more butter. Roast for a further 20 minutes. Turn the bird on to its back and baste well with the juices in the dish, roast for a final 20 minutes. In the hours cooking, the chicken will be golden brown all over and cooked. Remove the chicken. While the chicken is roasting, prepare the garnish.

Cook the peas in boiling salted water until tender, about 10–15 minutes, then drain. Cook the noodles in a large pan of boiling salted water for about 8 minutes. Drain.

Meanwhile, heat the cream with the saffron or turmeric, allow to stand 5 minutes. Melt the butter in the large pan, add the cream then the noodles, tossing to coat in the flavoured cream. Place over a very low heat for a few minutes, stirring every now and then.

Mix the noodles with the peas and cheese and place on a heated serving platter. Put the chicken, whole or jointed, on the mixture. It makes serving much easier to joint the chicken in the kitchen.

Add the chicken stock to the baking dish and stir to lift off the chicken drippings. Strain into a sauceboat and serve separately. *Serves 6*

Roast Chicken Chinese Style

•••

When honey and spices are rubbed into the skin of a chicken they not only give a lovely flavour to the flesh, but the skin crisps to a deep, mahogany colour during roasting. A very special chicken dish that's not too difficult to make.

1 roasting chicken, approx. 1.6 kg (3 lb 2 oz)
3 tablespoons soy sauce
1 tablespoon honey
½ teaspoon ground ginger
1 tablespoon dry sherry
6–8 spring onions, chopped
3 cloves garlic, crushed
1 teaspoon 5-spice powder
3 teaspoons salt

Remove any loose fat from inside the chicken and wipe inside and out with damp paper towels, pat dry. Combine the soy sauce, honey, ground ginger, sherry, spring onions, garlic, and ½ teaspoon of the 5-spice powder. Rub over the chicken and into the cavity. Loosen the skin on the breasts and thighs with a sharp, pointed knife, and rub the rest of the paste directly on to the chicken flesh. Cover and marinate in the refrigerator for 1 to 2 hours, turning occasionally.

Drain the chicken in a colander, reserving any marinade. Place on a rack in a roasting pan containing 2 cm (¾ inch) of water to prevent the drippings from burning. Roast in a moderate oven (180°C/350°F) for about 1¼ hours or until cooked, turning the chicken occasionally to brown all sides evenly, and brushing with the reserved marinade.

Chop the chicken into serving pieces, see below. Serve with the remaining 5-spice powder mixed with the salt for dipping. Rice is the usual accompaniment. *Serves 6*

Note: Five-spice powder is available from Chinese grocery stores and good delicatessens.

To chop the chicken: Place the chicken on a chopping board, and cut in half lengthways with a sharp cleaver. Each half is then chopped into 3.5 cm (1½ inch) strips and reassembled in the original shape on the serving platter.

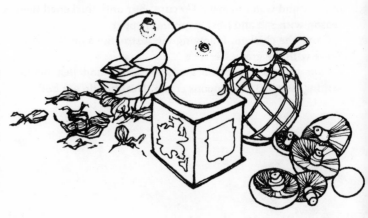

Cardamom Chickens

• • •

A party dish from India that serves 10 people. The spicy fragrance has all the flavour of an Indian curry without any of the fire. Garnish with pappadams which may be cut into strips before frying and accompany with Cashew Nut and Sultana Pilau (see the rice and pasta chapter, page 247).

2 × 1.5 kg (3 lb) chickens
3 teaspoons salt
½ teaspoon saffron threads
¼ cup boiling water
90 g (3 oz) ghee
cinnamon stick
2 whole cloves
2 medium onions, finely chopped
6 tablespoons cold water

Masala

1 small carton natural yogurt
seeds of 12 cardamom pods or 1 teaspoon cardamom seeds
1½ tablespoons grated fresh ginger
5 cloves garlic, chopped
½ teaspoon cayenne pepper

To garnish

4 pappadams, which may be cut into strips

Dry the chickens inside and out with paper towels and truss with string. Place all the ingredients for the Masala into a blender or food processor fitted with the double edged steel blade and combine at high speed for 30 seconds. If you do not have a blender or food processor pound the cardamom, ginger, garlic and cayenne pepper together using a pestle and mortar or the handle of a rounded rolling pin, then stir through the yogurt.

Rub the salt into the chicken skins and place them in a large shallow dish. Spoon the Masala over each bird. Cover with plastic wrap and leave to marinate at room temperature for several hours.

Place the saffron threads in a cup with the ¼ cup of boiling water. Leave to steep for 10 minutes.

Heat the ghee in a large shallow baking dish and add the cinnamon and cloves, stirring. Fry gently for 30 seconds, then add the onions and cook gently until they are soft and golden. Do not allow the onions to brown. Stir in the water. Place the chickens in the baking dish and spoon over the ghee and onion mixture. Cover with a large sheet of foil, crimping the edges to fit round the pan. Bake in a moderately hot oven (190°C/375°F) for 1 hour or until the chickens are tender. Baste with the pan juices every 10 minutes.

To serve, transfer chickens to a serving dish, discard the cinnamon stick and cloves and spoon the remaining sauce from the baking dish over the birds. If you have difficulty jointing a bird at the table, this can be done first in the kitchen. Garnish with pappadam strips and serve with Cashew and Sultana Pilau. *Serves 10*

Tandoori Chicken

• • •

Tandoori chicken is a North Indian dish marinated in spices and yogurt, threaded on a spit and cooked in a clay oven. In a modern kitchen it can be roasted in the oven or barbecued over hot coals. This recipe uses jointed chicken which I believe is convenient, especially when cooking for a crowd.

6–8 chicken pieces, legs or breasts

Yogurt Masala

3–4 cloves garlic
2.5 cm (1 inch) piece green ginger
1 teaspoon cumin seeds
pinch nutmeg
1½ teaspoons salt
¾ cup yogurt
1 tablespoon peanut oil
1 tablespoon tomato sauce
2 teaspoons lemon juice
2–3 drops red food colouring

Lemon Spice Sauce

½ teaspoon freshly ground pepper
¼ teaspoon ground cardamom
1 tablespoon peanut oil
2 tablespoons lemon juice

First make the Yogurt Masala: Peel and finely chop the garlic and ginger. Purée in an electric blender with the remaining ingredients.

Wipe over the chicken pieces and remove the skin. Cut 2 slits about 1 cm (½ inch) deep in the thigh and breast pieces.

Spread the Masala evenly over the chicken pieces and marinate for 10–14 hours in the refrigerator. Place chicken on a rack in a shallow, lightly oiled roasting pan. Spoon over any remaining Masala. Roast in a moderate oven (180°C/350°F) for 30–40 minutes, basting frequently.

Mix the ingredients for the Lemon Spice Sauce together. Remove the chicken from the oven, and coat with any remaining Masala, then sprinkle with the Lemon Spice Sauce. Return to a hot oven (200°C/400°F) for 10–15 minutes or until a dark reddish brown and crisp.

Serve the chicken on a large platter with onion rings, radishes, sliced green or red pepper, lemon and tomato wedges and for those who appreciate something hot, a few chillies. The dedicated will want to make one of the wonderful Indian breads, Naan the tear-drop shaped leavened bread or Chapati. For casual barbecues or picnics the flat Lebanese bread is ideal. Cut it in two and use the pocket to hold the chicken and salad vegetables. *Serves 6–8*

Chicken Sauté Bercy

• •

Chicken is sautéed until golden brown and tender, then served with a wine and mushroom sauce. This method is suitable for a whole, jointed chicken or economical chicken pieces.

1.2 kg (2 lb 10 oz) chicken or 4–6 chicken pieces
60 g (2 oz) butter
1 tablespoon oil
salt
freshly ground pepper
1 teaspoon chopped parsley
extra butter

Bercy Sauce

1 tablespoon chopped spring onions
½ cup white wine
squeeze of lemon juice
125 g (4 oz) mushrooms, finely chopped
30 g (1 oz) butter
chopped parsley

If using a whole chicken, cut into joints. Dry the chicken pieces thoroughly with paper towels (they will not brown if they are moist).

Heat the butter and oil in a heavy frying pan. When the foam has subsided, add the chicken pieces, skin side down, in one layer. Sauté for 2 to 3 minutes, and when the underside is golden, turn the pieces and brown the other side. Do not crowd the pan or the chicken will steam rather than sauté.

As the chicken browns, remove to a warm plate and add more pieces to the pan until all are browned. Season with salt and pepper, and sprinkle with the parsley. Add a little more butter to the pan if necessary, and replace the leg and thigh joints. Cook slowly for 8 to 9 minutes then add the breast and wing joints. Cover the pan and continue cooking for about 15 minutes, turning and basting several times during cooking. Place cooked chicken pieces on a serving dish and keep warm while making the sauce.

Brown the spring onions in the same pan the chicken was cooked in, then add the white wine. Stir well to loosen any crusty bits at the bottom, then boil rapidly until the sauce is reduced by half. Add the lemon juice and mushrooms. Simmer for 5 minutes, swirl in the butter and spoon over the chicken. Sprinkle with chopped parsley to serve. For a creamy finish swirl in 3–4 tablespoons cream. *Serves 4–6*

Note: If using only one kind of chicken piece, for example legs or breast, there will be no difference in timing, just sauté gently until cooked.

Chicken Majorca

• • •

All the flavours of the Mediterranean are in this dish. The chicken is sautéed in both butter and olive oil and flavoured with colourful peppers, garlic, tomatoes and, of course, sherry. The finishing touch is the julienne strips of orange rind – all very Spanish!

Chicken Sauté

6 chicken pieces
30 g (1 oz) butter
2 tablespoons oil
2 teaspoons tomato paste
1 tablespoon flour
2 tablespoons Madeira or sherry
1 cup stock
1 teaspoon fresh tarragon
1 sprig parsley
salt
freshly ground pepper

Sauce

2 tablespoons olive oil
1 clove garlic, chopped
4 mushrooms, sliced
½ red pepper, diced
½ green pepper, diced
2 tomatoes, skinned, seeded and diced
1 orange

Garnish

4–6 sautéed potatoes

Dry the chicken pieces thoroughly with paper towel. In a heavy sauté or frying pan, heat the butter and oil. When the foam has subsided, add the chicken pieces, skin side down in one layer. Sauté for 2 to 3 minutes and when golden, turn and sauté the other side. Remove the chicken and keep warm. Stir in the tomato paste and flour and pour over the Madeira or sherry and the stock. Bring to the boil, stirring. Return the chicken to the pan with the tarragon, parsley and a little salt and pepper. Cover and cook gently for 35 minutes. Remove and keep warm.

While the chicken is cooking, make the Sauce. Heat the oil in a pan. Add the garlic and the mushrooms and sauté for 1 to 2 minutes. Add the red and green peppers, and cook for a further few minutes. Add the tomatoes, toss lightly and cook for 5–10 minutes, stirring.

Using a swivel-bladed vegetable peeler, peel the rind from the orange. Remove any white pith and cut the rind into thin julienne strips, add to the sauce. Spoon the sauce over the chicken and garnish with the sautéed potatoes. *Serves 6*

To make the garnish: Cook the potatoes in boiling salted water until almost tender, drain. Peel and quarter each potato. Heat 30 g (1 oz) butter and 2 tablespoons oil in a pan (just enough to cover the pan) and sauté the potatoes until a brown crust appears, tossing the potatoes from time to time.

Chicken Mayan Style

(Pollo Pibil)

• • •

The distinctive flavour of cumin tends to dominate any dish in which it is included. When combined with garlic, oregano and fresh citrus juice you can count on a richly flavoured, very Latin American dish. If you have individual clay pots then cook each joint in its own little pot . . . just as the early Mayans would have done.

6 chicken pieces, breasts or Marylands
4 cloves garlic, chopped
1½ teaspoons salt
1 teaspoon chopped oregano or ½ teaspoon dried
½–1 teaspoon ground cumin
1 teaspoon freshly ground black pepper
¼ cup orange juice
¼ cup lemon juice
oil

Wipe the chicken pieces with damp paper towels and place in a large bowl. Combine the garlic, salt, oregano, cumin, pepper and fruit juices. Pour over the chicken and marinate, covered, for 24 hours in the refrigerator, turning 2 or 3 times.

Cut aluminium foil into large squares, about 30 cm (12 inch). Brush each square with oil. Divide the chicken pieces among the squares, and spoon the marinade equally over each, holding the edges up to avoid spilling. Fold the foil over the chicken and seal the edges tightly. Arrange the foil envelopes in a baking dish and bake, covered, in a moderate oven (180°C/350°F) for 1½ hours, or until the chicken is very tender. Open a parcel carefully and check at the end of an hour. Slit open the envelopes and serve, one to each person, with hot tortillas or crusty bread to mop up the juices. Flat Lebanese bread can be served instead of the tortillas. *Serves 6*

Chinese Steamed Chicken

• •

The Chinese way of steaming chicken is the best way I know, they call it White Chicken. It is best made with a fresh unfrozen bird. The bird is 'steeped', rather than cooked, in a lightly flavoured stock. Once you learn to cook chicken this way you will never boil or overcook it, for it emerges white, tender, succulent and flavoursome, tasting as it should, of chicken. This technique has been used throughout the book whenever cooked chicken is called for. It has also converted me to never buying a boiling fowl, which seems tasteless and stringy by comparison. The stock is useful for light soups, sauces and gravies, so nothing is wasted.

1 × 1.6 kg (3 lb 2 oz) chicken
water
1 teaspoon salt
2 spring onions, chopped
¼ cup peanut oil
extra salt

Wipe the chicken with paper towels. Place the chicken in a saucepan or large pot just big enough to hold it. Add enough water to cover the chicken. Take the chicken out, as at this stage you just want to establish the amount of water required.

Add salt and spring onions to the water and bring to the boil. Lower the chicken into the pan, bring back to the boil and cook for 5 minutes. Cover the pan and remove from the heat. Let the chicken stand in the liquid for 2 hours.

Lift the chicken out, rinse under cold water, drain and pat dry. The cold water rinse helps set the chicken skin. Brush all over with peanut oil and sprinkle generously with additional salt. When ready to serve, chop the chicken into pieces about 5 × 2 cm (2 × 1 inch). *Serves 6*
Note: A Chinese cleaver makes short work of chopping chicken, and if you like Chinese-style cooking you will find it invaluable. Failing a cleaver in your kitchen, joint the chicken and cut through the bones with poultry shears. For instructions on chopping a chicken, Chinese style, see page 138.

Sesame Chicken

•

This is a delicate and fascinating way of serving chicken as part of a buffet, or as a luncheon dish in its own right, with a hot sauce poured over cold chicken. The basis of the dish is Chinese Steamed Chicken which is chicken cooked only briefly, but allowed to cool in the stock. Chinese Steamed Chicken lends itself to the many fragrant and pungent sauces which the Chinese make so well.

1 Chinese Steamed Chicken, chopped (see page 141)
2 tablespoons light soy sauce
2 tablespoons bottled Teriyaki sauce
2 teaspoons sesame oil
1 tablespoon finely chopped fresh ginger
2 teaspoons sugar
3 tablespoons toasted sesame seeds
a handful of fresh coriander (Chinese parsley)

Arrange the chicken on a serving platter. Mix the soy and Teriyaki sauces, oil, ginger and sugar together in a small pan, and heat gently. When hot, pour the sauce over the chicken and sprinkle with the sesame seeds. Garnish the platter lavishly with coriander, which should be eaten with the chicken, not used merely for decoration. *Serves 6*

Variation

Instead of the sesame sauce, you can serve a fresh ginger sauce. The ginger should be young, fresh and free of fibres.

6–8 spring onions
4 cm (1½ inch) fresh ginger
1 teaspoon salt
4 tablespoons oil

Peel the ginger, cut in very thin slices then shred into fine needle like strips. Shred the spring onions finely on a diagonal slant and place with the ginger and salt in a heatproof bowl (not glass). Heat the oil until very hot and pour over the ginger and onion. Allow to stand for 10 minutes, then spoon the flavoured oil with the onion and ginger shreds over the chopped chicken.

Chicken in a Pot

••

The French have taught us how good chicken tastes when cooked in a heavy casserole with young spring vegetables. In France, this dish is known as Poulet en Cocotte Bonne Femme because it is the way many good cooks like to prepare chicken.

1.5 kg (3 lb) chicken
45 g (1½ oz) butter
60 g (2 oz) streaky bacon, rinded and diced
12 button mushrooms, quartered
12 baby white onions, peeled
2 tablespoons plain flour
2 cups chicken stock
salt
freshly ground pepper
bouquet garni
2 potatoes
chopped parsley

Remove the giblets from the chicken. Wipe the chicken inside and out with paper towels. Truss with string into a neat shape.

Melt the butter in a casserole and brown the chicken all over on a gentle heat, turning frequently. Remove from the pan and keep warm. Add the bacon, mushrooms and whole onions to the pan and sauté until golden. Remove to a plate. Sprinkle in the flour and cook until straw-coloured. Add the stock, season with salt and pepper and bring to the boil, stirring. Add the bouquet garni.

Replace the chicken and vegetables. Cover and bake in a moderate oven (180°C/350°F) for 1 hour or until the chicken is tender. Meanwhile peel the potatoes, cut into small pieces and pare each into shape of a large olive. Add to the casserole 15 minutes before the end of the cooking time. Sprinkle with parsley and serve. *Serves 6*

The New Wave Look

Breast of chicken Normandy with walnut sauce is a dish so special it deserves careful presentation. In the colour photograph on page 122, you can see my suggestion, a tomato rose with stems and leaves of spring onion.

You will find this type of decoration – not fussy or pretentious, but simple and beautiful in its own right – is part of the philosophy of 'new wave' cooking.

The old garnishes that often took more time to make than the recipe itself have been replaced with one or two touches that complement the colours and flavours of the food, and delight the eye.

If you would like to present your Chicken Normandy as you see in the photograph, here are step-by-step instructions for making a tomato rose.

Tomato Rose for Garnishing Cut across the base of a firm, red tomato, but do not sever the slice. Use a small, sharp paring knife and proceed as for peeling an orange. With the base still attached, continue cutting round the skin of the tomato, in a narrow strip, about 2 cm (¾ inch) wide. Move the knife in an up and down movement to give a wavy effect as you cut (this will make the edges of the tomato 'petals' look natural). When the strip is about half way down the tomato, taper it off to a point and remove.

Cut another straight strip from the tomato skin as long as the first one.

Curl the first strip of skin into its attached base with the flesh side on the inside of the flower and the bright red skin outside.

Roll the second strip into a tight scroll and place in the middle to make the heart of the rose.

To make the stems and leaves, blanch the green parts of a leek, shallot or spring onion by plunging into boiling water for 30 seconds then cooling at once under cold water. This makes it very green and manageable. Dry, lay flat on a chopping board and cut long strips for stalks and a wider strip with a pointed end for the leaf.

Arrange the tomato rose on its stalk and add other stalks and leaves to suit the shape of your platter.

Breast of Chicken Normandy with Walnut Sauce

• • •

The word Normandy in a recipe title means you can expect apple flavour in the dish, and here it comes in three ways – from the apple brandy called Calvados, apple cider and the accompaniment of lightly sautéed apple slices. A creamy sauce with the crunch of walnuts completes this superb main course for a special dinner party – as lovely to look at as it is to eat.

8–12 half-breasts of chicken
seasoned flour
60 g (2 oz) butter
1 tablespoon oil
salt
freshly ground pepper
3 tablespoons Calvados (apple brandy) or brandy
1½ cups apple cider
1 cup cream
2 tablespoons chopped walnuts

Garnish

2 large green apples
30 g (1 oz) butter

Carefully remove the chicken breasts from the bones and remove the skin. Cut the breasts diagonally into two, in even shaped fillets. Dust lightly with the seasoned flour. Heat the butter and oil in a large pan that has a tight-fitting lid. Brown the chicken breasts on each side, and season with salt and freshly ground pepper. Cook the chicken in batches, without crowding the pan.

Heat the Calvados or brandy in a small saucepan, set alight and pour over the chicken. Shake the pan until the flames subside, then pour in the cider. Cover and simmer gently for 5 minutes, or until the breasts are cooked and tender, remove and keep warm.

Reduce the liquid in the pan to half by boiling briskly. Taste and adjust the seasoning and stir in the cream and walnuts. For a very smooth sauce, put through a blender. Reheat, but do not boil.

Meanwhile prepare the garnish. Cut the apples into quarters, remove the core, then cut each quarter into three wedges, do not peel. Melt the butter in a large frying pan, and sauté the wedges on each side until heated through but not soft – about two minutes.

Place the apple wedges down the centre of a heated serving platter and arrange the sautéed chicken in overlapping rows over them, leaving some of the green skins and wedge shapes showing. Spoon some walnut sauce over the breasts and serve the remaining sauce separately. *Serves 4–6*

Chicken Tetrazzini

• • •

*This dish was named after Luisa Tetrazzini, the
great Italian coloratura soprano. Some dishes are great for
entertaining and this, like its namesake, is one of
them. Sufficient for 12 generous servings, the entire dish can
be prepared a day in advance and stored in the
refrigerator – ready to place in the oven an hour before
serving. The recipe may also be halved successfully
for six servings.*

2 large roasting chickens
1 carrot, halved
½ onion, stuck with 2 whole cloves
1 bay leaf
1 stalk celery
sprig fresh thyme or pinch dried thyme
6 peppercorns
salt

To finish

6–8 baby carrots
4 stalks celery, sliced
12 small onions, peeled
250 g (8 oz) butter
6 tablespoons flour
1 cup cream
500 g (1 lb) button mushrooms, sliced
500 g (1 lb) ribbon noodles
6 tablespoons grated Parmesan cheese
salt
freshly ground pepper

Garnish

1½ cups toasted, slivered almonds

Remove any excess fat from the chickens and place in a large
saucepan. If you haven't a saucepan big enough for two, use
two saucepans and divide the ingredients. Add the remaining
ingredients with enough water to barely cover the chickens
and salt to taste. Bring to the boil, cover and simmer gently for
about 30 minutes. Remove the pan from the heat, and cool the
chickens in the stock. Remove the chickens and strain the stock
into a bowl. Chill 5 cups of the stock in the refrigerator so that
fat rises to the top, and is then easily removed.

To finish: Remove the skin from the chickens and break the
flesh into large chunks, discarding the bones. Set aside,
covered, until required.

Cut the carrots in two if large, and place in a saucepan with
the celery, onions and just enough salted water to cover. Bring
to the boil, reduce the heat then cook until the vegetables are
tender, about 15 minutes, strain.

Melt 125 g (4 oz) of the butter in a large saucepan, blend in the
flour and cook for 2 minutes, stirring. Add the reserved
chicken stock and bring to the boil, stirring constantly. Season
with salt and pepper to taste, then add the cream, chicken and
cooked vegetables.

Melt 60 g (2 oz) of the remaining butter and toss the
mushrooms lightly in it until tender, then add to the chicken
mixture.

Cook the noodles in a large pan of boiling, salted water until
tender, about 10–15 minutes, then drain. Melt the remaining
butter and toss with the noodles, adding salt and pepper to
taste.

Divide the noodles between two shallow, greased casseroles
or baking dishes. Top with the chicken mixture and sprinkle
with Parmesan cheese. Cover with aluminium foil or plastic
wrap, cool, then chill in the refrigerator.

About 1½ hours before serving, remove from the refrigerator and take off the foil or plastic cover. Bake in a moderately
hot oven (190°C/375°F) for 1 hour, or until completely heated
through. Top with the toasted almonds, which may be slivered
before toasting. Serve with crusty bread and butter and a green
salad. *Serves 12*

Spiced Chicken Breasts

• • •

*Chicken breasts are baked until golden brown and tender in
yogurt flavoured with garlic and spices, making this
a marvellous party dish. For a more economical, but just as
delicious family meal, you can use chicken pieces.*

8 whole chicken breasts
125 g (4 oz) ghee or butter
2 small onions, finely chopped
2 cloves garlic, crushed
8 whole cardamom pods
2 sticks cinnamon
1 cup water

Marinade

2 cups natural yogurt
2 cloves garlic, crushed
1 onion, grated
2 tablespoons ground coriander
2 teaspoons finely chopped green ginger
2 teaspoons salt
2 teaspoons turmeric
½ teaspoon ground black pepper

Allow 1 whole chicken breast per person. Remove all the tiny rib bones, leaving the main breastbone. Combine all the ingredients for the Marinade in a large bowl, add the chicken pieces and stir to coat well. Marinate for at least 2 hours or overnight, in a refrigerator.

Melt 60 g (2 oz) of the ghee or butter in a large frying pan. Sauté the onions, garlic, cardamom pods and cinnamon sticks for 5 minutes, until the onions are soft and golden. Add the water and stir well. Spoon as much marinade as possible from the chicken breasts and reserve. Place the chicken in a baking dish and spoon a little of the onion mixture on top of each one. Dot with the remaining ghee or butter and bake in a hot oven (200°C/400°F) for 10 minutes. Spoon the reserved marinade over the breasts. Continue cooking until the chicken is tender, about 10 minutes longer.

Place the chicken on a serving dish and keep warm. Remove the cardamom pods and cinnamon sticks from the sauce, bring to the boil and spoon over the chicken to serve.

Serve with plain boiled or yellow rice, and interesting accompaniments. Tiny cherry tomatoes, poppadums and cucumber slices in yogurt would be nice – and don't forget the chutney! *Serves 8*

Chicken in Yogurt

••

Yogurt stems from the Balkans, and here as in the Near East, it is consumed several times daily, either as it is or in cooking. Apart from being a refreshing and nourishing food, yogurt is said by many to have excellent medicinal properties. Once you get a taste for it in marinades you will want to experiment further. This recipe is a good start.

1.5 kg (3 lb) chicken pieces
1 cup natural yogurt
2 cloves garlic, crushed
salt
freshly ground black pepper

Trim chicken pieces of excess fat, and remove all the skin.

Pour the yogurt into a deep bowl. Combine the yogurt with the garlic and season with salt and pepper. Add the chicken pieces and stir to coat with the mixture. Marinate for at least 4 hours, preferably overnight, turning the pieces every now and then.

Transfer the chicken pieces to a shallow ovenproof dish, spooning the marinade over the top. Bake in a moderately hot oven (190°C/375°F) for 50 to 60 minutes, basting occasionally. Increase the oven temperature to very hot (230°C/450°F) to brown the chicken quickly, or place under the grill. Serve with Rice Pilaf (see page 249) and a bowl of plain yogurt plus a spicy chutney and a tomato sambal if liked. *Serves 6*

Variation

You may like to add powdered cardamom, grated green ginger, a little curry powder, ground coriander or lemon juice to the marinade.

Note: The same marinade is delicious with lamb. Use boneless lamb from the leg or shoulder, cut into cubes, and marinated for 4 hours or overnight. To cook, thread the meat on skewers and cook under a hot grill. Gently heat leftover marinade and use as a sauce.

Lime Grilled Chicken

••

Once a luxury imported from California or the Pacific Islands, limes are appearing in shops for those devotees who appreciate their fresh and distinctive flavour. They make a refreshing difference not only to drinks, but to many fish and poultry dishes and marry well with tarragon which is the natural herb for chicken.

6 half-breasts of chicken
salt
freshly ground pepper

Sauce

½ cup oil
½ cup lime juice
1 onion, finely chopped
2 teaspoons dried tarragon
1 teaspoon salt
½ teaspoon Tabasco sauce

Garnish

2 limes (optional)
small bunch watercress or parsley

Combine all the Sauce ingredients and marinate the chicken breasts in this for 1–2 hours, or overnight for a stronger flavour.

Place the chicken on a lightly oiled sheet of aluminium foil, the edges turned up to make a tray and catch the juices. Place on the grilling rack under a preheated grill. Sprinkle with salt and pepper and brush with the sauce. Grill, skin side up, for about 8 minutes to brown the skin. Turn the chicken, baste again with the sauce and lower the grilling rack a little or reduce the heat. Cook for a further 8–10 minutes, basting often. Turn the chicken, skin side up, and cook for a further 5 minutes, basting, or until tender and the skin is golden and crackling.

Garnish if liked with wedges of lime and a small bunch of watercress or parsley.

Serve with creamed potatoes or boiled rice and a crisp green salad. *Serves 6*

Grilled Lemon Chicken

•

This is an excellent way of cooking chicken – quick, easy and good when something simple is called for. Dieters will appreciate this recipe; if on a serious weight-control programme remove the skin before grilling.

juice of 1 large lemon
½ onion, grated
1–2 cloves garlic (optional)
salt
freshly ground black pepper
4 chicken pieces, half-breasts or legs
1–2 tablespoons oil
1 lemon, sliced

Combine the lemon juice, onion, garlic crushed with salt if using and pepper to taste. Marinate the chicken pieces in this mixture for at least an hour, turning several times.

Heat the grill and lightly oil the grid. Place the chicken on the grid and grill for 10 to 14 minutes, about 7 minutes each side. Turn the chicken, skin side up and arrange 2 slices of lemon on top. Continue to grill for another 10 minutes or until the juice runs clear when the chicken is pierced with a fine skewer.

Serve with a green salad and for non-dieters, buttered baby potatoes or buttered rice. *Serves 4*

Note: If cooking skinned chicken breasts (for weight-watchers) place the chicken on a sheet of foil smeared with oil. Protect with lemon slices and grill without turning. The foil will heat through and help to cook the chicken from the underneath as the top grills.

Dijon Grilled Chicken

• •

A genuine French mustard in the Dijon manner (look for names like Grey Poupon, Maille, Vert Pre) has an interesting taste, and using it is one way of getting that elusive 'French flavour' in your food. Experiment with different flavours such as tarragon or green herbs if you like, although the mustard with white wine is probably the most useful and versatile.

6 chicken pieces, breasts or legs,
or 2 × 500 g (1 lb) chickens
90 g (3 oz) butter
1 tablespoon oil
2–3 tablespoons Dijon mustard
2 tablespoons chopped spring onions
¼ teaspoon thyme
salt
freshly ground pepper
pinch of cayenne pepper

Split the small chickens, if using. Heat the grill and arrange the chicken pieces on the rack, skin side up. Melt the butter in a small pan, add the oil, and brush the chicken pieces with some of the butter mixture.

Grill the chicken for 10 minutes on each side, brushing or basting frequently with the butter and oil.

Blend the mustard with the spring onions, thyme and salt and pepper to taste and slowly add the rest of the oil and butter mixture, drop by drop, to thicken it.

Turn the chicken skin side up, and spread with some of the mustard mixture. Grill for a further 10 minutes, reducing the heat if necessary, until the chicken is golden brown and tender, basting with the marinade from time to time. Small chicken pieces will take less time to cook, 15 to 20 minutes approximately, so time accordingly. *Serves 4*

Spiced Grilled Chicken

•

For those who enjoy variety and spice, here's the very thing – chicken pieces grilled in a devilish-hot sauce. Serve hot with rice straight from the grill or take cold on a picnic, when they should be eaten with the fingers. Provide plenty of paper napkins, of course!

4–6 chicken pieces or 2 × 500 g (1 lb) chickens
60 g (2 oz) butter
3 tablespoons chutney
1 tablespoon Worcestershire sauce
1 tablespoon soy sauce
dash of Tabasco sauce
stock or wine
watercress or spring onion to serve

Spiced Seasoning

1 teaspoon salt
2 teaspoons sugar
1 teaspoon ground pepper
1 teaspoon ground ginger
1 teaspoon dry mustard
1 teaspoon curry powder

Wipe over the chicken pieces with damp paper towels. If using whole chickens split in half and cut away the back and rib bones.

Mix the Spiced Seasoning ingredients together and rub into the surface of the chicken. Allow to stand for at least an hour.

Melt the butter in a small saucepan, brush the chicken pieces all over, and grill under a medium grill until brown and crisp, about 15 minutes, turning from time to time. Remove the rack from the grill pan and place the pieces in the pan, skin side up.

Mix the chutney, Worcestershire, soy and Tabasco sauces together with the remaining butter, in a small saucepan. Heat gently, then spoon some over the chicken. Continue cooking slowly under the grill for 15 to 20 minutes, basting frequently with the remaining sauce.

Arrange the chicken in a serving dish. Dilute the sauces which have gathered in the pan with a little stock or wine and spoon over the top. Garnish with watercress or spring onion to serve. *Serves 4–6*

Note: In Eastern countries where hot, spicy dishes are served, green or raw white onion is often offered to enhance the flavour, and also for its decorative appeal.

To make what the Chinese call spring onion brushes, trim spring onions of their tougher green leaves, shred the tender green ends finely, and drop into iced water. The green shreds curl up and look very fetching.

Honey Basted Chicken Wings

•

These are delicious at a barbecue or picnic, and can be served with rice or noodles. Supply plenty of paper napkins for these are best eaten with the fingers.

1 kg (2 lb) chicken wings
2 tablespoons soy sauce
2 tablespoons lemon juice
2 slices fresh green ginger
2 tablespoons honey
2 tablespoons tomato sauce
freshly ground black pepper

Cut off and discard the tips from the chicken wings. Mix the soy sauce, lemon juice and ginger in a bowl. Add the chicken, turn to coat and leave to marinate in the refrigerator for several hours or overnight.

Drain the wings and combine 1 tablespoon of the marinade mixture with the honey, tomato sauce and pepper. Cook under a preheated grill for 10 minutes, turn and brush with the honey mixture. Grill for a further 10 minutes or until cooked. *Serves 4–6*

Note: The wing tips can be used for making stock.

Green Peppercorn Chicken

•

Green peppercorns in small cans, labelled Poivre Vert, are available from health food shops and large stores. They are little berries from the same trees as the black peppercorn but are canned in their soft, undried state and have a more vibrant flavour than black peppercorns.

4 small whole chicken breasts
1 clove garlic
salt
1 tablespoon green peppercorns
45 g (1½ oz) butter, softened
lemon juice

Wipe the chicken breasts dry with paper towels. Crush the garlic with a little salt. Crush the peppercorns with the back of a spoon. Combine the peppercorns and garlic with the butter and lemon juice to make a smooth paste. Spread chicken on both sides with the peppercorn mixture and push a little between the flesh and skin. Leave to stand for several hours. Put chicken in a shallow roasting pan and place under a preheated grill.

Cook skin side up for 5 minutes. Turn chicken and cook for a further 10–15 minutes until tender, turning once or twice. Finish with the skin side up so the skin is crisp and golden. Brush during cooking with the juices. Serve with buttered noodles and a crisp salad or green vegetables. *Serves 4*

Fried Chicken Maryland

••

This American specialty is as good as the pictures we conjure up. There are a few tricks to learn, first the chicken, dusted with seasoned flour or cornmeal, is fried in hot fragrant butter until brown. The heat is then reduced and the chicken cooks more slowly and is turned frequently until done. The crispy chicken is then served with a creamy gravy – an American friend says preferably made with buttermilk.

6 Marylands (legs with thighs)
½ cup evaporated milk or buttermilk
½ cup (2 oz) plain flour or cornmeal
salt
pepper
60 g (2 oz) butter
3 tablespoons oil
6–8 mushrooms, sliced
½ cup boiling water
⅓ cup cream or buttermilk
¼ teaspoon paprika
chopped parsley

Dry the Maryland pieces well. Dip each piece in the evaporated milk or buttermilk, then in the flour or cornmeal, seasoned with 1½ teaspoons of salt and a pinch of pepper.

Heat the butter and oil in a large heavy frying pan, and when sizzling add the chicken. Fry over a medium heat until golden on both sides. Take care as the chicken often spits when frying. Reduce the heat, and continue to cook until done, turning frequently. The chicken pieces will take approximately 30 minutes to cook. Remove to a heated platter and keep warm.

Sauté the mushrooms in the pan for a few minutes. Gradually add the boiling water to the pan. Stir frequently until the brown bits dissolve and the mixture thickens slightly. Gradually add the cream or buttermilk, stirring until smooth and thickened, do not boil. Add salt, pepper and paprika pepper to taste. Spoon the sauce over the chicken and garnish with chopped parsley. Serve with hot garlic bread, potato crisps and a salad. *Serves 6*

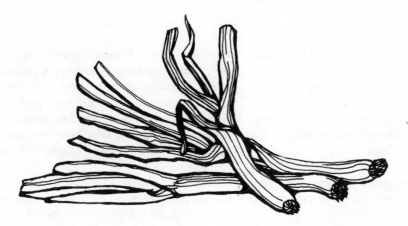

Chicken Wings Chasseur

•

Everyone seems to like chicken wings and they are inexpensive enough to serve often – for the family as well as special occasions. Here they star in a richly-flavoured sauce and are accompanied by golden rice, but would also be delicious with jacket potatoes or buttered noodles. Incidentally, be sure to have plenty of paper napkins on hand for those who, like me, can't resist picking up the wings in their fingers!

1 kg (2 lb) chicken wings
salt
freshly ground pepper
plain flour
60 g (2 oz) butter
2 tablespoons oil
1 clove garlic, crushed
1 small onion, chopped
½ cup chopped spring onions
125 g (4 oz) mushrooms, finely sliced
1 tablespoon chopped parsley
½ teaspoon dried thyme
½ cup each dry white wine and chicken stock,
or 1 cup chicken stock
½ cup canned tomatoes, chopped
chopped parsley to serve

Cut off and discard the tips from the chicken wings, use the tips to make the stock. Pat the wings dry with paper towels, sprinkle with salt and freshly ground pepper, and toss in the flour to coat.

Melt the butter and oil in a large heavy frying pan and sauté the wings, a few at a time, until browned. Transfer with a slotted spoon to a plate, keep warm. Add the garlic, onion and spring onions to the pan, and sauté until the onion is soft. Add the mushrooms and cook for a further 2–3 minutes.

Add the remaining ingredients, except the parsley, and season with salt and freshly ground pepper. Bring the mixture to the boil, return the chicken wings to the pan, and cover. Simmer for 20 minutes, or until the chicken is tender. Sprinkle with chopped parsley to serve. This dish goes particularly well with Saffron Rice, see page 246. *Serves 6*

Chicken Newburg

• • •

A popular wedding breakfast dish and now that chicken breasts are readily available at a reasonable price, serving this dish to a crowd is within the reach of everyone. Fluffy boiled rice is the perfect partner followed by a good salad.

12 half-breasts of chicken
salt
freshly ground pepper
1 bay leaf
1 small carrot, scraped
few parsley sprigs
60 g (2 oz) butter
½ cup sliced mushrooms
¼ cup sherry

Newburg Sauce

½ cup milk
½ cup cream
3 egg yolks
paprika pepper

Gently poach the chicken breasts in water to cover, with the salt, freshly ground pepper, bay leaf, carrot and parsley. Simmer very gently for 6–8 minutes then cool in the liquid.

Lift the chicken breasts from the stock and carefully remove the meat from the breastbones in one piece. With a sharp knife, slice the chicken breasts in half diagonally. (For a fork buffet cut in half again.)

Melt the butter in a large heavy saucepan and cook the mushrooms until softened. Add the chicken to the pan with half the sherry. Season with salt and freshly ground pepper, cover and heat for 2 minutes. Keep warm while making the sauce.

Combine the milk and cream and heat gently. Beat the remaining sherry with the egg yolks in a small bowl and add a little of the hot sauce. Pour the egg yolk mixture into the hot sauce and heat gently, stirring until thickened, but do not let it boil. Taste and adjust the seasoning and fold into the chicken mixture.

Serve sprinkled with a little paprika and accompany with a dish of fluffy boiled rice. *Serves 12*

DUCK

'Christmas is coming, the ducks are getting fat,
Please put a penny in the old man's hat'

For many people, Christmas certainly wouldn't be Christmas without roast duck – the dark flesh with its rich, distinctive flavour and the special joy of the crispy, golden skin.

Luckily, modern production and marketing techniques have tended to bring prices to a point where we can enjoy duck more than once a year. Local poulterers usually have fresh ducks in permanent supply, and frozen ducks are always available from larger supermarkets.

When buying duck, look for a plump breast and a good, creamy colour to the skin. The carcass is large in proportion to the meat, so you can count on an average duck, about 1.5 kg (3 lb), feeding only three people. For a dinner party, I think it's pleasant (and certainly very convenient for the carver) to serve half a small duckling to each person.

In choosing accompaniments for duck, consider sharp flavours that will complement its richness. Fruit sauces – like those made from sour cherries and peaches – provide wonderful contrast, also highly flavoured vegetables such as turnips and onions. A fresh green salad is an interesting idea instead of a hot green vegetable – cool and crisp, it seems just right with duck.

To Prepare for Roasting

As duck contains a lot of fat compared to chicken, be sure to remove all the loose fat from the cavity and neck. The tail area is also very oily, and any yellow residue should be carefully removed. The bird should then be rubbed all over with salt and perhaps a little lemon juice to reduce oiliness, and if very fat, pricked with a skewer along the back, thighs and below the breast. This helps release the fat during cooking.

If using stuffing, don't fill the cavity too tightly, allow room for expansion. Instead of stuffing, a few lemon slices and a quartered green apple may be placed in the cavity to flavour the bird.

Truss after stuffing, using the same method as for chicken (see page 29). Place the duck, breast side up, in a roasting pan and cook according to the following time chart.

To Roast

Set the oven at moderately hot (190°C/375°F). After 15 minutes of cooking time, reduce the oven temperature to moderate (180°C/350°F) and complete roasting at this temperature.

Ready to Cook Weight	Cooking Time	Serves
1.5 kg (3 lb)	1 hour, 5–15 mins	2 people
2 kg (4 lb)	1 hour, 25–35 mins	3–4 people
2.5 kg (5 lb)	1 hour, 35–40 mins	4–5 people

Unlike the French most of us like duck well done.
Note: If you have any doubts at all about the tenderness of your duck I would advise braising it instead of plain roasting. With braising you can still achieve a crispy skin if you leave the bird uncovered for the last 15 minutes of cooking, but the slower, longer cooking in liquid ensures moist, tender flesh.

Cutting a cooked duck into portions

Halve the bird by slicing along the breastbone. Use poultry shears to cut through the bones.

Slice the halved bird into two sections then cut through the bone with shears. Repeat on other half.

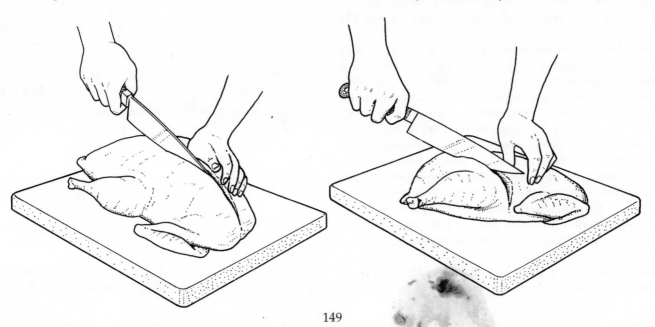

Braised Duckling with Turnips

••

This method of cooking duckling ensures melting tenderness, and sugar-glazed turnips and onions make a delightful contrast to the rich duck flavour. One large duckling should be sufficient for four people, but remember that duck contains a large proportion of bone to flesh. If a large duckling isn't available, choose two of medium size and serve half to each person.

1 × 2.5 kg (5 lb) duckling
90 g (3 oz) lean pork belly
30 g (1 oz) butter
1 onion, chopped
1 cup dry white wine
sprig or pinch of thyme
salt
freshly ground black pepper
1 kg (2 lb) small white turnips
1 kg (2 lb) small white onions
2 tablespoons sugar
60 g (2 oz) butter
1 cup water

Wipe the bird inside and out with damp paper towels and truss. If using pickled pork, cover with cold water, bring to the boil, and boil for 5 minutes, then rinse in cold water.

Melt the butter in an oval, flameproof casserole big enough to take the duckling. When hot, brown the duckling on one side, then turn to brown all over. Remove the duckling and pour off all but 1 tablespoon of the fat.

Dice the pork and fry in the fat until crisp and golden, stirring occasionally. Add the onion and continue frying gently until the onion is soft. Place the duckling in the pan, and pour over the wine. Add the thyme and season with salt and freshly ground black pepper. Cover the casserole tightly and cook in a moderately hot oven (190°C/375°F) for approximately 1½ hours.

About 30 minutes before the bird is cooked, peel the turnips and cut into quarters or wedges and peel the onions. Place in a heavy saucepan with the sugar, butter and water. Cover with a lid and cook until just tender, about 20 minutes. Remove the lid and allow the liquid to evaporate over a high heat until a thick syrup remains and the vegetables are glazed. Turn the vegetables with a spoon to coat evenly with the syrup.

Remove the cooked duckling to a serving dish, cut off the trussing strings and keep warm. Strain the liquid from the pan into a small saucepan, and skim off the fat. Reduce over a high heat until the sauce is thickened, or thicken with a little cornflour mixed with water. Surround the duckling with glazed turnips and onions and serve the sauce separately in a gravy boat. *Serves 4*

Note: If you are cooking two ducklings, I find it quite convenient to use a roasting dish as a casserole, with another one inverted on top as a lid. Otherwise, aluminium foil can be shaped into a lid and crimped tightly around the sides of the roasting dish.

Roast Duckling with Green Peppercorn Sauce

••

1 × 2.5 kg (5 lb) duckling
salt
pepper
1 small onion
4 tablespoons red wine vinegar
½ teaspoon dried tarragon, crumbled
1 teaspoon chopped fresh thyme
2–3 tablespoons green peppercorns
2 teaspoons French mustard
1½ cups Duck Stock
2 tablespoons chopped parsley

Cut off the neck and remove excess fat from the duckling. Wipe the duckling inside and out with a damp cloth and season with salt and pepper. Place, breast side up, on a rack in a roasting pan and bake in a moderately hot oven (190°C/375°F) for 1½ hours or until the duckling is cooked, basting occasionally.

Meanwhile, finely chop the onion and place in a small saucepan with the vinegar, tarragon and thyme. Boil uncovered, stirring, until all the liquid has evaporated.

Rinse the peppercorns and add to the onion with the mustard and duck stock. Bring to the boil and cook until reduced slightly, set aside. Remove duckling from the roasting pan and keep warm. Spoon, or siphon with a basting bulb, as much fat as possible from the pan. Pour the pan drippings into the peppercorn sauce, reheat if necessary and stir in the parsley.

Cut the duckling into portions and serve with a little of the sauce spooned over. Serve the remaining sauce separately.
Serves 4
Duck Stock Heat a little oil in a saucepan and brown the neck and giblets of the duck. Pour off all the fat and add 2 cups water, a bouquet garni and a little salt and pepper. Simmer for 1 hour and strain before using.

Right: Fragrant Cardamom Chickens (page 139) is a party dish for 10. Accompany with Cashew and Sultana Pilau (page 247).

TURKEY

Turkey breeding has changed over the years, and the present-day bird has more tender breast meat in proportion to dark meat than the same-size bird of years ago.

Turkeys are available now from a tiny 2.5 kg (5 lb) up to a giant 12.5 kg (26 lb). It is also possible to buy half turkeys and turkey hind quarters – so there's a turkey size to fit almost every family's size and budget.

Most turkeys are purchased frozen, and will take up to three days to thaw in the refrigerator. It is most important that the bird is properly thawed before it is stuffed and cooked, and that the stuffing is added just at the last moment, before baking.

Two Stuffings for Turkey

A turkey is usually stuffed with two different flavoured stuffings – one in the crop and one in the main body cavity. When the turkey is cooked, the stuffing in the crop is carved into slices, so everyone gets a piece of stuffing surrounded by white breast meat and crispy skin. The stuffing from the main body cavity is spooned around the carved meat. Be careful to stuff the crop lightly as the stuffing will expand during cooking and too much may cause the skin to split, spoiling the appearance of the turkey. One important point to remember – if you are cooking a very large turkey do make sure your oven is large enough to hold it. There is nothing worse than having a turkey that won't fit into the oven!

To roast turkey

Use a moderate oven (180°C/350°F) for the whole cooking time.

Ready to Cook Weight	Cooking Time	Serves
3–4 kg (6–8 lb)	3–3½ hours	8–10 people
4–5 kg (8–10 lb)	3½–4 hours	10–14 people
6–8 kg (12–16 lb)	4–6 hours	14–16 people

How to tell when the turkey is cooked

If a meat thermometer pushed into the thickest part of the thigh registers 85°C (190°F), the turkey is cooked.

If you don't own a thermometer, pierce the thickest part of the thigh with a fork or fine skewer. If the fork goes in easily and the juice which runs out is clear, the turkey is cooked. If the juice has a pink tinge, further cooking is required.

Left: Serve Parsleyed Packs of Lamb (page 171) with Béarnaise Sauce (page 45) and vegetables in season.

How to carve a turkey

First make sure your carving knife is razor sharp. Remove the trussing strings and skewers and set the bird on a large board or serving plate. Place a long-bladed sharp knife between the thigh and body of the bird and cut through the joint. Remove the leg by pressing it outward with the knife and bending it back with the fork. Separate the thigh and drumstick, and slice off the dark meat. Repeat with the other leg.

Remove the wings and cut into two if desired. Carve down the breast on each side with straight, even strokes.

Carve the stuffing in the crop including some of the white breast meat into thin slices, and remove stuffing from the body with a spoon.

To serve The white meat is usually arranged in overlapping slices at one end of the heated platter, with slices of dark meat at the other. Stuffing may be served on two separate heated plates or, if your platter is large enough, arranged with the turkey meat.

Roast Turkey

•••

6 kg (12 lb) turkey
1 quantity Fresh Herb Stuffing, see page 160,
or Sausage and Bacon Stuffing, see page 160
1 quantity Sweet Potato Stuffing, see page 159
60 g (2 oz) butter
salt
freshly ground pepper
2 cups stock, made from the turkey giblets

Gravy

2 tablespoons plain flour
extra 3 cups turkey giblet stock
1 turkey liver or 3 chicken livers

Wipe the turkey cavity with a damp kitchen cloth and place the herb or sausage and bacon stuffing lightly into the neck or crop, being careful not to pack it too tightly. Press the outside of the breast to give it a good shape and bring the skin over the back and secure it with small skewers.

Spoon the sweet potato stuffing into the body of the turkey. Tuck the wings under the turkey to give the bird a neat shape. Tuck the turkey flap under the wings to hold it.

Insert small skewers around the opening and lace together with fine string. Fasten the legs close to the body by tying the ends of the drumsticks together. Wipe well with a damp kitchen towel.

Soften the butter and spread all over the turkey, making sure that the breast and legs are well covered. Season with salt and pepper. Place on a rack in a roasting pan and pour in the stock.

Cover the roasting pan tightly with aluminium foil and roast the turkey in a moderate oven (180°C/350°F) for about 3½ to 4 hours or until the turkey is tender, basting it every 25 minutes (see chart above). Remove the foil for the last 30 minutes of cooking, to allow the turkey to brown. Test the turkey to see if it is cooked by piercing the thickest part of the thigh and drumstick with a fine skewer. If ready, the juice should run clear. If the juice has a slightly pink tinge, cook longer until it runs clear.

Remove to a heated serving platter and allow the turkey to rest in a warm place for 15 minutes while you make the gravy and serve the vegetables. This resting period gives the flesh time to set and makes carving easier. This may be done in the warming drawer, or on top of the steaming pudding if it's Christmas time, or on top of the vegetables. *Serves 14*

Giblet Stock • Giblets are usually contained in a plastic bag tucked inside the frozen turkey. Wash the giblets, place in a saucepan with a chopped onion and salt and pepper, cover with water, and bring to the boil. Simmer gently, covered, for 30 minutes, then strain and use to baste the turkey or for adding to the pan gravy.

To make pan gravy • Pour off all but ½ cup of juices from the pan. Add the flour and stir well over a medium heat, until thickened and brown. Add giblet stock or stock cubes and

water to make 3 cups. Bring to the boil and stir until smooth. Season with salt and freshly ground pepper.

A tablespoon of brandy or redcurrant jelly, or a few tablespoons of cream may be stirred into the gravy, if desired. Add after the gravy is cooked, stirring well to blend.

GOOSE

Roast goose challenges duck and turkey for popularity at Christmas time among many European and English people, and is becoming more readily available now we have specialty poultry shops. Some butchers will also get it for you if ordered in advance.

Although a goose has a large carcass in proportion to flesh, its meat is richer than that of turkey. Consequently, a goose and a turkey of comparable size will serve roughly the same number of people.

A goose is not always stuffed because it releases a large quantity of fat during cooking, which gives the stuffing a strong fatty flavour. Some cooks prefer to place whole apples or peeled onions inside the bird. These add their own flavour, and help to cut the richness of the goose. (They are discarded when the goose is cooked.) However, stuffing may be made and cooked with some of the drippings from the pan in a separate dish. Apples can also accompany the goose when you serve it, in the form of whole apples baked with a raisin stuffing (see page 158). A wonderful accompaniment!

To carve goose

Remove trussing strings and skewers and place the goose on a board. Cut off the legs with a sharp knife. (1) The leg joint of a goose is found further back on the body than that of a chicken.

Slip a long-bladed sharp knife under the wings and breast to raise them, then slide it along the carcass down to the wing bones. Slice off the wings with a piece of breast meat attached.

Carve breast by making the first cut along the breastbone, then making parallel cuts down the breast. Take care that the knife is well slanted towards the inside. To remove slices, cut upwards towards the breastbone, starting from the last cut.

To serve Place legs at one end of a heated serving platter and wings at the other end. Arrange the slices of breast in the centre. Spoon a little gravy over the meat to give a light glaze. Stuffing may be served separately or on the same platter.

Roast Goose

With Apple and Prune Stuffing
• •

This recipe calls for a delicious fruit stuffing

1 × 3 kg (6 lb) goose
Apple and Prune Stuffing (see page 159)
2 tablespoons flour
1 tablespoon oil
¼ cup brandy

Remove any excess fat from the inside of the goose and wipe inside and out with a damp towel. Using kitchen scissors remove the oil sac from the parson's nose. This has a strong taste and if not removed can flavour the flesh of the bird.

Fill the cavity of the goose loosely with the stuffing and sew up with a trussing needle or poultry pins. To truss the goose, tuck the wing tips underneath the goose. Pull the loose skin over the neck and fasten it to the back of the bird with small skewers. Tie the ends of the legs with a piece of string, drawing them close to the parson's nose, with a bow.

Wipe the goose over with a clean towel to dry thoroughly. Lightly dust the goose with the flour and place in a roasting pan lightly greased with the oil. Sear the goose over a high heat. Heat the brandy, set alight and pour flaming over the bird. This adds flavour and at the same time sears off the tiny pin feathers.

Roast in a preheated hot oven (200°C/400°F) for 15 to 20 minutes. Baste and cover with aluminium foil. Reduce the oven temperature to moderate (180°C/350°F) and cook for a further 2¼ hours. Remove the aluminium foil about 30 minutes before the end of the cooking time to give the goose a good golden colour.

When the goose is cooked, transfer to a serving platter or a carving board and remove trussing strings. Keep warm.

To make the Gravy: Pour off the pan juices and fat into a jug, reserve. Return about 2 tablespoons to the roasting pan and stir in 1 tablespoon of flour, cook over a moderate heat until the roux turns a golden brown, stirring and scraping up the crusty bits from the bottom of the pan. Skim off the fat from the reserved pan juices and stir the juices into the roux. Add more stock, made from the neck and giblets, if necessary. You need about 1½ cups liquid altogether. Bring to the boil, stirring, and simmer for 2–3 minutes. Serve the gravy in a sauceboat.

Serve the goose with red cabbage or Brussels sprouts and steamed parsleyed potatoes. *Serves 6–8*

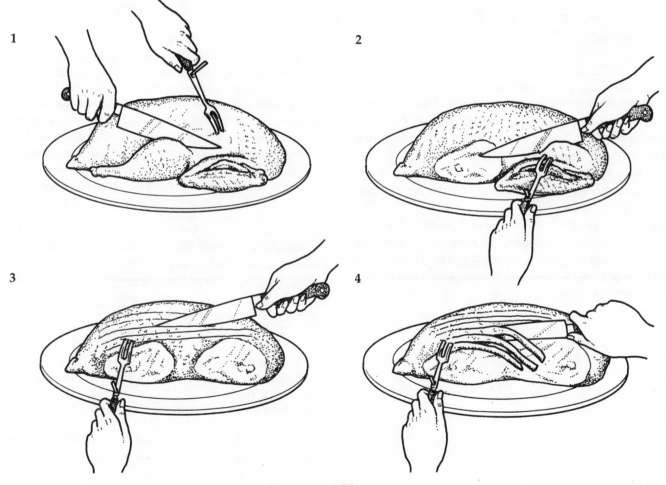

QUAIL

These delectable little birds are now being produced commercially in many areas, and if your local poulterer doesn't have a regular supply he should be able to order them for you. The flesh has a deliciously gamey flavour – strong without being overpowering.

Because the birds are tiny, one whole bird is the minimum serving per person. They are the perfect treat for special occasions.

Quail may be roasted in the oven, casseroled, grilled or poached on top of the stove. To keep them moist and tender they are frequently wrapped in vine leaves and a thin slice of pork fat or streaky bacon, which is removed before serving.

Roast Quail

•

*Quail simply roasted make a delightful light luncheon dish, they are the perfect thing to serve for a late Sunday brunch. Serve with toast as in this recipe or omit the toast and serve a Bread Sauce (see page 159) as well as gravy. An additional touch would be a bowl of redcurrant jelly – the fruity flavour goes so well with game.
You might also like to add canned, pitted cherries or small white grapes to the pan gravy, and the quail may be garnished with the crumbled bacon in which they were roasted.*

4–6 quail
4–6 pieces of pork fat or streaky bacon, thinly sliced, about 6 cm (2½ inch) square
60 g (2 oz) butter
salt
freshly ground black pepper
4–6 slices hot buttered toast

Wipe the birds inside and out with damp paper towels and season with salt and freshly ground pepper. Truss the legs and wings close to the body.

Cover each breast with a square of pork fat or streaky bacon and tie securely with white string.

Melt the butter in a flameproof dish and brown the birds on all sides. Cover the dish, and roast the birds in a preheated hot

156

oven (230°C/450°F) for 20 minutes. Take the birds out and remove the trussing strings and the pork fat, which may be kept and served with the quail.

Return the dish to the oven, but do not cover it. Continue roasting the quail for 5 minutes to give a golden finish.

To test if the birds are cooked, lift one up. If the juice that runs out is clear, with no pink tinge, the quail is done.

Remove the birds to a platter and keep warm.

To make a pan sauce, add a cup of water – or half wine and half water – to the dish. Stir over direct heat, stirring all the brown crusty bits from the bottom. Cook briskly until the sauce is reduced and slightly thickened, then add a knob of butter, and salt and freshly ground pepper to taste.

Serve each quail on a slice of hot, buttered toast, spread with pâté if desired, and spoon the gravy over each bird. *Serves 4–6*

Quail Borghese

••

A most delectable dish for a special occasion, presenting quail at their very best – roasted in a covered dish then finished off on a bed of green pea purée.

6 quail
salt
freshly ground pepper
2 strips orange rind, peeled very thinly, so no white pith remains
fresh thyme and parsley
6 small vine leaves
6 pieces pork fat or streaky bacon, thinly sliced about 6 cm (2½ inch) square
90 g (3 oz) butter
4 slices ham (optional)
Green Pea Purée
500 g (1 lb) shelled green peas, fresh or frozen
1 lettuce, shredded
60 g (2 oz) butter
½ cup cream

Wipe the birds with damp paper towels and season with salt and pepper. Put a small piece of orange rind and a small sprig of thyme and parsley inside each bird. Place a vine leaf covered with the pork fat or bacon over the breasts, tie securely or secure with poultry pins.

Heat the butter in a heavy flameproof casserole, and brown the quail on all sides. Cover the casserole and bake the birds in a very hot oven (230°C/450°F) for 15–20 minutes, basting several times during cooking with the juices.

Meanwhile, prepare the purée. Place the peas in a heavy saucepan with the shredded lettuce and the butter. Cover and cook over a gentle heat until the peas are tender, shaking the pan from time to time. Season with salt and pepper to taste, and purée in a mouli or food processor fitted with the double

edged steel blade, or push through a sieve. Return to the pan, taste and adjust the seasoning and fold in the cream, heat gently.

Spoon the green pea purée into a heatproof serving dish. Cut the ham, if using, into julienne strips and sprinkle over the purée. Remove the bacon, leaves and trussing strings from the quail and arrange on the purée. Return to a moderate oven (180°C/350°F) for 10 minutes. *Serves 6*
Note: When vine leaves are mentioned in a recipe, the processed leaves are intended – sold packed in cans, or in glass jars or loose from Continental delicatessens.

Quail on Vine Leaves

•

In this recipe the birds simmer to juicy tenderness in a spicy-sweet stock. Polenta is a traditional accompaniment for quail cooked in this way.

6 quail
30 g (1 oz) butter
¾ cup beef stock
¼ cup port
2 tablespoons raisins
2 whole cloves
6 canned vine leaves

Tie the wings and legs to the bodies of the quail with white string. Melt the butter in a wide-based saucepan, add the quail and brown on all sides. Pour off excess fat. Add the stock, port, raisins and cloves and bring to the boil. Place a lid on the pan, lower the heat, and simmer gently for 30 minutes. Meanwhile, snip stems from the vine leaves and blanch in boiling water for 1 minute, then drain.

To serve, remove trussing strings from quail, place each quail on a vine leaf and spoon the sauce over. Serve with Polenta. *Serves 6*

Polenta

•

2 cups water
½ teaspoon salt
½ cup fine polenta (yellow maize meal)
1 tablespoon oil
30 g (1 oz) butter

In a thick, heavy saucepan bring the water and salt to the boil. Gradually add the polenta, stirring constantly with a wooden spoon to keep it smooth. Cook over a moderate heat, stirring frequently, for about 20 minutes or until the polenta comes away cleanly from the sides of the pan.

Turn the polenta into a greased square cake tin, allow to cool, then cut into little squares and lightly fry on all sides in the hot oil and butter.

STUFFINGS FOR POULTRY

Stuffings can add interest and a change of flavour to roast birds, and are fun for the cook as well.

For example, turkey is often filled with two entirely different stuffings – one in the neck (the crop) and one in the main body cavity.

Breadcrumbs or diced bread are the usual base for stuffings, but cooked rice, chestnut purée or sausage mince may also be used.

Many people like to cook stuffing separately from the bird, so it crisps on top as it bakes. In this case, some of the pan juices may be spooned over the stuffing as it cooks, to add a lovely poultry flavour.

Individual containers (such as custard cups or muffin tins) make a pleasant change, as each diner then gets his own serving, or hollowed-out apple or orange shells may be used for an interesting presentation.

If there is stuffing left over after filling the bird or separate container, you may like to roll it into little balls and place around the bird for the last 20 minutes or so of cooking, basting once or twice with the juices. Children seem to enjoy these little stuffing balls, and they're also nice cold.

Of course, stuffing is not essential when roasting poultry. Chicken roasted the French way has a lovely flavour of its own, and for rich birds such as duck and goose, a few quartered, tart apples placed in the cavity help to cut the richness.

Just a few general hints to keep in mind first:

Don't soak the bread in liquid for stuffing. Blend with the other ingredients just before you are ready to stuff the bird –this gives a lighter texture.

Handle the stuffing lightly – mix just until the ingredients are combined. Again, this is to keep the texture light. Over-mixing results in a compact stuffing, which is not as appetizing.

Fresh white breadcrumbs are usually called for in stuffings. You can push the bread through a colander, or use your blender or food processor fitted with the double edged steel blade. Process just until crumbs are evenly formed – don't have them too fine, or the stuffing will be too compact.

Allow plenty of space when stuffing, so the mixture can swell and stay light. If you pack the bird too tightly, you again run the risk of a compact, hard stuffing. A useful rule of thumb in judging the amount of stuffing required is to allow half a cup of stuffing for each 500 g (1 lb) of bird.

Add the stuffing to the bird just before placing it in the oven. Never stuff the bird hours beforehand even if leaving it in the refrigerator. The cold may not penetrate to the stuffing, and it could go off without your knowing it – a disaster when it comes to serving time.

Finally, don't save stuffings just for festive occasions – use them for interest and variety in everyday family meals. There's even a sense of excitement for most people about 'what's in the stuffing', so I have included quite a few for you to try.

Apple and Raisin Stuffing

(For Goose)

•

8 small green apples
1 cup soft white breadcrumbs
½ small onion, chopped
30 g (1 oz) butter, melted
½ cup seeded raisins
salt
freshly ground black pepper
1 teaspoon sugar

Wash the apples and hollow out as much as possible from the top with a sharp spoon, leaving a shell of apple. Make sure all the core and seeds are removed, but take care not to pierce the base of the apple. Chop the apple flesh finely, and mix with the remaining ingredients. Spoon into the apple shells. Place around the goose for the last 45 minutes of cooking.

Sage and Onion Stuffing

(For Duck – a Traditional Stuffing)

•

2 medium onions, sliced
60 g (2 oz) butter
2 cups fresh white breadcrumbs
1 teaspoon dried sage
2 teaspoons finely chopped parsley
salt
freshly ground black pepper
1 beaten egg to bind, or a little milk

Simmer the onions for 15 minutes in salted water. Drain, and stir in the softened butter. Add the breadcrumbs, sage and parsley, season with salt and pepper, and mix together with beaten egg or a little milk.

Apple and Prune Stuffing

(For Goose or Large Duckling)

•

4 cups day-old bread, cut into small cubes
185 g (6 oz) butter
1 onion, chopped
2 Granny Smith apples
1 cup chopped, pitted, ready-to-eat prunes
¾ cup pine nuts
⅓ cup chopped parsley
salt
freshly ground pepper
½ teaspoon chopped fresh thyme

Lightly toast the bread cubes in a moderately slow oven (160°C/325°F) for 10 minutes. Meanwhile, melt the butter in a heavy frying pan and sauté the onion until soft. Peel, core and cube the apples and add to the pan, cook for a further 2 minutes. Combine the onion mixture with the toasted bread cubes and the prunes in a bowl. Use the onion pan to lightly toast the pine nuts. Add to the breadcrumb mixture with the parsley. Season well with salt and freshly ground pepper and add the thyme. Toss well.

Cognac Raisin Stuffing

(For Duck)

•

½ cup raisins
¼ cup Cognac or brandy
¼ cup chopped spring onions
6 tablespoons butter
½ teaspoon salt
1½ cups cooked rice
¼ cup chopped, shelled pistachio or pine nuts

Soak the raisins in the brandy for 10 minutes. Sauté the spring onions in the butter until tender. Combine the raisins, spring onions and butter, salt, rice and nuts in a large bowl and toss lightly to combine.

Bread Sauce

•

If you are serving a bird without stuffing, it is a pleasant idea to serve Bread Sauce separately. This goes with chicken or indeed any poultry.

1 cup milk
1 onion, chopped
1 bay leaf
6 peppercorns
1 cup soft white breadcrumbs
½ teaspoon salt
1 teaspoon butter

Put the milk, onion, bay leaf and peppercorns in a small saucepan and simmer for 30 minutes. Strain. Add the breadcrumbs and salt to the seasoned milk and simmer gently until a creamy consistency. Stir in the butter and serve in a sauceboat.

Sweet Potato Stuffing

(For Turkey)

•

2 tablespoons olive oil
500 g (1 lb) pork and veal mince
1 large onion, chopped
1½ cups chopped celery
4 cups fresh white breadcrumbs
4 cups cooked, mashed sweet potato
1 cup sliced mushrooms
4 teaspoons salt
black pepper
grated nutmeg to taste
generous pinch each dried thyme and
powdered cloves

Heat the oil in a large pan and cook the pork and veal mince until lightly browned, stirring to brown evenly. Remove meat from the pan with a slotted spoon, and add the onion and celery to the fat remaining. Cook for a few minutes, stirring, then add the breadcrumbs, sweet potato, mushrooms, salt, pepper, nutmeg, thyme and cloves. Stir over a gentle heat until well combined, then stir in the browned pork and veal mince. Take off the heat and allow to cool before filling the turkey. The mixture may be refrigerated in a covered bowl, and used to stuff the turkey just before baking.

Sausage and Bacon Stuffing

(For Turkey)

•

3 rindless bacon rashers, diced
1 cup diced celery
1 cup finely chopped onion
750 g (1½ lb) pork sausage mince
2 tablespoons chopped parsley
3 cups lightly-packed, soft white breadcrumbs
1 egg, lightly beaten
grated rind of ½ lemon
salt
freshly ground black pepper

In a large frying pan, over medium heat, sauté the bacon, celery and onions together for about 10 minutes, add the mince and stir until combined.

Place the sausage mixture in a large bowl and add the parsley, breadcrumbs, egg and lemon rind. Mix lightly but evenly with a fork, and taste for seasoning, adding salt and freshly ground pepper as required.

Note: This amount of stuffing is sufficient for a turkey weighing about 5–6 kg (10–12 lb). Use it to stuff the neck cavity or body cavity, but don't pack too tightly. Any leftover stuffing may be baked in a separate small ovenproof dish or made into balls and placed around the turkey for the last 30 minutes of baking.

Fresh Herb Stuffing

(For a Small Turkey or Large Chicken)

•

What makes this stuffing so good is the fresh herbs – the recipe may sound simple, but the result is deliciously fresh-tasting and interesting. If you don't have the fresh herbs, don't substitute dried herbs in this particular case. It is better to choose a different stuffing.

2 cups soft white breadcrumbs
125 g (4 oz) butter
3–4 tablespoons chopped parsley
1 teaspoon chopped fresh thyme or lemon thyme
1 teaspoon chopped fresh marjoram
2 eggs, beaten
salt
freshly ground pepper
grated rind and juice of 1 lemon

Toast the breadcrumbs in a moderate oven (180°C/350°F) until golden – about 15 minutes. Watch carefully, and don't allow to burn. They may also be toasted over a gentle heat in a heavy frying pan. Toss or stir constantly to prevent burning.

Melt the butter and combine in a large bowl with the toasted crumbs and the remaining ingredients. If the lemon is large and very juicy, use the juice of only half the lemon. Allow the mixture to cool, and stuff the bird just before roasting.

Right: Lamb Cutlets en Cuirasse are lamb cutlets and mushrooms duxelles wrapped in crisp filo pastry. See the recipe on page 176.

Above: Hearty, satisfying and full of flavour, Pork Chops with Onions typify the good cooking of the Lyonnais area of France (recipe page 180).

Right: Tripe à la mode de Caen starts with simple ingredients and careful seasonings then bakes slowly into a superb dish. (Recipe page 190.)

162

MAKING THE MOST OF MEAT

Most of us who have cooked for a family or kept house over a long period are price-conscious about the food we buy, and in particular about meat prices.

The good thing about meat is that there is a cut for every purse. The nutritional value of all meats is about the same. The proteins, minerals and vitamins are contained in the lean tissue of the meat and the amount of these is practically the same in all cuts of meat, so nutritionally speaking it doesn't matter whether you eat choice cuts or an inexpensive cut. So, while your purse may dictate what you buy, there are wonderful ways to cook every cut and type of meat.

Consider too, ways of stretching meat with rice and beans or making a whole meal from a piece of meat or chicken as the French do with their Pot-au-feu. For example, make a super meat loaf lighter and more tender with breadcrumbs, or serve a purée of mashed potatoes or turnips to mop up the lovely juices of boiled or grilled meat.

The more we learn from other people and other countries, the better it is for those intent on getting 'the best value' rather than 'the best' for their meat dollar. An international look at meat cooking shows us how to make minced meat into delicious Meatballs Avgolemono.

Barbecued Spareribs make a dazzling informal meal and there is no sweeter yet inexpensive dish than lamb neck chops with a caper sauce. The Chinese have introduced us to quick stir-fried dishes, and the Spice Islands to those delicate little morsels on a stick – satays.

In the same way many countries have given a national stamp to their native dishes; sour cream in Russia, spices in India, yogurt in the Middle East, paprika in Hungary, olive oil in Spain, butter and cream and sometimes wine or Cognac in France. In Great Britain the emphasis is on absolute simplicity, stressing the fine quality and flavour of the meat.

It is a good idea with such an expensive food to learn the basics of meat first. What to buy, how much and how best to cook each cut. This information is in the first chapter on pages 31 and 32.

For variety and insight into how the other half lives read on . . . it's a pot-pourri of simply great meat dishes.

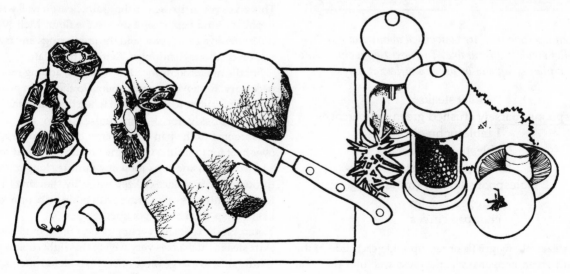

Left: Add a simple sauce of buttered crumbs and hard-boiled eggs to fresh asparagus to make Asparagus Polonaise (see page 197).

Scotch Fillet

••

Easy to prepare, cook, carve and serve – this is an ideal buffet dish. Scotch fillet is cheaper than eye fillet and preferred by some for its full flavour. Don't overcook this cut and it will be every bit as tender as true fillet.

1.5 kg (3 lb) piece Scotch fillet
freshly ground pepper or 2 tablespoons crushed
green peppercorns
30 g (1 oz) butter
2 tablespoons oil
3 tablespoons brandy

Trim the fillet and tie with string to keep a good shape. Season well with freshly ground pepper or press the crushed green peppercorns firmly on to the meat. Melt the butter and oil in a flameproof baking dish and sear the meat quickly to brown the surface, turning with two spoons. Heat the brandy and flame, pouring over the meat and shaking the pan so the meat burns with the flame.

Roast in a hot oven (220°C/425°F) for 10 minutes then reduce the temperature to moderately hot (190°C/375°F) and roast for a further 25 minutes. The smaller yearling beef will not take as long. Serve in slices accompanied with mustard, horseradish sauce and a crisp green salad. *Serves 8*

Steak au Poivre Vert

••

When it's time you are concerned about and not money, fillet steak is unbeatable. The next two recipes show how fillet steak can be used in different ways.

4 fillet steaks
3 teaspoons coarsely crushed green peppercorns
1 tablespoon oil
2 tablespoons butter
lemon juice to taste
2 tablespoons brandy (optional)
chopped parsley
chopped chives

Trim the steaks of any gristle or fat. Sprinkle each side of the steaks with green peppercorns and press well into the meat with the heel of your hand. Let it stand for 30 minutes.

Heat half the oil in a heavy frying pan, then place over a high heat. Add the steaks and cook until brown on one side, turn and cook until done. For rare steaks, cook on a high heat for a short time and for medium steaks, lower the heat to moderate and cook for longer. They should take only 3–4 minutes on each side.

Put one quarter of the butter on each steak and add lemon juice to taste. Warm the brandy, if using, ignite and pour over the meat. Sprinkle the steaks with parsley and chives and serve at once.

For a creamy sauce, stir 2 tablespoons of cream into the pan juices. *Serves 4*

Beef Stroganoff

••

There are different opinions on what makes a true Stroganoff – some claim no onions, some no mushrooms. Sometimes I sauté the beef strips, season the meat, add tomato paste and cream (no onions, no mushrooms) and then just before serving, add half a grated onion, and it is delicious. This recipe below seems to be more universally accepted.

750 g (1½ lb) fillet steak
salt
freshly ground pepper
1 tablespoon flour
60 g (2 oz) butter
2 medium onions, finely sliced into rings
185–250 g (6–8 oz) button mushrooms,
finely sliced
1 tablespoon tomato paste
⅔ cup sour cream
hot boiled rice

Trim the fillet of any fat and sinews. Cut into slices then into strips about 4–5 cm (1½–2 inch) long and 5 mm (¼ inch) wide. This gives you strips across the grain. Season well with salt and freshly ground pepper and toss in the flour. Melt 30 g (1 oz) of the butter in a frying pan, add the onion rings and fry until just coloured, about 10 minutes. Remove to a plate.

Fry the mushrooms for a few minutes, adding more butter if necessary. Remove the mushrooms to the onion plate, add the remaining butter to the pan and when hot put in the beef strips and fry briskly for 3–4 minutes. Return the onions and mushrooms to the pan with plenty of salt and pepper, shake over heat for 1 minute. Combine tomato paste and sour cream, add to the pan and cook for a few minutes longer until heated through. Serve at once or keep warm by standing in hot water for 10–15 minutes only. Serve with boiled rice or noodles or, if liked, crisp-fried straw potatoes. *Serves 6*

Note: A less expensive version of Beef Stroganoff is made with skirt steak which takes very well to this light cooking. As there is little skirt to a large piece of beef it is all too often snapped up by those who know the value of this inexpensive cut. It should be cut across the grain.

Russian Beef Casserole for a crowd

● ● ●

This is a great dish for entertaining a crowd. It is known
among friends as 'Stroganoff for a crowd' as it
indeed resembles that wonderful dish. I first made it for
weekends at a ski-lodge, because it travels well
and improves on keeping, especially if made up to the final
stage, adding the cream and the grated onion when
the base is heated through.
Serve with fluffy boiled rice stirred with a lavish addition of
parsley or hot buttered noodles with poppyseeds.
To give a true Stroganoff finish, serve a bowl of heated straw
potatoes (the prepackaged commercial ones will do)
as they give a pleasant crunchy contrast. Stroganoff was
originally served over crisp and golden straw potatoes,
made at the last moment of course.

2 kg (4 lb) skirt, round or chuck steak
½ cup flour
1 teaspoon salt
freshly ground pepper
4 tablespoons oil
4 onions, sliced
4 cloves garlic, crushed
2 × 400 g cans peeled tomatoes
1½ cups water and 1 beef cube
500 g (1 lb) button mushrooms
60 g (2 oz) butter
3 cups light sour cream
2 tablespoons tomato paste
1 small onion, grated
6–8 dill pickles, chopped

Cut the beef into thin strips and dredge in the flour seasoned
with salt and pepper. Heat 2 tablespoons of the oil in a frying
pan and sauté the meat in 3 or 4 batches until brown. Add the
remaining oil when required. Put the meat into a large
saucepan.

Cook the onions and garlic in the oil remaining in the pan
until soft and golden, add to the beef. Add the tomatoes and
juice, water and beef cube; simmer for 1 hour. Wipe the
mushrooms over with a damp cloth, trim stalks and slice. Heat
the butter in a frying pan and toss the mushrooms over a high
heat for a minute or two.

Remove the large saucepan from the heat and stir in the
mushrooms, sour cream, tomato paste and grated onion. Place
over a low heat, stirring until the mixture is hot. Do not allow to
boil. Taste and adjust the seasoning.

Serve with hot buttered Poppyseed Noodles or Parsleyed
Rice. *Serves 10–12*

Poppyseed Noodles

●

1 kg (2 lb) tagliatelle or noodles
salt
4 teaspoons oil
250 g (8 oz) butter
2 tablespoons poppyseeds

You will need 2 large saucepans. It is probably easier and more
successful to cook the pasta in 250 g (8 oz) batches at a time.

In each saucepan bring 12 cups of water to the boil, add 3
teaspoons salt and a teaspoon of oil and drop the pasta in,
keeping the pieces separate. Stir well and boil rapidly until the
pasta is tender but firm when tested between the teeth. This
will take about 8 minutes. Drain the pasta thoroughly, add 60 g
(2 oz) of the butter and keep warm while repeating with the
remaining noodles. Combine all the buttered noodles, lightly
toss the poppyseeds through the noodles and turn into a large
serving dish. For additional information on cooking pasta see
page 35. *Serves 10–12*

Parsleyed Rice

● ●

The rice can be cooked 1 or 2 days before the party. To reheat,
place in a greased baking dish and pour 1 cup hot milk over,
dot with a little butter. Cover and bake in a hot oven (200°C/
400°F) for 20 minutes.

3 cups rice
1 scant tablespoon salt
½ cup chopped parsley

Fill 2 large saucepans with water and bring to the boil, adding
half the salt to each pan. Add 1½ cups of rice to each pan. Keep
the water boiling rapidly and cook the rice until tender, about
15–20 minutes. Drain well and serve hot with the parsley
lightly stirred through the rice. *Serves 10–12*

Beef and Burghul Casserole

•	•

Throughout the world the phenomenon of the health food shop is changing our way of eating. With a reliable source of supply we can introduce unusual grains, flours, oils and nuts into our daily food. Burghul, the crushed wheat of the Middle East, adds a delicious nutty flavour to a beef casserole.

1 kg (2 lb) stewing beef
60 g (2 oz) butter
1 tablespoon oil
1 large onion, chopped
3 cups water
3 tablespoons tomato paste
salt
freshly ground pepper
½ cup burghul or cracked wheat
1 teaspoon salt
1 cup natural yogurt

Trim excess fat from the meat and cut into 3 cm (1½ inch) cubes. Melt 30 g (1 oz) of the butter and the oil in a large flameproof casserole, add the meat and brown on all sides. Remove the meat and keep warm. This is best done in several batches; do not overcrowd the casserole otherwise you get a stewed effect. Add the chopped onion to the pan and cook until softened. Return the meat to the pan. Stir in the water, tomato paste, and salt and pepper to taste. Bring to the boil, cover and simmer for 1 hour.

Melt the remaining butter in a medium saucepan, add the burghul and salt. Sauté over a medium heat, stirring constantly. Add burghul to the meat and bring to the boil. Cover and simmer for a further 30 minutes. Remove from heat and stand, covered, for 10 minutes before serving.

Serve with a salad and a bowl of natural yogurt. Each diner tops his or her portion with a spoonful of yogurt. *Serves 6*

Summertime Brawn

•	•

Homemade brawn, richly flavoured but light and spicy, is an old-fashioned treat for a summer's day.

2 large knuckles of veal
500 g (1 lb) shin of beef
1 onion, sliced
¼ teaspoon mixed spice
2 cloves
few peppercorns
salt
2 tablespoons gelatine
2 gherkins, chopped

Ask the butcher to saw through the knuckles of veal. Place the meats in a large saucepan and cover with water. Add the onion, spice, cloves, peppercorns and salt to the pan. Bring to the boil and simmer gently for 3 hours or until the meat is coming away from the bones. Remove the meat from the bones and chop finely, strain the stock.

Dissolve the gelatine in ½ cup of the hot stock. Make the liquid up to 2½ cups, adding water if necessary. Add the meat and gherkins. Taste and adjust the seasoning. Spoon into a loaf tin and refrigerate until firm. Unmould and serve with salad, tomatoes and spring onions.

If liked, a little strained stock may be spooned into the bottom of the tin or mould and a decoration of thinly sliced carrot, green ends of spring onions, gherkins or any decorative food arranged on the setting jelly. Place in the refrigerator until set then top with meat mixture. A little hot English mustard and vinegar complement this brawn. *Serves 6*

Meatballs Avgolemono

•	•

The good cooks of Greece do wonderful things with lemon and eggs. They beat them together to make a foamy sauce that is added to all kinds of different food. A clear broth becomes Avgolemono with this light and piquant addition; Dolmades, the delicious packages of rice and vine leaves take on an added dimension with this sauce and so do meatballs.

500 g (1 lb) lean minced steak
1 small onion, chopped
2 teaspoons chopped fresh mint
1 tablespoon chopped parsley
2 tablespoons raw rice
salt
freshly ground pepper
1½ cups beef stock
1 cup water
2 teaspoons cornflour
2 eggs
juice of 1 lemon

In a bowl, mix together the beef, onion, mint, parsley, rice, salt, pepper and ¼ cup of the beef stock. Mix well and form into balls the size of a walnut. Bring the remaining stock and water to the boil and drop in the meatballs. Simmer for 10 minutes. Blend the cornflour with a little water, add some hot stock then return to the meatballs.

Beat the eggs and lemon juice together until thick. Slowly add about 1 cup of the hot stock, beat constantly. Stir the egg mixture into remaining stock in pan, cover and stand for 5 minutes off the heat. Serve immediately. *Serves 4*

Meat Loaf

••

Every cook needs a really good meat loaf recipe. This one makes a loaf that is moist, tender and well flavoured and can be varied to give changes of taste and texture. The same mixture makes excellent hamburgers.
What you pay for you usually get and nothing is truer when it comes to minced meat. It is worth while getting a good minced steak, not too fatty and not too finely minced, then using it cleverly. This basic meat loaf is inexpensive and uses a cheaper cut of meat to the best advantage.

1 cup evaporated milk
2 tablespoons tomato sauce
1 tablespoon Worcestershire sauce
5 slices white bread
1 kg (2 lb) lean minced steak
½ teaspoon dry mustard
½ onion, chopped
1 teaspoon chopped mixed fresh herbs or
¼ teaspoon dried mixed herbs
2 teaspoons salt
freshly ground pepper
2 eggs, beaten
2 bacon rashers

Combine the evaporated milk and sauces. Trim the crusts from the bread, add to the seasoned milk and soak for 10 minutes, then beat with a fork.

Mix meat, bread, mustard, onion and herbs together with salt and pepper to taste. Mix in the eggs. Pack lightly into a greased 23 × 13 cm (9 × 5 inch) loaf tin. Remove the rind from the bacon rashers, arrange on top of the meat loaf and bake in a moderate oven (180°C/350°F) for 1 hour, or until the loaf shrinks slightly from the sides of the tin. Serve hot with vegetables or cold with a salad. *Serves 6–8*

Variations

Add one of the following to the meat, bread and onion mixture.
1 clove garlic, crushed
½–1 cup shredded cheese
½ cup finely chopped green olives
½ cup sliced or chopped sautéed mushrooms
½ cup chopped green pepper or celery
Hamburgers Use the basic meat loaf mixture or the mixture with any of the variations suggested above, and shape lightly into patties about 2 cm (¾ inch) thick and 8 cm (3 inch) across. Sauté quickly in a little oil and butter until well-browned outside but still a little rare inside.

Serve between hamburger buns, top with fried onion rings, mustard, lettuce, tomato slices or vegetables of your choice.

Spiced Beef

•••

Spiced beef used to be a regular Christmas dish in a great many English country houses and farms. This dish brings a change from the more usual cold cuts such as ham or pork that come in so handy during the holiday period. Cure is specified in this recipe and is similar to saltpetre giving the beef an appetizing pink colour. Butchers and some delicatessens sell it.

3 kg (6 lb) piece of beef silverside
½ cup brown sugar
4 tablespoons black peppercorns
2 tablespoons whole allspice
4 tablespoons juniper berries
1½ tablespoons cure
½ cup rock salt

Rub the beef all over with brown sugar and place in an earthenware bowl or crock. Leave for 2 days, turning frequently.

Crush the spices in a mortar with the cure and rock salt, or grind roughly in a blender. Rub the spice mixture thoroughly over the beef each day for 9 days, keeping it covered in a cool, airy place. Refrigerate in very hot weather.

After 9 days the beef is ready to cook. Take it from the bowl and lightly wipe off any of the spices still sticking to it. Place the beef in a heavy deep casserole into which it just fits and pour in about 1½ cups of water. Cover well with a double layer of aluminium foil and cover with a lid. Bake in a slow oven (150°C/300°F) for about 4 hours. Remove from the oven and leave to cool for a few hours. Before the fat sets, pour off all the liquid and put the beef on a board. Wrap in aluminium foil and put a plate with a 2 kg (4 lb) weight on top. Leave until the next day. Carve into very thin slices to serve. *Serves 10–12 generously*

Roast Racks of Lamb

••

A rack of lamb makes a compact joint which is easy to cook and carve. It is the best end of the neck joint and usually consists of 6–7 cutlets. The rack is trimmed exactly the way cutlets would be prepared if they were to be cut separately for grilling or frying, with the chine bone and most of the fat removed. They may be cut into small racks of 3 or 4 cutlets each, for 1 serving, or cooked whole in one piece and then cut into portions or single cutlets. Allow 3–4 cutlets per person.
Sauce Béarnaise is a wonderful accompaniment for racks of lamb. Serve creamed potatoes and just one other special vegetable such as Tomatoes Provençale or Tomatoes Garni (see pages 218 or 219).

4 small racks of lamb, each consisting
of 3 or 4 cutlets
salt
freshly ground pepper
2 cloves garlic, peeled

Ask the butcher to cut away the chine bone and saw between every second cutlet, for easier carving. Trim the cutlets, if your butcher has not done so, by cutting away the flesh from the top of the bone leaving about 5 cm (2 inch) of bone exposed. Slice away the skin and most of the fat, leaving a good even layer of fat. Sliver the peeled garlic and, using a small sharp knife, insert a few slivers just under the fat of each rack. Score the lamb with shallow diagonal cuts in a lattice pattern. Season well with salt and freshly ground pepper.

Place the lamb in a baking dish and roast in a preheated moderately hot oven (190°C/375°F) for 25–30 minutes. The meat will be pink and juicy after this time, cook for a further 5–10 minutes for medium to well done. Transfer to a heated serving dish, and serve with vegetables of your choice. *Serves 4*

Parsleyed Racks of Lamb

• •

Once you have mastered the technique of cooking a rack of lamb, you will want to try it in different ways and here are two different methods of preparing it. Try it with herbs or with a parsley flavoured crunchy crumb crust. The rack is cooked in one piece and requires careful preparation by the butcher or yourself.

2 small racks of lamb, each consisting
of 6–7 cutlets
salt
freshly ground pepper
60 g (2 oz) butter
3 tablespoons chopped parsley
1½ cups soft breadcrumbs
juice of ½ lemon
Béarnaise sauce (page 45), to serve

Trim the racks as described in the above recipe, then score and season with salt and pepper. Melt the butter and combine with the parsley, breadcrumbs and lemon juice, toss lightly. Cover the scored side of the lamb with a thick compact layer of the breadcrumb mixture, pressing the crumbs on to the meat.

Place the lamb in a baking dish and roast in a preheated moderately hot oven (190°C/375°F) for 25–30 minutes when the meat will be pink and juicy, allow a further 5–10 minutes for well done.

Transfer the meat to a heated serving dish. If liked, one of the racks can be cut into cutlets, and the other left whole. Small paper cutlet frills make a decorative finish on the ends of the cutlets. Serve with Béarnaise Sauce.

If the racks have been well prepared it is a simple matter to cut through the rack at the table. Cut singly or allow 2 or 3 cutlets (in one piece) for each serving. *Serves 6*

Grilled Rack of Lamb

• •

Cooking a rack of lamb (6 or 7 cutlets) for two doesn't justify heating an oven unless you propose to use it for other dishes or vegetables. With care it is possible to grill the rack. Prepare the rack as described above. Season both sides with salt and freshly ground pepper; a sprinkling of fresh herbs gives extra flavour. Make up a small tray with a sheet of foil, turning the edges up to catch the drippings.

Set the rack underside up and grill for 7–8 minutes, turn and cook on the top or fatty side for 10 minutes. The ends of the bones may char a little, if this bothers you protect with a strip of foil. Remove the foil and serve the rack with paper cutlet frills.

Boiled Leg of Lamb

• • •

When you serve this dish be prepared for two surprises. First, the lamb looks rather sad and grey even when sitting on a bed of watercress but when cut, the slices are rosy and running with juice – a pleasant surprise that shows just how delicious boiled leg of lamb can be. The watercress will be sufficient to serve as a green vegetable and tastes very good with the juices from the meat. Turnips may be the white turnip with a touch of purple in the skin or for a robust taste use the yellow swedes.

1 leg lamb, boned
2 cloves garlic, peeled
1 lemon
few sprigs of thyme or lemon thyme
1 teaspoon salt
1 kg (2 lb) turnips
60 g (2 oz) butter
freshly ground pepper
1 tablespoon capers

Garnish

large bunch watercress or green beans or
broccoli, lightly cooked

Ask the butcher to bone the leg of lamb. Cut each clove of garlic into 4 or 5 slivers. Peel the lemon and finely chop the rind and strip the leaves from the thyme, reserving one sprig. If lemon thyme is available, it is the best to use.

Open the leg of lamb and sprinkle the garlic, lemon rind and thyme over the cut surface. Roll or tie the leg into a neat shape and weigh.

Half fill a large saucepan with water, add the salt and bring to the boil, add the sprig of thyme. Carefully lower the lamb in, and quickly return to boiling point. Cover the pan, reduce the heat and simmer the lamb for 15 minutes for each 500 g (1 lb). The average leg of lamb will be from 1.5–2 kg (3–4 lb), so it should take about 45 minutes to 1 hour.

Meanwhile, prepare the turnips. Peel the turnips and cut into large dice, drop into boiling salted water and cook until tender, about 8–12 minutes. Drain. Add the butter and mash well to make a purée, season with salt and pepper and fold in the capers. Turn into a small vegetable dish and keep warm.

Pick off the leafy sprigs of watercress and gather into small bunches. Wash the watercress well, secure with a rubber band and set in a bowl of water until required. Arrange the lamb on a heated serving dish, surrounded by the watercress and accompany with the turnip purée. *Serves 6*

Lamb Casserole with Turnips

(Ragoût de Mouton aux Navets)

● ● ●

The best-known lamb in France comes from the salt flats of Normandy. The salty herbs and grasses that the animals eat give a characteristic tang to the meat. This ragoût is an excellent Norman method of cooking one of the cheaper cuts, even when the lamb is not from Normandy.
Shoulder of lamb can be used in place of breast of lamb, and small parsnips can replace the turnips if the latter are not available or are too large.

2 kg (4 lb) breast of lamb
1 tablespoon flour
4 onions, quartered
bouquet garni
1 clove garlic, peeled
1 cup stock or water
1 kg (2 lb) white turnips
60 g (2 oz) lard or mixture of butter and oil
salt
freshly ground pepper
6–8 small potatoes

Remove excess fat and bones from the lamb and cut into strips. Cook the strips slowly in a lightly greased heavy frying pan until brown on all sides, drain and transfer to a flameproof casserole. Sprinkle the flour over the meat and allow it to brown over a low heat, stirring continuously. Add the onions, bouquet garni, garlic and stock or water. Bring rapidly to the boil then cover and simmer slowly.

Meanwhile, peel the turnips and quarter. Heat the lard or butter and oil in the pan used to brown the lamb and cook the turnips slowly, until lightly browned, then add to the casserole. Season generously with salt and pepper and cook, covered, on a gentle heat or in a moderate oven (180°C/350°F) for about 1¼ hours. Peel the potatoes and add to the ragoût, cook for a further 20–30 minutes or until the potatoes are tender. *Serves 6*

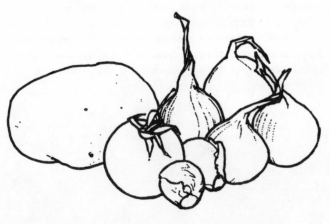

Shoulder of Lamb Dijonnaise

● ●

Give the butcher warning and he will bone the meat for this dish. Loin or shoulder both respond well to this treatment. Buy the true Dijon mustard, the imitations bear little resemblance to the original – lacking that special and distinctive flavour. Choose a brand like Grey Poupon or Maille although other very good brands are appearing.

1 shoulder or loin of lamb, boned
30 g (1 oz) butter
¾ cup stock or wine
3 teaspoons flour

Seasoning
2 tablespoons Dijon mustard
2 tablespoons soy sauce
1 clove garlic, crushed
2 teaspoons finely chopped rosemary or thyme
½ teaspoon olive oil

Have the butcher bone the shoulder of lamb. Trim off all the fell (the tough outer skin). If using a loin remove the heavy chine bone – the butcher will do this. Then cut away the piece of gristle which lies between the fat and the meat. Remove the fell and cut away the heavy fat. Lay out the shoulder or loin. Combine all the Seasoning ingredients and mix to a paste. Spread two-thirds of the mixture on the inside of the meat. Roll up tightly (starting from the thick end of the loin) and tie with pieces of string at regular intervals. Spread the remaining mixture on the surface of the lamb and allow to stand for at least 2 hours.

Preheat the oven to moderately hot (190°C/375°F). Place the meat in a baking dish, add the butter to the dish and pour in the stock or wine. Roast for 1½ hours or until the meat juices run clear.

Remove the meat to a serving platter and keep warm. Allow the meat to stand in a warm place for 10 to 15 minutes 'to set' before serving. The juices will be re-absorbed by the meat making carving easier. Meanwhile make a gravy.

Skim fat from the pan juices. Mix 1 tablespoon of fat with the flour in a small bowl and stir into the pan juices. Bring to the boil, scraping any brown sediment from the bottom of the pan and simmer for a few minutes. Season with salt and pepper. If the gravy is too thick add a little stock, water or wine.

Remove the string from the meat and carve into thick slices, serving the gravy separately.

Serve with creamy mashed potato and a cooked green vegetable or green salad. *Serves 6*

Right: When spring arrives, we look forward to a bounty of bright, tender young vegetables to enjoy in various ways.

Baby eggplant are well seasoned and baked with tomato slices for flavour and colour. See Baked Tomato Stuffed Eggplant on page 207.

Lamb with Caper Sauce

•

Everyone knows that the sweetest meat is close to the bone, and the Irish use sweet neck chops to advantage in their famous Irish stew. In this, an adaptation using new potatoes, the sauce is finished with capers, lots of parsley and lemon juice for the light freshness that is today's style.

1 kg (2 lb) lamb neck chops
1 kg (2 lb) new potatoes
1½ cups water
salt
pepper
1 tablespoon flour
2 teaspoons lemon juice
½ cup chopped parsley
1 tablespoon chopped capers

Trim chops of excess fat and skin, and lightly scrub the new potatoes. Place the chops and potatoes in a saucepan with the water and salt and simmer gently for 1 hour. Drain, reserving the liquid, and remove chops and potatoes to a warm plate. Season with salt and pepper and keep warm.

Blend the flour with a little cold water and add to the cooking liquid, stirring. Bring to the boil, stirring constantly, and simmer for 3 minutes. Add the capers, lemon juice and parsley and spoon over the chops. Serve with the potatoes. *Serves 4–6*

Pilau of Lamb

••

From time to time one is apt to go through a domestic crisis and feel the need for economy. Here is a dish that reminds you that you can still eat well on a budget when you cook with care.

1 kg (2 lb) boned shoulder lamb
60 g (2 oz) butter
2 tablespoons oil
4 onions, peeled and quartered
1 cup rice, well washed
3 cups stock or water
a good sprig thyme or oregano
salt
freshly ground pepper
½ cup raisins

Remove any gristle and trim excess fat from the lamb; cut into cubes. Melt the butter and oil in a heavy pot or flameproof casserole, add the onions and cook gently until golden brown but do not allow to burn. Add meat and toss over a high heat until nicely browned. Add the well washed rice and cook, stirring, until the rice is coated with butter.

Add stock or water, thyme or oregano, 1 teaspoon of salt and a grinding of pepper. Bring to the boil, stirring gently. Once the pilau comes to the boil do not stir. Cover, reduce heat and cook over a gentle heat for about 20 minutes. By this time the rice will have absorbed all the liquid with its flavour and the meat will be tender.

Take off the lid, add the raisins and fluff up the rice with a fork, using a gentle lifting movement. Serve on very hot plates as an entrée for 6 or as a light luncheon or supper dish for 4. If liked, cashew nuts or almonds tossed in butter may be added to the pilau. For a rose tinted, tomato flavoured pilau add 1 tablespoon of tomato paste to the stock. *Serves 4–6*

Herbed Loin of Lamb

••

Give your butcher warning and he will bone the loin for this dish. The pungent flavour of garlic, parsley, rosemary and thyme gives a deliciously aromatic and gamey flavour to the lamb. Serve with creamy mashed potatoes and, if liked, Tomatoes Provençale (see page 218).

1.5 kg (3 lb) loin of lamb
3 cloves garlic
salt
2 tablespoons chopped, mixed parsley,
rosemary and thyme
freshly ground pepper
30 g (1 oz) butter
¾ cup white wine or stock
3 teaspoons flour

Ask the butcher to bone the loin of lamb. Otherwise, trim the meat of any excess fat, remove fillet and bone. Crush the garlic to a fine paste with 1 teaspoon of salt. Mix the garlic and herbs together and spread over the inside of the lamb. Place the fillet on the loin, roll up and tie at 2.5 cm (1 inch) intervals. This can be done several hours ahead for a more 'gamey' taste.

Place the meat in a baking dish, sprinkle with salt and freshly ground pepper, add the butter to the dish and pour in the wine or stock.

Roast in a moderately hot oven (190°C/375°F) basting often, for 1–1½ hours or until the meat juices run clear.

Remove the meat to a serving platter and keep warm. Allow it to stand in a warm place for 10–15 minutes so the meat will 'set' before serving. The juices will be re-absorbed by the meat, making the carving easier.

Skim the fat from the pan. Mix 1 tablespoon of the fat with the flour in a small bowl. Stir into the pan juices, bring to the boil and simmer for a few minutes. Season with salt and pepper. If the gravy is too thick, add a little extra stock or water. Remove the string from the meat and carve into thick slices serving the gravy separately. Garnish with a small bunch of watercress or sprigs of parsley. *Serves 6*

Lamb Cutlets en Cuirasse

•••

A cuirasse is a breastplate and lamb cutlets in their little golden breastplates of pastry look glamorous enough for a dinner party. The thin, crisp filo wrapped around the tender lamb and the mushroom duxelles within give marvellous contrasting textures.

12 lamb cutlets
155 g (5 oz) butter
1 tablespoon oil
12 sheets (about half a 375 g packet) filo pastry
1 egg, beaten

Duxelles

15 g (½ oz) butter
·2 spring onions, chopped
90 g (3 oz) mushrooms, chopped
2 teaspoons chopped parsley
salt
freshly ground pepper

Trim the cutlets to a good shape and check that they have no tough pieces of yellow sinew near the top of the bone or small splintery pieces of bone left by the butcher – food to be wrapped in pastry must contain no unhappy surprises for the eater.

Heat 30 g (1 oz) of the butter with the oil and when very hot brown the cutlets quickly on both sides, they should remain rare inside. Place on crumpled kitchen paper to drain and leave them to get quite cold. Make the duxelles: Melt the 15 g (½ oz) of butter and cook the chopped spring onions over a low heat until soft but not brown. Add the mushrooms and stir until the moisture has evaporated. Stir in the parsley and season to taste with salt and pepper. Turn the duxelles on to a plate to get cold and divide into 12 equal portions.

Melt the remaining butter. Spread a dry tea-towel on a work surface, unfold the filo pastry on to it, cover with another dry tea-towel and then with a damp one, so that the pastry will not dry out and become brittle while you are working.

Take one sheet of pastry, brush it with butter, place another sheet on top and brush with butter. Continue until 6 sheets have all been brushed with butter. Cut the pastry in halves lengthwise then each half crosswise into thirds, ending up with 6 squares of layered filo. Take 6 cutlets and season with salt and pepper. Place one portion of duxelles on to each cutlet and wrap each cutlet in a square of pastry, leaving the bone out. Repeat with 6 more sheets of filo and the remaining cutlets. Brush all the cutlets with beaten egg and place on a rack in a baking tin. Bake in a hot oven (200°C/400°F) for 15 minutes and serve with green vegetables. *Serves 6*

Lamb Biriani

•••

Biriani is a Mogul dish and a fine example of the way Indian cooks use a wide variety of seasonings to enliven a dish and bring out its flavour without destroying its essential character. The basic formula is layers of delicately perfumed Pilau rice and lamb in spiced gravy. Chicken and fish can be used but these are not what make the dish great or traditional.
First, the lamb is prepared, then cooked in the Masala or gravy, which is rich with spices and made a little acid with curd (yogurt). Finally, the Pilau rice is cooked. The cooked lamb and the Pilau rice are then layered together in a heavy pot, with the Masala poured over, then baked.
The Biriani emerges fragrant with saffron and is unexpectedly subtle considering the spices used, it is garnished with a mixture of fried nuts and sultanas. For gala or festive occasions top with little leaves of edible gold or silver leaf (available at specialty shops providing artists' supplies).

1 leg lamb, boned
60 g (2 oz) ghee

Masala

90 g (3 oz) ghee
3 onions, thinly sliced
2 teaspoons grated fresh ginger
3 cloves garlic, chopped
½ teaspoon ground cumin
piece of cinnamon stick
8 whole cloves
6 cardamom pods
¼ teaspoon freshly grated nutmeg
1 teaspoon salt
1 cup chicken stock
½ cup natural yogurt
½ cup cream

Pilau rice

500 g (1 lb) Basmati rice
60 g (2 oz) ghee
½ teaspoon saffron threads
6 cardamom pods
1 teaspoon salt
4 cups chicken stock

Garnish

½ cup cashew nuts
¼ cup slivered almonds
¼ cup pistachio nuts
2 tablespoons sultanas
ghee for frying
edible silver leaf (optional)

176

Lamb: Have the butcher bone the leg of lamb. Trim the lamb of any excess fat, sinews or skin and cut into 2.5 cm (1 inch) cubes. Heat the ghee in a pan and fry the lamb until lightly browned on all sides, set aside.

Masala: Heat the ghee in a heavy pan, add the onions and fry over a gentle heat until soft and golden brown. Remove and set aside.

Add the ginger, garlic, cumin, cinnamon, cloves, cardamom, nutmeg and salt to the pan, adding more ghee if necessary, and fry lightly for a few minutes. Add the stock. Mix the yogurt and cream together and stir into the stock and spices. Cook for a minute or two. Add the lamb and half of the fried onion to the pan, stir in, cover and cook over a low heat for about 15 minutes more. When cooked, allow to stand for about 10–15 minutes.

Pilau Rice: Wash the rice well until the water runs clear and drain in a colander. Heat the ghee in a heavy saucepan, add the saffron and cardamom pods, fry for a few seconds then add the rice and fry until the rice is coated with the ghee. Add the salt and stock and bring to the boil, stirring once or twice. Once it comes to the boil, do not stir. Reduce the heat and cook gently for about 10–15 minutes, in which time the stock will have evaporated and the rice will be almost cooked. Cover and set aside.

To put together: Melt a little ghee in a large heavy flameproof casserole, swirling it up the sides. Spoon in half the rice (fork it up lightly to loosen and separate the grains first) and smooth over evenly with the back of a spoon.

Transfer the lamb cubes to the casserole using a slotted spoon, and place evenly over the rice. Top with the remaining rice. Push the Masala liquid through a sieve and drizzle over the rice. Top with the remaining fried onion rings. Cover the casserole with a sheet of foil, crimping the edges to keep it in place. Cover with a lid and bake in a preheated moderately hot oven (190°C/375°F) for 20 to 30 minutes or until the rice and lamb are tender.

If preparing the Biriani for a party it can be prepared up to this stage and stored covered in the refrigerator for up to 2 days. It will then take 45 minutes to finish cooking in the oven.

Garnish: Fry the nuts and sultanas in a little ghee until lightly browned. Sprinkle over the Biriani.

To serve: Fluff up the rice with a fork and heap the entire contents of the casserole on a large heated dish. Sprinkle with the nuts and sultanas.

For a festive finish, top with a few sheets of edible gold or silver leaf. If the Biriani has been cooked in a good looking casserole it can be taken to the table in its casserole, and served from it, each guest getting a portion complete with layers.

Serves 8

Note: Gold and silver leaf comes in small squares, fitted in between leaves of a paper tissue pad. These are best kept in a refrigerator wrapped in a plastic bag. To use the foil, lift off with the tip of a paint brush and gently lay on the food. It is unbelievably thin, so take care to handle it out of a breeze, even a quick swishing movement will have the foil folding and crimping into unwanted shapes.

Roast Pork

..

The day I learnt to cook roast pork with crispy crackling and tender succulent meat like my husband's mother used to do, was a great day indeed. The secret is in this recipe . . . the timing and temperatures.

1 loin of pork, weighing 2 kg (4 lb) or 1 leg of pork
coarse salt

Ask the butcher to score the skin at 5 mm (¼ inch) intervals. Rub all over with coarse salt. Place in a very hot oven (260°C/ 500°F) and roast for 30 minutes or until the skin is crisp and golden. Reduce the heat to moderate (180°C/350°F) and roast until cooked through (see below). Serve hot with vegetables and apple sauce or baked apples.

Cooking times: Pork should always be well cooked. Allow 30–35 minutes for each 500 g (1 lb) plus an extra 30 minutes.

Roast Loin of Pork with Plums

..

One of the best cooks I knew had the happy knack of serving fruit with meats. She was French, and cooked for a French ambassador and assured me that in her native province it was widely accepted. Tart fruit seems especially good with rich meats like pork. When fresh plums are in season use them with pork or lamb. Good quality canned or bottled plums may also be used. Rhubarb is also excellent with pork – just how good you'll just have to believe me – until you have tried for yourself!
No gravy is offered. The fruit provides the necessary soft sauce – another example of New Wave cooking.

1.5–2 kg (3–4 lb) loin of pork
salt
freshly ground pepper
2 cloves garlic, peeled and slivered
Plums for pork
500 g (1 lb) Mirabelle or any violet
or dark red plums
½ cup sugar
½ cup water
rind and juice of 1 lemon
15 g (½ oz) butter

Ask the butcher to bone the loin of pork and score the fat in narrow strips or a diamond pattern. Season the inside of the pork with salt, pepper and garlic, then roll and tie the loin. Preheat the oven to very hot (230°C/450°F). Put the meat, skin side up, on a rack in a roasting pan. Roast for 25 minutes in a very hot oven to crisp the skin. Reduce the oven temperature to moderate (180°C/350°F) and continue to roast the meat, allowing 25 minutes per 500 g (1 lb) in all, about 2 hours.

Transfer the meat to a serving platter and keep warm for 10 minutes. Carve the meat into thick slices and serve with the plums or baked rhubarb. *Serves 6*
Plums: Wash the plums and place in a small buttered baking dish, sprinkle over the sugar and add water, lemon juice and rind. Cover with foil. Bake in a moderate oven with the pork for 15–20 minutes.

If using canned or bottled plums, drain off most of the liquid and heat through with a little lemon juice and rind.
Baked Rhubarb: Wash a large bunch of rhubarb, about 1 kg (2 lb). Do not peel the stalks or the rosy colour will be lost. Discard the leaves and cut the stalks into 5 cm (2 inch) lengths. Put rhubarb in a buttered baking dish with the rind and juice of 1 orange and ½ cup sugar. Cover with foil. Bake in a moderate oven, with the pork, for about 20 minutes.

Roast Loin of Pork with Summer Rice Salad

..

Roast pork always seems rather special, but here it is even more so when served with a rice salad and a sauce which combines the classic ingredients of Cumberland Sauce with the piquant tang of sour cherries. The pork would make a good dish for the buffet table or summer luncheon or as an informal meal for entertaining. Although the pork is not meant to be served hot in this recipe, neither should it be chilled. Cook the pork in the morning if you plan to serve it for lunch, and let it stand, covered, at room temperature – not in the refrigerator. This is the way to enjoy the full succulent flavour and texture.

2 kg (4 lb) boned loin of pork, with the
rind removed
3 cloves garlic, crushed
1 tablespoon salt
freshly ground pepper
1 teaspoon fresh thyme
watercress or parsley to garnish

Have the butcher bone the pork and cut off the thick skin. Mix the garlic with the salt, pepper and thyme. Rub the garlic mixture over the boned surface of the pork, and let stand for at least 2 hours. Wipe off the mixture with a paper towel, and roll and tie the pork with string at 5 cm (2 inch) intervals. Place the pork in a roasting pan and roast in a preheated hot oven (200°C/ 400°F) for 30 minutes. Reduce the heat to moderately slow (160°C/325°F), and roast for a further 1½ hours. Let the meat stand at room temperature until cool. Remove the string, and arrange the roast, either whole, or with half cut into thick slices, on a bed of the Summer Rice Salad. Garnish the platter with watercress or parsley and serve the Cumberland Sauce and Sour Cherries separately. Serve with a green salad. *Serves 6–8*

178

Note: If you like crackling with your pork, score the rind, rub it with salt and cook it separately in a baking dish during the 30 minutes the oven temperature is set at high.

Summer Rice Salad

2 cups white long-grain rice
1 teaspoon Dijon mustard
salt
freshly ground pepper
1 tablespoon vinegar
4 tablespoons oil
¼ cup Mayonnaise (see page 45)
½ cup thinly sliced radishes
½ cup thinly sliced spring onions
1 small green pepper, seeded and chopped
2 tablespoons each chopped gherkin, fresh dill,
chives and parsley

Wash the rice well then drain in a colander. Bring 4 cups of salted water to the boil in a heavy saucepan. Add the rice, sprinkling it in slowly so that the water remains at a boil. Boil for a few minutes then cover tightly. Turn the heat to very low and cook, without lifting the lid, for 17–20 minutes, or until the rice grains are tender when tested. Remove from the heat, uncover for a few minutes to allow the steam to escape, then fluff up with a fork. Re-cover and cool to room temperature.

Mix the mustard, salt, pepper and vinegar in a small bowl then slowly whisk in the oil. Combine the vinaigrette with the mayonnaise. Toss the cooled rice with the dressing. Add the radishes, spring onions, pepper, gherkin, parsley, dill and chives, season to taste with salt and freshly ground pepper and stir lightly to combine.

Cumberland Sauce and Sour Cherries

1 large bottle sour cherries, drained
(see Note below)
½ cup port
¼ cup redcurrant jelly
1 tablespoon Dijon mustard
⅓ cup lemon juice
¼ cup orange juice
1 teaspoon grated orange rind

Put the cherries and port in a saucepan and simmer for about 10 minutes, let the mixture cool completely. In another small saucepan, soften the redcurrant jelly over a gentle heat but do not melt. Stir the mustard, lemon juice, orange juice and grated rind into the redcurrant jelly, then stir the jelly into the cherry mixture. Serve in a sauceboat with the loin of pork.

Note: The syrup from the cherries may be used in fruit salad, or may be used to poach fresh fruit such as plums, apples or quinces.

Pork Chops Charcutière

(Côtes de Porc Charcutière)

••

A favourite French way of cooking pork chops, particularly in the central and eastern provinces. The name means cooked in the manner of the pork butcher, and came about because pork chops cooked in this way were usually available, ready to eat or take away, at any charcuterie.

6 pork chops, trimmed
30 g (1 oz) butter
1 small onion, finely chopped
⅓ cup white wine
1 tablespoon vinegar
1 tablespoon tomato purée (optional)
1 tablespoon water
salt
freshly ground pepper
2 teaspoons mustard
1 pickled gherkin
1 tablespoon chopped parsley

Sauté the pork chops in their own fat. Transfer to a serving dish when cooked and keep warm. Pour off all but 1 tablespoon of the fat from the pan and add the butter. Cook the onion in the fat until soft and golden. Add the wine and vinegar and boil rapidly to reduce the liquid by one quarter. Add the tomato purée, if using, and the water and cook slowly for 10 minutes longer. Season with salt and pepper to taste and add the mustard, sliced pickled gherkin and parsley. Swirl in the remaining butter. Return the chops to the pan to heat through but do not allow to boil. Serve immediately with the sauce poured over the chops, and accompany with creamy mashed potatoes. *Serves 6*

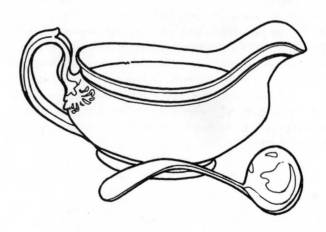

Pork Chops with Onions

(Côtes de Porc aux Oignons)

• •

*Onions are a feature of Lyonnais cooking,
typified by this hearty dish which should be served with lots
of mashed potatoes to absorb the flavoursome juices.*

6 pork chops
salt
freshly ground pepper
1 kg (2 lb) onions, finely chopped
3 tablespoons cider vinegar
3 tablespoons dry white wine
1 sprig thyme

Trim any excess fat from the chops, and season with a little salt
and pepper. Melt a little pork fat in a heavy pan and cook the
onions slowly, stirring, until starting to turn brown. Remove
from the pan and keep warm. Melt a little pork fat if necessary
and fry the pork chops on both sides until cooked through,
about 20 minutes. Remove to a serving platter and keep warm.
Add the vinegar and wine to the pan, bring to the boil, and
scrape up any pan sediments. Reduce the liquid to half by
rapid boiling. Reduce the heat, add the onions, season with
salt and pepper and thyme. Cook, stirring, for 3–4 minutes
then pour around the chops. Remove the thyme, and serve the
pork with creamy mashed potatoes. *Serves 6*

Barbecued Spareribs

• •

*There was a time when spareribs were as cheap as sin but
now that we have learnt how to cook and enjoy
them, like the delicacy they can be, we have to pay the price.
The secret is a bake in a high heat to rid the
spareribs of excess fat then reduce the heat, basting them
with a sweet and savoury barbecue sauce. Best
eaten with fingers, so provide dampened towels or
plenty of paper napkins.*

1.5 kg (3 lb) pork spareribs
2 tablespoons oil
2 onions, chopped
2 cloves garlic, crushed
2 tablespoons tomato paste
2 tablespoons soy sauce
3 tablespoons vinegar
2 tablespoons golden syrup
½ teaspoon ground ginger
1 beef stock cube
1¼ cups water

Cut rib section into single ribs and place in a shallow roasting
dish in a single layer. Heat the oil in a frying pan, add the
onions and sauté until translucent. Stir in the garlic, tomato
paste, soy sauce, vinegar, syrup and ginger. Dissolve the stock
cube in the water. Add to the pan and simmer for 15 minutes.

Brush ribs with the sauce and bake in a hot oven (220°C/
425°F) for 30 minutes. Pour off excess fat from the roasting dish.
Spoon over the remaining sauce and bake for 1 hour at 190°C
(375°F), turning the spareribs occasionally and basting with the
sauce. *Serves 6*

Cassoulet

• • •

This hearty dish of beans with several kinds of meat has its origins in south-western France, at least three towns lay claim to the first and true Cassoulet. Pork, duck, preserved goose, mutton and garlic sausages are among the meats used in a Cassoulet; which of these are added to the beans depends on which versions of Cassoulet you follow. This one, typical of Toulouse, uses pork, lamb and sausages and will serve 10–12 people.

1 kg (2 lb) white haricot beans
1.25 kg (2½ lb) pork spareribs
250 g (8 oz) bacon
1 onion
bouquet garni
2 cloves garlic, bruised
750 g (1½ lb) breast or shoulder of lamb, boned
500 g (1 lb) garlic flavoured boiling sausage
(such as clobassi)
¾ cup breadcrumbs

Soak the beans in cold water overnight. Trim the rind from the pork and bacon as thinly as possible, and cut the rind into small squares. Drain the beans and place in a heavy saucepan with the rind, bacon, onion, bouquet garni and garlic. Cover with water and simmer for 1½ hours. Meanwhile, roast the pork and lamb in a moderately slow oven (160°C/325°F). Add the sausage to the beans for the last 15 minutes cooking.

When the beans are almost cooked, drain them and reserve the liquid, discarding the onion, bouquet garni and garlic. Place half the beans in a deep casserole. On top place the sausage, thickly sliced, then the lamb and pork, cut into serving size pieces. Cover with the remaining beans and moisten with 1 cup of reserved liquid. Sprinkle the breadcrumbs on top. Bake in a very slow oven (120°C/250°F) for 1½ hours, adding more liquid if the dish becomes too dry. The breadcrumbs should have formed a fine golden crust on top by the end of cooking. *Serves 10–12*

Ham Baked in Guinness with Spiced Peaches

• • •

A glistening rosy pink baked ham can take star billing on a buffet table. Although expensive it is an ideal choice for the busy home caterer, providing one splendid dish that is easy to serve and people will enjoy. Although this recipe calls for a precooked ham, the long baking allows the wonderful flavour of Guinness stout and fragrant spices to flavour the meat.

1 × 7.5 kg (15 lb) cooked leg ham
1½ cups plus an extra 2 to 3 tablespoons
Guinness stout
1 cup sugar
2 teaspoons dry mustard
1 teaspoon ground ginger
2 teaspoons ground cardamom
1 bunch watercress, to garnish

Peel the skin off ham, leaving a portion around the bone. Place the ham, fat side up, in a roasting pan and pour over 1½ cups of the stout. Bake in a moderately slow oven (160°C/325°F) for 3 hours, basting occasionally with stout. Remove the ham and baste with the drippings. Score the fat diagonally to form a diamond pattern. Mix the sugar, mustard, ginger and cardamom and add the extra stout to form a paste and spread over the ham. Increase oven temperature to hot (200°C/400°F) and bake the ham for a further 15 minutes. Serve warm or hot, garnish with watercress. Accompany with Spiced Peaches. *Serves 20 to 30*

Spiced Peaches

3 × 825 g cans peach halves
½ teaspoon whole cloves
2.5 cm (1 inch) piece cinnamon stick
8 whole allspice
½ cup sugar
¼ cup white vinegar
2 oranges, sliced
extra cloves (optional)

Drain the peaches and reserve 1 cup of the syrup. Put the syrup, cloves, cinnamon, allspice, sugar, vinegar and orange slices into a saucepan. Bring to the boil, add the peaches and simmer for 5 minutes. Cover and allow to cool. Chill. Remove the spices before serving. If liked, stud the fruit with extra cloves.
Note: The flavour of the fruit will improve if made 4 or 5 days in advance and kept in the refrigerator.

Veal Chops with Mushrooms

••

European veal is more tender and has a better flavour than
that found in other parts of the world and the
things good European cooks do with it are worth copying.
This recipe is quite simple and utterly delicious.
Serve with creamed potatoes or noodles and
offer a green salad.

4 veal loin chops, trimmed
½ teaspoon salt
1 teaspoon paprika
60 g (2 oz) butter
6–8 mushrooms, sliced
2 teaspoons flour
¼ cup cream
few drops lemon juice
2 tablespoons white wine or 1 tablespoon brandy
2 tablespoons chopped parsley
4 slices Swiss or Gruyère cheese

Sprinkle the veal chops on both sides with salt and paprika. In
a heavy frying pan sauté the chops in 30 g (1 oz) of the butter
until lightly browned. Place the chops on a heatproof platter.
Sauté the mushrooms in the same pan as the chops, adding
more butter if necessary. When lightly browned, stir in the
flour, allow to cook for 30 seconds then add the cream, lemon
juice and wine or brandy. Simmer for about 4 minutes. Add the
chopped parsley and spoon over the chops. Place a slice of
cheese, cut to fit, over each chop. Place under a preheated grill
or in a hot oven (200°C/400°F) until the cheese is melted but
not browned.

If preferred, the chops can be boned and pounded before
cooking. *Serves 4*

Veal with Vegetables

(Veau à la Jardinière)

••

The French welcome the arrival of spring and the first of the
new season's vegetables. Fresh young peas, tiny
white onions and baby carrots make their appearance on
every vegetable stall at the markets, and they are
often combined with veal for this
delicious casserole.

1.5 kg (3 lb) breast of veal
¼ cup olive oil
bouquet garni
salt
freshly ground pepper
1 kg (2 lb) fresh peas
500 g (1 lb) small white onions
500 g (1 lb) small new carrots
1 teaspoon sugar
60 g (2 oz) butter

Remove the bones and skin from the veal and cut into small
cubes. Brown the veal in the olive oil, in a heavy saucepan.
Add the bouquet garni, salt, pepper and boiling water to
almost cover the meat. Cover and simmer over a low heat for
1½ hours.

Shell the peas and peel the onions and carrots, add them to
the casserole with the sugar. Continue to simmer slowly until
the vegetables are tender. Remove the bouquet garni and stir
in the butter, keep warm without boiling. Serve warm with
boiled new potatoes. *Serves 6*
Note: This casserole can also be made with frozen or canned
vegetables if desired. It is just as good reheated as it is freshly
made.

Sauté of Veal Marengo

••

There are some who claim this is an improvement on the
original sauté of Chicken Marengo. Try it and
decide for yourself. The original dish was created for
Napoleon by his chef, Dunand, after the Battle
of Marengo and I don't want to go into battle on the question
of which is the better dish . . . I enjoy them both.

750 g (1½ lb) veal steak, cut 2.5 cm (1 inch) thick
4–5 tablespoons oil
1 large onion, chopped
1 tablespoon plain flour
¾ cup white wine
2 cups chicken stock
1 clove garlic, crushed
½ teaspoon salt
bouquet garni
500 g (1 lb) ripe tomatoes, peeled and seeded
or 1 × 425 g can tomatoes
250 g (8 oz) button mushrooms

Garnish

4 slices white bread
30 g (1 oz) butter
finely chopped parsley

Trim and cut the meat into large pieces. Heat the oil in a frying
pan and sauté the meat until coloured on all sides. Drain off all
but 1 tablespoon of oil, add the onion and cook gently until
translucent. Sprinkle over the flour and cook slowly, stirring,
for 3–4 minutes or until golden. Add the wine and stock and
bring to the boil, stirring. Reduce the heat, add the garlic, salt,
bouquet garni and tomatoes. If using canned tomatoes, drain
the liquid. Cover and simmer gently for about 45 minutes.

Meanwhile prepare the mushrooms; wipe with a damp cloth
and trim the stems. If the mushrooms are large, halve them.

Lift the meat from the pan with a slotted spoon and boil the liquid down over a high heat until there is about 2 cups of liquid left. Return the meat, add the mushrooms and simmer very gently for 15 minutes.

To make the garnish: With a heart-shaped biscuit cutter, cut heart shapes from the bread and fry in the hot butter until golden. Drain. If you don't have a heart-shaped cutter, cut the bread into triangles. Garnish the veal dish with the croûtes and finely chopped parsley. *Serves 4*

Veal Escalopes

If you want those tiny little escalopes of veal you find in good Italian restaurants you can prepare them yourself.

Order a loin of veal, about 5 or 6 chops but ask the butcher to keep them whole making sure he does no chining or chopping between the bones. Cut the fillet of lean meat from the bones, then cut the fillet into 2 cm (¾ inch) slices. They should be about 8 cm (3 inch) across and weigh about 90 g (3 oz). Place each escalope between two sheets of plastic wrap and gently beat out to about 10 cm (4 inch) in diameter. Remove to a plate and cover with plastic or foil.

The escalopes are ready for cooking – use to make schnitzels, veal birds, saltimbocca, or other dishes calling for veal steaks.

Use the bones and trimmings to make veal stock for gravies or soup or else they can be put in a freezer bag and frozen and used to supplement other bones for stock.

Veal Escalopes in Mustard Cream

•

This is a quick and simple recipe, which has an elegant flavour provided you can use the best French mustard. Tarragon flavoured mustard is superb, but you might also experiment with mustard with poivre vert or simply the classic white wine mustard of Dijon.

8 veal escalopes or 4 veal steaks, beaten thin
seasoned flour
1 tablespoon oil
30 g (1 oz) butter
½ cup cream
1 tablespoon good French mustard
salt
freshly ground pepper

Dust the veal lightly with seasoned flour. In a heavy frying pan, heat the oil and butter and cook the veal quickly until lightly browned on both sides. Do not crowd the pan, brown the escalopes in batches, transferring to a hot serving dish as they are done, keep warm.

Pour the cream into the pan, stir in the mustard and cook, scraping and stirring to remove all the pan sediments, until the sauce is coffee-coloured and thickish. Season with salt and pepper and spoon over the escalopes. This dish is very good served with creamed potatoes or buttered noodles and a crisp green salad as the only accompaniments. *Serves 4*

Veal with Marsala

•

Veal steak can be bought conveniently from the delicatessen already beaten thin. Or, if your butcher has good veal, remember to ask him to flatten the steaks out thinly for this dish.

750 g (1½ lb) veal steaks, cut into thin even slices,
or veal escalopes (see left)
seasoned flour
60 g (2 oz) butter
4 tablespoons Marsala
squeeze lemon juice
4 tablespoons cream
salt
freshly ground pepper

Pound the veal steaks lightly until very thin. If large steaks are used, cut into smaller pieces. Dust the veal lightly with seasoned flour. In a heavy frying pan, heat the butter and cook the veal quickly until lightly browned on each side. Pour over the Marsala and let it bubble for a few minutes until it looks syrupy. Add the lemon juice and cream. Stir well, scraping up the veal juices from the pan, season with salt and freshly ground pepper. Simmer for a minute longer until you have a delicious coffee-coloured sauce.

Serve with noodles or boiled rice and a tossed green salad. *Serves 6*

LIVER

Liver well cooked is a delicacy but for all too many it is a dreaded dish, reminiscent of bad nursery food – dry, tough and totally lacking in flavour. Calves' liver is considered by many the finest, but lambs' liver is easier to find and if prepared and cooked with care is quite delicious.

Liver should not be overcooked. Long cooking will toughen it. Liver that is sautéed and cooked only to the rare stage should be done by the time both sides are browned, so watch it carefully as it cooks. Before cooking, liver should be soaked in salted water for half an hour. Wipe with a damp cloth and remove thin outer tissue and any veins.

Cut in thin slices, cut evenly or they will cook unequally! Pat each slice dry before coating with flour, otherwise the liver will steam or stew and not fry to a dry outside with a tender pink inside.

Prepare the liver in readiness for cooking but have the family seated before you start to cook it, any vegetables should be ready and kept warm.

Sliced liver may be cooked in any of the following ways:
Grilling Line a grilling rack with foil, lightly oil. Place slices of liver on foil. Season with salt and freshly ground pepper and drizzle with oil or melted butter. Cook for 3–4 minutes on both sides under a very hot grill. Brush with oil or butter when the liver is turned. Serve immediately. Serve with grilled bacon if liked or lemon wedges.
Frying Season sliced liver with salt and freshly ground pepper and a squeeze of lemon juice. Dust lightly with flour to give the slices a crisp surface. Heat a little bacon fat or butter and oil in a frying pan. Fry liver on each side for 2–3 minutes only. Serve with grilled bacon or lemon wedges.
Chinese Style Coat slices of liver with a light dusting of cornflour. Heat 3 tablespoons of peanut oil in a frying pan. Add 3 thin slices of green ginger and 2 stalks of spring onion cut into short lengths and allow to heat through and season the oil. When hot, add the liver slices and fry for 2–3 minutes on each side. Serve immediately.
Italian Style Season slices of liver with salt and freshly ground pepper. Coat with a light dusting of flour. Thinly slice a peeled onion and fry in a little olive oil until soft and golden, push to one side of the pan then add the liver and fry for 2–3 minutes on both sides. Lightly combine the liver and onions.
With Herbs Sage and basil are two herbs that go well with liver. Allow 2 sage or sweet basil leaves per person, heat them in the oil first then proceed with directions above for frying liver. Serve with lemon wedges.
With Gravy Liver should not need a gravy but for those who enjoy a light gravy it's easy enough to make. Add ½ cup stock, wine or water to the pan after the liver is cooked. Cook gently scraping up the brown bits in the pan, season with salt and pepper, add a knob of butter and swirl around, spoon gravy over the liver.
Cream Gravy Make as above but instead of butter swirl in ¼–⅓ cup cream, cook until sauce takes on body.

KIDNEYS

In winter most of the kidneys seem to find their way into steak and kidney stew and to buy a dozen or so seems well-nigh impossible. But once winter is over kidneys, whether veal, lamb or pig, are plentiful, usually very cheap and make nourishing and quickly cooked meals. All kidneys have the same food value, so choose which work out best for your dish.

Kidneys, if they are to have a good flavour, must be eaten quickly and should not be stored longer than 24 hours in the refrigerator, or well wrapped for up to a month in the freezer. If you buy kidneys in packets at the supermarkets, put the packet into a freezer bag, as they develop an 'off' flavour in the freezer if not properly packed.

Kidney, Mushrooms and Toast

••

This is a dish I plan to serve if I know I will be late home, as the men in my family love it. You can use veal kidneys if they are available, but whatever you use, remember to heat gently when cooking them or they will be tough.

2 rashers rindless streaky bacon, chopped
30 g (1 oz) butter or 1 tablespoon oil
1 small onion, thinly sliced
6 lamb kidneys, skinned, quartered and cores removed
¼ cup plain flour
1 × 425 g can tomatoes
salt
freshly ground pepper
250 g (8 oz) mushrooms
melted butter
8 triangles toast or fried bread

Fry the bacon gently in the butter or oil. Add the onion and kidneys and fry for a few minutes until lightly browned. Add the flour, then stir in the tomatoes. Bring to the boil, season with salt and pepper, reduce heat and simmer for 10 minutes. Brush the mushrooms with a little melted butter and grill for a few seconds.

Turn the kidney mixture into a hot dish and arrange the mushrooms down one side of the dish and the triangles of toast down the other. If you prefer crispy croûtes, simply fry the triangles in a little oil until crisp and golden on both sides, drain on kitchen paper and lightly salt. *Serves 3–4*

Veal Kidneys with Cream Sauce

(Rognons de Veau à la Crème)

• •

Mustard and cream sauces are common in French cookery, especially in the area around Dijon, the home of the best mustard. Dijon mustard is available in most countries and one of the most common brands is Grey Poupon. Veal kidneys are a great delicacy and consequently very expensive. If you can't get them from your butcher, substitute lamb kidneys.

1 kg (2 lb) veal or lamb kidneys
60 g (2 oz) butter
¼ cup brandy
salt
freshly ground pepper
grated nutmeg
1 teaspoon cornflour
¾ cup cream
1 teaspoon strong French mustard

Remove fine skin from the kidneys, cut in halves lengthwise and remove the cores. Melt the butter in a heavy pan and cook the kidneys until coloured on both sides. Sprinkle over the brandy and cover with a tight fitting lid. Cook for 1 minute then remove and keep warm. Reduce the pan juices to half by rapid boiling, and season with salt, pepper and a grating of nutmeg. Combine the cornflour and cream and add to pan and stir, scraping up any sediments in the pan, until boiling. Return the kidneys to the pan, they should be slightly pink in the centre as overcooking makes them hard and tough. Stir in the mustard and blend well. Heat through over a gentle heat, basting the kidneys with the sauce. Serve hot with boiled rice. *Serves 4–6*

Devilled Kidneys

•

8 lamb kidneys
60 g (2 oz) butter
1 tablespoon flour
1 teaspoon French mustard
1 teaspoon curry powder (optional)
¼ teaspoon Worcestershire sauce
½ cup stock or water
salt
freshly ground pepper
squeeze of lemon juice
hot buttered toast, to serve

Skin the kidneys, halve and remove the cores, then cut into thin slices. Heat 30 g (1 oz) of the butter in a frying pan and quickly brown the kidneys on both sides. This should take about 1½ minutes. Do not overcook or the kidneys will be hard and tough. Remove to a heated dish. Add the flour, mustard and curry powder (if using) to the frying pan and stir well. Add the Worcestershire sauce, stock or water and cook for 2 minutes. Season with salt and pepper and a squeeze of lemon juice. Add the remaining butter and kidneys and toss well until heated. There should be very little sauce. Serve immediately on hot buttered toast. *Serves 4*

SEVEN GREAT AND CLASSIC DISHES

The names of certain dishes are on every good cook's lips .... Boeuf à la Bourguignonne, Beef Wellington, Tripe à la Mode de Caen, Hungarian Goulash, Crown Roast of Lamb, Pot-au-feu, Paella.

What makes these dishes great? Time! The years that have gone into building and refining the flavour, the hours that have gone into perfecting and simplifying each step by great chefs or generations of good cooks.

Why is it then that although many cook books contain recipes for these greats, they are not cooked very often? The recipes may *seem* long and complicated but that is only because the first time you attempt anything new it takes much longer.

Many years ago I read the book *The Garrulous Gourmet* by William Wallace Irwin, in which he describes the making of the splendid French peasant dish Pot-au-feu. This was put on early in the day and cooked while the peasant worked all day in the fields. Our author directed us to go, like the peasants, into the fields for the day – he supplied the alternative of going off to a movie. I slavishly followed his recipe and by the end of the day I began to wonder when I was ever going to get out of the kitchen, let alone into the fields or to a movie. I have discussed this with other cooks and we all agreed that any time we attempt a totally new dish, it will be a long job. As you make and remake a dish you get to know what processes are done first, what things can be cooking while you prepare the next step. You soon get a clear picture of the dish and every step falls into place naturally and you do get to go to a movie . . . if not into the fields.

I have selected seven great dishes that I now make often and with ease. My cooking friends and I agree that it was well worth the time spent learning to make such specialties and when we serve them the really great thing is that everyone knows why generations of people have loved them.

Tournedos Wellington

•••

Beef Wellington, named after the victor of Waterloo, usually indicates a whole fillet of beef spread with fine pâté and then baked in a puff pastry wrapping. For Tournedos Wellington, I suggest a variation on the usual pâté topping and also the fillet is cut into thick steaks and each is encased in its own beautifully decorated puff pastry covering. This makes for a more glamorous appearance on each plate and is also far easier for a host or hostess to serve at the table.

8 fillet steaks, cut 4 cm (1½ inch) thick
salt
freshly ground pepper
1 tablespoon oil
60 g (2 oz) butter
125 g (4 oz) small mushrooms
180 g (6 oz) good smoked ham, finely chopped
or minced
1 tablespoon brandy
500 g (1 lb) commercial puff pastry
1 egg, separated
2½ cups Madeira Sauce (see page 43) to serve

Trim the steaks of all fat and gristle. Shape with your hands into round, high shapes and tie string round each to keep a neat shape. Season with salt and pepper. Heat the oil with 30 g (1 oz) of the butter in a frying pan and when it is very hot, brown the steaks well all over. Set aside to get quite cold and remove the string.

Wipe the mushrooms, trim and slice thinly. Add to the pan with the remaining butter and cook gently until lightly browned. Add the ham and heat thoroughly, stirring. Season to taste, then stir in the brandy. Spread on top of each steak and allow to get cold.

Roll out half the pastry thinly on a lightly floured surface. Cut into 8 circles, 2.5 cm (1 inch) larger than the meat. Using a small fluted and a small plain round cutter cut crescent shapes out of the pastry scraps, see note below, and set aside for decoration. Place the steaks on the circles of pastry and brush the edges with slightly beaten egg white. Roll out the remaining pastry thinly and cut into eight circles, 4 cm (1½ inch) larger than the meat. Gently mould over the meat, joining up with the other piece of pastry and pressing the edges to seal, trim the edges. Brush the pastry with the slightly beaten egg yolk and arrange the pastry crescents in a pattern round the edge of the top and brush these also with egg yolk. Bake in a very hot oven (230°C/450°F) for 15 minutes until the pastry is golden. Serve with Madeira Sauce (double quantity of the recipe on page 43) in a separate sauceboat. *Serves 8*

★ Sauté the steaks two or three at a time; don't crowd the pan or they will steam and will not be well sealed by the initial browning. It is essential that the meat should be well sealed and quite cold before it is encased in the pastry or it will make the inside of the pastry damp, giving a covering that is doughy and heavy when baked instead of crisp and airy-light.

★ Tournedos Wellington may be prepared well in advance. Have the beef browned and covered with the pastry, ready to glaze and decorate just before baking. Refrigerate if keeping overnight but take out and leave at room temperature for 2 hours before baking so that timing will be accurate.

★ To make a crescent, press one side of a small round fluted cutter down on the pastry then press the side of a slightly larger plain round cutter down just behind the fluted cut.

Boeuf à la Bourguignonne

• • •

Boeuf à la Bourguignonne, or simply Beef in Burgundy, is almost as well known around the world as it is in France.

It's a great favourite with small restaurants and with the French housewife who makes it with a cheap cut of meat and allows it to stew slowly to develop a wonderful aroma and rich sauce.

This dish has been popular for many years and is believed to have originated in Burgundy, a province famous not only for its wine and Charolais beef but for its richly flavoured dishes. Plain boiled rice sprinkled with parsley is its usual accompaniment but potatoes are good too.

1.5 kg (3 lb) chuck steak or gravy beef
2 tablespoons olive oil
60 g (2 oz) butter
125 g (4 oz) salt pork, diced
18 small onions, peeled
¼ cup brandy
1 tablespoon flour
1 cup red wine
1 cup beef stock
1 bouquet garni, containing 1 garlic clove
salt
freshly ground pepper
250 g (8 oz) button mushrooms

Cut the beef into 5 cm (2 inch) cubes and dry well. Heat the oil and 30 g (1 oz) of the butter in a heavy flameproof casserole and brown the salt pork. Remove pork and brown the onions. Place on one side with the pork.

Brown the beef. Warm the brandy, set alight and pour over the beef. Stir in the flour then add the red wine. Allow it to bubble for a minute and then add the stock and bouquet garni.

Season with salt and pepper, cover the pan and cook in a slow oven (150°C/300°F) for 3–3½ hours.

Sauté the mushrooms in the remaining butter for a few minutes and then add to the beef with the reserved onions and salt pork. Cover and cook for a further 30 minutes. Remove the bouquet garni and serve with boiled rice sprinkled with parsley. *Serves 8*

★ The cheaper cuts of beef given here are the best for Boeuf à la Bourguignonne, they have excellent flavour and become very tender and melting with the long slow cooking.

★ The flavour of this dish depends very much on the wine and the richness of the beef stock. The most suitable wine is a soft fruity red style often called 'burgundy'.

★ When peeling the onions, leave the root end intact so that the onions will hold together throughout cooking. Browning the onions and pork first gives the pan juices excellent flavour.

★ Brown the meat in batches, not too many pieces at a time, to prevent the meat sweating and releasing the juices.

★ Warmed brandy flames very easily. Pour over the meat and shake the pan over the heat until the flames die down completely.

★ The flavour of this dish is improved when heated up for a second time. Reheat in a slow oven.

★ A boned joint of beef may be browned, cooked whole and served with the same sauce.

Crown Roast of Lamb

••

We tend to think of Europe as the home of the starring dishes of Western cuisine, but Crown Roast is of American origin. The neat design of cutlets with their little curved bones has inspired other lovely presentations, such as England's Guard of Honour, which is two racks of cutlets standing upright with the bones interlaced or the French way of laying single cutlets in two straight rows down a long platter with the bones herringboned. However, for real drama and sense of occasion, Crown Roast is a winner.

1 crown roast of lamb (see below)
1 quantity Mushroom or Kidney, Ham and
Spinach Stuffing

Gravy

1 small onion, finely chopped
1 tablespoon flour
1 cup stock or vegetable water
salt
freshly ground pepper

Make one quantity of either the Mushroom Stuffing or Kidney, Ham and Spinach Stuffing.

Wrap the ends of the bones of the crown roast in aluminium foil. Stand the lamb in a roasting pan and roast in a hot oven (200°C/400°F) for 30 minutes. Spoon the stuffing into the centre and roast for a further 30 minutes or until the juices run pale pink when the meat is pricked with a skewer. Transfer to a heated platter and allow to stand in a warm place for about 10 minutes while making the Gravy. When ready to serve, the foil is removed and a cutlet frill may be placed on the end of each bone. Carve at the table straight down between two bones into double cutlets. *Serves 6–8*

Gravy Pour all except 1 tablespoon of fat from the pan. Add the onion to the pan and stir over a moderate heat until browned. Add the flour and stir until a good brown colour then add the stock or vegetable water. Stir until bubbling gently, season with salt and pepper and allow to cook for a few minutes. Strain and serve in a sauceboat with the lamb.

Notes

★ A crown roast is simply 2 racks of lamb bent round and sewn together at each end with the bones on the outside and the meat on the inside. A rack consists of the 6 to 7 rib chops or cutlets which adjoin the shortloin chops on one end and the forequarter on the other. For a crown roast or other dish using rack of lamb, the joint is chined (see Words You Should Know), the skin and some of the thick fat covering are trimmed off and the meat is cleaned away from around the bones for about 4 cm (1½ inch) from the ends. Your butcher will usually do all this for you if you give him a little notice.

★ Order your crown roast by the number of cutlets, according to how many people you plan to serve. It is usual to allow 2 cutlets per serving, although for small Spring lamb you may wish to serve 3.

★ When the juices run pale pink, the lamb will be moist and pink inside. If you prefer it well-done, cook for a little longer until the juices run clear when the meat is pierced.

★ Spinach in many greengrocers' shops often means silverbeet. Use six leaves of this but if you can get the smaller-leafed English spinach which has a far more delicate texture and flavour then use it, the equivalent quantity is about half a bunch.

Mushroom Stuffing

60 g (2 oz) butter
2 spring onions, finely chopped
375 g (12 oz) mushrooms, finely chopped
1 tablespoon chopped fresh thyme or 1 teaspoon
dried thyme
1 tablespoon finely chopped parsley
1 cup fresh white breadcrumbs
salt
freshly ground pepper

Melt 30 g (1 oz) of the butter and cook the spring onions gently for 1 minute, then add the mushrooms, thyme and parsley. Cook briskly for 5 to 6 minutes then remove from the heat and add the remaining butter and breadcrumbs. Season with salt and pepper to taste.

Kidney, Ham and Spinach Stuffing

2 lambs' kidneys
¾ cup finely chopped ham
½ clove garlic, crushed
1 cup fresh breadcrumbs
6 spinach leaves
1 small egg, lightly beaten
salt
freshly ground pepper

Remove skin, halve and core the kidneys, chop finely. Mix with the ham and crushed garlic then stir in the breadcrumbs. Remove stalks and centre ribs from the spinach leaves and chop the leaves very finely. Add to breadcrumb mixture and stir in the egg to bind. Season with salt and freshly ground pepper.

Hungarian Goulash

••

*There are many versions of this famous, centuries-old dish,
and in fact the original recipe didn't include paprika.
It is said that the Hungarians added the paprika during the
18th century to give it spice and heat.
Goulash is a peasant's dish, a nourishing and wholesome
stew. It was invented for men who had to wander
far from home because it could be made from previously dried
ingredients that could be transported easily.*

2 tablespoons lard or olive oil
4 onions, finely chopped
2 cloves garlic, finely chopped
1.5 kg (3 lb) neck of veal
1 tablespoon paprika
2 green peppers, seeds and ribs removed
2 tomatoes, peeled and chopped
salt
freshly ground pepper
noodles and sour cream to serve

Heat the lard or olive oil in a flameproof casserole and add the onions and garlic. Cover and cook gently for about 10 minutes until soft and transparent, stirring occasionally. Cut the veal into large cubes, add to the onion and sauté until golden. Turn the heat down, sprinkle with the paprika and simmer gently for about 10 minutes.

Chop peppers and add to the casserole with the tomatoes. Bring to the boil, cover and cook for 2 hours in a slow oven (150°C/300°F).

Serve with a dish of buttered noodles and a bowl of sour cream handed separately. *Serves 6–8*

Notes

There have been many cooks' feuds over which is the correct version of Hungarian Goulash but it seems that everyone agrees to the following principles:

★ The meat should be cut into large cubes or pieces, about 5 cm (2 inch). Veal is a very tender meat and smaller pieces might be inclined to break up too much with the long, slow cooking.

★ Paprika must never be cooked over high heat without liquid. If it is overheated it will become bitter.

★ Goulash should never be thickened except with the use of a diced potato which is added to make it even more wholesome. Things that might go into the making of a French stew are never used, so there should be no confusion. Never a glass of wine, a bouquet garni or a sprinkling of chopped parsley.

★ Sour cream is often added to the goulash just before serving, but authorities say this is incorrect, so let the diner add it himself if he wants to.

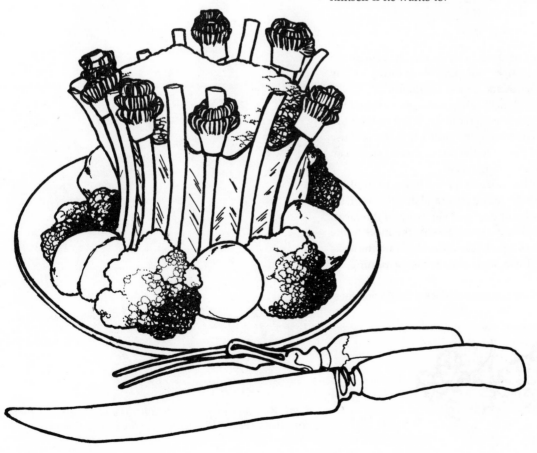

Tripe à la Mode de Caen

•••

*Tripe fanciers owe tribute to Benoit, the great chef of the
French city of Caen. It was he who created this dish
with the carefully calculated seasoning that puts savour into
the otherwise bland and tasteless tripe. To be at its
best it should be cooked in large quantities with an ox foot,
Calvados (the apple brandy of Normandy) and
cider, then simmered for many hours.
Our version simplifies the making of this
exquisite dish without losing any of its fine flavour and
succulence.*

4 onions

4 carrots

1 kg (2 lb) shin of beef on the bone or 2 pig's trotters

2 kg (4 lb) tripe

2 leeks

bouquet garni

4 cloves garlic, peeled

1 teaspoon salt

a little freshly ground pepper

6 whole allspice

½ cup cider

2 tablespoons Calvados or brandy

1 cup water

Luting Paste

2 cups flour

¾ cup water

Peel, halve and slice the onions and carrots and lay them on the
bottom of a heavy, large flameproof casserole or stew pan. Lay
the shin of beef or pig's trotters, on the vegetables.

Cut the tripe into 5 cm (2 inch) squares and place around the
shin, then add the remaining ingredients. Bring to the boil.
Make a thick paste by combining the flour and water and use
this to seal the edges of the lid to the pot so that no steam can
escape. This is known as a luting paste.

Bake in a slow oven (160°C/325°F) for 5–8 hours or until the
tripe is tender. Break off the luting paste and discard, skim off
any fat. Take out the shin of beef and cut away all the meat,
discarding the bone and fatty tissue. Return the meat to the
casserole, strain off excess liquid, take out and discard the leeks
and bouquet garni. Taste and adjust the seasoning, if
necessary.

Serve the tripe from the casserole with jacket baked potatoes.

Serves 8 generously

Notes

★ The essential ingredient is tripe, some prefer honeycomb
though this is a matter of taste. To this is traditionally added an
ox foot to provide a gelatinous substance, a little fat and a good
meaty flavour. As ox foot is very difficult to get use whole
shin of beef, making sure that the hoof end near the joint is
included. Pig's trotters may also be used.

★ Bouquet garni for this dish should consist of several pieces of
celery, 2 parsley sprigs, 2 bay leaves and a sprig of thyme. Bind
all together with cotton or string.

★ In principle, the liquid should be all cider strengthened with
a few spoonfuls of Calvados, the Normandy brandy made from
apples, but as this makes the tripe rather dark I prefer to use
some water with the cider and brandy.

★ As Tripe à la Mode de Caen should be cooked in a
hermetically sealed dish, use a flour and water paste to seal the
lid to the dish. Mine is a heavy cast iron pan coated with enamel.
The sealing ensures all the flavour stays in the meat, in the dish,
and this is why comparatively little liquid is needed.

*Right: Ripe tomatoes baked with herbs and garlic make Tomatoes
Provencale (page 218). Serve from the baking dish with grills or
roasts.*

Paella

• • •

My introduction to Paella was in the home of Don Carlos
Zalapa whose practice it was to have all the
ingredients prepared in bowls and plates.
The charcoal fire was lit out of doors and the large **paellera** –
in which the Paella was to cook – set on the glowing
coals and then the ritual began. The chicken and pork were
fried in golden Spanish olive oil, then the onions
and rice were fried and seasonings, stock and vegetables
added. Delicate seafoods were added last.
Meanwhile, we sipped wine, nibbled on Spanish chirozo and
olives and watched our host with admiration.
The skill is to gently cook the Paella without burning the
bottom yet still cooking the top, so it may be taken
on and off the fire adding more stock when needed. This can
be done over a gas burner or if the paellera is large
use two burners, turning the pan to get an even
distribution of the heat.
The hot Paella is placed in the centre of the table and the
diners usually help themselves, offering little tid-
bits to a neighbouring guest. It's all very informal and
great fun.
Like a good many dishes, Paella is a poor man's food that has
become a rich man's treat. Our recipe originated
in the country regions of Spain where all the delicacies would
be on hand; today and in big cities we may have to
go further afield for all the ingredients.

¼ cup olive oil

3 pork loin chops, trimmed of excess fat

3 half-breasts of chicken

1 onion, chopped

1 clove garlic, chopped

½–1 teaspoon saffron

2½ cups long-grained rice

2 tomatoes, peeled and chopped

5 cups chicken stock

1 cup green peas

salt

freshly ground pepper

250 g (8 oz) large prawns

1 jar pickled mussels or 500 g (1 lb) fresh mussels
in their shells

1 squid, cleaned with skin removed (optional)

2 canned pimientos, cut in julienne strips

Heat the oil in the paella pan or in a large frying pan and when hot add the pork chops. Cook for about 5 minutes on each side. Remove the chops from the pan and keep warm. Add the chicken breasts and brown. Add the onion and garlic to the pan with the saffron and when the onions are lightly coloured, add the rice. Mix with the onions and fry for a further 5 minutes. Add the tomatoes to the rice with the stock and green peas and season with salt and pepper. Spread the rice to the edge of the pan.

Cut the pork chops into small pieces removing the bone. Remove the chicken breasts from the bone and cut each into two long fillets. Arrange the pork and chicken on the rice in an attractive pattern pushing in so that they are level with the rice and continue cooking.

Shell the prawns leaving the tails intact. Drain the mussels and slice the squid into rings. When most of the liquid has been absorbed into the rice add these ingredients arranging them decoratively. Cook over a moderate heat for a further 10 minutes adding more stock if necessary. Finish off with the julienne pimiento strips. *Serves 6–8*

Note: If using fresh mussels scrub well. Discard any with open shells.

Note: Look for a Spanish paellera in good kitchen shops. Failing that use a large frying pan. Electric frypans do an excellent job of Paella.

Left: There is coconut milk, coriander and ginger in the sauce
for Corn Cobs with Mixed Vegetables in Coconut Milk (recipe
page 206).

Pot-au-feu

● ●

In France, in the country regions, the peasant woman has always taken an active part in the labour on the farm. Due to this, there are a number of dishes that are prepared then left to cook over a smouldering fire. These preparations often include soup, vegetables and meat all cooked together in one dish. Being savoury, nourishing and economical, and easy to prepare, several of these dishes have climbed the social ladder from the fireplace of the farmer to the banquet of the banker.

Pot-au-feu, or pot on the fire, is one of the great dishes from France and it does vary from region to region but the way of serving is always the same. The broth is served first and the meat and vegetables follow as a second course. Sometimes a chicken is added, but this takes a large pot, not often found in today's households. The dish is then called Petite Marmite Henri IV but that is another story.

1.5 kg (3 lb) fresh brisket, silverside or topside of
beef, in one piece
few beef or veal bones
12 cups (3 litres) beef stock or water
and stock cubes
1 plump chicken (optional)
salt
4 carrots
2 small turnips
2 parsnips
6 small onions
6 cloves
2 leeks
bouquet garni

Put the beef and bones into a large pan, adding cold water to cover. Bring to the boil and simmer very slowly for 10 minutes, drain off the water. Add the stock, or water and stock cubes and 1 tablespoon of salt (use less salt if the cubes are salty). Bring slowly to the boil and remove the scum as it rises to the surface. Lower the heat, cover the pan with a lid and simmer very gently for 2½ hours.

Meanwhile, peel carrots, turnips and parsnips and cut into chunks. Peel onions and stud each with a clove. Wash leeks thoroughly and cut into 5 cm (2 inch) lengths. Add all these to the soup with the bouquet garni; if using the chicken, add it now. Simmer very slowly for a further 1 hour. Skim all fat from the soup, discard the bouquet garni and bones then taste and adjust the seasoning. Remove the meat and vegetables and keep warm.

Ladle the clear soup into bowls, adding a piece of carrot for colour and some dry crusty bread broken into bits. Serve with a bowl of grated Gruyère cheese. In France this is placed in the bowl and the soup is poured over. Follow with the meat and vegetables as a second course. The meat is cut in thick slices and the chicken is jointed. *Serves 6, or 8 if chicken is used*

Notes

★ The soup may be strained through a sieve, lined with several layers of cheese cloth, into a tureen for serving and the meat and vegetables served on a separate dish.

★ Because the meat is mild in flavour from the long cooking mustard or horseradish sauce and sour pickles are often served with it. A dish of Maldon salt or crushed rock salt should be supplied to sprinkle on the meat and vegetables.

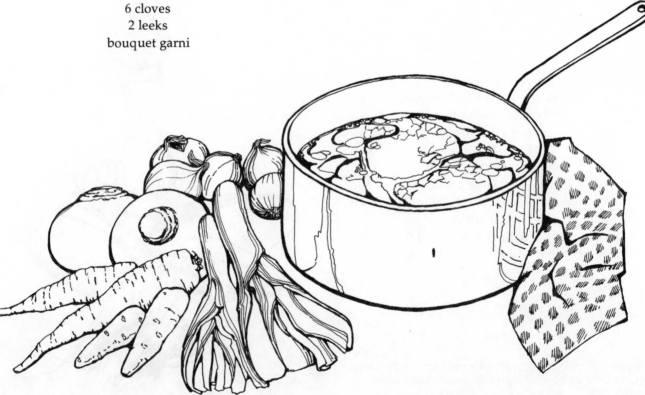

THE WONDERFUL WORLD OF VEGETABLES

On my very first visit to the East the glamour of exotic and colourful confrontations at every turn left my head spinning. But what struck me most was the reverence given to vegetables. No self-respecting Oriental or Asian cook would consider anything but the very freshest vegetables. They market twice daily, morning and afternoon, and will haggle and harangue, getting the very best the market can supply. My own Scottish upbringing wasn't much different. Many a time an embarrassed young girl had to return tomatoes that were soft, beans that wouldn't snap, green peas that weren't green. My mother, like those women of the East, would brook no deceptions.

Today, I find more people are discovering the joys of vegetables, not simply as an accompaniment to meat, fish or poultry but as stars in their own right. The range of fresh vegetables that come to the market is quite overwhelming. Tiny patty pan squash, pearly white pink gilled mushrooms, the beautiful globe artichoke, tender asparagus spears, peppers red, green, gold and yellow in all shapes and sizes vie with many varieties of string beans, potato, spinach, broccoli and marrow.

There seems to be no end to the delights our greengrocers have to offer.

There are ways to get the best out of vegetables. Shop on days when supplies reach your store and buy only as much as you can hold in the refrigerator or a cool place for the least time possible. Wash just before cooking. Cook as quickly and lightly as possible (there are a few exceptions). Old vegetables take well to being dressed with herb butters, spices and sauces. Young tender ones need only a light toss with butter or a squeeze of lemon juice.

One of the great delights is discovering a good vegetable dish, whether it is a simple one like the tenderest young green beans tossed in butter and lemon juice or a wonderful combination like herbed new potatoes with fresh peas or Indian corn cobs with mixed vegetables. With these in your repertoire you will be joining the happy band of people who claim to, and DO enjoy a whole meal of beautiful vegetables.

For the basics of cooking vegetables see pages 33 to 34, as it helps to know all you can about individual vegetables.

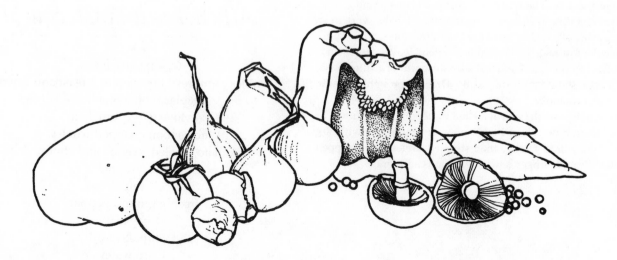

195

Artichokes

*The artichoke is a member of the thistle family
and comes on the market in early summer in various sizes.
Some are green and some almost purple.
The Italian artichoke with its slender elongated head
appears first and it is usually quartered or halved
and then fried or stewed in wine or stock. When cooked it
resembles a beautiful flower with crisp bronze petals.
The large, round artichoke is the kind most suitable for
serving plain, just boiled, to be eaten leaf by leaf
with melted butter or a sauce. When prepared, with the
clipped leaves spread out and the centre freed of
its 'choke', it resembles a handsome flower.
Artichokes may be served as a separate course, as a first
course, or as a dressed vegetable with the main course.
The most prized part of the artichoke is the 'fond' or
bottom which is used as a garnish for many
classical French dishes.
The regal globe artichoke should not be confused with the
small cream tuberous Jerusalem artichoke, which
is a winter vegetable, most often puréed and used to
make an excellent soup.*

To prepare and cook

Remove the tough outside leaves, then cut one-third off the top of the artichokes and trim the stalk and outer leaves with scissors.

As each artichoke is prepared, place into a bowl of cold water, into which is squeezed plenty of lemon juice to prevent them discolouring. This method of preparing them gives a most attractive shape. Otherwise, the sharp points of the leaves may simply be trimmed with scissors and the stalk cut off level with the base. Place in water with lemon juice as you prepare them.

To cook: Place the artichokes in boiling salted water with a slice of lemon and simmer for 20 to 45 minutes, depending on the age and size. The artichoke must not be overdone.

The exact time will depend on the size – a baby, very fresh young artichoke will be tender in 15 to 20 minutes, while larger ones will require up to 45 minutes. A good way to test them is to pull off an outer leaf and test with the point of a knife. Also, the leaves should pull off easily. Drain thoroughly upside down in a colander.

Serve with a small bowl of melted butter or lemon butter. To make lemon butter: heat 1 tablespoon of lemon juice with 60 g (2 oz) butter until frothy, then stir in 1 tablespoon chopped parsley. Provide finger bowls, teaspoons and forks.

How to Eat an Artichoke

Pull the leaves off, one at a time and dip the succulent base into the butter. Gently prise the soft fleshy base of the leaf between the teeth; the leaf is then discarded on the side of the plate. When the outer leaves have been eaten, scrape away the hairy choke with a teaspoon and discard (very young artichokes will not have one).

What remains is the heart and 'fond' (base) of the artichoke, the delicate and prized part which can be eaten whole, dipped in the accompanying sauce.

Artichokes Vinaigrette

••

Cook artichokes as described above, chill. Serve with small bowls of vinaigrette for dipping. Make the dressing by beating 3 tablespoons oil and 1 tablespoon vinegar with salt and pepper to taste and a teaspoon of French mustard.

Italian Artichokes in Wine

••

Use the young Italian artichoke with its slender elongated head.

Cut the artichokes lengthwise into quarters. Put in cold water to cover, with some lemon slices, as you prepare them. Drain on paper towels.

Heat a little olive oil in a heavy pan with a sprig of fresh or a pinch of dried oregano and 1 clove garlic, bruised. Add the artichokes and cook over a moderate heat, turning and tossing the artichokes until they are burnished and crispy on the outside. Remove the garlic clove. Add ½ cup white wine, season with some salt and freshly ground pepper, cover the pan and simmer gently until the artichokes are tender, about 10 to 15 minutes. Serve warm as a first course.

Artichokes à la Grecque

••

4–6 globe artichokes
1 tablespoon fresh tarragon or 1 teaspoon dried
1 tablespoon lemon juice
1 clove garlic, crushed
1 tablespoon chopped parsley
1 tomato, peeled, seeded and chopped
pinch thyme
salt
freshly ground pepper
1 bay leaf
⅓ cup olive oil
1 cup water

Prepare the artichokes as described in the introduction (see To cook artichokes at left). Combine with the remaining ingredients in a flameproof casserole and cook gently for 30–45 minutes. Allow to cool. Serve the cooking sauce with the artichokes. *Serves 4–6*

Asparagus

Asparagus is considered the most luxurious of all vegetables. It is a member of the lily of the valley family from which the rarest perfumes, fit for a queen, are made. Great chefs have created some of their finest and most complicated dishes with asparagus. Most of us, however, enjoy this exotic little 'grass' as a separate course, cooked until just al dente, *that is, when tender but still retaining texture. It should never be overcooked until soft and limp.*
Among the virtues of asparagus is that it not only tastes excellent with any kind of food, it can also be served hot, warm or cold, starring on its own. Perhaps the most popular ways of serving asparagus are boiled and hot with melted butter or Hollandaise sauce, or cold with Vinaigrette.

To prepare and cook

Allow 6 to 8 stalks per person. Cut asparagus all the same length and, only if they seem woody, scrape each stem from below the head in the direction of the root. Put into cold water and soak for a few minutes. Tie the asparagus in small bundles of 6–8 spears. Stand in a pan of fast boiling salted water so only the white stems are in the water, the tender green tips need only steam.

A special asparagus boiler is available, it is small in diameter but very deep. A good substitute is a deep round cake tin that sits, inverted, on top of a saucepan, this allows the tips to steam covered. Alternatively use a double boiler, the asparagus sits in the bottom, the top half inverts over the bottom giving you a deep receptacle. Failing this make a foil dome like a chef's hat around the saucepan.

The cooking time will depend on the age and size of the asparagus but after 10 minutes test the white part, if the tips of a fork penetrate easily they are done. Lift out and drain.

Remove the strings and serve in the simplest way with melted butter and lemon juice and a quick grinding of pepper or with Hollandaise sauce, see page 44, or cold with Vinaigrette, see page 46.

There are other delicious ways of serving asparagus. A few recipes are given on the right.

Asparagus Polonaise

• •

1 large bunch asparagus
60 g (2 oz) butter
3 tablespoons fine white breadcrumbs
2 hard-boiled eggs, finely chopped

Cook the asparagus as described above, drain and serve with Polonaise sauce.

Make the sauce while the asparagus is cooking. Melt the butter in a frying pan and sauté the breadcrumbs until golden brown. Mix with the finely chopped hard-boiled eggs and spoon over the asparagus. *Serves 2*

Asparagus Flamande

• •

1 large bunch asparagus
1 hard-boiled egg yolk
90 g (3 oz) butter, melted

Cook the asparagus until tender. Mash the egg yolk with a fork and very slowly add the melted butter, stirring all the time. This will become a flowing sauce, which blends admirably with asparagus. *Serves 2*

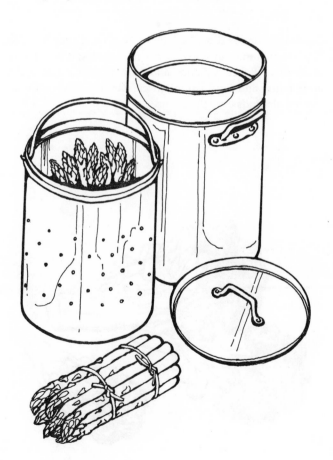

Green Beans

There are a great variety of green beans on the market and now that many of these are stringless, beans are a vegetable to be enjoyed often, no matter how busy we are. The old snap test is still the best assurance of youth and freshness.

To prepare and cook

Beans are at their best when young and fresh and cooked whole. Simply break off the ends, drop into a little boiling salted water, then simmer for 6 to 15 minutes, depending on the age and size, or until they are barely tender. Test after 6 minutes, it will give you an idea on how much longer they will take – do take care not to let the vegetable cook dry. Practice will help you gauge the right time and required heat.

If the beans have to be kept, drain and plunge them briefly into cold water to halt the cooking process. When required reheat in a little butter. The aromatic herb winter savoury goes well with beans, just add a few chopped sprigs to the pan when reheating in butter.

Beans Almandine

••

Cook the beans as described above, drain and keep hot. Melt 30 g (1 oz) butter in a pan, toss in 2 tablespoons slivered almonds or flaked almonds and brown lightly. Add a little more butter and swirl around in the pan, pour the butter and toasted almonds over the beans.

Beans with Lemon

••

This is a recipe for slimmers. Cook beans as described left, drain and keep hot. Serve with a squeeze of lemon juice and a fresh grinding of black or white pepper or, if liked, a little freshly grated nutmeg. Garnish with lemon wedges for extra juice if needed.

Beans Provençale

••

750 g (1½ lb) green beans
4 ripe tomatoes
2 tablespoons oil
2 cloves garlic, crushed
1 onion, chopped
6 sage leaves or winter savoury
salt
freshly ground pepper

Trim the beans, cook, drain and plunge into cold water to halt the cooking process.

Meanwhile, drop the tomatoes into boiling water, count to 10 and remove. Cut out the blossom end, peel, halve, remove the seeds and chop.

Heat the oil in a large saucepan over a medium heat. Add the garlic and onion and cook until the onion begins to colour. Add the tomatoes and sage, season with salt and pepper and simmer for about 5 minutes. Add the beans, toss them lightly with the tomatoes, taste and adjust the seasoning. Simmer for 2 or 3 minutes until the beans are reheated and then turn out into a hot vegetable dish. *Serves 4–6*

Beans Lyonnais

••

750 g (1½ lb) green beans
2 tablespoons oil
2 onions, finely chopped
salt
2 tablespoons chopped parsley
freshly ground pepper

Trim the beans, cook lightly and drain as described in the introduction.

Heat the oil in a pan, add the onions, cover and cook gently for about 5 minutes. Add the beans and sauté by tossing over a moderate heat until the flavours blend. Add salt to taste, turn on to a hot vegetable dish and sprinkle with the parsley and pepper. *Serves 4*

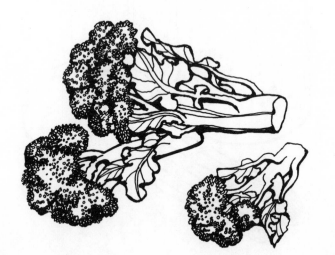

Beetroot

Beetroot would have to be one of Australia's most popular salad vegetables. If you can get some fresh beetroot do try it, as it is absolutely delicious and tastes quite different to canned beetroot. Beetroot is easy to cook, but does take a while. Take care when washing the beetroot not to break the skin as this will cause them to 'bleed' in the cooking water and so lose colour.

To prepare and cook

When cooking whole beetroot, leave 2.5 cm (1 inch) of the stem and the root ends. Wash well and cook in unsalted water to cover, in a covered pan, until tender when tested with a fork. Small young beets take 30 minutes to 1 hour, older beets 1–2 hours. When tender, drain and slip off the skins.

Baked beetroot Beetroot may be baked like jacket potatoes in the oven. Preheat the oven to 180°C/350°F. Trim the top stalks off the beetroot, wash, place in a baking dish and bake until tender, about 45 minutes for young beetroot and 1–1½ hours for older ones. Slip off the skins, season with salt and pepper or use in any of the recipes calling for cooked beetroot.

Beetroot in Sour Cream

•

In the top part of a double boiler or in a heavy saucepan, mix 3 cups cubed or sliced cooked beetroot with ½ cup sour cream, 1 tablespoon prepared horseradish, 1 teaspoon grated onion and a pinch of salt. Heat, stirring occasionally, over a hot pan of water or a gentle heat until the mixture is at serving temperature. Garnish with snipped chives or parsley. A delicious accompaniment to grilled meats or chicken. *Serves 6*

Beetroot with Fresh Herbs

•

6 beetroot, cooked and cut into cubes
1 tablespoon butter
1 tablespoon oil
1 onion, chopped
salt
½ cup mixed chopped fresh herbs (parsley, marjoram, basil, chervil, mint, etc.)

Heat the butter and oil in a saucepan over a medium heat until melted, add the onion and cook until it is soft. Add the beetroot, season with a little salt, stir until very hot, and then add chopped herbs. Stir lightly for 1 minute and turn out into a hot vegetable dish. *Serves 6*

Gingered Beets

•

2½ cups sliced canned beetroot
⅓ cup sugar
2 teaspoons cornflour
½ teaspoon ground ginger
grated rind and juice of 1 orange
1 tablespoon vinegar
30 g (1 oz) butter

Drain the beetroot, reserving ¼ cup of the liquid. Combine the sugar, cornflour and the ginger and stir in the orange rind and juice, vinegar and beetroot liquid. Cook, stirring, over low heat until the mixture is thickened. Add the beetroot and the butter and cook until heated through. *Serves 4–6*

Broccoli

Broccoli is an attractive vegetable that complements many other foods. It has a particular affinity with Hollandaise sauce, and is excellent with poached fish.

To prepare and cook Trim tough ends from 1 large bunch of broccoli, weighing about 1 kg (2 lb). Peel stems and make 2 slits crosswise in the stems to speed cooking. Stand the broccoli upright in a saucepan containing a little lightly salted boiling water. Cover and cook until the stalks are just tender, about 12–15 minutes. Drain and keep warm. Melt 60 g (2 oz) butter and add 2 tablespoons lemon juice, pour over the broccoli and serve. *Serves 4*

Brussels Sprouts with Caraway Seeds

•

750 g (1½ lb) Brussels sprouts
chicken stock
1 tablespoon butter
½ teaspoon salt
freshly ground black pepper
2 teaspoons whole caraway seeds

Wash the Brussels sprouts, trim off the tough outer leaves and cut a small cross in the bottom of each.

Pour chicken stock to a depth of 2.5 cm (1 inch) in a saucepan. Bring the stock to a boil and add the sprouts. Return to the boil and simmer, uncovered, for 5 minutes. Cover and cook for 6 to 10 minutes longer, or until just tender. Drain if necessary. Add remaining ingredients, toss lightly and serve at once. *Serves 6*

199

Braised Cabbage

• •

There are many excellent Middle European ways of cooking cabbage. In contrast to the modern trend of lightly steaming cabbage, older recipes braise it for many hours and the result is different but quite delicious, especially with pork, goose or duck. This is an Italian recipe.

1 green cabbage
250 g (8 oz) pickled pork belly
2 carrots, sliced
salt
freshly ground pepper
1 onion stuck with 1 clove
1 cup stock

Bouquet garni

3 sprigs parsley
2 sprigs thyme or ½ teaspoon dried
1 bay leaf

Remove the core from the cabbage and the rough outer leaves. Cook in boiling salted water for 3 minutes, then rinse under cold water and loosen the leaves. Cook the pork belly in boiling water for 15 minutes, drain and slice.

Line the base of a heavy flameproof casserole with half the sliced pork. Scatter the carrots over the pork, add the loose cabbage leaves and season with a little salt and pepper. Place the onion and bouquet garni, tied with string, over the cabbage, cover with the remaining sliced pork and pour in the stock. Bring to a boil over a medium heat, cover the casserole, and cook in a moderate oven (180°C/350°F) for 1½ hours. Discard the onion and bouquet garni and serve in the casserole. *Serves 6*

Note: For a smoky taste to the cabbage use 250 g (8 oz) smoked speck in place of the pickled pork; it is not necessary to boil the speck, it is better however to cut it into small strips and use it in layers between the cabbage. Bacon rashers may also be used in this recipe.

Spiced Red Cabbage

•

1 small red cabbage
60 g (2 oz) butter
1 cup water
2 whole cloves
2 cooking apples, peeled, cored and sliced
1 tablespoon sugar
white vinegar to taste

Remove the outer leaves of the cabbage, cut in half, remove the core and wash. Shred the cabbage finely. Put 30 g (1 oz) of the

butter and the water in a saucepan. Add the cabbage, cloves and apples, cover tightly and simmer slowly for 45 minutes. Add the remaining butter, the sugar and vinegar to taste, about 1–2 tablespoons. Simmer for another 5 minutes. Serve with duck, goose, pork or turkey. *Serves 4–6*

Red Cabbage Fiammingo

• •

The deep plum-coloured cabbage that comes to the markets is much prized by European cooks. A red cabbage responds well to slow braising with a touch of vinegar as in this Italian recipe. Serve with pork, goose, duckling or pot-roasted beef.

1 head red cabbage
60 g (2 oz) butter
salt
freshly ground pepper
1 tablespoon wine vinegar
1 cup stock or wine
3 tart apples, peeled, cored, and quartered
1 tablespoon brown sugar

Remove the core of the cabbage and shred. Melt the butter in a heavy flameproof casserole over a low heat. Add the shredded cabbage and season with a little salt and pepper. Cover the casserole, and simmer for 10 minutes, stirring occasionally. Add the vinegar, stock or wine, apples and brown sugar, lightly mix into the cabbage, cover and simmer for 3 hours. Check occasionally to make certain the stock has not evaporated and add a little more if necessary. Serve in the casserole or in a vegetable dish. *Serves 6*

Right: Colourful Zucchini and Tomato Medley (recipe page 220) includes green beans, onions and herbs and is almost a meal in itself.

Above: Tomatoes with Basil (page 229) are natural partners. Add Spanish onions and a light dressing for an easy salad.

Right: New Potatoes and asparagus make a salad that is the essence of spring (page 230). When asparagus is out of season use green beans instead.

Carrots with Brandy

••

Carrots take on an expensive air when finished off with a flame of brandy. Very young carrots should be left whole, larger carrots cut into slices or finger-length strips, larger and thicker than julienne.

1 kg (2 lb) young carrots
60 g (2 oz) butter
salt
freshly ground pepper
2 teaspoons sugar
2 tablespoons brandy
2 tablespoons chopped parsley

Scrub the carrots and leave whole if young. Slice or cut into thick julienne strips if large. Heat the butter in a heavy frying pan over a moderate heat and add the carrots. Season with salt, pepper and the sugar.

Cover the pan and cook them slowly for about 15 minutes or until tender, shaking the pan occasionally. Julienne strips will take only 7–10 minutes. Remove the cover, add the brandy, heat for a few seconds, ignite and shake the pan until the flames subside. Turn the carrots out into a hot vegetable dish and sprinkle with the parsley. *Serves 6*

Carrots à la Crème

••

Prepare in the same manner and with the same ingredients as Carrots in Brandy, omitting the brandy. When the carrots are tender, remove the pan from the heat and add ¾ cup cream mixed with 1 lightly beaten egg yolk. Return the pan to a very low heat and shake pan gently until the cream is slightly thickened. *Serves 6*

Vichy Carrots

••

Scrape 500 g (1 lb) young carrots and cut into thick slices. Place in a heavy saucepan with ½ cup water, 15 g (½ oz) butter and 2 teaspoons sugar. Cover the pan and cook for about 5 minutes until carrots are tender. Remove lid, add a pinch of salt and continue cooking until liquid has evaporated, leaving a syrupy glaze on the carrots. Serve sprinkled generously with chopped parsley. *Serves 4*

Carrots Flamande

••

Prepare Vichy carrots but add 1 cup young peas (frozen peas will do nicely) and ½ cup stock. Cook, covered, over a gentle heat for about 10 minutes or until the peas are tender. Add a sprig of mint for the last few minutes of cooking. Remove the mint, season with a little pepper and serve. *Serves 4*

Cauliflower with Almonds

••

1 cauliflower
30 g (1 oz) butter
¼ cup whole almonds, blanched
and shredded
1 cup fresh white breadcrumbs
1 clove garlic, crushed

Cook cauliflower whole or in florets in 2 cups lightly salted water for about 10 minutes or until tender. Drain well and place on a warm serving dish, keep warm. Melt the butter in a frying pan and fry the almonds and breadcrumbs until golden brown, adding the garlic as the crumbs start to turn colour, stir constantly. Sprinkle over the cauliflower and serve. *Serves 4–6*

Mexican-style Cauliflower

•

1 medium head of cauliflower
3 tomatoes, peeled, seeded and chopped
2 tablespoons chopped parsley
⅛ teaspoon cloves
¼ teaspoon cinnamon
1 tablespoon capers
2 tablespoons chopped olives
3 tablespoons grated cheese
2 tablespoons fine breadcrumbs
1 tablespoon olive or salad oil

Trim the cauliflower and divide into florets. Cook the florets, covered, in a small amount of boiling salted water until barely tender. Drain. Mix the tomatoes, parsley, cloves, cinnamon, capers and olives and heat gently to make a sauce. Pour a little of the sauce into an ovenproof serving dish, add the cauliflower and cover with the remaining sauce. Sprinkle with the cheese, breadcrumbs and oil and bake until brown in a hot oven (220°C/425°F), about 20 minutes. *Serves 6*

Left: Corkscrew shaped pasta, known as fusilli, add interest to Pasta e Fagioli (page 240), which also contrains beans, cheese and vegetables.

Corn Cobs with Mixed Vegetables in Coconut Milk

••

This colourful and very delicious vegetable dish is of Indian origin. Cut the vegetables into large chunks or thick slices and be careful not to overcook them – the crisper they are, the better. The fresh coriander and coconut milk added to the dish create a subtle aromatic flavour.

3–4 corn cobs
1 kg (2 lb) mixed vegetables (French beans, potatoes, butternut pumpkin (optional), sweet potato, carrots, cucumber, cauliflower)
½ bunch spinach
small bunch fresh coriander
2.5 cm (1 inch) piece fresh green ginger
2 green chillies
2 tablespoons oil
2 teaspoons salt
1–1½ cups Coconut Milk

Remove the outside leaves and as much of the silk as possible from the corn and cut each cob into three pieces. Peel and cut all the vegetables into large chunks or cubes. Remove the white stalks and chop the spinach and coriander. Wash them both and set aside. Place the other vegetables in a colander and wash well. Peel and grate the ginger and seed and chop the chillies.

Heat the oil in a large heavy saucepan. Add the ginger and chillies and stir in the corn pieces. Scatter over half the chopped spinach and coriander, spoon in all the vegetables and scatter over the remaining spinach and coriander.

Add salt to the Coconut Milk and pour half over the vegetables. Cover with a tight-fitting lid and simmer very gently for 10–15 minutes or until vegetables are cooked but still crisp. Remove the lid and add the remaining milk. Serve immediately. Garnish with fresh coriander, if liked. *Serves 4–6*

Coconut Milk

•

1 teaspoon ground coriander
½ teaspoon ground cumin
1½ cups desiccated coconut
1½ cups milk

Heat the milk with the coriander and cumin, add the coconut and bring slowly to the boil. Allow to cool slightly. Put into blender at high speed for 2–3 minutes.

Pour into a sieve over a bowl and knead the coconut well to extract all the milk. This is the first extract or thick milk which is used in the above recipe. Repeat process with same coconut and 1½ cups fresh milk; this will give a thinner milk, which will still have good flavour and can be used in curries or served as a flavoured milk.

Dolmades with Lemon Sauce

••

This version of a popular Mediterranean dish has been praised by friends who ought to know. Minced lamb is easy if you are a lucky owner of one of the new food processors, otherwise give your butcher plenty of notice and he'll mince it for you. I make the same dish using minced beef and cabbage leaves.

500 g (1 lb) lean minced lamb
1 onion, peeled and finely chopped
1 clove garlic, peeled and finely chopped
¼ teaspoon ground nutmeg
¼ teaspoon cinnamon
½ cup raw rice
1 tablespoon olive oil
salt
freshly ground pepper
1 tablespoon chopped mint
2 tablespoons chopped parsley
12–18 grapevine leaves
2 cups stock or water and stock cubes
1 tablespoon tomato paste

Sauce

2 eggs, separated
juice of 2 lemons
1 cup cooking liquid from dolmades

Place the meat in a large bowl. Add the onion, garlic, nutmeg, cinnamon, rice and oil to the meat. Season with salt and pepper, add the mint and parsley and lightly mix with a fork until well combined.

Rinse the canned or packet grapevine leaves thoroughly in warm water and place on a flat surface, shiny side down. Place a spoon of meat mixture on each leaf and roll up, folding in the ends to seal in the filling and form a parcel shape. Arrange folded side down in a flameproof casserole.

Heat the stock with the tomato paste and pour over the dolmades. Simmer, covered, for 45 minutes or until cooked through. Carefully drain the dolmades, place on a heated serving plate and keep warm.

To make the sauce: Beat the egg whites until stiff and combine with the egg yolks. Add the lemon juice and stir into the reserved cooking liquid. Reheat *without* allowing the sauce to boil. Spoon the sauce over the dolmades and serve at once. *Serves 6*

Variations

Yogurt Sauce If liked, replace the egg-lemon sauce with a simple yogurt sauce. In a bowl, combine 1 cup natural yogurt, 1 crushed clove garlic and ½ teaspoon salt. Beat the sauce thoroughly. Serve in a sauceboat with dolmades made from grapevine leaves or cabbage.

Cabbage Rolls Make as for dolmades but substitute 12 cabbage leaves for the vine leaves and minced beef for the lamb. Blanch the cabbage leaves in boiling salted water for 7 minutes (it is best to do this in 2 batches), drain and cut out the thick centre. Very large leaves can be cut in half. Fill with prepared stuffing and simmer gently for 1 hour.

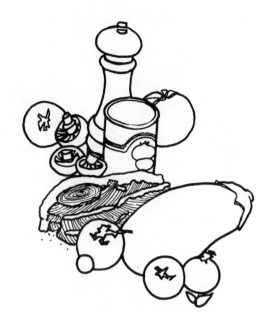

Baked Tomato Stuffed Eggplant

••

When baby eggplants come to the market, it is a nice idea to cook them whole or dressed up in a special way. This recipe shows off to good advantage the appealing shape of the tiny vegetable, a secondary consideration perhaps to taste, which goes without saying. Serve as a first course, entrée or as a separate vegetable dish. Good, too, with barbecued meat.

8 small eggplants
1 tablespoon salt
2 large onions
3 cloves garlic
3 tablespoons olive oil
salt
freshly ground pepper
6 small tomatoes
¼ cup olive oil
¼ cup chopped parsley or basil

Starting just below the stem, carefully insert a sharp knife and make three lengthwise cuts in each eggplant, leaving the slices attached to the stem. Lightly salt the layers and leave to degorge on a plate for 1 to 2 hours. Before using, rinse out the excess salt and liquid.

Slice the onions thinly and crush the garlic with a large pinch of salt. Lightly oil a shallow baking dish with the 3 tablespoons oil. Scatter the onion and garlic over the bottom of the dish and season with salt and freshly ground pepper. Cut the tomatoes into 4 slices each and put 1 slice in each cut of the eggplant. Carefully arrange over the onions in the dish, spreading the slices slightly apart, and pour over the olive oil. Sprinkle with the chopped parsley or basil. Cover and bake in a preheated moderately hot oven (190°C/375°F) for 1 hour or until they are soft. Cool the eggplants and serve at room temperature garnished with sprigs of Italian parsley or basil. *Serves 8*

Eggplant Parmigiana

•

Eggplants are available all year round now, and are relatively inexpensive. They team well with many meat dishes, or, as here, may play the main role themselves. Serve this dish as a first course, as an accompaniment to grills or roasts, or as a meal in itself with the addition of a salad and crusty bread.

⅓ cup olive oil or melted butter
½ teaspoon salt
freshly ground black pepper
2 cloves garlic, chopped
1 onion, thinly sliced
1 medium eggplant
3 medium tomatoes, sliced
grated Parmesan cheese
thin slices Mozzarella or mild Cheddar cheese

Heat a little of the oil in a heavy frying pan and season with salt, pepper and garlic. Add the onion and cook gently until soft. Remove the onion and add the remaining oil to the pan, heat.

Cut the eggplant into thick slices and fry until golden brown on both sides. Divide the onion slices over the slices of eggplant, then cover with a layer of sliced tomato. Season with salt and pepper and sprinkle generously with grated Parmesan cheese.

Top each piece with a thin slice of Mozzarella or mild Cheddar cheese. Arrange each eggplant slice in an ovenproof serving dish. Carefully slide each slice off an egg slicer so the layers do not topple over. Cook in a moderately hot oven (190°C/375°F) for 20 minutes, then serve from the dish at the table. *Serves 4*

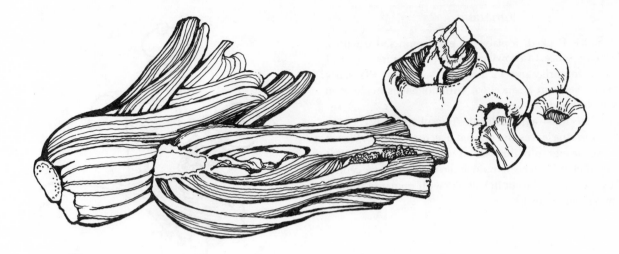

Braised Fennel

•

The lovely Florence fennel with its celery-like bulb has a refreshing aniseed flavour. It may be eaten raw in salads, as part of an antipasto tray with a vinaigrette dressing or as a cooked vegetable. Before using it remove and discard any tough outside leaves.

4 heads fennel
6 tablespoons olive oil
2–3 cloves garlic, crushed
½ cup stock or wine
salt
freshly ground pepper

Trim fennel and remove any tough outer leaves. If large cut into two or four pieces.

Heat the oil in a large heavy flameproof casserole, add the garlic and cook until it begins to colour. Add the fennel, stock or wine and season with salt and pepper. Cover and braise gently for about 30–40 minutes until it is very lightly browned and tender. Serve in the casserole or transfer to a vegetable dish. *Serves 6*

Fennel au Gratin

•

Prepare Braised Fennel as above. When cooked, arrange the fennel in an ovenproof serving dish. Melt 60 g (2 oz) of butter and combine with 1½ cups breadcrumbs and ½ cup grated Parmesan cheese, sprinkle over the fennel. Bake in a moderate oven (180°C/350° F) for about 20 minutes or until top is golden brown. *Serves 6*

Fennel Parmigiana

•

Prepare Braised Fennel as above and transfer to a flameproof serving dish when cooked.

Top with thin slices of Mozzarella or Gruyère cheese, sprinkle with ½ cup grated Parmesan cheese and place under a preheated grill for 2 or 3 minutes to brown the surface. *Serves 6*

Stuffed Marrow

••

Members of the marrow family have never been more popular than now – from the tiny, button-size squash through dark green zucchini to the large marrows big enough to take generous fillings. This is a meal in one dish, because it combines meat, rice and vegetables and is served with a flavourful tomato sauce. Buy a good quality minced meat.

1 large vegetable marrow
salt
1 cup raw rice
3 tablespoons oil
1 onion, finely chopped
125 g (4 oz) streaky bacon, diced
250 g (8 oz) minced beef
freshly ground black pepper
chopped parsley

Tomato Sauce

500 g (1 lb) tomatoes or 1 × 400 g can tomatoes
2 tablespoons oil
1 small onion, chopped
1 clove garlic, crushed
salt
freshly ground pepper
pinch sugar
60 g (2 oz) butter

Cut marrow in half horizontally and remove the seeds. Scoop out some of the flesh with a spoon, leaving a shell. Chop the flesh and reserve. Sprinkle the inside of the marrow with salt and turn upside down to drain.

Cook the rice in boiling salted water until just tender and drain. Heat the oil in a frying pan and cook the onion gently until it is soft. Add the bacon and fry for a few minutes, then add the beef and cook until brown, stirring often. Add the rice and the chopped marrow and cook for a further 10 minutes, stirring. Season well with salt and pepper.

Divide the mixture between each half of the marrow and cover the tops with greased aluminium foil. Place in a baking dish and bake in a moderate oven (180°C/350°F) for about 1 hour or until the marrow is soft.

Meanwhile make the Tomato Sauce: Peel and chop the tomatoes. Heat the oil and cook the onion and garlic gently until soft. Add the fresh tomatoes, or the drained canned tomatoes; season with salt, pepper and a pinch of sugar and cook gently for 10 minutes. Stir in the butter.

Remove the foil for the last 10 minutes of cooking so the tops can brown. Sprinkle with chopped parsley and serve with the Tomato Sauce, either poured over or served separately. *Serves 8* **Note:** This filling and sauce may also be used for other vegetables such as cabbage, pepper and eggplant. Only the final cooking time will vary.

Mushrooms

Avoid the Destroying Angel like the plague (what a name for poisonous mushrooms!) – not that anyone except those intrepid mycophiles who wish to find their own mushrooms in the woods need to be warned.
Today most of us are delighted to shop for pearly pink gilled mushroom caps or more flavoursome cocoa-brown gilled flats, assured that we are getting a remarkable flavour to enjoy alone or enhance other foods.
Mushrooms have always been highly prized as a vegetable, for their versatility and the wonderful flavour they add to rich savoury meats or light delicate chicken.
They team well with eggs – mushroom omelette is an all-time favourite. They can star on their own cooked in a delicate manner or in a robust Italian way with that aromatic herb, oregano.

To prepare mushrooms

Do not wash or peel mushrooms as the skin has a great deal of flavour. If they have specks of soil wipe them clean with a damp kitchen towel, first dipped in water with a squeeze of lemon juice. Trim the stalks. Store lightly covered in the refrigerator. They should keep at least a week.

Here is an outline of simple ways of cooking mushrooms which may add interest to many meals:

Sautéed Mushrooms Mushrooms absorb a lot of fat when cooking; when too much fat is used the mushrooms become soggy. To avoid this use only enough butter or oil, or a mixture of both, to cover the surface of the pan. Slice the mushrooms or cook whole and toss lightly in butter over a gentle heat about 2–3 minutes – no longer. Do not overcrowd the pan or they will steam. Season with salt and pepper. Chopped parsley or other herbs may be added just before serving. Serve with crisp toast, as a filling for omelettes or with grilled steak. Add to chicken gravy or a chicken or beef casserole.
Grilled Mushrooms Brush mushrooms with a little melted butter or oil and place under a gentle grill for about 5 minutes. Turn halfway through cooking.
To Flute Mushrooms Choose very white fresh mushrooms. Hold rounded side up and with a small, sharp, pointed knife make deep swirling cuts. The slivered peeling falls off and the petals are revealed (see below). Use in any recipes where the mushrooms remain uncut or as a garnish for main course dishes with mushrooms.

Mushrooms with Oregano

• •

Serve as an entrée, first course or as an accompaniment to grilled meat or poultry.

750 g (1½ lb) mushrooms
5 tablespoons oil
2 cloves garlic, crushed
2 tablespoons chopped oregano (or any desired fresh herb)
salt
freshly ground pepper
pinch nutmeg

Wipe over the mushrooms with a damp cloth and trim the stalks, then slice.

Heat the oil in a large frying pan over a fairly high heat and quickly brown the mushrooms, a few at a time. As they brown remove them to a plate and add more fresh ones. When all the mushrooms are browned return to the pan, reduce the heat and add the garlic and oregano, season with salt and pepper and a pinch of freshly grated nutmeg. Cook slowly for about 2 minutes longer, stirring occasionally. Spoon into a heated serving dish.

This may be served with hot buttered toast as a light luncheon dish. *Serves 6*

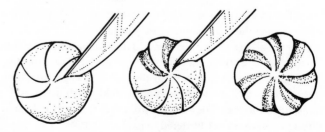

Mushrooms Bordelaise

••

This is a classical way to enjoy mushrooms in their own right.

500 g (1 lb) mushrooms, sliced
60 g (2 oz) butter
8–10 spring onions, chopped
salt
freshly ground pepper
juice of 1 lemon
4 tablespoons chopped parsley

Heat the butter in a very large frying pan over medium heat until almost golden and sauté the mushrooms for about 4 minutes, or until they are lightly browned. Do not crowd them in the pan as they will steam rather than sauté. Cook only a few at a time, remove them with a slotted spoon when they are browned, and add fresh ones to the pan – or use two pans with slightly more butter. When they are all browned, return them all to the pan, add the spring onions and cook for 2 minutes longer, shaking the pan briskly to toss the mushrooms.

Season the mushrooms with salt and pepper, turn them out on to a hot serving dish, squeeze the lemon juice over and sprinkle with the chopped parsley. *Serves 4*

Variation

Mushrooms with fresh herbs Prepare Mushrooms Bordelaise adding 2 tablespoons chopped mixed fresh herbs such as basil, oregano, savory, marjoram and 2 tablespoons chopped parsley instead of the 4 tablespoons parsley. The herbs should be mixed through the mushrooms just before serving. If liked ½ cup of cream can be added; heat through for a minute or two.

Mushrooms Neapolitan

••

500 g (1 lb) button mushrooms
1 clove garlic
salt
3 tablespoons olive oil
3 ripe tomatoes, peeled, seeded and roughly chopped
freshly ground pepper
1 tablespoon chopped parsley

Wipe the mushrooms with a damp paper towel and trim the stalks. Crush the garlic with a pinch of salt.

Heat the oil in a frying pan and add the mushrooms, cap side down. Sauté until golden brown for about 2–3 minutes, turning once. Add the garlic to the pan and cook for a few seconds then add the tomatoes and sprinkle with the parsley. Cook until the mushrooms are tender and the dish is heated through. Serve on hot buttered toast. *Serves 3–4*

Onions au Gratin

•

500 g (1 lb) small whole white onions, or
3 large onions, sliced
2 tablespoons butter
1 tablespoon flour
1 cup milk
salt
freshly ground black pepper
¼ cup chopped parsley or capsicum (optional)
1 cup coarse breadcrumbs
½ cup grated Cheddar cheese

Peel the onions and cook them in a little lightly salted boiling water until just tender. Drain.

Melt 1 tablespoon of the butter in a saucepan, add the flour and blend with a wire whisk. Add the milk to the mixture, while stirring vigorously with the whisk. Stir until boiling, add salt, pepper and parsley, or capsicum, if using.

Add the onions to the sauce and turn the mixture into a casserole. Melt the remaining butter and lightly toss the breadcrumbs until buttered, sprinkle over the onions with the cheese.

Brown under a preheated grill. If the dish has been prepared ahead, bake uncovered in a preheated moderately hot oven (190°C/375°F) until heated through and brown on top. *Serves 4*

Variation

Vegetables au Gratin Substitute any cooked vegetable such as peas, spinach, or celery or a mixture of vegetables for part of the onion.

Onions Stewed in Wine

•

8 large onions, peeled
1 tablespoon olive oil
½ cup red or white wine or vermouth
water
salt
freshly ground pepper

Put the oil in a flameproof casserole into which the onions will fit neatly in one layer. Place over a moderate heat and add the onions. When the oil begins to sizzle, pour in the wine and let it boil briskly for a few minutes. Add water to come halfway up the onions. Transfer to a slow oven (150°C/300°F) and cook uncovered for about 1½ hours. Return to the top of the stove and cook over a high heat for 2–3 minutes until sauce is thick and syrupy. Season to taste with salt and pepper. Serve as a separate vegetable or with a roast. *Serves 8*

Grilled Onions

•

Select flat white or, if possible, the mild purple onions no more than 2.5 cm (1 inch) thick but as large as possible. Skin and slice in two across the onion, *not* from stem to base. If very large onions are used cut in 3 or 4 thick slices. Place cut side down on a grilling pan lined with foil, dot with a little butter or oil, then place under a preheated grill and cook for 5–6 minutes. Turn and cook for another 5–6 minutes. Serve with a dot of butter, pepper and salt.

Peas and Cucumber with Dill

•

1.5 kg (1½ lb) fresh peas or 1 packet frozen peas
1 cucumber
½ cup sour cream
2 tablespoons snipped dill or 1 tablespoon dried dill

Cook the shelled peas in boiling salted water until barely tender. Drain.

Peel, seed and dice the cucumber. Cook the cucumber quickly in boiling water for about 2 minutes, taking care not to overcook it, the vegetable should remain crisp.

Just before serving, combine the cooked peas and cucumber with sour cream and dill in the top of a double boiler. Heat slowly over hot water until the vegetables are warm. *Serves 4*

Fresh Peas French Style

• •

2 cups shelled peas (about 1 kg/2 lb in the shell)
6 tiny white onions, peeled, or 2 onions, quartered
5–6 lettuce leaves, shredded
3 sprigs parsley, tied together
½ teaspoon salt
pinch of sugar
2 tablespoons butter
¼ cup stock or water
1 teaspoon flour

In a saucepan combine the peas, onions, lettuce, parsley, salt, sugar and 1 tablespoon of the butter. Mix together and add the stock. Cover closely and cook over medium heat until almost all of the moisture has evaporated, about 20 minutes.

Cream the remaining butter and flour together. Add the flour mixture to the liquid in the pan and shake the pan in a circular movement to mix it in, as stirring with a utensil breaks the peas. When the liquid has thickened and returned to the boil, remove the pan from the heat. Remove the parsley and serve. *Serves 6*

Mousse of Green Peas

••

750 g (1½ lb) peas, fresh or frozen
salt
½ cup hot milk
½ cup dried breadcrumbs
¾ cup chicken stock
60 g (2 oz) butter
2 egg yolks
freshly ground pepper

Shell and cook the peas in boiling salted water until tender, about 5–6 minutes. Drain well, shaking to remove as much moisture as possible. Combine the milk and breadcrumbs, set aside until ready to use. Push peas through a sieve or purée in a blender, or food processor fitted with the double edged steel blade, adding the stock to make blending easier. Add milk mixture to peas, beating with a wooden spoon. Soften the butter and add to the pea mixture with the egg yolks and salt and pepper to taste. Pour mixture into a greased 3 cup ring tin or mould.

Place in a dish of water and bake in a moderate oven (180°C/350°F) for 1 hour or until firm to the touch. Turn out on to a serving plate and fill the centre with julienne strips, prepared as below. *Serves 4–6*

Julienne strips Use half a bunch of celery and 2 large carrots. Cut into about 6 cm (2½ inch) lengths, then into fine matchstick strips. Melt 30 g (1 oz) of butter in a saucepan, add ½ cup stock and the vegetables and cook covered for about 5 minutes, tossing every 2 minutes.

Frozen Peas

Frozen peas are the great standby green vegetable for many of us, and are an excellent product, but they can give your meals an air of 'prepared in a hurry' if you always serve them just boiled. Vary them with a few quick tricks.

French Peas

Drop 2 cups of frozen peas into boiling salted water, bring to the boil and drain. Wash and finely shred half a small lettuce or outside leaves of lettuce, and chop 1 small onion. Melt 60 g (2 oz) butter in a saucepan and cook the onion gently until tender. Add the peas and stir in the lettuce and 1 teaspoon tarragon. Cover, cook until just tender, about 5 minutes. Season with salt and pepper. *Serves 6*

Oriental Peas

Heat 2 tablespoons oil in a saucepan, add a 2.5 cm (1 inch) piece of fresh ginger peeled and very thinly sliced and 3 spring onions chopped. Sauté for 30 seconds then add 2 cups frozen peas, tossing constantly for 1 minute. Add 1 cup water and 1 crumbled stock cube.

Bring to the boil, reduce heat then simmer, covered, for 8 minutes or until the peas are tender. Season with salt and pepper. *Serves 6*

Peas with Bacon, Onion and Cream

In a saucepan fry two or three slices of rinded bacon until crisp. Remove and break into small pieces. Sauté 1 chopped onion in the bacon fat in the pan. Add 2 cups cooked peas and ½ cup of water and cook, covered, for 5 minutes. Add ½ cup of cream. Return the bacon to the pan, season and cook gently for a few minutes until the cream thickens slightly. Serve very hot. *Serves 6*

Epicurean Peas

Put 2 cups frozen peas with just 2 tablespoons of water and 1 tablespoon of butter in a heavy pan, packed below and above with shredded lettuce (outside leaves will do) and flavoured with crushed garlic, 1 small chopped onion and a little rosemary. Cover and cook gently for 10–15 minutes. *Serves 6*

Herbed New Potatoes with Fresh Peas

•

In Scandinavia summer is heralded with tiny pearly new potatoes – they are eagerly awaited and treated almost with reverence. I feel the same way about the new season's mint or basil and fresh garden peas – so why not combine them and have one superlative vegetable dish.

750 g (1½ lb) new potatoes
1¼ teaspoons salt
1 cup shelled peas
2 tablespoons shredded mint or basil
freshly ground pepper
30 g (1 oz) butter
¼ cup cream
fresh parsley

Scrape the potatoes and cook, covered, in boiling salted water until tender, about 20 minutes. Ten minutes before the potatoes are completely cooked, add the peas. When the peas are cooked remove from the heat and drain if necessary. Add the mint or basil, pepper, butter and cream and heat for a few seconds. Turn into a serving dish and garnish with fresh parsley. Serve immediately. *Serves 6*

Right: Richly flavoured Saffron Pilau (page 247) can be served hot or cold, piled into a dish or heaped in tomato cases.

Lamb Biriani (page 176) is a festive rice dish; spiced lamb and rice are topped with nuts, sultanas and edible gold leaf.

Potatoes Colombia

••

Red and green peppers have outstanding nutritional value, but as green pepper ripens to a deep, glowing red it gives a bonus – it becomes doubly rich in vitamin C. Red peppers are sweeter and milder than green, and combine well with other vegetables. I am sure you will find this dish good to eat and so bright and colourful it can't help lifting your spirits on a cold day.

60 g (2 oz) butter
1 kg (2 lb) potatoes, peeled and sliced
salt
freshly ground black pepper
2 red peppers (prepared as directed)
3 tablespoons oil
2 tablespoons chopped parsley

Heat the butter in a large frying pan over medium heat until almost golden, add the sliced potatoes and season with salt and pepper. Cover the pan and cook for about 15 minutes, or until the potatoes are tender. Toss them frequently with a spatula, so they will partially brown.

Meanwhile, prepare the peppers as described below then slice. Heat the oil in another frying pan and sauté the peppers gently for about 5 minutes or until tender. Remove from heat and keep warm. When the potatoes are tender, add the peppers to the potatoes and toss lightly. Transfer to a hot serving dish and sprinkle with parsley. *Serves 6*

To Prepare Peppers: Before cooking, peppers are better skinned. The simplest way to do this is to hold them by a long fork over a gas flame until they are charred and black on the outside, or char halved peppers, skin side up, under a hot grill. Rinse under cold water, then scrape the charred skin away with a knife. The core end should then be cut out and the pith and seeds removed. This sounds a little tedious, but is well worth the time spent – and red peppers skin more easily than green. **Note:** Canned red pimiento may be used to replace red peppers – use 3 whole pimientos.

Creamy Mashed Potatoes

•

Overcooking potatoes or cutting them too small makes them water-soaked and they lose flavour. They should break under pressure of a fork, but not be too mushy. Adding cold milk to potato makes it sticky so always add hot milk for fluffy mashed potato.

6 medium potatoes
salt
freshly ground pepper
½–1 cup milk
30 g (1 oz) butter

Peel the potatoes and put into a saucepan with cold, lightly salted water to cover. Cook, covered, until the potatoes are easily pierced with a fork, about 20–30 minutes. Drain thoroughly, then shake pan over a low heat for a few minutes until all surplus moisture has evaporated and the potatoes are quite dry. Mash with a potato masher or put through a potato ricer.

Beat the potatoes with a wooden spoon until very smooth. Scald the milk. Add the butter to the potatoes, then gradually beat in the hot milk until the potatoes are light and fluffy. Season to taste with salt and pepper.

To keep mashed potato hot without spoiling: Cook potatoes as described above, then mash and press down well in the saucepan with the potato masher. Pack tightly, levelling the top. Add the butter and spoon about 4 tablespoons hot milk over. Cover with well-fitting lid and leave in a warm place. Before serving beat well, adding more hot milk if necessary. The potatoes will keep for up to 20 minutes. *Serves 4–6*

Variations

Cheesed potatoes Spread mashed potatoes in a buttered flame or ovenproof dish. Sprinkle the top generously with grated cheese such as Parmesan, Gruyère or Cheddar and brush with melted butter. Or spread with cream to which the grated cheese has been added. Place under a hot grill or in a hot oven until the cheese has melted.

With chives or spring onions Snip chives or chop spring onions and fold through potatoes just before serving.

Egg Gratin

Grease four individual ramekins. Fill with hot buttered mashed potatoes and make a depression in each one. Drop an egg into each depression, spoon over a little cream or cream and grated cheese. Bake in a preheated moderately hot oven (190°C/375°F) until the eggs are just set.

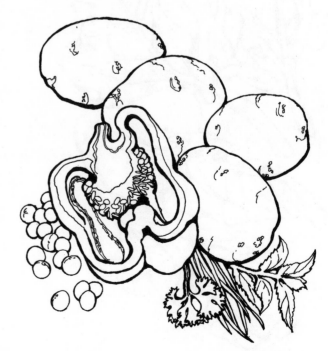

Spinach and Silverbeet

Spinach has the virtue of being a very agreeable accompaniment to a wide variety of meat, poultry, chicken and egg dishes. Silverbeet with its intense green leaves and robust flavour and its more delicate counterpart true spinach should be lightly cooked. The flavour of these vegetables is at its best when steamed for a short while in the water that clings to the leaves after washing.

To prepare and cook

The well washed leaves should be trimmed of the thick whiter stalks and excess water shaken off. Roughly chop the leaves before cooking. Put the spinach in a large enamel or stainless steel pot and cook, covered, for 3–4 minutes over a low heat.

Never cook spinach in aluminium as it induces a chemical reaction that brings out a bitter flavour.

It should be stirred frequently or the pot given a good shake until steam is formed. Cook for only 3–4 minutes. Remove to a colander, squeeze off excess water and chop finely. This can be done in a food processor fitted with the double edged steel blade.

Return the spinach to the pan and heat through with a little butter. A fresh grating of nutmeg and, if liked, a squeeze of lemon juice, is a simple way of enjoying this vegetable. For variations try the two following recipes.

Look, too, for the Italian spinach sometimes available at Italian greengrocers.

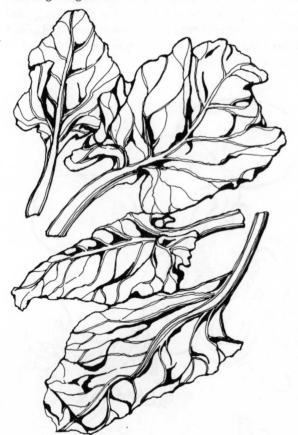

Spinach with Anchovies

•

1 kg (2 lb) spinach or silverbeet
1 clove garlic, peeled and halved
60 g (2 oz) butter
salt
freshly ground pepper
4 anchovy fillets, chopped
pinch grated nutmeg

Wash spinach well, remove the stalks and put into a saucepan. The water clinging to the leaves is enough to cook the spinach. Cook over low heat for about 3–4 minutes or until softened. Turn into a colander and press out as much water as possible.

Melt the butter in a small saucepan with the anchovy fillets and garlic over a very low heat. Add the spinach, a little salt, a grinding of pepper and the nutmeg. Remove the garlic and serve. *Serves 4*

Viennese Spinach

•

1 kg (2 lb) spinach or silverbeet
½ cup light sour cream
1 tablespoon butter
1 teaspoon grated onion
2 teaspoons flour
salt
freshly ground pepper

Wash and trim the spinach and cook, covered, until just tender – about 3–4 minutes. Drain thoroughly and chop.

Melt the butter and blend in the flour. Add the sour cream and onion and cook, stirring constantly, until the mixture thickens. Add the spinach to the mixture and heat gently. Season with salt and pepper to taste. *Serves 4*

Danish Spinach Ring

• •

This is a lovely dish for special occasions. It may be made ahead ready to be baked, it always looks good when turned out – just the thing for a dinner party.

1 kg (2 lb) spinach
¼ cup cream or milk
4 eggs, beaten
pinch nutmeg
½ teaspoon sugar
½ teaspoon salt

Wash and trim the spinach well and place in a deep saucepan. Cover and cook without additional water until tender, about 2 minutes. Remove to a bowl and chop, or process in a food processor fitted with the double edged steel blade. Return to the pan. Add the cream or milk and heat to simmering, do not boil. Stir a little of the spinach into the eggs, then return this mixture to the pan. Add the sugar, nutmeg and salt.

Turn into a greased ring mould and cover with buttered paper. Place on a rack in a saucepan and add a little boiling water to the saucepan. Cover the pan and steam for about 30 minutes, or set in a pan of boiling water and bake in a moderate oven (180°C/350°F) until set, about 30 minutes. The ring is cooked when a knife inserted in the centre comes out clean. *Serves 4–6*

Brandied Sweet Potatoes

•

A vegetable dish for those who don't have to watch their waistline. Good with turkey, baked ham or roast veal.

6 medium sweet potatoes
½ cup brown sugar, firmly packed
½ cup water
60 g (2 oz) butter
¼ cup raisins
¼ cup brandy

Wash the sweet potatoes but do not peel. Cook in boiling water to cover until barely soft, about 15 minutes. Drain, cool and peel. Slice into a greased casserole or ovenproof dish.

Bring the brown sugar, water, butter and raisins to the boil. Add the brandy and pour the mixture over the potatoes. Bake, uncovered, in a moderate oven (180°C/350°F) for 30 minutes, basting several times with the syrup in the casserole. *Serves 6*

Orange Sweet Potato Casserole

•

Something special for that Christmas turkey or baked ham.

1 kg (2 lb) sweet potatoes (about 6 medium)
125 g (4 oz) butter, melted
4 tablespoons brown sugar
2 tablespoons dark rum
½ teaspoon salt
2 oranges
2 tablespoons chopped walnuts

Wash the sweet potatoes, cut into chunks and cook in boiling water to cover for about 20 minutes. Drain, cool and peel. Whip the sweet potatoes, 60 g (2 oz) of the butter, 2 tablespoons of the sugar, the rum and salt together.

Peel two or three thin strips of rind from one of the oranges and cut into fine julienne strips. Peel all the oranges, removing the white membrane. Segment the oranges by cutting in between each and every membrane; remove the seeds. Fold the orange segments into the sweet potato mixture. Turn into a greased casserole dish. Combine the remaining butter with the sugar, julienne orange rind and walnuts. Sprinkle over the top and bake covered in a moderately hot oven (190°C/375°F) for 30 minutes. Uncover for the last 10 minutes. *Serves 6*

Glazed Butternut Squash

•

1 kg (2 lb) butternut squash
½ cup brown sugar, firmly packed
½ teaspoon cinnamon
¼ teaspoon grated nutmeg or ground ginger
¼ teaspoon salt
60 g (2 oz) butter, melted

Peel, seed and slice the squash. Put sufficient water in a saucepan to cover the bottom. Place a rack in and put the squash on the rack. Cover with a tight-fitting lid, bring to the boil and steam for 12–15 minutes or until the squash is nearly tender. Drain the squash well.

Arrange the squash in one or two layers in a greased shallow baking dish. Mix the sugar, cinnamon, nutmeg or ginger and salt together and sprinkle over the squash. Drizzle with the melted butter. Bake in a preheated hot oven (200°C/400°F) until the squash is tender and slightly glazed, about 15–20 minutes. For a deeper glaze, put under the grill for a few minutes. *Serves 4–6*

Baked Butternut Squash with Bacon

•

2 small butternut squash
90 g (3 oz) butter
salt
freshly ground pepper
3 bacon rashers
6 teaspoons brown sugar

Cut each squash into three wedges and spoon out the fibre and seeds. Arrange the squash, cut side up, on a baking sheet. Drop a little butter into the cavity of each and season with salt and pepper to taste. Bake in a moderate oven (180°C/350°F) for 30 minutes.

Cut the bacon into strips and add to each piece of squash with 1 teaspoon of brown sugar. Return to the oven for a further 15 minutes. *Serves 6*

Stuffed Butternut Squash

••

2 medium butternut squash
1 cup broken noodles
500 g (1 lb) good minced meat
1½ tablespoons flour
½ cup water
3 tablespoons brown sugar
¼ teaspoon dry mustard
salt
freshly ground pepper

Cut the squash in halves lengthwise and remove the seeds and fibres. Place, cut side down, in a baking dish, add water to cover the bottom of the dish and bake in a moderately hot oven (190°C/375°F) for 30 minutes or until tender.

Meanwhile, cook the noodles in boiling salted water until tender then drain. Brown the minced meat in a saucepan and pour off excess fat. Mix the flour with the meat, add the water and bring to the boil. Add the noodles.

Mix the sugar and mustard with salt and pepper to taste. Brush the cut surfaces of the squash halves with fat from the frying and sprinkle with half the sugar mixture. Pile the noodle mixture into the squash and sprinkle with the remaining sugar mixture. Return to the oven and bake for 15 minutes. *Serves 4*

Tomatoes

Tomatoes are indispensable in a kitchen whether fresh, canned or in pastes. They are quickly made into a tasty soup with finely chopped spring onions and garlic, a little chicken stock and a handful of chopped herbs then served hot or cold (see page 88). A quick sauce is made in minutes for pasta, grilled meats or poultry and practically everyone has a favourite way of cooking them for breakfast, lunch or dinner.
Learn to peel a tomato, it makes a difference to many dishes. This is most simply done by pouring boiling water over them, count to 10, lift out and cool under a running tap. Cut out the little blossom and then peel off the skin. To seed a tomato (for sauce, soups), cut in two, squeeze out the seeds, flipping out any obstinate ones.

Tomatoes Provençale

•

A most versatile yet simple dish, adding a touch of colour and robust flavour to roast chicken or a mixed grill.
The amount of garlic used depends on personal liking for this pungent little bulb.

6 ripe tomatoes
1–2 cloves garlic, chopped
2 tablespoons chopped herbs (basil, parsley, thyme)
¾ cup fresh breadcrumbs (optional)
30 g (1 oz) butter
salt
freshly ground pepper

Cut off the top of each tomato and season generously with salt and pepper. Sprinkle each with a little of the garlic and herbs and top with breadcrumbs (if using). Put a generous dot of butter on top of each tomato. Arrange in a buttered gratin dish and bake in a moderate oven (180°C/350°F) for 10 minutes. Serve from the dish. *Serves 4*

Tomatoes au Gratin

•

4 ripe tomatoes
4 tablespoons oil
salt
freshly ground pepper
1 cup fresh breadcrumbs
¼ cup Parmesan cheese

Cut the tomatoes into thick slices and arrange them overlapping in a lightly oiled flameproof dish. Season generously with salt and pepper, sprinkle with the breadcrumbs, then the cheese, and finally the oil. Place the dish under a medium grill for 5–6 minutes, or until the tomatoes are tender and the surface is lightly browned. Serve from the dish. *Serves 4*

Tomatoes and Eggplant au Gratin

•

Prepare in the same manner as the preceding recipe, except before grilling, intersperse the overlapping slices of tomatoes in the dish with eight slices of eggplant, which have been dusted with flour and very quickly browned in a frying pan over a fairly high heat. *Serves 4*

Tomatoes Garni

●

This special way with tomatoes is often used as a garnish for dishes such as roast chicken, rack of lamb or roast fillet of beef.

Cut the tops from 6 medium sized tomatoes, scoop out the seeds using a teaspoon or grapefruit knife.

Sprinkle inside with salt and a pinch of sugar, invert the tomatoes and drain for 30 minutes. Pat the insides dry with paper towels, put a teaspoon of butter in each tomato and arrange on a buttered baking dish. Fill with buttered fresh peas. Bake in a preheated moderately hot oven (190°C/375°F) for 10 minutes, brushing the skins once or twice with butter. *Serves 6*

Tomatoes with Mixed Herbs

●

4 large ripe tomatoes
2 tablespoons butter
½ cup mixed chopped fresh herbs (parsley,
marjoram, oregano, basil, tarragon, etc.)
2 cups fresh breadcrumbs
salt
freshly ground pepper

Cut the tomatoes into thick slices. Heat 1 tablespoon of the butter in a large frying pan, over a fairly high heat, and very quickly sauté the tomato slices, a few at a time, for about 2 minutes on each side. Transfer them to a hot serving dish and keep warm until all of the tomatoes have been sautéed. Season the slices with salt and pepper and sprinkle with the chopped herbs. Fry the breadcrumbs for a few seconds in the remaining butter and spoon over the tomatoes. Serve hot, from the serving dish. *Serves 4–6*

Sicilian Stuffed Tomatoes

●

6 medium tomatoes
2 tablespoons olive oil
1 onion, chopped
4 anchovies, chopped
1 tablespoon capers, chopped
1 tablespoon chopped parsley
1 cup fresh breadcrumbs
1 tablespoon dry white wine
¼ teaspoon salt
freshly ground black pepper

Cut the tops from the tomatoes and scoop out the centres. Chop the centres and drain. Heat 1 tablespoon of the oil in a pan, add the onion and brown lightly. Add the tomato pulp, anchovies, capers, parsley, ¾ cup of the breadcrumbs, the wine, salt and pepper and mix. Fill the tomatoes with the stuffing. Mix the remaining crumbs with the remaining oil and spread over the top. Place in a greased baking dish and bake in a moderate oven (180°C/350°F) about 20 minutes. *Serves 6*

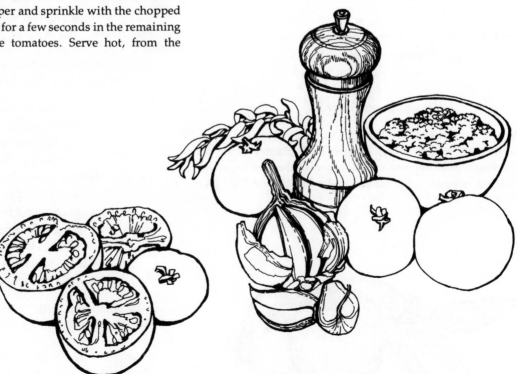

Turnips

Once you get a taste for turnips, either the pretty white ones with their purple tinged skin or the yellow swedes, it's easy to understand how these vegetables have featured in many classical dishes of haute cuisine as well as the provincial greats. Turnips are a particularly fine accompaniment to the more strongly flavoured poultry such as duck, goose and turkey – try them with boiled lamb, for the recipe see page 171.

Turnips in Butter

•

500 g (1 lb) turnips
salt
60 g (2 oz) butter
freshly ground pepper

Peel the turnips and cut into wedges, quarters or thick slices. Cook in boiling lightly salted water for about 10–15 minutes or until they are tender. Drain and cool. Heat the butter and brown the turnips, a few at a time. Do not crowd the pan. Season them with salt and pepper as they cook. Remove to a hot serving dish and keep warm while browning the remaining slices, adding more butter when necessary. *Serves 4*

Turnips in Sour Cream

•

4 white turnips
2 teaspoons caraway seeds
¼ cup light sour cream
paprika
lemon juice

Peel the turnips and dice. Cook the turnips in 1 cup of boiling salted water with the caraway seeds for 5 minutes. Drain off any water. Add the sour cream, return to the heat for a few minutes. Sprinkle with paprika and a little lemon juice and serve hot. *Serves 4*

Zucchini (Courgette)

These wonderful little vegetables of the marrow family have been enjoyed by the French and Italians for many years. I don't know why they took so long to be adopted by the rest of the world as a favourite vegetable.

To prepare and cook

Zucchini only need to be washed, both ends cut off, then cut into slices. They are frequently cooked in just a little lightly salted water, taking great care not to overcook. Zucchini are deceptive in that they soften considerably after being drained, so 3–4 minutes is often enough to tenderize them.
★ Zucchini may be cut into long strips, thin or thick slices, cut straight or on the bias to give an oval shape. Toss them in oil, or butter and oil mixed, and gently pan fry until tender but still crisp.
★ Raw zucchini are also delicious in salads.
★ Coarsely grated, or put through the julienne cutter in a food processor, they can be lightly steamed in a little butter. A spoonful of cream with a fresh grating of nutmeg gives them a mysterious flavour.
★ Zucchini and that other new member of the squash family, patty pan squash, are a busy cook's dream vegetable and a great standby for the smart hostess.

Zucchini and Tomato Medley

•

For those who enjoy vegetables lightly cooked with a natural fresh flavour, this is a dish that is good on its own, or may be served as an accompaniment to grilled chicken or meats. Topped with grated cheese, it is a meal in itself for a light lunch or supper.

1 large onion, sliced
1 clove garlic, crushed
2 tablespoons olive oil
large pinch of salt
freshly ground black pepper
¼ cup chopped parsley
1 teaspoon chopped fresh thyme or sage
500 g (1 lb) green beans
500 g (1 lb) zucchini
4 large tomatoes, quartered
¼ cup water

Sauté the onion and garlic in the oil in a heavy frying pan. Season with salt and freshly ground black pepper and add the herbs.
Cut the beans into lengths, and the zucchini into chunks. Add the beans, zucchini, tomatoes and water to the pan and simmer, covered, for 10 minutes or until just tender. *Serves 4*

Sautéed Zucchini

•

*The delicate flavour of this tender vegetable is enhanced
by quick cooking in olive oil.*

750 g (1½ lb) zucchini
3 tablespoons oil
salt
freshly ground pepper
1 tablespoon chopped parsley
1 tablespoon chopped oregano (optional)

Wash zucchini, do not peel. Trim off the ends and cut into thin
crosswise slices. Heat the oil in a large frying pan. Cook the
zucchini until the slices are translucent and the edges are
lightly browned, turning with a spatula to cook uniformly.
This should only take 3–4 minutes. Add more oil if needed.
Sprinkle with salt, pepper and the herbs. Serve with grilled
meats or poultry. *Serves 6*

Zucchini Omelette

••

*When a quick but simple meal is called for the
answer is often an omelette. Here is a variation of that
popular dish.*

3 tablespoons olive oil
3 small zucchini, washed and sliced
1 garlic clove, crushed
2 fresh tomatoes, peeled and chopped
4 eggs, beaten
2 tablespoons grated Parmesan cheese
½ teaspoon fresh oregano or pinch dried
salt
freshly ground pepper

Heat 2 tablespoons of the oil in a saucepan and sauté the
zucchini for a few minutes. Add the garlic and cook a few
seconds, then add the tomatoes. Cook, covered, for about 5
minutes.

In a heavy frying pan, heat the remaining oil and add the
beaten eggs. As the omelette begins to set lift the edges and
let the uncooked mixture run into the pan; keep lifting the
edges until the omelette is just setting. Spoon over the zucchini
mixture, top with cheese and sprinkle with the oregano.
Season with salt and pepper. Continue to cook over a gentle
heat until the omelette is just set.

Lift edges of set omelette up to make sure it will slip off the
pan. Slide on to a hot round serving plate.

Serve in wedges to 4 people for a light lunch or supper, or 2
people as a main dish. Good with crusty bread or hot toast.

Stuffed Zucchini

•

8 zucchini
1 cup grated cheese
salt
freshly ground pepper
2 tablespoons cream (optional)
2 tablespoons Parmesan cheese
2 tablespoons breadcrumbs
2 teaspoons butter

Wash the zucchini and trim off both ends. Drop into a little
boiling salted water and steam for 3–4 minutes. Refresh under
cold running water. Cut off a thin slice along each zucchini,
from top to tail. Scoop out the centre with a teaspoon and chop.

Combine the chopped zucchini and grated cheese with salt
and pepper to taste. Add cream to moisten, if liked. Fill the
zucchini shells with the cheese mixture, top with a mixture of
the Parmesan cheese and breadcrumbs, and dot with the
butter. Place under a hot grill until brown and heated through.
Serves 4

White Beans with Rosemary

••

A dish of beans is a welcome accompaniment to roast lamb or veal. Topped with Parmesan cheese, it makes a satisfying light luncheon.

2 cups dried haricot or cannelini beans
1 onion, stuck with 2 cloves
1 bay leaf
2 tablespoons oil
2 cloves garlic, bruised
1 small sprig rosemary or 1 teaspoon dried
1 × 500 g can tomatoes
salt
freshly ground pepper

Cover the dried beans with cold water, bring to the boil and cook for 3 minutes. Remove from the heat and let stand, tightly covered, for 1 hour. Drain. Then cook in fresh lightly salted water with the onion and bay leaf for about 1 hour or until tender. Drain.

Heat the oil in a large saucepan. Fry the garlic until brown, then discard. Add beans, rosemary and drained chopped tomatoes. Season with salt and freshly ground pepper and cook for 20 minutes or until sauce is thick. *Serves 6*

White Haricot Beans in Tomato Sauce

••

Dried haricot beans make a delicious entrée or simple meal or accompaniment to roast lamb. The time for cooking beans varies, largely depending on the age of the beans; they can take from 30 minutes to 2 hours. Never add the tomatoes until the beans are cooked as the acid in tomato will prevent softening of beans.

500 g (1 lb) dried white haricot beans
salt
freshly ground pepper
1 kg (2 lb) ripe tomatoes
1 small onion
1 celery stalk
6 parsley stalks
90 g (3 oz) speck or fatty bacon
30 g (1 oz) butter
2 tablespoons olive oil

Cover the dried beans with cold water, bring to the boil and cook for 3 minutes. Remove from the heat and let stand, tightly covered, for 1 hour. Drain, cover with fresh cold water, add a good pinch of salt and cook slowly for about 1 hour or until the beans are tender.

While the beans are cooking, peel, seed and chop the tomatoes. Finely chop the onion, celery stalk and parsley stalks. Chop the speck or bacon. Put the speck, butter and olive oil into a frying pan and cook until the fat runs from the speck. Add the onion, celery and parsley stalks and sauté until they begin to colour. Add the tomatoes, season with salt and pepper and cook briskly for 30 minutes. Drain the beans and add the tomato sauce. Lower the heat and continue to cook for about 20 minutes to allow the beans to absorb the flavour of the tomatoes.

Serve hot accompanied by a bowl of grated Parmesan cheese. *Serves 6*

Indian Spiced Lentils

(Dhal)

•

A purée of intriguingly spiced lentils accompanies many Indian meals; it is spooned over rice or meat balls, eaten with Chapatis and kebabs, and is nutritious as well as delicious. Don't wait for a curry to serve lentils; they give zest to grills and roasts Western style.

1 cup brown lentils
60 g (2 oz) butter
2 onions, finely chopped
1 clove garlic, crushed
2 teaspoons ground coriander
1 teaspoon finely chopped green ginger
½ teaspoon crushed red chilli pepper
½ teaspoon turmeric
2½ cups water

Pick over the lentils and rinse well. Melt the butter in a large saucepan, add the onions and cook until golden. Stir in the garlic, coriander, green ginger, crushed red chilli and turmeric. Cook over a gentle heat for 1 minute. Add the lentils and sauté for 5 minutes, shaking the pan at intervals. Add the water and bring to the boil over a moderately high heat. Reduce the heat and simmer the mixture, covered, for 45 minutes, or until the lentils are soft and most of the moisture has evaporated. Mash the lentils and season with salt. *Serves 4–6*

Sautéed Red Lentils

•

Red lentils team with other vegetables plus walnuts for an interesting texture contrast to make a dish many a vegetarian would consider a meal. Nutritionally, it makes a sound dish but most would consider it can stand on its own – just for the flavour!

1 cup red lentils
4 cups water
2 teaspoons salt
90 g (3 oz) butter
1 onion, finely chopped
½ green pepper, finely chopped
2 sticks celery, sliced
¼ cup chopped walnuts
salt
freshly ground pepper
2 tablespoons chopped parsley

Pick over the lentils and rinse in several lots of water. Place in a large saucepan with the water and salt. Bring to the boil over a moderately high heat, reduce heat, and simmer the lentils for 5 to 8 minutes, or until they are just tender. Drain the lentils in a sieve.

Melt half the butter in a saucepan, add the onion, green pepper and celery and cook over a gentle heat for about 5 minutes. Add lentils and walnuts, salt and freshly ground pepper to taste, and cook the mixture, stirring, for 3 minutes, or until the lentils are heated through. Stir in the remaining butter. Turn into a vegetable dish and top with chopped parsley. *Serves 4*

Lentils with Tomatoes

•

250 g (8 oz) lentils
2 onions, finely chopped
2 cloves garlic, finely chopped
2 tablespoons olive oil
3 tomatoes, peeled, seeded and sliced
1 tablespoon chopped fresh coriander or
1½ teaspoons dried coriander
salt
freshly ground pepper
extra fresh coriander to garnish

In a large saucepan cook the lentils in water to cover for about 1 hour or until they are almost tender, then drain. In a frying pan, sauté the onions and garlic in the oil until they are tender. Add the tomatoes. Stir in the coriander, salt and pepper. Cook the mixture long enough to make a light sauce. Add the sauce to the lentils and cook the mixture over a low heat for about 5 minutes. Top with additional coriander. Serve as an accompaniment to curried food, grilled meat or chicken. *Serves 4–6*

SALADS

from all things bright and beautiful

Salads have come a long way since they were simply edible greens and herbs dressed with salt. A decade ago, a hostess would glow with pride if complimented on her excellent dressing or fresh crisp greens . . . that is now all taken for granted. Today, interest is shown in innovative combinations and unusual and imaginative dressings. The search is on for a wide variety of greens; cos, mignonette, tiny corn or lambs tongue lettuce, watercress, escarole or curly endive, Belgian endive or witloof and fresh garden herbs all add interest and distinction to green salads.

There is hardly an edible food that cannot be made into a salad but it is worth using only the best; gently poached chicken breast, freshly cooked seafood, rare roast beef. Learn to use food in season, oranges feature in Mediterranean, Californian and Australian salads so much because of the orange groves providing cheap and plentiful supplies. Apples, potatoes, dried beans and pasta are all inexpensive and can boost the more luxurious asparagus, smoked salmon or ham. It's not the price that counts, quality is everything.

The oils used to make a salad should be in a good condition. Oil in a large bottle exposed to the air will soon become rancid. If you buy in quantity, transfer to smaller bottles. Look for walnut oil, a robust Spanish olive oil, or the gentler virgin (first pressing) olive oil, sesame oils for that Oriental touch, and for those watching their hearts, the polyunsaturated oils. Keep oil in a cool place – the refrigerator if necessary. Use a good vinegar, the herb vinegars of France are excellent. And encourage garden herbs, they grow well even in a window box.

Salads can provide that wonderful feeling of sunshine. It may be a simple salad of impeccably fresh washed and dried lettuce dressed with a good olive oil, a squeeze of lemon, salt and a grinding of pepper or it may be an elaborate seafood salad of pink, luscious and varied seafood. All salads should have that fresh, light and bouffant 'just made' look. The foods settle down if mixed too far ahead of serving.

Consider salad as a first course, and there are salads that are a meal in themselves. When including a salad as part of a meal make sure that it provides the right balance. A light salad for a rich or heavy meal, a rich, fuller salad for a light meal like poached or grilled fish or an omelette. A rich dish of pork or goose needs a tart salad.

Experiment with salads, use your imagination with dressings but don't go overboard. The dressing and the seasoning used should enhance not overpower the flavour of your salad.

For information on the basic dressings and care of salad greens see pages 46 and 33 then branch out into the exciting world of salad fantasia.

Green Salad with Chapons

•

French bread cut in thick slices, flavoured liberally with garlic, good olive oil and salt and pepper is tossed with a salad of mixed greens to add a distinct garlic flavour. Much better than merely smearing the serving bowl with garlic – the crunchy crusts let you mop up the good flavour of the dressing. The French call these garlicky breads chapons.

Wash, dry and chill a selection of salad greens – lettuce, curly endive, spinach, spring onions, parsley, watercress and green pepper. Tear into bite-size pieces and slice the green pepper into strips or squares. Crush 2 garlic cloves, put in a small bowl with a few tablespoons of olive oil and a grinding of black pepper. Mix well. Brush the garlic oil on slices of French bread. Add to bowl with salad greens and just before serving toss with a little Vinaigrette, see page 46.

Green Salad with Cream Dressing

•

Before the general use of salad oils and fancy vinegars (and I can remember those days in a small country town), people still made excellent salads from the simple farm foods they had on hand. Like this country salad with class.

1 lettuce
3 hard-boiled eggs
8–10 spring onions
3 slices bread
45 g (1½ oz) butter
salt
freshly ground pepper
paprika

Dressing

½ cup light sour cream
1 tablespoon cider vinegar
1 teaspoon sugar

Rinse and pat dry the leaves from 1 head of lettuce like cos or 2 heads mignonette. Tear into bite-size pieces, leaving the tiny centre leaves whole.

Roughly chop 2 of the hard-boiled eggs. Trim the spring onions, remove outer leaves and cut into shreds, about 8 cm (3 inch) long. Trim crusts from bread, cut into cubes and fry in butter to make crisp, golden croûtons.

In a salad bowl, combine the lettuce, chopped eggs, spring onions and croûtons. Season to taste with salt and pepper. Make the Dressing by combining the sour cream, vinegar and sugar in a small bowl. Toss the salad in the dressing. Top with slices of hard-boiled egg and sprinkle with a little paprika. *Serves 4*

Chicken Salad Chinoise

••

Lightly poached chicken breasts are folded through an oriental inspired mayonnaise. This makes a perfect light luncheon for 4 or serve as a first course for 6.

4 half-breasts of chicken
½ cup canned water chestnuts
2 celery stalks, diced
½ teaspoon salt
freshly ground black pepper
2 teaspoons vinegar
2 tablespoons oil
¾ cup Mayonnaise (page 45)
2 teaspoons soy sauce
1 lettuce
6–8 green olives

Poach chicken breasts in salted water to cover for about 6–8 minutes. Remove the flesh from the bones and shred into small finger lengths.

Drain the water chestnuts and slice. Combine chicken with water chestnuts, celery, salt and pepper. Beat the vinegar and oil together until slightly thickened and use to moisten the chicken mixture, chill in the refrigerator. Flavour the mayonnaise with soy sauce and fold through the chicken mixture. Pile into crisp lettuce cups and garnish with the olives. *Serves 4–6*

Curate's Salad

••

Who the curate was and why this salad was named after him is pure conjecture. Perhaps a European version of tea and cakes when the curate called unexpectedly.

2 heads Belgian endive or 1 lettuce
6 slices of French bread
1 clove garlic, halved
125 g (4 oz) sliced Gruyère or Swiss cheese
60 g (2 oz) Gorgonzola or other blue cheese
8 radishes, sliced
½ cup Vinaigrette (page 46)

Separate the endive or lettuce, wash, dry, wrap in a tea-towel and place in the refrigerator to crisp. If using lettuce, prepare as above but tear into bite-sized pieces.

Rub the bread with the garlic and place in a moderate oven (180°C/350°F) to become a little dry but not coloured. Failing a French loaf, any bread can be used. Cut the slices a little thicker than usual, then when baked, break into small pieces.

Cut the Gruyère into strips and dice the Gorgonzola. Combine the greens, radish, cheese and bread and toss lightly with vinaigrette. *Serves 6*

Endive, Beet and Avocado Salad

•

Endive and beetroot are a well-known combination in France and the addition of creamy nut-like avocado is a good break with tradition. Serve this salad as a first course or as a luncheon salad. It is particularly good after a creamed seafood or chicken in pastry cases or quiche.

2 cooked beetroot, peeled and diced
half recipe Chive Vinaigrette (page 227)
4 Belgian endives
2 avocados

Toss the beetroot with ¼ cup of the Chive Vinaigrette and chill for 1 hour. Trim the endives and cut crosswise into 2 cm (¾ inch) pieces, leaving 6 whole small leaves for garnish. Peel and seed the avocados and cut into small wedges or dice.

Arrange the vegetables, in bands, on 6 chilled salad plates or a large platter. Drizzle the remaining Chive Vinaigrette over endives and avocado and serve. *Serves 6*

Fennel and Citrus Salad

• •

The fresh flavour of citrus fruits marries well with the crispy aniseed tang of Florence fennel. If you can get the pink fleshed grapefruit and the soft leaved mignonette lettuce you will be adding the touches that make a simple dish great.

2 grapefruit, pink flesh if possible
1 orange
⅓ cup natural yogurt
½ teaspoon salt
2 small bulbs fennel
soft leaf lettuce (mignonette or cos)

Peel the grapefruit and orange over a bowl to catch any juice then remove the pith and membrane. Section the fruit by cutting segments out between the membranes and squeezing the membranes to release the juice, there should be ⅓ cup juice in all. In a large bowl whisk the yogurt, fruit juice and salt together, add the fruit segments.

Remove the outer leaves of the fennel, reserving them for other use (they are delicious sliced and braised in a little oil or butter) and cut the bulbs across into thin slices. Add the fennel to the bowl and toss well. Serve in a bowl or divide among 6 chilled salad plates lined with lettuce leaves. *Serves 6*

Cauliflower Salad

• •

This will be a creamy or piquant salad depending on whether you use the mayonnaise or vinaigrette. Try the special French mustard containing the whole grains of mustard and spices with this salad, it gives a robust taste and look.

1 cauliflower
salt
4–6 anchovies
1 cup Mayonnaise (page 45) or ⅔ cup Vinaigrette (page 46)
1 tablespoon French mustard
freshly ground pepper
paprika or chopped parsley, to garnish

Wash the cauliflower, break into florets and cook in boiling salted water until barely tender, about 5 minutes. Drain and refresh under cold water. Dry thoroughly and arrange in a salad bowl or dish.

Chop the anchovies and fold into the mayonnaise or dressing with the mustard. If mayonnaise is too thick, dilute with a little milk or cream. Spoon over cauliflower, season with freshly ground pepper, toss lightly, then sprinkle with paprika or chopped parsley to serve. *Serves 6*

Greek Salad

•

Roast chicken, veal or lamb and one or two salads is a great way to celebrate luncheon on a sunny weekend. Serve something robust like this Greek Salad with the black Kalamati olives and slightly acid Feta cheese.

1 lettuce
6–8 spring onions, cut in lengths
1 cucumber, sliced
2 tomatoes, cut in wedges
6–8 black olives
4–6 sardines, salted not canned, soaked for a few hours to remove excess salt
125 g (4 oz) Feta cheese, cubed
½ cup Vinaigrette (page 46)

Wash the lettuce, pat dry with a towel and tear into bite-size pieces. Mix all the salad vegetables, olives, fish and cheese together in a large bowl and add the dressing just before serving, otherwise it wilts. *Serves 4*

Vegetable Batons Vinaigrette

••

A vegetable platter that says New Wave. It's the new way to lightly cook vegetables which are all cut into the same length 'baton' size strips. These batons are then arranged in a patchwork design on a pretty plate and dressed with a herby vinaigrette. Serve as a salad in its own right, a first course or cold vegetable accompaniment to baked ham, roast chicken or any cold meat.

1 beetroot, cooked
250 g (8 oz) green beans
1 white turnip
2 carrots
1 red pepper
250 g (8 oz) zucchini

Chive Vinaigrette

2 tablespoons lemon juice
1 tablespoon Dijon-style mustard
½ teaspoon sugar
⅔ cup olive oil
3 tablespoons snipped chives

Prepare each vegetable in the usual way then cut each into 'batons', about 2.5 cm × 6 mm (1 × ¼ inch). Cook each vegetable, except the beetroot, separately in boiling salted water until just tender; when cooked drain in a colander and refresh under cold running water and pat dry with paper towels.

To make the Chive Vinaigrette: Combine the lemon juice, mustard and sugar in a small bowl. Beat with a fork or small whisk and add the oil in a stream, whisking vigorously until smooth. Whisk in the chives, salt and a fresh grinding of pepper to taste.

Arrange the vegetables in separate bundles on a platter or serving dish and drizzle the Chive Vinaigrette over them. *Serves 6*

Italian Pasta Salad

••

A creamy salad of pasta, ham, black olives and green peas. It makes a nice accompaniment to grilled chicken or cold cuts for a luncheon menu.

2 cups macaroni or fancy pasta (shells, bows)
2 tablespoons oil
125 g (4 oz) black olives, halved and stoned
250 g (8 oz) ham, cut in thick slices and cubed
1 cup green peas
½–1 cup Mayonnaise (see page 45)
2 teaspoons French mustard
salt
freshly ground pepper
2 tomatoes

Cook the macaroni in boiling salted water with 1 tablespoon of the oil for 15 minutes or until just tender. Drain and rinse well. Sprinkle the remaining oil over to prevent the macaroni sticking.

Add the olives and ham to the macaroni. Cook the peas in boiling salted water, drain and add to the macaroni. Combine ½ cup of the mayonnaise with the mustard and stir through the macaroni mixture, adding a little more mayonnaise if necessary to give a creamy salad. Add salt and pepper to taste and spoon into a salad bowl. Peel and quarter the tomatoes and arrange around the salad. Serve chilled. *Serves 4–6*

Watercress and Beet Salad

•

I can think of nothing nicer after roast beef or veal than watercress salad. The next day make a light luncheon salad or super sandwich with any leftover beef and watercress . . . delicious!

1 large bunch watercress
3 beetroot, cooked
Walnut oil dressing
2 tablespoons wine vinegar
1 tablespoon Dijon-style mustard
salt
freshly ground pepper
½ cup walnut oil

Pick leafy sprigs from watercress, wash and tie in little bundles with a rubber band or hold together with foil. Stand in water to keep fresh until required. Dice the beetroot.
To make the dressing: beat the vinegar and mustard together with salt and pepper to taste. Add the oil in a steady stream, beating the dressing until well combined.
Just before required, twist tops off watercress from the bundles into a salad bowl and combine with the diced beetroot. Lightly toss in the dressing. *Serves 4–6*

Watercress and Pear Salad

•

An unexpected combination but a really lovely salad to serve with roast pork, goose or duckling.

Make as for Watercress and Beet Salad but replace the diced beetroot with 2 ripe pears, cut into slices. This should be done at the very last moment as the pears discolour quickly after they are sliced. Whether you peel the pears is a matter of personal choice.

Watercress and Walnut Salad

•

There is often a call for a light and elegant salad after a rich main course. When watercress is available nothing is nicer than the peppery cress dressed with a walnut dressing and finished with the crunch of buttery walnuts. Walnut oil is available at most health food shops.

1 large bunch watercress
2 teaspoons Dijon-style mustard
2 teaspoons wine vinegar
3 tablespoons walnut oil
½ teaspoon salt
½ cup shelled walnuts

Pick leafy sprigs from watercress, wash and tie into little bundles with a rubber band or hold together with foil. Stand in water to keep fresh until required.
Combine the mustard, vinegar, walnut oil and salt, beating well until thickened.
When ready to serve, twist off the tops of the watercress from the bouquets into a salad bowl. Lightly toss in the dressing and sprinkle with the walnuts. *Serves 4–6*
Note: Care should be taken to ensure walnuts are absolutely fresh – nothing is more distasteful than a rancid walnut! Those in tins are often the best, kept airtight, the rich oils in the flesh are kept fresh. Freshly opened walnuts are also good. Storing opened walnuts is best done, well protected, in the freezer.

Tomatoes with Tabbouli

• •

Burghul or cracked wheat gives a delicious nutty flavour to this variation of Tabbouli. Serve as a first course, to accompany barbecued food or on the buffet table.

1 cup burghul
6 tomatoes
salt
2 tablespoons finely chopped spring onions
freshly ground pepper
1 cup finely chopped parsley
¼ cup finely chopped fresh mint
3 tablespoons olive oil
3 tablespoons lemon juice

Soak burghul in water for about 2 hours before preparing the salad, it will swell to at least double its volume. Drain and squeeze out as much water as possible with your hands, then spread out on a tea-towel to dry further.
Meanwhile, peel the tomatoes if liked, remove tops and scoop out the centres. Sprinkle with salt and stand upside down to drain.
Chop the flesh of the scooped out tomatoes and combine with the spring onions and burghul, adding salt and pepper to taste. Add the parsley, mint, oil and lemon juice and mix well. Taste to see if more seasoning is required – the salad should taste lemony.
Fill the tomatoes with Tabbouli. Arrange on a plate, cover with plastic wrap and refrigerate for 1 hour. *Serves 6*

Tomatoes with Basil

••

When tomatoes are in season it is fortunate that the basil shrubs are thriving and we can get the lovely mild Spanish or salad onion with its purple skin. They are a formidable threesome and need the lightest dressing of good oil.

4–5 large ripe tomatoes
½ Spanish onion or 6 spring onions
5–6 large basil leaves
1–2 tablespoons olive oil
freshly ground pepper
salt (flaky Maldon salt for preference)
squeeze of lemon juice

Peel the tomatoes, remove the cores and cut into wedges. Finely slice the onion or cut the spring onions into long slivers. Shred the basil leaves but do not chop as they tend to bruise.

Combine the tomatoes, onion and basil in a bowl. Drizzle over a little oil, season with salt, a fresh grinding of pepper and a squeeze of lemon juice. Toss lightly. *Serves 4*

Tiny Toms with Basil When those full flavoured but tiny round cherry or tiny tom tomatoes are in season serve as above; simply wash and dry the tomatoes. Do not peel.

Tomatoes Pesto

(Tomatoes Stuffed with Basil)

••

Pesto, the famous green sauce from Genoa, is a mixture of fresh basil, pine nuts, oil and Parmesan cheese. It is traditionally served with freshly cooked pasta. Here, a variation of that famous sauce is used to stuff ripe tomatoes.

Serve as a first course or as part of a salad to accompany grilled meats or the cold buffet. When basil is hard to get, use fresh parsley and oregano which are almost as good.

6–8 ripe tomatoes
salt

Pesto

1 cup fresh basil leaves, closely packed, or
1 cup parsley and ¼ cup oregano
1 clove garlic
½ cup olive oil
¾ cup breadcrumbs
¾ cup pine nuts
½ cup freshly grated Parmesan cheese

Peel the tomatoes, if liked, remove the cores and scoop out the centres. Squeeze the tomatoes gently to remove most of the seeds. Sprinkle with a little salt and turn them upside down to drain.

Meanwhile make the Pesto; put all the ingredients in the container of an electric blender or food processor fitted with the double edged steel blade. Blend on low speed until well puréed, or pound to a purée with a pestle and mortar.

To finish, salt the tomatoes both inside and out and spoon equal portions of the Pesto mixture into the centre of each. Chill and serve cold, decorated with a fresh basil leaf. *Serves 6–8*

Mushrooms Pesto • When young tender mushroom cups are available, prepare them with Pesto as above.

Wipe mushrooms over with a damp cloth, fill with Pesto and chill. If liked, bake the mushrooms in a moderate oven (180°C/350°F) for 15 minutes and serve warm as a first course or include on a hot hors d'oeuvre tray.

Salad Périgordine

••

The success of this salad is in finishing it off at the very last minute, the hot bacon and bacon fat give a wonderful taste to the lettuce, eggs and walnuts.

1 lettuce
1 tablespoon wine vinegar
2 tablespoons walnut oil
3 hard-boiled eggs, quartered
2 tomatoes, cut into wedges
½ cup shredded walnuts
3 rashers bacon

Wash and dry a crisp lettuce then tear the leaves into bite-size pieces. Combine the vinegar and oil in a small bowl to make a dressing. Combine the lettuce, eggs, tomatoes and walnuts and lightly toss in the dressing.

Remove the rind from the bacon, cut into strips and fry in a dry pan until the fat runs and the bacon becomes crisp. Quickly mix the hot bacon with the fat through the salad and serve immediately. *Serves 6*

Asparagus with Potato Salad

•••

When baby new potatoes and asparagus are in season it makes sense to enjoy these two Spring vegetables in one dish. This excellent salad depends on fresh asparagus, canned just isn't the same. Serve the salad at room temperature, not chilled.

500 g (1 lb) asparagus
2 tablespoons Vinaigrette (page 46)
500 g (1 lb) new potatoes
½ cup Mayonnaise (page 45)
½ cup cream
salt
chopped parsley

Wash the asparagus, remove the woody ends and tie into bundles. Stand in boiling salted water and cook for 12–15 minutes. Drain and allow to cool. Cut into lengths and toss lightly in the vinaigrette.

Cook the potatoes, in their skins, in boiling salted water until just tender. Skin while still hot and leave whole if small or cut into slices. When cold toss the potatoes in the combined mayonnaise and cream, season with salt. Add asparagus to the potatoes and toss lightly, reserving a few of the tips for garnishing. Turn into a serving bowl, sprinkle with chopped parsley and the asparagus and serve. *Serves 4*

Potato and Bean Salad •• The asparagus season is an all too short one, so use fresh green beans with ½ Spanish onion and follow as above. Cook the beans until just tender-crisp, refresh under cold running water. Thinly slice the onion.

Moroccan Beetroot Salad

••

Morocco is a land of surprises. This salad combines the unexpected, beetroot with orange-flower water (available at pharmacies) and not unexpectedly that fresh tasting spice, cumin.

4 beetroot
2 teaspoons sugar
1 tablespoon orange flower water
1 teaspoon ground cumin
1 tablespoon chopped coriander or parsley

Cook the scrubbed and trimmed beetroot in water to cover for 30 to 40 minutes or until they are tender. Drain, slip off the skins under cold running water and cut into small cubes.

In a bowl combine beetroot with the remaining ingredients. Cover and chill for 1 hour before serving. *Serves 4*

Finnan Haddie and Potato Salad

••

1 kg (2 lb) new potatoes
500 g (1 lb) smoked haddock
1 onion, chopped
2 apples, chopped
¾ cup light sour cream
2 tablespoons capers
1 tablespoon prepared horseradish
¼ cup chopped parsley
freshly ground black pepper

Place the potatoes in cold salted water and bring to the boil. Cover and simmer until tender to the point of a sharp knife. Drain and peel then slice thickly and set aside in a salad bowl.

Poach the haddock and onion in just enough water to cover for about 10 minutes or until the fish flakes easily when tested with a fork. Drain the fish and onion and flake the fish into large pieces. Combine the fish and onion with the potatoes and chopped apples.

Combine sour cream, capers and horseradish. Toss lightly with potatoes and fish and sprinkle liberally with parsley. Season well with freshly ground pepper. Serve warm. *Serves 4–6*

Right: Pasta Genovese (page 246) combines noodles with basil in flavoured Pesto sauce. Fresh Tomato Sauce (page 47) is also good with pasta.

Creamy Potato Salad with Ham

••

An old way of making and a new way of serving this popular salad. The usual sharp vinaigrette flavours the potatoes, sour cream and mayonnaise give a creamy finish. This may be served as a first course at dinner, or as the main course for lunch. Cold sliced tongue, corned beef, or any of the continental type sausages can replace the more expensive ham.

500 g (1 lb) new potatoes
3 tablespoons oil
1 tablespoon vinegar
1 small onion, chopped
salt
freshly ground pepper
½ cup Mayonnaise (see page 45)
½ cup sour cream
3 thick slices ham or cooked tongue
chopped parsley
1–2 canned pimientos (optional)

Cook the potatoes in boiling, salted water until just tender. Peel while hot and cut into thick slices. Put the oil, vinegar and onion in a bowl, beat until thick and add salt and pepper to taste. Add the warm potatoes, folding them into the dressing. Allow to cool.

Combine the mayonnaise and sour cream in a bowl and lightly fold into the potatoes. Turn into a salad bowl. Cut the ham into julienne strips and arrange on top of the potatoes.

Sprinkle with chopped parsley to serve, and, if liked, strips of red pimiento and sprigs of parsley. This salad is best served at room temperature, that is, not chilled in the refrigerator. *Serves 4*

Italian Orange Salad

••

Mediterranean people enjoy fruit with meat, and this lovely salad is a perfect example of just how good the combination can be. Serve with cold, sliced meats, hot grilled meats, or poultry.

4 medium-sized oranges
1 small onion
¼ cup dry sherry
juice of ½ lemon
1 tablespoon olive oil
pinch white pepper
6–8 black olives, halved, seeded and slivered
crisp lettuce leaves

Left: Choose from Duck and Chicken Liver Pâté in the terrine (page 252), Mackerel Pâté in the bowl (page 256) or Potted Shrimps (page 52).

Peel the oranges, remove the pith and cut into 1 cm (½ inch) slices. Peel and thinly slice the onion and separate into rings. Place both in a bowl with the sherry and marinate for 1 hour.

In a small bowl, blend the lemon juice, oil, pepper and sherry marinade. Whisk well. Arrange the lettuce leaves in a serving dish. Place the orange slices on top, then the olives and onion. Pour on the dressing and toss carefully. *Serves 4*
Note: For a special occasion, you may like to try the addition of 1 tablespoon of Pernod or anisette liqueur to the dressing. Look for the miniature bottles, which are reasonably priced.

Mussel and Eggplant Salad

•••

The sweet, delicate flavour of mussels can be highlighted by simply steaming in wine with aromatics or they can be combined with a variety of ingredients to produce a dish of great complexity. Here we settle for something in between.

1.5 kg (3 lb) mussels, cleaned
2 medium eggplants
salt
⅓ cup oil
1 sprig fresh thyme or ½ teaspoon dried
1 red salad onion or 6–8 spring onions
freshly ground pepper
½ cup pine nuts, toasted
¼ cup chopped parsley
lettuce leaves

Dressing

2 tablespoons lemon juice
½ teaspoon anchovy paste or essence
1 clove garlic, crushed
3 tablespoons oil

Arrange the mussels in one layer in a large baking dish. Put in a preheated very hot oven (230°C/450°F) for 7–8 minutes or until the shells have opened. Discard any unopened shells. Shell the mussels, discard any dark rims and place in a bowl. Cover and chill.

Peel and dice the eggplant. Place on a plate, sprinkle with salt, place a second plate on top and weight lightly, stand for 1 hour. Rinse off salt and squeeze any liquid from the eggplant.

Place the eggplant in a gratin or ovenproof dish with the oil, 1 teaspoon of salt and leaves from the sprig of thyme. Bake in a preheated hot oven (200°C/400°F) for 30 minutes, or until tender. Let the eggplant cool. Make the Dressing by combining all the ingredients in a small bowl, beat with a fork until thick.

In a salad bowl, combine the eggplant, mussels, finely sliced onion, or spring onion shredded lengthwise, and salt and pepper to taste. Lightly fold in the dressing and chill the salad for at least 2 hours. Add the pine nuts just before serving.

Garnish the salad with chopped parsley, a few extra slivers of onion or spring onion and serve on lettuce cups on a platter. *Serves 4 as an entrée, 6 as a first course*

Orange Rosewater Salad

••

From Morocco comes this refreshing salad, which may also be served as a dessert. The rosewater is available from pharmacy shops.

4 navel oranges
4 teaspoons rosewater
3 teaspoons caster sugar
1 teaspoon cinnamon

Peel and section the oranges, detaching each segment from the membrane with a grapefruit knife. Divide the oranges between 4 salad plates, arranging them in a decorative pattern. Sprinkle each salad with a teaspoon of rosewater. In a small bowl combine the sugar and cinnamon and sprinkle over each serving. Cover and chill the salads for 1 hour. Just before serving sprinkle each salad with a pinch of cinnamon. *Serves 4*

Herring Salad

••

A wide range of herrings from Sweden and Denmark are readily available and they make wonderful Scandinavian type salads. This salad is just the thing to take on a picnic or for any alfresco lunch. Serve with dark rye bread or black bread. Cold lager would be the perfect accompaniment.

8 matjes herring fillets
3 beetroot, cooked
2 potatoes, cooked
2 apples
2 large dill pickles
½ cup vinegar
1 teaspoon sugar
½ cup cream
½ teaspoon salt
3 hard-boiled eggs
1 tablespoon snipped dill or chives

Finely chop the herrings, beetroot, potatoes, apples and dill pickles. Combine together. Mix the vinegar and sugar and fold through the herring mixture. Transfer the salad to a glass bowl.

Whip the cream with the salt until it holds its shape and pile on the salad. Decorate with quartered hard-boiled eggs and sprinkle over the snipped dill or chives. *Serves 6–8*

Seafood and Vegetable Salad

•••

This is something special for those who like to serve a beautiful salad as a luncheon dish. No tart, herby dressing for this salad but the creamy mayonnaise seems just right for a seafood combination. In France this is garnished with diced pâté de fois gras; ham or prosciutto is an interesting substitute.

500 g (1 lb) cooked prawns
250 g (8 oz) scallops
2 large carrots
2 stalks celery
250 g (8 oz) zucchini
12 mushroom caps
soft leaved lettuce (mignonette or cos)
125 g (4 oz) sliced ham or prosciutto

Dressing

⅔ cup cream
½ teaspoon salt
½ cup Mayonnaise (page 45)

Shell and devein the prawns. Trim the scallops of any brown bits, retain the coral and poach in a little salted water for 3–5 minutes.

Scrub the carrots and shred coarsely, or cut into fine julienne strips. Remove strings from celery and cut into julienne strips. Finely slice the zucchini. Blanch the carrot and celery in boiling salted water for 2 minutes and the zucchini for 1 minute, drain in a colander and refresh under cold running water. Pat dry with a paper towel. Slice the mushrooms. Combine the seafoods and vegetables, except the lettuce, in a bowl. Make the Dressing: Whip the cream with salt until it holds soft peaks, fold in the mayonnaise. Pour the dressing over the prawn mixture and toss the salad lightly.

Arrange several leaves of lettuce on a plate (failing soft lettuce use small leaves of a crisp lettuce or shredded lettuce). Mound the salad on the lettuce. Cut the ham or prosciutto into fine julienne strips and sprinkle over the salad. *Serves 4 as a main course or entrée, or 6 as a first course*

Ham, Cheese and Watercress Salad

•

There is a growing interest in entrée salads and this is an example of how good they can be. A favourite follow-up would be creamed chicken in pastry, a quiche, or loin of lamb served with potatoes only.

1 large bunch watercress
6 slices ham, cut about 3 mm (⅛ inch) thick
125 g (4 oz) Gruyère cheese
Mustard Dressing
2 tablespoons Dijon-style mustard
2 tablespoons lemon juice
½ cup olive oil
salt
freshly ground pepper

Pick leafy sprigs from watercress, wash and tie in little bundles. Stand in water to keep fresh. Make the Mustard Dressing: Combine the mustard and lemon juice in a small bowl. Add the oil in a stream, whisking until the dressing is well combined and thickened slightly. Add salt and pepper to taste.

Cut the ham and cheese into julienne strips. Twist the tops off the watercress into a salad bowl, add the ham and cheese and toss in the Mustard Dressing. *Serves 6*

Note: If watercress is hard to find look for mignonette lettuce or cos; sometimes the tiny corn or lambs tongue lettuce are available and they can be used in this salad.

Lentil and Anchovy Salad

••

Lentils were among the first plants ever cultivated and they are believed to be the 'red potage' for which Esau sold his birthright. Lentils have always been popular in the Middle East, but today's cooks are doing imaginative things with them, like this economical but delicious salad.

1 cup brown lentils
4 cups water
½ teaspoon salt
½ cup diced dill pickles
6–8 chopped spring onions
3 tablespoons chopped capers
2 tablespoons parsley
4 anchovy fillets, chopped
2 hard-boiled eggs
extra anchovy fillets, to garnish
Dressing
¼ cup tarragon vinegar
2 teaspoons Dijon-style mustard
½ teaspoon salt
freshly ground pepper

Rinse and pick over the lentils and place in a large saucepan with the water and salt. Bring to the boil over a moderately high heat, reduce the heat and simmer the lentils, covered, for 25 to 30 minutes or until just tender. Drain the lentils in a sieve, transfer to bowl and cool. Stir through the pickles, spring onions, capers, parsley and anchovies. Make the Dressing: In a small bowl beat the vinegar with the mustard and salt. Add the oil in a steady stream, beating. Season with pepper to taste.

Toss the lentil mixture with the dressing, add salt and pepper to taste, and cover and chill the salad for at least 2 hours. Garnish the salad with the chopped or sliced hard-boiled eggs and the remaining anchovy fillets. *Serves 4–6*

Chick Pea Salad

••

*Rich in protein, and with a delightful firm texture, chick peas
can be used in dips and in many hot and cold
dishes. They are available already cooked, in cans and are
sometimes labelled Garbanzos. Or you can start
with the dried variety and cook them yourself. The first
method is easier, the second more economical.
To cook dried chick peas: Soak the required amount of chick
peas overnight in cold water to cover. Remove
any peas which float. Drain, cover with fresh water and
bring the peas to a slow boil, reduce the heat and
simmer until tender. This will take anything from 30 minutes
to 1 ½ hours, depending on the age of the peas.
If you have forgotten to soak the peas, a quick method to
tenderize them is to cover with cold water, bring
to the boil and simmer for 5 minutes. Remove from the heat
and leave tightly covered for 1 hour. Cook in
the usual way until tender. Blanching the peas in this fashion
is equal to almost 8 hours of soaking.*

1 cup dried chick peas
2 small onions
1 bay leaf
1 clove garlic
1 teaspoon salt
1 orange
2 stalks celery, sliced
½ green or red pepper, sliced
4 tablespoons Vinaigrette (page 46)

Soak the peas in water to cover overnight; next day, drain.
Place in a saucepan, cover with fresh water, add 1 of the onions
halved, the bay leaf, garlic and salt.

Bring to the boil and skim off any scum that rises to the
surface. Simmer for 1–1½ hours or until tender. Drain and
leave to cool.

Prepare the orange as described below. Cut the remaining
onion into slices and separate into rings. Mix the orange
segments, celery, pepper and onion rings. Toss with about 4
tablespoons of vinaigrette. *Serves 4*

To section oranges: Hold the fruit over a bowl to catch all the
juice, and use a sharp, serrated knife to remove all the rind and
white pith. Pare around and around like an apple, so the fruit is
exposed. Loosen the sections by cutting down along each side
of the membrane. Lift out the segments in one piece and
remove any seeds. Squeeze the core with remaining membrane over the segments. This juice may be added to the
dressing.

Zucchini Salad

••

750 g–1 kg (1½–2 lb) zucchini
2 tablespoons white vinegar, preferably tarragon
6 tablespoons olive oil
salt
freshly ground pepper
2 spring onions, finely chopped
1 tablespoon capers, chopped (optional)
2 tablespoons chopped parsley
1 tablespoon snipped chives
extra parsley and chives to garnish

Trim ends of zucchini and cut into diagonal slices. Drop into
boiling, salted water and cook uncovered for 1 minute. Drain
and refresh under cold water.

Blend the vinegar with the oil and remaining ingredients,
and whisk until the dressing is thick and combined.

Toss the zucchini in the dressing, allow to cool, then chill.
Serve topped with extra chopped parsley and chives. *Serves 6*

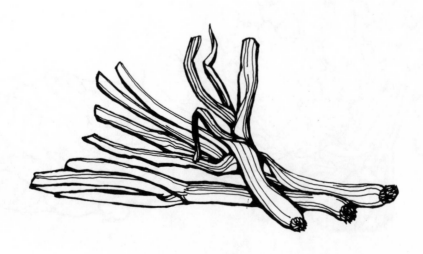

RICE AND PASTA

The Chinese and Indians are probably born knowing how to cook rice perfectly and the Italians seem to cook pasta to perfection as if by second nature. The art of cooking rice and pasta doesn't come as easily to many of us. However we can learn to cook rice so that every grain is separate and dry yet not gummy or sticky. And once you learn to cook pasta in *plenty* of boiling salted water until just 'al dente' you have the makings of a superlative and quick meal.

With a jar of rice and a packet of pasta in the cupboard you can enjoy the kind of food that is daily bread to one-third of the world's population. Exotic Birianis, Pilaus and Risotto, fried rice of infinite variety and pasta dishes of Italian, Chinese and European origin, from everyday fare to party dishes – all these dishes and many more are now accepted by the rest of the world, as once potatoes were an accepted essential part of a meal.

For the basics of cooking rice and pasta, see page 35.

Macaroni with Ham and Eggs

• •

Any shaped macaroni or spaghetti can be used for this Roman dish. The simple sauce of ham and eggs is a pleasant change from the more usual tomato or spicy sauces.

500 g (1 lb) macaroni
salt
125 g (4 oz) ham or bacon
90 g (3 oz) butter
2 eggs
grated Parmesan cheese

Cook the macaroni in a large pan of boiling salted water for about 15 minutes or until tender but still firm. Drain and turn into a heated serving dish.

While the macaroni cooks, cut the ham or bacon into julienne (matchstick size) strips and cook gently in a small pan in some of the butter for about 5 minutes. Beat the eggs lightly. Just before serving, stir the eggs into the ham and cook over a low heat, stirring, until the eggs just start to thicken. Before they turn into scrambled eggs, toss with the macaroni and remaining butter. Top with grated Parmesan cheese and serve more Parmesan separately. *Serves 4*
Note: There is another way to make this dish. Cook the pasta and drain. Add the cooked ham or bacon and while the pasta is still very hot, add the beaten eggs and stir. The heat of the pasta is sufficient to cook the eggs.

Vermicelli Napoletana

•

Neapolitans prefer the fine spaghetti known as vermicelli rather than the thicker spaghetti most people eat. In Italy, pizza and spaghetti are synonymous with Naples and throughout the world they have become a synonym of Italy itself. This sauce is the classic accompaniment for spaghetti.

¼ cup olive oil
45 g (1½ oz) butter
½ onion, finely chopped
750 g (1½ lb) tomatoes, peeled, seeded and chopped
salt
freshly ground pepper
500 g (1 lb) vermicelli
1 tablespoon fresh basil, chopped
1 cup freshly grated Parmesan cheese

Heat the oil and 15 g (½ oz) of the butter in a heavy frying pan. Add the onion and cook until softened. Add the tomatoes, salt and pepper and simmer uncovered for 15 minutes.

Cook the vermicelli in plenty of boiling salted water until 'al dente', then drain. Place in a shallow serving dish and dot with small pieces of the remaining butter. Sprinkle with the basil and 2 tablespoons of the Parmesan cheese and pour the sauce on top. Mix carefully and serve the remaining Parmesan cheese separately. *Serves 4*

Spaghetti Caruso

••

Surely one of the most triumphant ways to present liver, that highly nutritious food. Basil is especially good as a foil to the rich flavour of liver and mushrooms.

2 cloves garlic, split
4 tablespoons olive oil
2 medium onions, chopped
250 g (8 oz) chicken livers, chopped
250 g (8 oz) mushrooms, sliced
1 small can (140 g) tomato paste
½ cup water
2 cups canned tomatoes, with juice
¼ teaspoon thyme
¼ teaspoon basil
1 bay leaf
1 teaspoon salt
¼ teaspoon pepper
½ teaspoon sugar
500 g (1 lb) spaghetti
1 cup grated Parmesan cheese

Sauté the garlic in 3 tablespoons of the oil for 2 minutes then discard. Sauté the onions in the oil for 3 minutes, add the liver and mushrooms, and brown for 5 minutes. Add the tomato paste mixed with the water, tomatoes and juice, thyme, basil, bay leaf, salt, pepper and sugar. Simmer, covered, for 30 minutes.

Cook the spaghetti in boiling salted water with the remaining olive oil. Drain and put on a heated platter with ½ cup of the cheese. Spoon over half the sauce and toss. Pass the remaining sauce and cheese separately. *Serves 6*

Canneloni

••

There are many fillings for canneloni, the big pipes. This one is typical and simple.

250 g (8 oz) canneloni tubes
125 g (4 oz) Mozzarella cheese, thinly sliced

Sauce

1 onion, chopped
1 clove garlic, crushed
¼ cup oil
1 teaspoon chopped parsley
1 teaspoon salt
pepper to taste
1 medium can (400 g) tomatoes
2 cups boiling water

Filling

500 g (1 lb) minced steak
2 eggs, beaten
2 tablespoons oil
2 tablespoons grated Parmesan cheese
1 tablespoon chopped parsley
1 teaspoon salt
pepper to taste

Cook the canneloni in boiling, salted water for 5 minutes. Rinse in cold water and drain. The canneloni should be just flexible enough to handle.

Sauce: Sauté the onion and garlic in the oil until brown. Add the parsley, salt and pepper, and stir in the tomatoes. Pour in the water slowly, cover and simmer for 20 minutes. Pour half the sauce into a shallow baking dish.

Filling: Combine all the filling ingredients and season to taste with salt and pepper.

Fill the canneloni with the filling using a pastry bag and plain nozzle or a small teaspoon. Arrange side by side in the sauce. Cover with the remaining sauce and thin slices of Mozzarella and cook in a moderate oven (180°C/350°F) for about 45 minutes. Serve with a green salad. *Serves 4*

Rigatoni alla Carbonara

••

*This is a Roman specialty and translated literally means
'charcoal-burner's style'. Try to find rigatoni for
this dish (these are the ribbed noodles) otherwise, spaghetti is
a good substitute.*

500 g (1 lb) rigatoni or spaghetti
125 g (4 oz) bacon or speck
1 tablespoon oil
4 eggs
¾ cup freshly grated Parmesan cheese
1 teaspoon salt
freshly ground black pepper
¼ cup cream
60 g (2 oz) butter

Cook the pasta in plenty of boiling salted water until 'al dente'.
Drain. Meanwhile, cut the bacon into 2.5 cm (1 inch) pieces and
fry in the oil until crisp and brown. Remove. Beat the eggs in a
bowl, add the cheese, salt, pepper and cream and mix well.
Melt the butter in a frying pan, add the egg mixture and stir
constantly until it begins to thicken. Add the drained spaghetti
and bacon, mix together quickly and serve at once. *Serves 4*
Note: It is important to cook and drain the spaghetti before
cooking the eggs and to add the spaghetti to the eggs just as
they thicken. They must not overcook and should be moist.

Spiced Rice

•

*Spices and flavourings of South East Asia make this a good
side dish with curries and other Asian foods.*

2 tablespoons peppercorns
2 teaspoons cardamom seeds
1½ teaspoons whole cloves
2 cups long-grain rice
¼ cup peanut oil
4 cups boiling water
salt
3 tablespoons lemon juice
¼ cup chopped cashew nuts
desiccated coconut and chopped coriander

Place the peppercorns, cardamom seeds and whole cloves in a
heavy frying pan and roast gently over a low heat, shaking
frequently to prevent scorching. When well roasted, transfer to
a blender or a mortar and grind them finely.

In a large heavy saucepan, sauté the rice and spice mixture in
the oil until the rice is transparent. Stir in the boiling water and
salt to taste and cook for 5 minutes. Cover and transfer to a
moderate oven (180°C/350°F) for 15 minutes or until the rice is
tender. Add the lemon juice, toss rice with a fork and sprinkle
with the chopped cashew nuts, sautéed in peanut oil until
golden, coconut and coriander. *Serves 8*

239

Pasta e Fagioli

(Pasta with Beans)

••

Pasta, beans, cheese and lots of herbs and vegetables –
a glorious mixture that you might serve with no more
addition than salad and bread for a luncheon, or it would
follow beautifully after a light first course such as
prosciutto with fresh fruit.

1 cup haricot beans
4½ cups cold water
1½ teaspoons salt
3 cups macaroni (fusilli)
2 tablespoons olive oil
1 large onion, chopped
2 large carrots, sliced
1 cup celery, chopped
1 clove garlic, crushed
2 cups peeled, chopped tomatoes
1 teaspoon sage leaves, chopped
1 teaspoon oregano leaves
salt
¼ teaspoon freshly ground black pepper
chopped parsley
grated Parmesan cheese

In a large bowl combine the beans with the water and salt and
refrigerate overnight. Next day, transfer to a large saucepan.
Bring to the boil, reduce the heat and simmer, covered, for 1–2
hours, or until the beans are tender, stirring several times
during cooking. Drain and reserve 2½ cups of liquid.

Cook the macaroni in boiling salted water until 'al dente',
drain.

In a large, heavy saucepan heat the oil and sauté the onion,
carrots, celery and garlic until soft, but not coloured. Add the
tomatoes, sage, oregano, salt and pepper. Cover and cook over
a gentle heat for 20 minutes.

In a large saucepan combine the beans, macaroni and tomato
mixture. Add 1½ cups of the reserved bean liquid. Bring to the
boil, cover and simmer for 15 to 20 minutes, stirring
occasionally and adding more bean liquid if necessary. Season
to taste with salt and pepper.

Turn into a serving bowl or casserole. Sprinkle with chopped
parsley and Parmesan cheese and serve hot. *Serves 8*

Pasticcio

•••

This is a substantial and festive dish for a crowd.

500 g (1 lb) noodles
½–1 cup grated Parmesan cheese

Pasticcio Sauce

185 g (6 oz) lentils
salt
1 teaspoon oil
1 large eggplant
3 tablespoons olive oil
30 g (1 oz) butter
2 onions, chopped
½ teaspoon cinnamon
½ teaspoon oregano
salt
freshly ground pepper
1 clove garlic, crushed
8 tomatoes, peeled and chopped
125 g (4 oz) can tomato paste

Custard Sauce

30 g (1 oz) butter
3 tablespoons flour
3 cups milk, heated
3 eggs

Pasticcio Sauce: Wash the lentils, cover with 3 cups of boiling
water and allow to soak for 3–4 hours. Place the lentils in a
saucepan with the water, salt and olive oil and cook until the
water has almost completely evaporated – about 30–45
minutes.

Wash the eggplant and cut into small pieces. Heat the olive
oil and butter in a large heavy frying pan. Add the onions,
eggplant, cinnamon, oregano, salt and pepper to taste and
garlic. Cover the pan and simmer over a gentle heat for 10
minutes. Add the tomatoes to the pan with the lentils and
remaining lentil liquid. Allow to cook a little longer until the
mixture is thick. Stir in the tomato paste and correct seasoning.
Set the sauce aside.

Custard Sauce: Melt the butter in a saucepan, stir in the flour
and cook for a few minutes. Pour in the milk, stirring with a
whisk and cook until thickened. Beat the eggs in a bowl and
pour the sauce over them, beating with a whisk all the time.
Cover with wetted kitchen paper to prevent a skin forming.

Cook the noodles in plenty of boiling, salted water until they
are just tender. Butter a large casserole or oblong baking dish
and put half the noodles in an even layer across the bottom.

Sprinkle the Parmesan cheese over the noodles and cover
with half the Pasticcio Sauce. Top with the remaining noodles
then the sauce. Finally, pour the Custard Sauce over the top.
Sprinkle a little more Parmesan over and cover. Bake in a hot
oven (200°C/400°F) for 1 hour. Serve with a green salad and red
wine. *Serves 12–14*

There are many superb savoury fillings for quiches. Two favourites
are Asparagus (page 260) and Spinach (page 259).

Right: Rosti (page 264).

Below: Crêpes Polonaise at the rear (page 264), Blintzes served with strawberries (page 265) and Buckwheat Pancakes with caviar (page 266).

Spaghetti with Garlic and Oil

•

*To the true pasta fancier, the simplest treatment
is the best. Such an enthusiast would eat this spaghetti by
itself, but it would also be good with grilled beef,
lamb or chicken.*

500 g (1 lb) spaghetti
4–5 tablespoons olive oil
4 cloves garlic, finely chopped
4 tablespoons chopped parsley
125 g (4 oz) butter
salt
freshly ground pepper
grated Parmesan cheese

Cook the spaghetti in plenty of boiling salted water until firm
but tender. Drain and sprinkle with 1 tablespoon of the oil.

Fry the garlic and parsley in the hot butter and 3 tablespoons
of the remaining oil, until heated through. Do not allow the
garlic to colour. Stir into the spaghetti, turning with 2 forks to
evenly coat. If necessary add another tablespoon of the oil.
Season to taste with salt and pepper. Serve topped with
Parmesan cheese and, if liked, dots of butter. *Serves 4–6*

Tagliatelle all' Amatriciana

• •

*This recipe is one of the most famous of all pasta dishes,
the origin of which is said to be Amatrice, a little
village in the Sabine country near Rome. The sauce is based
on 'guanciale', a type of bacon, which is diced and
mixed with tomatoes, chilli peppers and onions – purists
omit the tomatoes. Try to find the very thin
tagliatelle ribbon noodles for this dish.*

250 g (8 oz) bacon or speck
2 tablespoons oil
1 small dried chilli or pinch cayenne
1 small onion, chopped
500 g (1 lb) tomatoes, peeled, seeded
and chopped
salt
freshly ground black pepper
500 g (1 lb) tagliatelle
1 cup freshly grated Pecorino or
Parmesan cheese

Cut the bacon into 2.5 cm (1 inch) pieces. Heat the oil in a heavy
frying pan, add the bacon and cook until brown and crisp.
Remove from pan, drain and set aside.

*Left: Fresh Plum and Peach Compote can be served with Pain Perdu
or Crème à la Vanille (page 286).*

Meanwhile, soak the chilli in hot water for 5 minutes, then
remove the seeds and finely chop. Add the chilli and onion to
the pan and sauté until the onion is softened. Stir in the
tomatoes, season with salt and pepper and simmer the sauce
for 10 minutes.

While the sauce is cooking, drop the tagliatelle into plenty of
rapidly boiling salted water and cook until 'al dente'. Drain and
place the pasta in a large shallow serving dish. Add the bacon
to the sauce and pour over the pasta. Sprinkle with the grated
cheese and serve at once. *Serves 4–6*

Piquant Vermicelli

•

*Marjoram adds piquancy to the combination
of mushrooms and parsley, whose flavour affinity has made
them classic partners. Serve with grills,
roasts or chicken.*

250 g (8 oz) vermicelli
2 tablespoons oil
125 g (4 oz) mushrooms
60 g (2 oz) butter
2 tablespoons chopped parsley
salt
freshly ground black pepper
1 teaspoon chopped marjoram

Cook the vermicelli in plenty of rapidly boiling salted water to
which the oil has been added. Drain, set aside and keep hot.

Slice the mushrooms finely and sauté in the butter until
tender. Add the vermicelli to the pan with the remaining
ingredients and heat thoroughly. *Serves 4*

Other Ideas

★ Cook pasta (tagliatelle or fettuccine are best) in plenty of
rapidly boiling salted water until 'al dente'. Drain and toss in
plenty of melted butter and chopped parsley or snipped chives
to flavour. Season to taste with salt and freshly ground black
pepper. Serve with meat or fish.

★ Mix cooked macaroni or penne with a smooth sauce made by
combining Ricotta cheese with a few tablespoonfuls of the
water in which the pasta was cooked, celery salt and cayenne.
Serve with meatballs.

★ Drain and dry pasta well. Mix with mayonnaise and
chopped fresh herbs. Serve with salads.

Pasta Genovese

•

The classic fresh basil and pine nut sauce called Pesto is used in all kinds of pasta dishes and also in Genoese vegetable soup. This recipe is the simplest possible way to eat pesto and is a dish for the gods.

500 g (1 lb) ribbon noodles
extra Parmesan or Pecorino cheese to accompany

Pesto Sauce

1 cup fresh basil leaves, closely packed
¼ teaspoon salt
2 cloves garlic
¼ cup pine nuts, toasted
½ cup grated Parmesan or Pecorino cheese
¾ cup olive oil

Cook the noodles in plenty of boiling salted water until firm but tender. While the pasta is cooking make the sauce.
Pesto Sauce: Place all the ingredients in the container of an electric blender or food processor fitted with the double edged steel blade. Blend on a low speed until well puréed. Failing a blender or processor, place the basil, salt, garlic and pine nuts in a mortar and pound to a paste then gradually add the Parmesan cheese while pounding. When smooth, gradually beat in the oil.

Drain the cooked noodles and toss with the Pesto Sauce. Pass the grated cheese separately. *Serves 4*

Fettuccine Verde alla Gargiulo

(Green Noodles with Chicken, Tomato and Prosciutto)

• •

A specialty of Gargiulo's Restaurant in New York and a sumptuous combination indeed.

250 g (8 oz) green ribbon noodles
60 g (2 oz) butter
60 g (2 oz) grated Parmesan cheese, to serve

Sauce

1 chicken breast
2 small onions
½ cup olive oil
125 g (4 oz) mushrooms, sliced
125 g (4 oz) butter
60 g (2 oz) prosciutto, cut into julienne strips
250 g (8 oz) ripe tomatoes, peeled, seeded
and chopped
½ cup cream
freshly ground nutmeg
salt
freshly ground pepper

To make the sauce: Steam the chicken breast over simmering water for 10 minutes and set aside to cool. It should be only barely cooked.

Peel the onions, halve then cut from the top to the bottom into thin strips. Sauté in the oil until golden. Add the butter to the pan and when it has melted add the prosciutto and tomatoes, simmer for 5 minutes.

Meanwhile, skin and bone the chicken breast and cut into thin strips. Add to the pan with the cream, nutmeg, salt and pepper to taste. Bring to a simmer over a high heat, stirring. Remove sauce from heat and keep warm.

Prepare the fettuccine: Cook the fettuccine in plenty of boiling salted water until just tender, about 8 minutes then drain in a colander. Toss with the 60 g (2 oz) of butter and place in a serving dish. Spoon the sauce over the pasta and serve with the grated Parmesan cheese. *Serves 4*

Saffron Rice

•

I find this one of the most useful of all recipes. I turn to it again and again when I'm looking for a simple but stylish accompaniment to meat, poultry or fish. Use Basmati, the fragrant rice of the Punjab, if you can. It is comparatively expensive but has a subtle nutty flavour like no other in the world. Saffron, too, is expensive but you need very little for any one dish and its fragrance, flavour and colour make rice memorable.

1½ cups Basmati or other long-grain rice
15 g (½ oz) butter
1 tablespoon oil
1 small onion, finely chopped
½ teaspoon saffron threads
3 cups boiling water or chicken stock
salt to taste

Soak the saffron in enough warm water to barely cover. Wash the rice well and drain thoroughly. In a deep saucepan with a tight-fitting lid heat the butter and oil and cook the onion until soft without colouring. Add the rice and cook for a further few minutes, stirring all the time until the rice is well coated by the butter and oil.

Pour on the stock or water, add the saffron and water in which it was soaked and a large pinch of salt (or less if your stock is salty). Stir once, cover and cook gently for about 20 minutes or until the rice is tender and the liquid has been absorbed. Remove the lid and stand for a few minutes to let the steam escape, fluff up with a fork and serve. *Serves 8*

Saffron Pilau

••

A party, barbecue or large luncheon is usually the signal for me to make Saffron Pilau, an intriguingly flavoured and spiced rice. It goes so well with roast Scotch fillet, a variety of poultry dishes or cold meats and is good served hot or cold. It looks marvellous piled into a big dish, heaped into tomato cases or moulded into a ring. I also like it because guests sing its praises and, even more important, the recipe is failproof. Adding the liquid in three parts ensures that the rice will not become soggy. The saffron is expensive but worth every cent for its lovely colour, fragrance and flavour.

3 tablespoons oil
2 onions, finely sliced
½ teaspoon saffron threads
2 cups long-grain rice
3½ cups stock or water and stock cubes
8 peppercorns
2 whole cloves
4 cardamom pods, bruised
2 teaspoons salt
1 stick cinnamon
½ cup sultanas or raisins
½ cup halved, toasted almonds

Heat the oil in a heavy pan and gently fry the onions until a pale golden colour. Make sure the onions are soft but do not allow to burn; this will take quite a while.

Add the saffron and cook for 1 minute, stirring. Add the rice and fry gently for 5 minutes until all the rice is coated with oil, stirring constantly until golden. Add 1¾ cups of the boiling stock, with the peppercorns, cloves, cardamom and cinnamon. Add the salt (reducing if the stock or stock cubes are salty). Bring back to the boil, cover and reduce the heat.

Simmer gently for 20–25 minutes, until the rice is tender, adding more stock as it is absorbed. Add the raisins, cover and allow to plump. Turn the heat off and keep covered until ready to serve.

A few minutes before serving, uncover pan to allow steam to escape, fluff up with a fork and add the almonds. Turn on to a large serving dish. For a main dish garnish with 6 hard-boiled eggs, halved. *Serves 8–10*
Note: Turmeric may be substituted for saffron, it gives good colour but not the same flavour, use 1 teaspoon.

Cashew and Sultana Pilau

••

30 g (1 oz) ghee
1 onion, finely chopped
2 cups long-grain rice
salt
freshly ground pepper
4 cups chicken stock
60 g (2 oz) cashew nuts
60 g (2 oz) sultanas
a little extra ghee

Melt ghee in a heavy saucepan. Add the onion and cook gently until soft and golden. Wash rice well, drain and dry on kitchen towel then stir into the onion mixture. Season with salt and pepper and cook slowly until the rice becomes translucent. Meanwhile, bring the stock to a boil. Pour stock over rice, stir once, bring back to boil then lower heat, cover and cook very gently for about 20 minutes or until the liquid is absorbed and the rice is tender with small holes appearing on the surface.

Remove the lid and cook uncovered for a minute or two. Fry cashews and sultanas in a little ghee and fork through the pilau. Serve as an accompaniment to Cardamom Chickens (page 139). *Serves 10*

Pilau-stuffed Tomatoes

•

Peel firm tomatoes, scoop out the centres with a teaspoon, salt inside and turn upside down on kitchen paper for 10 minutes to drain. Brush tomatoes lightly with oil, pile hot saffron pilau into the centres and place in a baking dish. Heat in a moderate oven (180°C/350°F) for 10 minutes.

Pilau Ring

•

Pack saffron pilau firmly into an oiled ring mould. Put a heated platter over the mould and invert, tap the mould to release the rice, and remove the mould. Fill the centre, if liked, with cooked mushrooms and peas, sautéed chicken livers tossed in a little cream or any other savoury filling.

Rice Salad

•

Prepare Saffron Pilau or Saffron Rice. Combine 2 tablespoons vinegar, 2 teaspoons prepared mustard (Dijon is best) and 6 tablespoons oil. Season with salt and pepper to taste and beat with a fork until thick. Toss through the rice. To this basic Rice Salad you can add 1 cup diced cooked chicken, ½ cup chopped green peppers and some chopped parsley. Shelled prawns and sliced canned water chestnuts for a crispy contrast make another good combination. For a creamy salad, fold in a little good mayonnaise.

Green Rice

•

Rice combined with fresh green herbs and vegetables, cream and cheese makes a colourful and complete accompaniment to meats or fish, or it could be an interesting part of a meatless meal.

½ cup olive oil
½ cup chopped green pepper
3 cups cooked rice
3 cups chopped cooked spinach
¾ cup chopped parsley
½ cup snipped chives
1 teaspoon salt
¼ teaspoon freshly ground pepper
½ cup cream
2 cups grated Parmesan cheese

Heat the oil in a large pan and sauté the pepper for 5 minutes. Stir in the rice, spinach, parsley, chives, salt and pepper and toss together until hot. Remove from the heat and toss with the cream and 1 cup of the cheese. Turn into a hot serving dish and sprinkle the remaining cheese on top. *Serves 8*

Fried Rice

••

The secret of fried rice, with every grain separate, is to cook the rice by the steam method, then spread it out on a flat dish or tray and allow it to dry and become quite cold before adding it to the other fried ingredients. The best idea is to cook the rice a day ahead and chill it overnight in the refrigerator.

60 g (2 oz) dried Chinese mushrooms
125 g (4 oz) cooked chicken breast
small piece barbecued pork or ham
6 tablespoons oil
2 eggs
salt to taste
6 spring onions, chopped
½ cup shelled small cooked prawns
6 cups steamed cold rice
½ cup cooked peas

Seasoning

1 tablespoon Chinese wine or dry sherry
¼ cup stock
2 teaspoons soy sauce

Soak the mushrooms in water to cover for 30 minutes, drain. Simmer gently in salted water for 5 minutes. Drain, remove stalks, slice mushrooms thinly and set aside. Cut chicken and pork or ham into small dice and set aside.

Heat 2 tablespoons of the oil in a wok or frying pan. Beat the eggs with a pinch of salt and add to the pan. Cook until firm, stirring so that cooked egg is broken into small pieces. Remove from pan and set aside.

Heat wok or pan and add remaining oil. When hot add the spring onions, meats, prawns and mushrooms. Fry for a few seconds, then add the rice, tossing constantly to mix and heat through. Season with salt and add peas and egg. Combine the Seasoning ingredients and sprinkle over rice. Mix well and serve. *Serves 8–10*

Curried Rice

●

Serve spicy curried rice as a main dish in a meatless meal, or to give savour to a barbecue or plain grill.

125 g (4 oz) ghee or butter
3 onions, finely sliced
2 teaspoons turmeric
1 tablespoon curry powder
1 kg (2 lb) long-grain rice
7 cups chicken stock
12 peppercorns
4 whole cloves
8 cardamom pods, bruised
1 stick cinnamon
1 tablespoon salt
2 cups cooked peas (optional)

Heat the ghee or butter in a large heavy saucepan or flameproof casserole. Fry half the onions until golden brown, add the turmeric and curry powder and stir well for a minute. Add the rice and fry for a few minutes, stirring, until golden in colour. Add boiling stock, peppercorns, cloves, cardamom, cinnamon, salt and remaining onions.

Stir well, cover and cook over a gentle heat for about 20 minutes. Turn off the heat and keep covered until ready to serve. A few minutes before serving, uncover pan to allow steam to escape. Fluff up with a fork and garnish with the peas, if liked. *Serves 12*

Rice Pudding

●

Butter a deep ovenproof dish and add 4 tablespoons of short-grain rice, 3½ cups of milk, 4 tablespoons of sugar, 15 g (½ oz) butter, ½ vanilla bean or ½ teaspoon vanilla essence and a pinch of nutmeg. Stir well and bake in a moderate oven (180°C/350°F) for about 2 hours or until the rice is soft and the milk is thickened and creamy with a thin golden crust on top. Stir once or twice during the first hour of cooking. Remove the vanilla bean and serve with pouring cream and stewed fruit.

Rice Pilaf

●

Melt 30 g (1 oz) butter in a heavy saucepan, add one small, finely chopped onion and cook gently until soft and golden. Stir in 2 cups of rice, season with salt and pepper and cook until the rice becomes translucent. Pour in 4 cups of boiling stock. Bring to the boil again then lower the heat, cover and cook very gently for about 20 minutes or until all the liquid is absorbed and the rice is tender (small holes will appear on the surface). Remove the lid and cook uncovered for a minute or two. Fluff up with a fork before serving.

Buttered Rice

●

This is a good way of using leftover cooked rice. It can be an accompaniment or a meal in itself, depending on what you add to the basic recipe.

For each cup of steamed rice, use 30 g (1 oz) butter. Melt butter in a heavy pan, stir in rice and mix well, tossing lightly over gentle heat, or heat through in a moderately slow oven (160°C/325°F), shaking occasionally until thoroughly heated through.

Flavouring: After buttering rice and before heating, any of the following may be added:
★ thinly sliced mushrooms
★ strips of pimiento
★ diced celery or pepper
★ any cooked vegetables
★ prawns, scallops or mussels
★ A little whipped yogurt can accompany this simple dish.

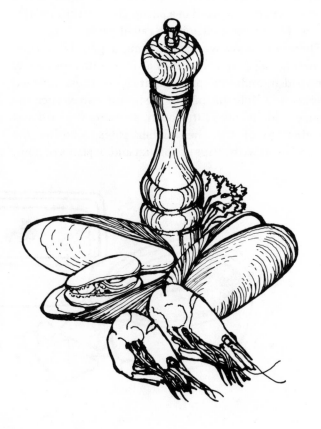

PRESENTABLE PÂTÉS AND TERRINES

To a Frenchman, pâtés are an indispensible part of good eating but you don't have to be a Frenchman to enjoy them.

Pâtés are not only easy to make, but come in a flavourful variety. Have you thought of rabbit or smoked mackerel pâté, and of course, there are the lovely terrines, country and home-style pâtés.

What is the difference between a pâté and a terrine, the question often crops up. Nowadays, the words are used interchangeably. Pâté and terrine mixtures are the same, it is how the mixture is treated that makes the difference. It is usual to describe a pâté as a mixture of any finely ground meats, liver, game etc., seasoned, flavoured and baked. When the mixture is placed in a dish that has been lined with pork fat or bacon it is a terrine, when it is baked in a pastry crust 'en croûte' it is a pâté. Most liver mixtures are called pâtés.

There are many ways of making a pâté or terrine. Sometimes all the meat is finely ground with other finely chopped ingredients, and this includes those labelled pâté maison. It is the 'pâté of the house' and as such the 'house' adds its own little touch, showing the skill and imagination of the chef. Other pâtés combine the ground meat with strips of pork fat and/or strips of ham,

tongue or other meats; these are marinated to give a distinctive taste then packed in the centre of the meat mixture to give a mosaic effect when cut. Pâtés and terrines are marvellous to have on hand, they keep well in the refrigerator for at least 2 weeks and they are one of the best dishes to serve as a first course at luncheon and some dinners.

Some pâtés or terrines are sealed with a *luting paste*, which is a stiff paste of flour and water used to seal the lid and base of a terrine or other oven-baked dish. Luting paste provides a very good seal and there is less shrinkage of the meat. Aluminium foil can be used in conjunction with the lid but a luting paste is far superior. After cooking, the luting paste is broken off and discarded. The proportions of 1 cup of flour to 4 tablespoons water will make enough paste to seal a smallish terrine.

Pâtés and terrines travel well to picnics and served with pickled cucumbers, a bowl of rose radishes, a green salad, some crusty bread and a bottle of wine, you have the makings of a delightful luncheon; if it can be taken 'alfresco' so much the better. I've included some simple fish pâtés in this chapter but the recipes for Potted Shrimps or Crab (page 52) also make good first courses.

Potted Pork

••

Potted Pork is traditionally served as a first course with hot toast. It can be made with shoulder of pork or belly of pork, in which case the extra fat is not necessary. Flavour it well to prevent the dish tasting bland, using plenty of freshly ground pepper. This dish keeps for weeks, when covered well and kept in the refrigerator.

375 g (12 oz) lean pork
125 g (4 oz) pork fat
½ teaspoon salt
freshly ground pepper
½ cup water
1 bay leaf
2 whole cloves

Cut pork into 1 cm (½ inch) cubes and place in a heavy casserole. Cut the pork fat into small cubes and add to the pork with the remaining ingredients. Cover and bake in a slow oven (150°C/300°F) for about 4 hours, or until most of the liquid has evaporated and the pork is very tender. Do not let the pork brown, if it begins to colour add a little more water.

Transfer the pork to a shallow bowl with a draining spoon. Discard the bay leaf and cloves and reserve the cooking liquid. Shred the pork as finely as possible using two forks then stir in the reserved cooking liquid. Check for seasoning with extra salt and pepper. Pack mixture tightly into a small stone jar or terrine. Cover with a lid or piece of aluminium foil and refrigerate for at least 24 hours before serving.

Pork Cheese

••

Serve this delicious cold meat with a green salad and spring onions. Offer a little hot mustard and vinegar, as both go extremely well with this dish.

1 fresh or pickled hand of pork
salt
freshly ground black pepper
4 sage leaves

If using pickled pork, soak in water to cover overnight. Drain, place in a heavy pot with enough fresh water to just cover. Cook covered over low heat for 4 hours or until tender. Remove the bones from the meat. Place the meat, including the skin, in a basin and season with salt (a pickled hand may not need salt, so taste first) and freshly ground black pepper. Chop the sage leaves finely and sprinkle over the pork. Strain a little cooking liquid on to the meat in the basin and leave to cool, pressing down with a weight. Chill and set. Turn out and serve with a green salad.

Pâté de Campagne

•••

This is a robust country-style pâté, strong with herbs and spices and of course Cognac or brandy. Vary the flavour by using Calvados or Armagnac just as a Frenchman would do.

60 g (2 oz) butter
1 large onion, finely chopped
500 g (1 lb) veal and pork mince
250 g (8 oz) pork fat, finely minced
250 g (8 oz) chicken livers
125 g (4 oz) ham, sliced thickly
2 eggs, slightly beaten
1 clove garlic, crushed
2 tablespoons brandy
¼ cup cream
2 teaspoons salt
1 teaspoon white pepper
¼ teaspoon each ground mace, allspice, thyme and rosemary
pinch ground cloves
1 bay leaf

Luting Paste

1 cup flour
4 tablespoons water

Melt the butter in a heavy frying pan and fry the onions until golden. Remove from the heat and place in a large mixing bowl together with the mince and pork fat. Mix together well. Remove the sinews from the chicken livers and slice them finely. Add them to the pork and veal mixture together with the remaining ingredients, except the bay leaf. Mix the ingredients together until well combined. Spoon the mixture into a 5–6 cup ovenproof dish and place the bay leaf on top. Cover with foil and a lid or seal the lid with Luting Paste made by combining the flour and water. Place the dish in a baking pan of hot water (water should come halfway up the sides of dish) and bake in a moderate oven (180°C/350°F) for 2 hours. Uncover and cook for a further 30 minutes. Remove from oven, cover with aluminium foil and place a weight on top. Store in the refrigerator overnight. Turn the finished pâté out of the dish and serve.

Note: To make this pâté into a terrine, line the dish with 3 mm (⅛ inch) strips or sheets of fresh pork fat back or fat from pork loin. Place a sprig of fresh thyme and bay leaf on top. Proceed as above but do not remove the lid during cooking.

Duck and Chicken Liver Pâté

• • •

*Most of us know and enjoy chicken liver pâté, but the
addition of duck livers is a little different –
adding a special richness of flavour. If the shop where you
buy your chicken livers hasn't duck livers on
hand, I am sure they will be happy
to order them in for you.*

250 g (8 oz) chicken livers
250 g (8 oz) duck livers
250 g (8 oz) butter
1 large onion, finely chopped
1 clove garlic, crushed
2 teaspoons chopped mixed fresh herbs
(thyme, sage, marjoram)
salt
freshly ground pepper
1 tablespoon brandy or Grand Marnier

Clarified Butter

90 g (3 oz) butter

Trim livers of fibres. Melt 30–45 g (1–1½ oz) of the butter in a
heavy frying pan and sauté the onion and garlic until very soft,
about 15–20 minutes. Using a slotted spoon remove the onion
and set aside. Quickly sauté the livers a few at a time in the
same pan, until still quite pink inside. Remove and purée in a
food processor or blender with the onions and fresh herbs until
smooth, or push through a sieve. Cool.

Cream the remaining butter in a large bowl and when the
liver mixture is cool, beat into the butter. Season well with salt
and freshly ground pepper and brandy or Grand Marnier and
spoon into a mould. Place a sage leaf, sprigs of fresh thyme or a
fresh bay leaf in the centre of the pâté, and spoon a layer of
Clarified Butter over the top. Cover and chill.

To clarify butter: Melt the butter in a small pan, and when
completely melted remove from heat and stand for a few
minutes, allowing the milk solids to settle to the bottom. Skim
off the butter fat from the surface and pour very carefully into
another container, leaving the solids behind. The clarified
butter is now ready to use. To cover the pâté in the quantity
given above, about 90 g (3 oz) of butter (before clarifying)
should be sufficient.

Terrine with Olives,
Pine nuts and Prosciutto

• • •

*This elegant terrine would start any dinner party
with a flourish. Olives, pine nuts and prosciutto add
intriguing texture as well as flavour and colour.*

500 g (1 lb) lean pork
125 g (4 oz) veal
125 g (4 oz) pork fat
⅓ cup pine nuts
¼ cup soft white breadcrumbs
2 tablespoons dry vermouth
90 g (3 oz) prosciutto, cut in one slice
1 clove garlic
1 teaspoon salt
⅓ cup black olives, finely chopped
1 tablespoon chopped, fresh basil or 1 teaspoon
dried basil
½ teaspoon dried thyme
freshly ground black pepper
1 egg, lightly beaten
6 slices fatty bacon, rinds removed

Cut the pork, veal and pork fat into small pieces, then mince
together in a food processor fitted with the double edged steel
blade. (If you don't have a processor, ask your butcher to mince
them together for you.)

Lightly toast the pine nuts on a tray in a moderate oven, or
under the grill. Soak the breadcrumbs in the vermouth. Cut the
prosciutto into small dice. Crush the clove of garlic with the
salt.

Combine all the prepared ingredients in a large bowl, with
the olives, basil, thyme, a grinding of black pepper and the
egg, mix well.

Line a 5–6 cup loaf pan or terrine with 3 slices of the bacon,
rinds removed. Turn the meat mixture into the pan and press it
down firmly. Cover with the remaining bacon. Bake the terrine
in a moderate oven (180°C/350°F) for 1¼ hours. Pour off any
excess fat or juices. Put a plate on top, and weight it down (an
iron makes a good weight). Cool, then chill for 12 hours. To
serve, unmould on to a platter and allow to come to room
temperature.

Note: Double – cured, smoked Canadian bacon, or ham de
luxe, may be substituted for the prosciutto. If you have a pork
butcher in your neighbourhood, thin slices of fat back may be
used to line the pan instead of fatty bacon, but in this case, you
should remove the fat back before serving, although some
people enjoy this on bread.

*Right: Delicate cold desserts include Apricot Orange Mousse
(page 274) and Petits Pots de Crème in various flavours (page 287).
Decorate the dishes for an attractive finish.*

Rabbit Terrine

• • •

The addition of Pernod gives this terrine an intriguing flavour. Use the food processor to mince the meats — but you can finely chop or mince the meat using a mincer if you wish. Buy 2 large or 3 small rabbits to obtain the amount of rabbit meat required.

750 g (1½ lb) rabbit meat, boned
375 g (12 oz) good sausage mince
3 rashers bacon
2½ cups soft white breadcrumbs
185 g (6 oz) chicken livers
30 g (1 oz) butter
1 tablespoon Pernod
1 small onion, finely chopped
1 clove garlic, crushed
½ teaspoon thyme
1 teaspoon salt
pepper
1 egg
250 g (8 oz) fresh pork fat back or fat from pork loin, or fatty bacon

Mince the rabbit meat and place in a large bowl with the sausage mince, finely chopped or minced bacon and breadcrumbs.

Trim the chicken livers of fibres and discard any which are discoloured. Melt the butter in a frying pan and sauté the livers for about 3 minutes until they are stiffened and lightly browned, but still quite pink inside. Place the liver and butter in a blender and blend until reduced to a purée, or process in a food processor fitted with the doubled edged steel blade. Add the liver to the meat mixture with the remaining ingredients, except the pork fat. Mix all the ingredients together thoroughly with a wooden spoon.

Slice the pork fat or bacon into 3 mm (⅛ inch) strips or sheets. Arrange lengthwise in a 10 cup terrine, completely covering the bottom and sides, leaving a sheet of pork fat for the top. Spoon the rabbit meat mixture into the terrine, levelling the top. Cut the remaining pork fat or bacon into thin strips and arrange on the top of the terrine – lattice fashion. Cover with foil and lid, or seal lid with luting (flour and water) paste made from 1 cup flour and 4 tablespoons water. Place the terrine in a baking dish of hot water and bake in a moderate oven (180°C/350°F) for 1½ hours. Take from the oven, remove the lid and place a weight on top. Leave until cool and set. Good accompaniments are tiny gherkins and crusty French bread.

Terrine Bourguignonne

• • •

Most terrines improve with being made a few days ahead of eating. Like cheese they ripen. This is an interesting terrine to make and most rewarding to serve. It's well worth the trouble you take, if you own a modern food processor then it's a breeze.

500 g (1 lb) veal steak
500 g (1 lb) pork fillet
500 g (1 lb) rabbit meat, boned
½ cup dry white wine
2 small onions, finely sliced
1 teaspoon fresh thyme or ½ teaspoon dried thyme
2 bay leaves
2 eggs, slightly beaten
½ cup Madeira
salt
freshly ground black pepper
250 g (8 oz) fresh pork fat back or streaky bacon

Slice half of the veal, pork and rabbit into long thin strips. Place them in a glass or earthenware dish and marinate in the wine, onions, thyme and one of the bay leaves for 2 hours.

Prepare a fine meat stuffing by mincing together or putting through a food processor fitted with the double edged steel blade, the remaining veal, pork and rabbit. Add the marinade liquid, eggs, Madeira, salt and pepper. Slice the pork fat or bacon into 3 mm (⅛ inch) strips or sheets and arrange lengthwise in a 10 cup terrine completely covering the bottom and sides, leaving a sheet of pork fat for the top. Press in one-third of the meat stuffing, then add half of the meat strips. Add another third of the meat stuffing, then the remaining sliced meat and the remaining stuffing. Cover the meat with the remaining sheet of pork fat or bacon.

Place the remaining bay leaf on top. Cover the dish and seal with a Luting Paste (see page 251). Place the terrine in a baking dish of hot water and bake in a hot oven (200°C/400°F) for 1¾ hours. Remove from oven, cover with aluminium foil and place a weight on top. Store in the refrigerator overnight. Turn the finished terrine out of mould and serve.

Note: Try to find a good pork butcher so that you have a reliable source of supply for pâtés and terrines. They should supply you with the pork, veal and fresh rabbits as well as the pork fat used to line the terrine. Failing pork fat use lean streaky bacon. The fat lining helps keep the meat moist.

Left: Strawberries are lovely by themselves or can be perfumed with oranges and liqueur to become Strawberries Romanov (page 295).

Pork Pâté

• • •

This simple pork pâté is one that is made every other week in Denmark and one I make regularly. The pork fat for lining the terrine is cut from the back. It can be ordered from some butchers. In place of pork fat, mild cured bacon rashers can be used.

strips of pork fat
750 g (1½ lb) minced pork
2 eggs, beaten
1 teaspoon dried tarragon
½ teaspoon ground cumin
1 teaspoon salt
black pepper
¼ cup brandy

Luting Paste

1 cup flour
4 tablespoons water

Line the bottom and sides of a 3½ cup terrine or other ovenproof dish with the pork fat. Mix the pork, eggs, tarragon, cumin, salt and freshly ground pepper to taste with a wooden spoon. Warm the brandy, ignite and add to the mixture when the flame subsides. If necessary pound the meat mixture in a mortar to get a smooth paste.

Fill the lined terrine with this forcemeat. Place a slice of pork fat on top and cover with foil and a lid. Seal the lid of the dish with the Luting Paste made by combining the flour and water. Bake the pâté in a moderate oven (180°C/350°F) for 1–1½ hours. For best results, stand the dish in a pan of boiling water. Remove from oven, break off the Luting Paste, take off lid and place a plate or flat board directly on top of the pâté with a weight on top. Leave until cold, then cover with a fresh piece of foil and chill.

Fish Pâté

Most of us are used to pâtés made with a meat base, but fish pâtés are also delicious – and give that touch of difference you often look for in a first course. Here are a couple of simple ones and a last minute recipe for unexpected guests. You will find smoked trout and eel available at most good delicatessen shops.

Mackerel Pâté

•

Imported smoked mackerel in foil and plastic packets makes a superb pâté that can be served as a first course or with drinks. It is unbelievably simple to make in a food processor.

1 smoked mackerel, weighing about 500 g (1 lb)
185 g (6 oz) butter
juice of ½ lemon
freshly ground black pepper
pinch paprika
2 tablespoons cream

Skin and remove the bones from the mackerel and flake the flesh, there should be approximately 375 g (12 oz) of fish or more. Beat the butter until soft and creamy, add the mackerel flesh and beat well. Add the lemon juice and season with freshly ground pepper and a small pinch paprika. Beat in the cream until just combined. Spoon into a small earthenware pot or dish and serve with hot toast, Melba toast or crisp crackers. *Melba Toast* Lightly toast thinly sliced bread; as soon as it is ready, remove crusts and halve diagonally, slice each piece through horizontally. Place on a baking tray and bake in a slow oven (150°C/300°F) until crisp and pale golden. Cool. If preparing in advance store in an airtight container.

Smoked Trout Pâté

• •

1 smoked trout
juice of 1 lemon
60 g (2 oz) butter
125 g (4 oz) packet cream cheese
½ teaspoon freshly ground black pepper
½ teaspoon paprika
salt (optional)

Skin and fillet the trout and mash the flesh with the lemon juice in a food processor fitted with the double edged steel blade, whirl in a blender or push through a mouli. Soften the butter and cream cheese, and beat together with a fork until creamy.

Blend the butter and cheese with the trout, and season with pepper and paprika. Taste and add salt if necessary. Pack into an attractive bowl and chill, covered, for several hours before serving. Serve with Melba toast, hot buttered toast or brown bread and butter.

Note: The pâté keeps well in the refrigerator if sealed with a layer of clarified butter (see page 252).

Smoked Eel Pâté

• •

250 g (8 oz) smoked eel
2 anchovy fillets
2 teaspoons onion juice
125 g (4 oz) butter
1 teaspoon lemon juice
few drops of sherry, Marsala or port
pinch each of black pepper, cayenne, grated
nutmeg and powdered thyme

Skin and fillet the eel and mash the flesh with a fork. Add the remaining ingredients and pound together to a smooth paste. This can also be done in a food processor fitted with the double edged steel blade. Pack the mixture into a bowl and chill for at least 3 hours in the refrigerator. Serve with brown bread and butter, hot buttered toast or Melba toast.

Note: To obtain onion juice, grate a peeled onion into a bowl to catch the juice. If the pâté is to be kept longer than a few days, seal the top with a thin layer of clarified butter (see page 252).

Salmon Pâté

(Last minute Pâté)

•

When you need something savoury, quick and delicious in a hurry, you should find all these ingredients waiting in the pantry. Serve with hot buttered toast, Melba toast, brown bread and butter or crisp crackers. A bowl of bright red radishes or celery stalks would be a pleasant, crunchy addition.

1 × 250 g (8 oz) can salmon or tuna
2 teaspoons anchovy essence or paste
90 g (3 oz) butter, softened
juice of ½ a lemon
1 tablespoon Worcestershire sauce
freshly ground black pepper

Remove any bones and skin from the fish and drain off oil or brine. Place in a bowl with all the other ingredients, mashing well with a fork to form a paste. You may also use a food processor fitted with the double edged steel blade. Pack the pâté into a small bowl and serve immediately, or chill in the refrigerator.

SAVOURY QUICHES AND TARTS

Quiche has become a standard in many homes including mine, and it's easy to see why. These savoury French tarts can do you proud as a casual meal, a first course, a picnic or with drinks.

They carry well, reheat well and, though a quiche is at its peak about 15 minutes after baking, they eat well at any temperature from hot to cool. What other dish can claim as much? I'm finding new directions for these favourites by using filo pastry as a change from shortcrust and interesting flavours like fresh herbs and finnan haddie (smoked haddock) for the fillings.

The flan case can be prepared ahead, the pastry made and the tin lined and stored in the refrigerator. The custard can be mixed and the filling prepared then both can be kept covered also in the refrigerator. It then becomes a simple matter of assembling the quiche and putting it into the oven.

Time the operation so that the quiche comes out of the oven 10–15 minutes before you intend to eat it – that's when the quiche is at its very best – when still warm. Don't let that deter you from taking it on a picnic, a quiche is still good served cool.

Flan case

(Rich Shortcrust Pastry)

•

1½ cups plain flour
pinch of salt
90 g (3 oz) butter
1 egg yolk
1 tablespoon water

Sift the flour and salt into a bowl. Rub the butter in lightly and evenly until the mixture resembles fine breadcrumbs. Mix the egg yolk and water and stir into the flour with a spatula or knife to form a dough; add more water if necessary. Knead lightly on a lightly floured board, wrap and chill for 30 minutes or until required. This allows the pastry to rest so that it loses all elasticity and will not shrink or lose its shape during baking. Roll out on a lightly floured board to fit a 20 or 23 cm (8 or 9 inch) fluted flan ring. Press the pastry well into the flutes, being careful not to stretch or tear it. Using a sharp knife, cut the pastry level with the top of the flan ring. Chill while preparing the filling. *Sufficient for a 20–23 cm (8–9 inch) ring.*
Note: The uncooked dough will keep for up to 3 or 4 days under refrigeration, or can be frozen for several weeks. In either case, wrap in greaseproof paper and then in plastic wrap or a freezer bag.

Herb Quiche

••

For those with a ready supply of fresh herbs or a good herb garden, here's a deliciously different and aromatic quiche.
If watercress is not available, substitute chopped parsley, plus a teaspoon of your choice of fresh herbs.

30 g (1 oz) butter
2 medium onions, or 8–10 spring onions, finely chopped
1 cup cream or milk
2 eggs
1 tablespoon snipped chives
1 tablespoon chopped watercress
1 tablespoon chopped parsley
salt
freshly ground pepper
1 flan case (left), chilled, or filo case (right)

Melt the butter in a heavy based saucepan and fry the onions until softened. Place the cream and eggs in a mixing bowl and beat together until well combined. Stir in the onions, herbs and seasonings and spoon into the flan case. Bake in a moderately hot oven (190°C/375°F) for 30–40 minutes or until the custard is set. *Serves 4–6*

258

Finnan Haddie Tart

• • •

A light yet satisfying luncheon dish. The filo pastry is just right with its fine flaky layers opening around a creamy custard filling.

Filo case

8 sheets filo pastry
90 g (3 oz) butter, melted

Filling

250 g (8 oz) smoked haddock
1½ cups milk
2 eggs
½ cup sour cream
2 hard-boiled eggs, chopped
2 tablespoons chopped parsley
½ teaspoon salt
¼ teaspoon freshly ground pepper
¼ teaspoon ground nutmeg

Filo case: Line a 20 cm (8 inch) metal flan tin or pie dish with the filo pastry, brushing each layer with the melted butter. Trim the edges with kitchen scissors.

Filling: Poach the haddock in 1 cup of the milk for 10 minutes or until tender. Remove the fish and cool slightly. Remove the skin and any bones and flake the flesh with a fork. Beat the eggs, add the remaining milk and sour cream. Fold in the hard-boiled eggs, parsley and haddock. Season with salt, pepper and nutmeg.

Spoon the filling into prepared pastry case. Bake in a moderately hot oven (190°C/375°F) for 15 minutes then reduce heat to moderate (180°C/350°F) for 25 minutes or until golden. Serve with a tossed salad. *Serves 4–6*

Spinach Quiche

• •

500 g (1 lb) spinach
30 g (1 oz) butter
1 small onion, finely chopped
1 prepared flan case (page 258) chilled,
or filo case (left)
1 egg
1 egg yolk
1 cup Ricotta cheese
½ cup sour cream
salt
freshly ground pepper
1 teaspoon fresh chopped oregano or a pinch
of nutmeg

Remove the tough centre stalks from the spinach, wash well under running water and shake off excess. Place in a saucepan, cover tightly and simmer for 4–5 minutes. Press the spinach between two plates to remove all the liquid. Chop finely or chop in a food processor fitted with the double edged steel blade. Set aside.

Melt the butter, add the onion and cook until soft but not coloured, add the spinach. Cook over a high heat for 2–3 minutes to remove any moisture, place in a bowl and allow to cool.

Prick the base of the flan case with a fork, line with kitchen paper, half-fill with dried beans and bake in a hot oven (220°C/450°F) for 10 minutes. Remove the beans and paper.

Beat the egg and egg yolk together, add the Ricotta cheese and sour cream, mix well. Season to taste with salt and pepper. Add the spinach and stir in the oregano or nutmeg, stir to combine. Bake in a moderately hot oven (190°C/375°F) for 30 minutes or until golden. *Serves 4–6*

Leek Filo Pie

••

Filo pastry, the special Mediterranean pastry of a thousand leaves, is now so universally available it needs no additional introduction. This pie makes use of the mild but aromatic flavour of leeks and is a change from the usual spinach filling.

6 medium leeks
1 egg
125 g (4 oz) Feta cheese
salt
freshly ground pepper
8 sheets filo pastry
3 tablespoons olive oil or melted butter

Slit the leeks right down one side and wash thoroughly under cold running water to remove all the grit. Trim the root ends and remove any coarse outer leaves. Slice the leeks 1 cm (½ inch) thick and simmer in a little lightly salted water for 8 minutes. Drain and refresh under cold running water. Drain again and set aside until cold.

Place the egg and Feta cheese in a blender or food processor fitted with the double edged steel blade and blend until smooth, or mash together with a fork. Combine with the cold leeks. Season to taste – but do not add too much salt, as Feta is a salty cheese.

Place the filo between two dry tea-towels with another dampened tea-towel on top. Brush a 20 cm (8 inch) shallow square cake tin with 1 teaspoon of the oil or butter. Brush one sheet of filo lightly with oil, fold in half and brush lightly with oil again and use to line the tin. Place two more sheets of filo, each lightly brushed with oil on top, overlapping them and allowing the ends to hang over the sides of the tin. Add the leek filling and spread evenly in the tin. Top with the remaining filo, folded in half and lightly brushed with oil as before. Tuck the overhanging ends down inside the tin, enclosing the filling completely, and brush the top with oil. Bake in a moderately hot oven (190°C/375°F) for 45 minutes or until the filo is golden. Cut into squares to serve. *Serves 4–6*

Asparagus Quiche

••

1 flan case (page 258) or filo case (page 259)
1 × 450 g (15 oz) can asparagus
salt
freshly ground pepper
60 g (2 oz) Gruyère cheese, thinly sliced
2 eggs
⅔ cup light sour cream

Prepare flan case and chill. Drain the asparagus and arrange in a cartwheel in the case; Season. Cover with the cheese. Beat the eggs and sour cream together, only until just combined. Spoon the egg mixture over the asparagus. Bake in a moderately hot oven (190°C/375°F) for 30–40 minutes or until the filling is set.

Allow to stand for 3–4 minutes before serving. *Serves 4–6*

Spring Onion Tart

••

For a luncheon or picnic, treat the family to this nutritious tart. It slices well so could be used in the lunch box.

Pastry
¾ cup self-raising flour
pinch of salt
¼ cup medium oatmeal
90 g (3 oz) butter
2–3 tablespoons water
beaten egg to glaze

Filling
6–8 spring onions
1 rasher streaky bacon, chopped
2 tablespoons grated Cheddar cheese
1 egg
¾ cup milk
salt
freshly ground pepper

To make the pastry: Sift the flour and salt together. Add the oatmeal and rub in the butter. Mix to a firm dough with about 2 tablespoons of the water. Line an 18 cm (7 inch) sandwich tin or springform tin with two-thirds of the pastry, reserving the remaining pastry for the top.

Wash and finely slice the onions into 6 mm (¼ inch) lengths. Arrange on the bottom of the pastry case. Sprinkle over the bacon and cheese. Beat the egg and milk together, add salt and pepper to taste and pour over the filling.

Roll out the remaining pastry and place on top, pressing down gently over the sides. Brush with beaten egg and make a small steam hole in the centre. Bake in a moderately hot oven

(190°C/375°F) for 45 minutes or until golden brown and crisp and the custard is cooked through. Serve with a green salad. *Serves 4–6*

Broccoli Quiche

• •

500 g (1 lb) broccoli
salt
60 g (2 oz) Gruyère cheese, thinly sliced
2 eggs
⅔ cup light sour cream
freshly ground pepper
1 flan case (page 258), chilled, or filo
case (page 259)

Wash and trim the broccoli and cut into small heads or branches. Cook in a small amount of boiling salted water, covered tightly, for 5 minutes. Drain well, and cool.

Arrange the broccoli in layers or cartwheel fashion in the flan case. Cover with the cheese. Beat the eggs and sour cream together only until combined, and add salt and pepper to taste.

Spoon the egg mixture over the cheese. Bake in a moderately hot oven (190°C/375°F) for 30–40 minutes or until the filling is set. Stand for 3–4 minutes before serving. *Serves 4–6*

Onion Quiche

• •

4–5 medium onions, finely sliced
30 g (1 oz) butter
1 tablespoon oil
½ teaspoon cumin
½ teaspoon salt
3 egg yolks, beaten
½ cup cream
1 flan case (page 258), chilled

Heat the butter and oil in a heavy pan, add the onions and cook over a gentle heat until the onions are soft and golden, shaking the pan from time to time; this will take 15–20 minutes. Remove from the heat and add the cumin and salt, then stir in the egg yolks and cream.

Spoon the onion mixture into the flan case. Bake in a hot oven (200°C/400°F) for 10 minutes, then reduce the temperature to moderate (180°C/350°F) for a further 20 minutes. *Serves 4–6*
Note: A less rich version can be made with 2 whole eggs and half milk, half cream, or use evaporated milk. Cumin may be replaced with nutmeg.

CRÊPES AND PANCAKES

Crêpes and pancakes are both made from the same basic ingredients, but crêpes usually have a higher proportion of eggs to flour, and are thin, tender and light. Rolled around a savoury filling they are a delicious first course when entertaining, and the perfect answer to the problem of what to have as a light lunch. With a sweet filling, or folded and basted in a liqueur-flavoured sauce, they become a marvellous dessert.

Pancakes are usually thicker in consistency and can also double as a sweet or savoury course. The traditional sweet topping is lemon and sugar, but in the USA they are served with butter and maple syrup, and in Scandinavian countries a topping of berries and sour cream.

Some of the savoury pancake dishes make a quite substantial main dish, as you will see from the recipe for Pork and Egg Pancake.

Like sandwiches, pancakes offer a field day for the creative cook to add his or her own imaginative touches.

The Pancake and Crêpe Pan

A pan especially designed for pancakes is made of cast iron and has straight sides about 1 cm (½ inch) high which makes the tossing of pancakes easy. A pan 18 cm (7 inch) across makes a good-sized, all-purpose crêpe or pancake.

This type of pan, like an omelette pan, should never be washed – just cleaned with a piece of oiled cloth or kitchen paper. If for some reason the pan should become burnt or sticky, take a damp cloth, dip it in salt, rub the pan well and then rub with an oiled cloth.

The French make a good omelette pan which can do double duty for both crêpes and omelettes. Select one the same size as a crêpe pan, 18 cm (7 inch).

To season a new pan Fill with oil, place on the heat and bring to the boil. Remove and allow to stand for 24 hours. Pour off the oil, wipe the pan out with kitchen paper, and it is then ready for use.

Basic Pancake Batter

•

A pancake is thicker than a crêpe and has a more cake-like texture. Many recipes, like this one, include baking powder which gives a slight 'rise' when the pancakes are cooked, making them especially light.
When should you choose a pancake, and when a crêpe mixture? You may often, of course, substitute one for the other, but crêpes are usually preferred for their lacy thinness if they are to be served folded or rolled.
Pancakes, however, are usually preferred for their delicate softness when they are to be served flat or in a stack and eaten immediately.

1 cup flour
1 teaspoon baking powder
½ teaspoon salt
1 egg
1½ cups milk
2 teaspoons butter, melted

Sift the flour with the baking powder and salt into a mixing bowl. Make a well in the centre and add the egg, milk and melted butter. With a wooden spoon gradually draw in the flour. Beat well, cover and leave to stand for 1 hour.

Heat a little butter in a pancake or crêpe pan. Pour off excess, reserving for when the pan needs regreasing. Use a small jug to pour in enough batter to coat the surface of the pan or you can measure it in from a large spoon – about 2 tablespoons is right for a 15 cm (6 inch) pan. Run the batter smoothly and evenly over the surface. Cook until small bubbles appear, about 1 minute, then use a metal spatula to turn the pancake over. Cook for 1 minute on the other side. *Makes about 14 pancakes*

Basic Crêpe Recipe

•

Crêpes can be freshly made each time they are required but they freeze so well it makes sense to keep a stock on hand.
This amount of batter should make 20–24 crêpes depending on size and thickness. Stack the crêpes in groups of 8 to 10 (depending on how many you intend serving at the one time) with a square of greaseproof paper separating each one. Wrap in aluminium foil and place in plastic freezer bags, store in the refrigerator or freezer. If frozen, defrost before using.

1¼ cups plain flour
pinch of salt
3 eggs, beaten
1½ cups milk
1 tablespoon brandy
2 teaspoons melted butter
extra butter

Sift the flour and salt into a mixing bowl. Make a well in the centre and add the eggs and milk. With a wooden spoon gradually draw in flour. Beat well and stir in the brandy and melted butter. Cover and leave to stand for 1 hour.

Heat a little butter in a pancake or crêpe pan. Pour off excess, reserving for when the pan needs regreasing.

Use a small jug and pour in enough batter to thinly coat the surface of the pan. Rotate pan quickly and run batter smoothly and evenly over the surface, pour off any excess.

The crêpes should be about 13 cm (5 inch) across. Cook until small bubbles appear, about 1 minute, then use a metal spatula to flip the crêpes over. Cook for 1 minute on the other side. *Makes 20–24 crêpes*

Spinach and Ricotta Crêpes

• •

1 kg (2 lb) fresh spinach
1 tablespoon softened butter
1½ cups Ricotta cheese
3 egg yolks, beaten
½ cup grated Parmesan cheese
pinch of nutmeg
1 teaspoon salt
¼ teaspoon freshly ground black pepper
8–10 Crêpes (see left)
30 g (1 oz) butter

Topping

½ cup light sour cream
½ cup grated Parmesan cheese

Remove the tough centre stalks and wash the spinach. Cook, covered, in a large saucepan in a little water for 10 minutes over a moderate heat. Drain thoroughly, squeezing the spinach in your hands to remove all moisture. Chop and purée in an electric blender with the butter.

Push the Ricotta cheese through a sieve and add to the cooled spinach with the egg yolks, Parmesan cheese, nutmeg, salt and pepper. Blend to a smooth paste.

Place one crêpe on a flat surface. Spoon a little of the filling over just below the centre then neatly roll up the crêpe, cigar fashion. Repeat with the remaining crêpes and filling. Place in a greased ovenproof dish, dot with the butter and cover with aluminium foil.

Cook in a moderate oven (180°C/350°F) for 20–25 minutes until well heated through. Remove the foil, spoon over the sour cream and sprinkle with the Parmesan cheese. Return to the oven and cook for a further 10 minutes. *Serves 4–6*

Crêpes Polonaise

• •

⅔ cup grated Gruyère cheese
125 g (4 oz) butter, softened
salt
freshly ground pepper
grated nutmeg
1 egg, lightly beaten
12 crêpes (page 263)
extra beaten egg
fine breadcrumbs
oil for deep-frying
parsley

Combine the cheese and butter, working to a smooth paste. Season with salt, pepper and nutmeg then stir in the egg. Divide into portions the size of marbles. Enclose a portion in each crêpe and roll up, folding the ends in to form crêpe 'parcels'. Dip the crêpes in extra beaten egg, then in breadcrumbs. Fry a few at a time in deep hot oil. Drain and serve sprinkled lightly with salt. Garnish with parsley. *Serves 6*

Rosti

• •

*Rosti is Switzerland's crusty, golden potato cake. It may be just potatoes or flavoured with onion or bacon.
The onion version here makes a satisfying simple lunch, accompanied by crisp fried bacon or cold meats
and a salad. Rosti is also an excellent accompaniment to meat dishes.*

1.5 kg (3 lb) old potatoes
3 tablespoons oil
30 g (1 oz) butter
2 medium onions, chopped
½ teaspoon salt

Scrub the potatoes and place in cold water to cover. Bring to the boil and cook for 10 minutes. Drain and when cool enough to handle, peel. Cover and leave to become cold.

Heat half the oil and butter in a medium-sized frying pan and fry the onion gently until transparent. Grate the potatoes coarsely and toss with the salt. Remove onions from the pan and set aside on a plate. Put half the potatoes in the pan, spread flat and smooth then spread the onions over them and cover with the other half of the potatoes.

Pat flat and cook uncovered over a low heat for about 10 minutes. Slip a spatula or fish slice under the Rosti from time to time to check that it is not becoming too brown. When it is golden brown, place a plate upside down over the frying pan. Wearing thick oven gloves on both hands grasp the pan and plate firmly together and invert them, the Rosti is now on the plate. Place the pan back on the heat, add remaining butter and

oil and when the foam has subsided, slide the Rosti, brown side up, into the pan. Cook for 8 minutes over low heat, checking that it does not become too brown, then slide on to a large heated platter and serve at once. *Serves 6–8*

Canneloni

• • •

Let the uninitiated be warned, special shopping has to be done for the ingredients in this canneloni. This recipe makes use of crêpes in place of the traditional canneloni tubes. The filling is time consuming – a food processor does the job in a flash, but the results more than justify the means for this is a very special dish with which you can expect to win some laurels.

16 Crêpes (page 263)
6 tablespoons grated Parmesan cheese

Filling

750 g (1½ lb) chicken breasts
250 g (8 oz) chicken livers
60 g (2 oz) butter
125 g (4 oz) ham
125 g (4 oz) Mozzarella cheese, cubed
2 tablespoons grated Parmesan cheese

Sauce

60 g (2 oz) butter
4 tablespoons plain flour
4 cups milk
½ cup cream
salt
freshly ground pepper
grated nutmeg

Make the filling: Skin and bone the chicken breasts. Halve the chicken livers and trim off the sinews. Melt the butter in a heavy frying pan and sauté the chicken breasts over a moderate heat until golden brown and cooked through, about 10 minutes. Push to one side of the pan, add the chicken livers and cook for 4 minutes, turning them to brown on all sides. Mince the chicken meat, livers and ham or chop finely or put through a food processor fitted with the double edged steel blade. Mix together with the Mozzarella and Parmesan cheeses.

Make the sauce: Melt the butter in a large saucepan, add the flour and stir for 2 minutes. Add the milk and stir until the sauce boils and thickens. Reduce the heat and cook for 5 minutes, stirring. Add the cream, salt, pepper and a pinch of freshly grated nutmeg. Blend 1 cup of the sauce with the meat mixture.

Lay the crêpes out flat and spoon about 2 tablespoons of filling on to each crêpe and roll up tightly. Spoon a little of the reserved sauce into a large shallow ovenproof dish and place the cannelloni on top in one layer. Coat with the remaining sauce and sprinkle with the Parmesan cheese. Bake in a moderate oven (180°C/350°F), for about 30 minutes or until golden. *Serves 8*

Pork and Egg Pancake

●●

This dish makes a substantial main meal. Serve with a tossed salad or lightly cooked green vegetable for a warming winter meal.

4 tablespoons oil
1 onion, finely chopped
1 small tomato, peeled and chopped
1 clove garlic, crushed
500 g (1 lb) lean minced pork
½ teaspoon salt
freshly ground black pepper
2 eggs, lightly beaten

Garnish

1 tomato, cut into eighths
parsley sprigs

In a heavy frying pan heat 2 tablespoons of the oil, add the onion, tomato and garlic. Cook for 5 minutes, stirring frequently until the vegetables are soft but not coloured. Stir in the pork, salt and pepper, and cook uncovered until the meat is tender and there is no trace of pink. Partially cover the frying pan and cook for 20 minutes or until most of the liquid has evaporated. Spoon mixture into a bowl. When it has cooled add the eggs.

In a heavy frying pan heat 1 tablespoon of the remaining oil. Pour in the pork and egg mixture and cook over a low heat for 1 or 2 minutes or until the top is firm to the touch. Loosen the edges with a metal spatula and slide the pancake on to a plate, add the remaining oil to the pan and return the pancake brown side upwards. Cook for a further 1 or 2 minutes. Loosen edges and bottom of pancake with a metal spatula and slide on to a heated platter.

Garnish with tomato and parsley. Serve cut in wedges. *Serves 4*

Blintzes

●●●

Blintzes, golden crêpes filled with creamy cheese and topped with jam and sour cream, make a perfect dessert or supper dish. They are good too, served with canned cherries or strawberries, or serve them plain accompanied with sour cream for brunch or lunch. Best of all, they can be filled several hours in advance, stored in the refrigerator and sautéed just before serving.

1 quantity crêpe batter (page 263)
butter for frying
sugar and cinnamon to serve

Cheese filling

1 egg yolk
2 tablespoons sugar
250 g (8 oz) softened cream cheese
500 g (1 lb) creamed cottage cheese
¼ teaspoon vanilla

Make the crêpes but cook them on one side only. Cook until golden on underside and the top is bubbly, about 1 minute. Remove and place each blintz on a damp tea-towel or kitchen paper, cooked side up.

Make the cheese filling: Combine the egg yolk and sugar together in a bowl and beat well until thick. Add the cheeses and vanilla and stir until well combined. Place 2–3 tablespoons of the filling in the centre of the cooked side of each blintz. Fold two opposite sides over filling to make a rectangle about 10 cm (4 inch) long, then overlap the other two ends, to cover the filling completely. The blintzes should be in the shape of a neat parcel.

Melt 1–2 tablespoons of butter in a large frying pan over a medium heat. Add 3–4 blintzes, seam side down making sure they do not touch. Sauté until golden then turn and cook the other side. Keep warm in a moderately slow oven (160°C/325°F) while cooking the rest. Serve hot, sprinkled with sugar and cinnamon. *Serves 10–12*

Buckwheat Pancakes

••

½ cup plain flour
¼ teaspoon salt
½ teaspoon baking powder
½ teaspoon bicarbonate of soda
1 tablespoon sugar
½ cup buckwheat flour
1 egg, beaten
2 tablespoons oil or 30 g (1 oz) butter, melted
1½–2 cups buttermilk

Sift the flour with the salt, baking powder, bicarbonate of soda and sugar into a bowl. Stir in the buckwheat flour and set aside. In a small bowl combine the egg, oil or melted butter, and buttermilk, mix well. Add the buttermilk mixture to the flours and stir only until combined. The batter will be lumpy. **Note:** For thinner pancakes add a little extra buttermilk.

Slowly heat a griddle or heavy based frying pan and oil very lightly. Place spoonfuls of batter on the hot griddle and cook until bubbles form on the surface and the edges become dry. Turn and cook the other side until nicely browned. Serve warm, as any of the suggestions below. *Makes approximately 20 pancakes*

These pancakes can also be topped with the following savoury or sweet suggestions.

Savoury toppings:

★ Red or black caviar, or the more common lump fish, served in a small bowl, accompanied by bowls of melted butter, sour cream, chopped onion and chopped capers. This is one of the most glamorous and delectable dishes for a light luncheon or supper meal. As a pre- or after-theatre snack nothing could be more special. Offer icy cold vodka and a tall glass of Pilsener or light ale.

★ Smoked salmon with the previous suggestions.
★ Creamed chicken, turkey or salmon with a bowl of pickled dilled gherkins and chopped olives.

Sweet toppings:

★ Lemon juice and sugar
★ Strawberries, raspberries, bananas or peaches sautéed in a little butter with cream
★ Apple purée and cinnamon sugar
★ Poached apricots and sour cream
★ Maple syrup and cream

Dessert Crêpes

Pancakes and crêpes are delicious with a dusting of sugar and a squeeze of lemon juice, or spread with a favourite fruit conserve, fruit or creamy custard filling.
For dessert crêpes, fill individual crêpes (recipe page 263) with any of the following suggestions.
★ *Sweetened stewed apple flavoured with cinnamon. Fold the crêpes in quarters (like a pocket handkerchief) or roll up loosely, place in a flame and oven proof dish and heat in a very slow oven (100°C/200°F) for 10–12 minutes. Sprinkle caster sugar and slivered almonds over the crêpes and place under a preheated grill for 1 minute to caramelize the sugar a little. Sprinkle a thick layer of icing sugar over the folded crêpes and make a lattice pattern over the top of the crêpes with hot skewers. Serve with whipped or pouring cream.*
★ *Sweetened stewed peaches, plums or apricots.*
★ *125 g (4 oz) Ricotta or cream cheese mixed with 1 tablespoon caster sugar.*
★ *Sweetened chestnut purée beaten with a little rum.*

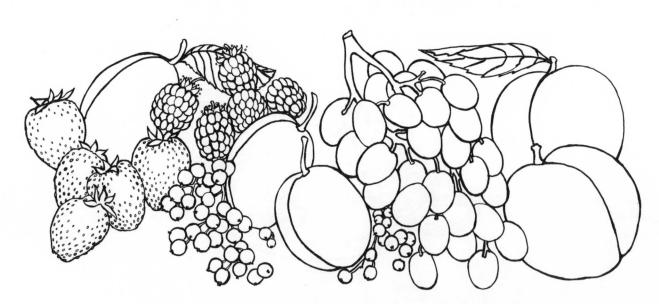

SANDWICHES

there are more than two sides to the story.

The name sandwich, as we all know, comes from John Montagu, Fourth Earl of Sandwich, who was playing cards in the 18th century and didn't want to leave the table. He asked for his cold beef to be placed between two slices of bread and was able to continue the game with one hand while he ate with the other. While many countries still commonly regard the sandwich as filling placed between two slices of bread, in Scandinavia and Germany the sandwich is more often 'open-face' – a single slice of bread with the topping uncovered.

Sandwiches can also be rolled around the fillings, or made in different sizes, and rolls or crispbread can take the place of bread. So can muffins, Lebanese bread and pancakes!

Sandwiches can be cold or hot. In America, hot gravy is poured over a cold meat sandwich, and in Australia grilled cheese on toast has become as popular as meat pies! A sandwich can be baked in a sandwich-maker, fried in a pan, or wrapped in foil and grilled on a barbecue.

In fact, almost anything that combines bread or a bread-type base and a filling follows the tradition made famous by the Earl of Sandwich, and it is probably one of the most versatile and popular foods in the world. In a documentary on China, it was fascinating to see Chinese eating bread with chopsticks! Despite their universal acceptance, there are still creative things to do with sandwiches.

Hero Rolls

•

For a picnic, bushwalk or any outing take these hearty rolls, you'll find they travel well tied with string to keep the filling intact. When ready to eat simply cut into three or four pieces and hand round.

Cut three long rolls of crusty bread in halves lengthwise. Scoop out some of the crumb from the bottom half and spread rolls with butter. Fill liberally with slices of ham, cheese, tomato and lettuce leaves. Season well. Replace top and tie both ends and the middle of each roll with string. Wrap in clear plastic food wrap or aluminium foil. *Serves 6*

Fillings

Any of these fillings may be used as an alternative for the Hero Rolls or for sandwiches.
★ Sliced ham and chutney
★ Cooked crumbled bacon and dill pickles
★ Sliced salami, teawurst or devon
★ Cooked sliced chicken and mayonnaise
★ Sliced cheese and cheese spreads
★ Salmon, tuna, sardines
★ Cooked sliced beef and horseradish

Shooter's Sandwich

•

For six to eight people grill a thick piece of rump steak (about 750 g/1½ lb) until medium rare. Have ready two crusty loaves of bread such as Vienna, sliced through the centre lengthwise, with a little of the crumb removed. Slice steak thinly across and place on the base of each loaf. Season with salt, freshly ground pepper and mustard. If liked, thinly sliced dill pickles can be added. Top with the loaf halves and tie with string. Wrap well with aluminium foil or plastic wrap. Place a heavy weight on top for about 6 hours. Cut across into slices to serve. *Serves 6–8*

Mozzarella in Carrozza

•

12 slices crusty bread
6 thick slices Mozzarella cheese
salt
freshly ground pepper
1 × 50 g tin anchovy fillets, drained and chopped
3 eggs, lightly beaten
¾ cup milk
olive oil for frying

Make 6 sandwiches, using the bread, cheese and anchovy fillets and season with a little salt and pepper.

The sandwiches can be left whole or cut into halves. Lightly beat the eggs and milk. Dip each sandwich into the egg mixture, letting the excess drip off. Fry in hot oil, turning once so both sides become golden brown. Drain on paper towels. Serve as a first course before something light or with a salad for a luncheon dish. *Serves 6*

Savoury Filled Breads

*Two classic breads from the Mediterranean
are served at simple out-of-doors luncheons, usually
accompanied only with a carafe of wine. If made
for a picnic, for which they are ideal, be sure to take along a
sharp bread knife and a small board for easy cutting.
I've included a hearty steak sandwich (page 267)
that is unbelievably good, especially eaten in a
bushland setting.*

Patafla

• •

4 tomatoes
⅓ cup black olives
⅓ cup green olives
2 green peppers
1 large onion
3 tablespoons capers
3 small gherkins
1 long French loaf
olive oil
paprika
salt
freshly ground pepper

Peel and chop the tomatoes, stone the olives and place in a bowl. Remove core and seeds of the peppers and chop finely. Chop the onion, capers and gherkins finely. Add to the tomato mixture with the green peppers. Cut the loaf in half lengthwise and remove all the crumb from both halves. Mix the breadcrumbs with the tomato mixture, kneading it all together with a little olive oil, a pinch of paprika, salt and freshly ground pepper.

Fill the two halves with the mixture, wrap, then put into the refrigerator. The next day, cut into slices ready for lunch. *Serves 6*

Pan Bagna

•

Cut a long French loaf or round flat crusty loaf horizontally into halves. Sprinkle the cut sides liberally with olive oil and leave to soak for 30 minutes. Spread one half with tomato slices, halved black olives, anchovy fillets, pimiento or pepper strips, onion rings and radish slices. Chopped gherkins or hard-boiled eggs may be added. Sprinkle with freshly ground pepper and join the halves together. Wrap in plastic, greaseproof paper or foil and put under a weight for 30 minutes. Cut into thick slices for serving. *Serves 4–6*

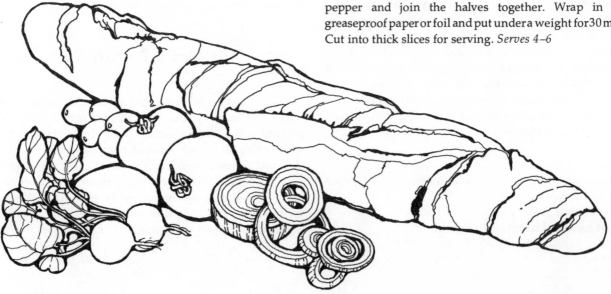

The Smørrebrød

*This is the Danish word for open sandwiches,
and in Denmark, like the Tivoli Gardens, they have been
raised to the status of a national institution. Some
of the finest Danish poets have even been moved to praise
Smørrebrød in verse and why not!*

Smørrebrød consists of a piece of bread, butter, some food to put on it (usually cold) plus a garnish of one kind or another. They may vary from the simple flat kind to the artistically piled high type, but to make attractive Smørrebrød it is necessary to have an eye for colour combinations and a tongue for taste harmonies.

Smørrebrød taste best when freshly made. If it is more convenient to make them ahead of time – for instance, if you want to have a delicious supper to come home to after the movies or theatre – they can still be kept fresh for a few hours. Cover the prepared Smørrebrød with pieces of damp greaseproof paper, then with a clean tea-towel, and place in the refrigerator. Add the final garnishing just before serving.

There is something very satisfying to the creative cook in assembling a big platter of Smørrebrød because the variations are literally endless. One famous Danish restaurant lists 177 varieties on its menu, and you can be just as imaginative at home.

Smørrebrød is also versatile in use. Though principally a lunch food, they are eaten with tea or coffee, for late suppers, and at odd moments when a 'little something' is necessary. They make an interesting first course before dinner, are perfect for a teen-age party, and can be carefully packed to take to picnics.

In Denmark they are usually eaten with a knife and fork, so the fillings can be as lavish as you like.

With your own Smørrebrød keep in mind whether they are to be served at the table or as finger food, because this will dictate your choice of toppings and garnishes to a certain

extent. For finger food, the flat type is more convenient than the piled high.

Whichever way you serve them, once you get into the habit of making Smørrebrød, you will enjoy them as much as the Danes do!

Bread for Smørrebrød

Rye bread in all its variations is a popular choice for Smørrebrød, but you may use any kind, or a mixture of breads. Crusty Italian bread, long French sticks, the chewy mixed-grain breads, high fibre breads and wholemeal breads are all good choices. Rye bread is always cut in thin slices, and one slice is used for each piece of smørrebrød. If bread is large then cut in two. If using a small diameter bread like a French stick, a whole slice is used and this is ideal for cocktail food.

Buttering the Bread

Butter is used for Smørrebrød, and I prefer unsalted butter for this purpose. Store it in a covered container away from strong smelling foods, because butter absorbs smells. It should be soft enough to spread without tearing the bread, but not too soft. Butter evenly and not too thinly – you want the butter to provide a good buffer between the bread and the filling, so the filling can't soak into the bread. After buttering each slice, cut in half if necessary and place the pieces side by side on a tray or flat dish, ready to add the toppings and garnishes.

Adding the Toppings

Before placing the Smørrebrød ingredients on the bread, a lettuce leaf can be put on first as a foundation. This gives added protection against the fillings soaking the bread and adds nice crispness and colour (do make sure the lettuce leaf is perfectly dry, of course). Then add the toppings, keeping a careful eye out for complementary colours, flavours and textures. Garnish as you go along, or add the garnishes later. Note that all toppings go on buttered bread and should completely cover the bread.

Practically anything makes a Smørrebrød, but here are some suggestions to get you started.

★ Top potato salad with herring tidbits and chopped, pickled beetroot. Garnish with sliced olives.

★ For a hot Smørrebrød, which makes a perfect luncheon dish, top hot scrambled eggs with slices of smoked eel and garnish with thinly-sliced raw leeks.

★ Top smoked herring fillets with a mound of chopped radishes. Make a hollow in the centre of the radishes and carefully drop in a raw egg yolk.

★ Top shredded lettuce with smoked salmon paste (bought in a tube). Pipe the salmon paste through a nozzle, making a decorative pattern with the paste and leaving a hollow in the centre. Carefully drop a raw egg yolk into the hollow and top with a little prepared horseradish.

★ Top lettuce with cold scrambled egg and garnish with thin slices of smoked salmon.

★ Spread bread with a thin layer of seasoned, scraped raw beef. Top with a lettuce leaf, slices of hard-boiled egg and garnish with capers.

★ Spread bread with mayonnaise and top with a lettuce leaf and cooked or pickled mussels. Garnish with a sprig of fresh dill.

★ Top bread with cooked prawns or canned shrimp and garnish with cucumber slices and a small spoonful of mayonnaise.

★ Arrange thin slices of smoked ham on bread. Garnish with alternating slices of pickled beetroot and cucumber and spoon a little prepared horseradish over.

★ Spread bread with liver pâté and top with drained flat anchovy fillets. Garnish with prepared horseradish and a sprig of parsley.

★ Arrange thin, hard salami slices in overlapping rows. Top with scrambled egg and thin slices of raw onion.

★ Top thinly sliced rare roast beef with mayonnaise and raw onion sliced into thin rings.

★ Top the bread with thin slices of cooked chicken alternating with slices of Gruyère cheese. Garnish with mayonnaise and thin slices of radish.

★ Arrange thin slices of smoked tongue on top of a lettuce leaf. Top with butter whipped with a little horseradish and garnish with sliced stuffed olives.

Garnishes

The suggestions just given include ideas for garnishing. When choosing your own, the principle is to use a garnish which contributes to taste as well as colour harmony. Sliced lemon goes well with fish, horseradish with meats, tomato and bacon with liver pâté. The bright green of unpeeled cucumber slices and the red and white of radish slices complement most toppings, and snipped chives or a sprig of watercress or parsley are used a great deal for decorative purposes.

Once the principle ingredient of a piece of Smørrebrød has been placed in position, add the garnishes for maximum effect. When using slices of tomato, lemon, cucumber or orange, it is a good idea to make a single cut from the centre out to the edge; then, twist the 'tails' in opposite directions, the slice can be made to stand up on the piece of Smørrebrød for a professional finish.

Miniature Smørrebrød

Smørrebrød may be made canapé-size to serve with drinks. Use slices of the special little savoury sticks sold in some bread shops, or cut small shapes with a sharp knife or round biscuit cutter from sliced bread. The tiny crisp squares of toasted bread sold as mani scoffs (mini toast) are ideal, so too are tiny disks of pumpernickel. For this purpose, Smørrebrød should be easy to manage with the fingers, and the toppings firm.

Cold Canapés

Use any of the above bases buttered and top with one of the following suggestions.

★ Top with a small wedge of Camembert cheese and garnish with a small halved radish with a little green leaf attached and a dab of mayonnaise.

★ Place a teaspoon of smoked eel or salmon paste on the base. Add a few tiny prawns and a parsley sprig.

★ Mash liver pâté and mix with grated onion, chopped ham and chopped stuffed olives. Spread mixture on base and garnish with slices of sweet pickle or a small pickle fan.

★ Top with a tiny lettuce leaf, and a mixture of mayonnaise and grated sharp cheese. Garnish with a walnut half.

★ Top with a thick slice of unpeeled cucumber, which has been hollowed out. Fill the hollow with smoked eel or salmon paste or a little red or black caviar.

★ Beat prepared mustard into butter, and spread on bread. Top with a thin slice of ham, an unpeeled slice of cucumber and quarter-slice of peeled orange. Add half a maraschino cherry for garnish.

Hot Canapés

When little hot nibbles are in order, it's easy to produce them on the run, using Smørrebrød toppings plus an extra topping which will turn golden-brown under the griller. Use half slices of bread or the bases suggested for miniature canapés plus a Mayonnaise Topping. Make this topping by beating 1 egg white until stiff, then stirring in 2 tablespoons mayonnaise.

Hot Ideas

★ Spread buttered bread with caviar and top with sliced hard-boiled egg. Cover with a spoonful of Mayonnaise Topping and put under the grill until brown and puffy.

★ Top buttered bread with a thick spear of asparagus. Spread with Mayonnaise Topping and grill until brown.

★ Mash sardines with lemon juice and a dash of Worcestershire sauce. Top with cooked, crumbled bacon, then spread with Mayonnaise Topping and grill until brown.

★ Top bread with thin slices of smoked eel and cover with slices of sharp cheese. Put under the grill until the cheese has melted and is bubbly.

★ Mix together grated onion, grated sharp cheese and a little chopped gherkin or pickle. Spoon on to bread and garnish with a criss-cross of flat anchovy fillets. Put under the grill until the cheese is melted and bubbly.

Open Crispbread Sandwiches

All Smørrebrød toppings may be placed on crispbread instead of bread if desired. There is a wide variety of crispbreads available today, from the very thin kind to the thicker, more substantial ones.

A crispbread Smørrebrød is a fine summer idea for weight-watchers and one or two make an appetizing winter lunch with the addition of a bowl of hot soup.

Serve lacy Brandy Snaps (page 276) for afternoon tea, or as a superb dessert with strawberries and whipped cream.

Fresh cherries covered with rich, sweet custard makes a delicious Cherry Quiche (page 295). Apples are also delicious cooked this way.

JUST DESSERTS

Many gourmets prefer hot desserts to cold. I know men particularly fond of hot desserts, and especially the old-fashioned puddings of their childhood days. Others claim they really don't care much for sweet things, hot or cold. For many years I blew hot and cold and, to be truthful, didn't care all that much whether I'd left enough space or not.

A turning point came when my daughter Suzanne returned from London with her Cordon Bleu Diploma tucked under one arm and under the other 12 months' experience as the sweets cook at the former Cordon Bleu Restaurant in Marylebone Lane, famous for its good food, fine cakes and exquisite desserts. From Suzanne I learnt what all sweet-tooths have always known, a good dessert is worth waiting for and can be the crowning glory to a good meal.

Today I appreciate all kinds of desserts and although there aren't many short cuts to making good desserts there are a few. Bought puff pastry perhaps, the advent of the food processor, a definite yes. Care with choice and use of ingredients really shows in the end result. The almond macaroons you make yourself, the tender buttery pastry are as important as blemish-free strawberries or perfumed peaches. When you can't get a genuine soft French cheese make your own fresh cream cheese rather than buy a second-rater. Serve it with quince cheese you've made from the fragrant fruit that comes in late autumn and you have a superlative but simple dessert.

I particularly enjoy freshly prepared desserts such as fruit pies, rice puddings, baked apples, but they must be freshly cooked and still warm. Ice creams and cold desserts, beautiful moulded Bavarian creams, soft and rich custards as a sauce, baked or as a base for floating islands have justifiably, many fans. There is much to be said for tender, light and delicate pastries and fruits, whether fresh, poached or used in puddings or little French tarts.

With so many delicious and variously flavoured desserts, fine fruit tarts and unconsciously rich or consciously delicate desserts in your repertoire, you may, like me, be found guilty of assault on the waistlines of the sweet-toothed. Their Just Desserts . . . what a way to go!!

Apricot Orange Mousse

•

Australian dried apricots are true gourmet fare. Nothing can quite match them for flavour. I know a Parisian, a most accomplished hostess, who keeps them in her store cupboard. In Los Angeles' famous Farmers' Market, they take pride of place with other world leaders. They make a mousse as rich and as welcome as a pot of gold.

500 g (1 lb) dried apricots
½ cup sugar
grated rind and juice of 1 orange
¾ cup cream
½ teaspoon vanilla
whipped cream and toasted slivered
almonds to decorate

Simmer the apricots in water to cover for 20 minutes. Stir in the sugar and cook for 5 minutes longer. Drain, reserving the liquid. Add the orange rind and 3 tablespoons of the juice to the apricots. Purée in a blender, using a little of the cooking liquid if necessary, or push through a sieve. Cool. Add any remaining orange juice if it needs a slightly more 'orangy' taste. Whip the cream until it holds soft peaks and fold in the vanilla. Fold the cream into the apricot purée. Spoon or pipe into mousse pots or other small dessert pots.

Decorate with whipped cream and sprinkle with toasted slivered almonds. *Serves 6*

Apricot Bavarian Cream

• • •

There are those who maintain that the bavarois was devised by a French chef who just happened to be employed at the Bavarian Court at the end of the 17th century. French or Bavarian, this delicious moulded fruit cream is enjoying a comeback. Decorate with strawberries, citrus slices, fresh garden leaves, as fits the occasion.

1 × 825 g can apricot halves
⅓ cup brandy
1½ tablespoons gelatine
1 teaspoon vanilla
2 cups cream
¼ cup sugar

Sauce

1½ cups apricot jam
⅓ cup brandy
¼ cup slivered, blanched almonds

Drain the apricots and reserve the syrup. Purée the apricots through a sieve, food mill or in a food processor. Cover and chill. Place the brandy in a small bowl, sprinkle the gelatine over and allow to soften for 10 minutes. In a saucepan bring ½ cup of the reserved syrup to the boil, remove from the heat and add the gelatine mixture. Stir until the gelatine has dissolved, allow to cool a little, then add the vanilla and stir into the apricot purée. Whip the cream and sugar until soft peaks form and fold into the apricot mixture.

Rinse a 6 cup mould with cold water and pour the bavarois mixture in; rap the mould on a hard surface to fill any air spaces and chill, covered, for several hours or overnight.

To make the sauce: Melt the jam with ½ cup of the reserved apricot syrup over a low heat, stirring. Sieve and add the brandy and, just before serving, the almonds.

To serve, dip the mould into hot water for 2–3 seconds. Place a wetted serving plate over it and invert, holding the mould and plate together, rap sharply on your working surface and the bavarois should drop on to the plate.

Serve with the sauce passed in a separate bowl. *Serves 6–8*

Apple Crisp

•

6 tart apples
1 cup sugar
¼ teaspoon ground cloves
½ teaspoon cinnamon
2 teaspoons lemon juice
¾ cup sifted flour
⅛ teaspoon salt
90 g (3 oz) butter
¼ cup chopped walnuts
whipped cream or ice cream

Apricot Sauce

250 g (8 oz) dried apricots, soaked for several hours
1 stick cinnamon
½ cup sugar

Peel, core and slice the apples into a bowl. Add ½ cup of the sugar, the cloves, cinnamon and lemon juice. Mix lightly and pour into a buttered 2½ cup ovenproof dish.

Blend the remaining sugar, flour and salt. Rub the butter in until the mixture has a crumbly consistency. Add the nuts and sprinkle over the apple mixture. Bake in a preheated moderate oven (180°C/350°F) for 45 minutes, or until the apples are tender and the crust is nicely browned.

To make the Apricot Sauce: Bring the apricots and soaking liquid to the boil with the cinnamon stick and simmer until soft. Remove cinnamon stick. Rub through a sieve and add the sugar. Return to the heat and cook until the sugar is dissolved. A little more water may be added if the sauce is too thick, also a little more sugar if the apricots are rather tart.

Serve the Apple Crisp with whipped cream or ice cream and the Apricot Sauce. *Serves 6*

Ambrosia

••

A light fluff of sour cream, perfumed very lightly with rum, lemon and vanilla – delicious.

1 tablespoon gelatine
¼ cup cold water
1½ cups sour cream
½ cup brown sugar
1 teaspoon vanilla
juice of ½ lemon
1 tablespoon rum
2 egg whites
½ cup cream, whipped
6 macaroons, crumbled (see page 297)

Sprinkle the gelatine over the cold water and leave until spongy, about 5 minutes, then dissolve over hot water. Beat the sour cream with the sugar. Add the vanilla, lemon juice and rum, then the gelatine. Chill until the mixture begins to thicken. Stiffly beat the egg whites and fold into the sour cream mixture with a rubber spatula or large metal spoon.

Turn into chilled, individual dishes and chill until set. Top with whipped cream and crumbled macaroons. *Serves 6*

Apple Snow

•

The best apple snow is made with apples baked in their skin. The apples are then pulped to a purée and stiffly beaten egg whites folded through. The rum flavour is just right for adult tastes. Make half-and-half so that the whole family can enjoy it.

6 semi-tart cooking apples
2 egg whites
½–¾ cup sugar
1 tablespoon rum or vanilla to taste
orange and/or lemon juice (optional)

Wash and dry the apples thoroughly. Do not peel or cut. Place in a baking pan with sufficient water to cover the bottom, do not cover the pan. Bake in a hot oven (200°C/400°F) for 45–50 minutes or until the apples are tender, but not falling apart. Remove the cores and push the apples through a colander, then through a sieve. If using a blender or food processor, remove the skin as well. Chill.

Beat the egg whites until stiff, gradually adding a few tablespoons of sugar. Fold through the apple purée, then add as much of the remaining sugar as is needed to sweeten, the rum or vanilla, and orange and/or lemon juice to taste, if using.

Beat vigorously until foamy, using an electric mixer or a rotary egg beater.

Turn into a glass serving bowl or individual glasses and chill for 3–4 hours before serving. *Serves 6*

Strawberry Snow

•

Like the lightest drift of pink snow, this unbelievably delicate yet fragrant dessert, served in a pretty bowl, makes the perfect finale to a rich meal.

500 g (1 lb) ripe strawberries, washed and hulled
2 egg whites
½ cup sugar or to taste
½ cup cream
vanilla

Push the strawberries through a sieve or purée in a blender or food processor fitted with the double edged steel blade. Combine the strawberry purée, egg whites and sugar, then beat vigorously until stiff and glossy; this is easily done in an electric mixer.

Whip the cream and flavour with vanilla to taste. Using a rubber spatula or large metal spoon, fold gently through the strawberry mixture. Turn into a pretty glass serving dish, or 6 individual dishes. Chill or serve at once. *Serves 6*

Ginger Soufflé

•••

Soufflés are easier to make than most people realise and ginger is one of the all-time favourites. Even without the classical straight-sided soufflé dish (any 8 cup ovenproof dish can be used) a soufflé is impressive.

90 g (3 oz) butter
3 tablespoons flour
1 cup milk
⅓ cup sugar
salt
1 tablespoon brandy
⅛ teaspoon ground ginger
½ cup drained preserved or crystallized
ginger, finely chopped
4 eggs, separated

Preheat oven to moderately hot (190°C/375°F). Melt the butter, add the flour and stir with a wire whisk until blended. Meanwhile, bring the milk to a boil and add all at once to the blended roux mixture, stirring vigorously with the whisk. Bring to the boil, stirring constantly, until the sauce is thick and smooth. Add the sugar, a pinch of salt, brandy and ginger. Remove from the heat and cool slightly.

Beat in the egg yolks one at a time. Cool. Beat the egg whites with a pinch of salt until they stand in peaks and fold into the mixture. Place into an 8 cup soufflé dish and bake for 35–45 minutes. Serve immediately. *Serves 6*

Chocolate Soufflé

• • •

*With today's excellent thermostatically controlled
ovens it is easier to succeed than to fail in making perfect
soufflés. There was, however, a time when the making
of a soufflé was a somewhat tricky affair. That was
in the days when stoves were wood-burning or coal-burning
and it was difficult to maintain a constant
oven temperature.*

60 g (2 oz) butter
2 tablespoons flour
¾ cup milk
salt
60 g (2 oz) unsweetened chocolate
⅓ cup sugar
2 tablespoons strong cold coffee
½ teaspoon vanilla
3 egg yolks
4 egg whites
whipped cream to serve

Preheat oven to moderately hot (190°C/375°F). Melt the butter,
add the flour and stir with a wire whisk until blended.
Meanwhile, bring the milk to a boil and add all at once to the
roux mixture, stirring vigorously with the wire whisk until
blended. Bring to the boil and cook, stirring, until the sauce is
thick and smooth. Add a pinch of salt.

Melt the chocolate with the sugar and coffee in a double
boiler. Stir the melted chocolate mixture into the sauce and add
the vanilla. Beat in the egg yolks, one at a time, and cool.

Beat the egg whites with a pinch of salt until they stand in
peaks and fold into the mixture. Turn into a buttered 8 cup
soufflé dish sprinkled with sugar. Bake for 30–45 minutes, or
until puffed and brown. Serve immediately with whipped
cream. *Serves 6*

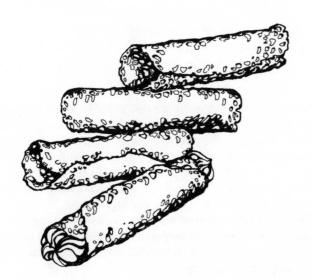

Brandy Snaps

• • •

*Crisp lacy brandy snaps are an English specialty served
with afternoon tea. They make a wonderful
accompaniment to fresh fruit compote or a bowl of fresh
berries and are often filled with whipped cream.
Practice makes perfect with most things and once you get the
knack with brandy snaps you'll want to make
them your speciality . . . just about
everyone loves them.*

60 g (2 oz) butter
⅓ cup lightly packed brown sugar
⅓ cup golden syrup
½ cup plain flour
1 teaspoon ground ginger
grated rind of ½ a lemon
¾ cup cream for filling

Put the butter, sugar and golden syrup in a pan and heat gently
until the butter melts. Remove from heat, cool until lukewarm
then stir in the sifted flour and ginger, and lemon rind. Mix
until smooth.

Brush baking trays with melted butter. Drop 2 teaspoonsful
of mixture on to each tray, allowing 10–13 cm (4–5 inch) space
between them for spreading. Bake one tray at a time in a
moderate oven (180°C/350°F) for approximately 10 minutes.

When the brandy snaps are a deep amber colour, remove
from the oven and allow to stand for a few seconds to set
slightly. Ease from the tray with a broad-bladed knife or
spatula. Wrap each one lightly around the handle of a greased
wooden spoon, putting the smooth side against the spoon so
that the lacy pattern of the top is on the outside. Do not press
too firmly against the handle as it will become difficult to slip
them off.

Place on a wire rack to cool and when set slip off the spoon
handle. Leave on rack to cool completely (if your container is
really airtight, they may be kept for a few days).

To fill the brandy snaps: Whip the cream until stiff, fill a large
greaseproof paper cone or a piping bag fitted with a star pipe
with the cream and pipe some into both ends of each brandy
snap. *Makes approximately 20 brandy snaps*

Note: Do not bake more than two brandy snaps at a time as the
biscuits must be rolled while hot and unless you are very
experienced and very quick, a third one will be too cold to
handle successfully. Use two wooden spoons. While you are
rolling the first batch, the second tray of snaps can be baking. It
is very important to store brandy snaps in an airtight container
and to fill only just before serving. Humidity can cause the
snaps to soften.

The Duchess's Christmas Trifle

● ● ●

*That popular T.V. series 'The Duchess of Duke Street'
revived many an interest in wonderful 'show off'
dishes. 'Any good cook should know how to make a good
trifle: good custard, good booze and a topping
like an Ascot hat', instructed Louisa. Well, I made this one
first for a television show and everyone loved it
and made it for special occasions – here is the recipe.
The decorations of sugared rose petals and violets
are edible.*

200 g (7 oz) dried apricots
¾ cup sugar
2½ cups milk
vanilla pod
1 teaspoon cornflour
5 eggs
10 sponge fingers
¼ cup sherry or Madeira
⅓ cup brandy
90 g (3 oz) glacé apricots
60 g (2 oz) angelica
12 almond macaroons (page 297)
1½ cups cream
125 g (4 oz) glacé cherries
split toasted almonds

Sugared rose petals and violets

1 fresh pink rose
small bunch violets
1 egg white
caster sugar

Soak the apricots overnight in plenty of water to cover. Drain and place in a saucepan with fresh water to cover. Simmer for about 30 minutes or until soft. Rub the apricots through a sieve or purée in a blender. Return to the pan and add ½ cup of the sugar and cook until sugar has dissolved, about 30 minutes. While the apricots are cooking, make the sugared rose petals and violets.

To make the sugared rose petals and violets: Carefully pluck the rose petals from the stem. Nip the violets, leaving a short stem. Beat the egg white until a little frothy but not white. With a small paint brush, paint the petals with the egg white, covering well. Large petals can be dipped in the egg white, but shake off any excess. Lightly coat with caster sugar. Place on a cake rack; the albumen of the egg white will set stiff, holding the sugar coating. Treat the violets in the same way. Allow to set and become firm.

Bring the milk to the boil with the vanilla pod. Mix the remaining sugar with the cornflour. Gradually add the eggs and beat well. Remove the vanilla pod from the milk and pour the hot milk on to the egg mixture, stirring constantly. Cook the custard in the top of a double boiler over simmering water until thickened. Place in a bowl and cover with dampened greaseproof paper. Cool.

Sandwich the sponge fingers together with a generous layer of apricot purée and cut into 2.5 cm (1 inch) pieces. Arrange half the pieces in the bottom of a trifle dish. Sprinkle with some of the sherry or Madeira and the brandy, and spread some purée over. Spoon over half the cooled custard. Repeat with the remaining sponge fingers, liquor, purée and custard.

Cut long leaves of angelica and quarter the macaroons. Whip the cream lightly and spread a thick layer over the custard. Place the remaining cream in a piping bag.

Starting at the outer edge of the trifle dish, make one circle of alternating cherries and macaroons around the dish. Pipe swirls of cream to make a second circle. Make a third circle of glacé apricots, cherries and angelica and a fourth circle of piped cream. Continue with the cherries and macaroons and cream until you reach the centre. Arrange the sugared rose petals to form a rose in the centre, arrange the violets on the cream.
Serves 8–10

Floating Islands au Chocolat

• • •

This is one of the most delectable of desserts. Mounds of egg white are poached in milk, then the milk is used to make a rich chocolate custard; the little 'islands' of egg white are then set to float on the custard. This is a variation of the traditional 'Île Flottante' where the custard is vanilla flavoured not chocolate.

3 cups milk
small piece vanilla pod or 1 teaspoon vanilla
1 cup caster sugar
6 egg whites, at room temperature

Chocolate Custard

½ cup sugar
90 g (3 oz) unsweetened chocolate,
roughly chopped
6 egg yolks
3 cups hot milk, reserved from the meringue

To decorate

chocolate caraque or curls (page 296) (optional)

Combine the milk with the vanilla pod and ¼ cup of the sugar. Slowly heat to simmering point.

Meanwhile, beat the egg whites until stiff. Continue beating, adding the remaining sugar gradually, until the meringue holds its shape.

Using two spoons, drop egg-shaped balls of meringue on the simmering milk and simmer until they are firm, turning once. Carefully remove and set on a clean tea-towel. Remove the pod and reserve the milk. If a pod is not used add the vanilla. **To make the Chocolate Custard:** Mix the sugar, chocolate, and egg yolks in a saucepan. Slowly add the hot milk, stirring, and cook over a very low heat, stirring constantly until the mixture coats the back of a metal spoon. Remove from the heat and cool. Pour into a glass serving bowl and float the 'islands' of meringue on top. Chill. Decorate, if liked, with chocolate caraque or curls. *Serves 8*

Lemon Compote

• •

A German dessert – this is fresh-tasting for those who like the tart-sweetness of lemons. It is excellent after grilled pork, ham or fish and is quick to make.

4–6 large lemons
½ cup caster sugar
¼ cup slivered almonds or pistachio nuts
2 tablespoons Curaçao or Madeira

Carefully cut all peel and pith off the lemons. Using a very sharp, thin knife cut the lemons into paper-thin slices. Arrange in circles on 4 individual glass dessert plates. Sprinkle with the sugar, nuts and liqueur. Chill, covered with a sheet of plastic film, in the refrigerator for 1–2 hours before serving. *Serves 4*

Fruit Salad with Honey and Wine

•

You can use your own choice of fruit for this salad; fresh cubed pineapple or melons or any ripe berries.
Do not use citrus fruit – the acid is too strong for the wine. Serve with light sour cream if liked.

¾ cup white wine
3 tablespoons honey
3 tablespoons mixed chopped nuts
1 large apple
1 large ripe pear
2 ripe peaches
3 ripe apricots
250 g (8 oz) strawberries

Mix the wine and honey together until well blended and stir in the nuts. Wash, peel and core the fruit as necessary and cut into thin slices. If strawberries are large, cut in half, otherwise leave whole. Combine all fruit in a large glass serving bowl and pour the honey sauce over. Toss gently with a wooden spoon until the sauce is mixed through the fruit. Chill for several hours before serving. *Serves 4–6*

Queen's Pudding

• •

A grand name for a very simple pudding that is ideal for using up stale cake or biscuit crumbs. Excellent served either hot or cold with an apricot sauce or stewed fruit.

1 cup stale cake or biscuit crumbs
2½ cups milk
2 eggs
¼ cup sugar
vanilla
caster sugar
Apricot Sauce (see page 274)

Rub cake or biscuit crumbs through a fine sieve or whirl in a blender or food processor. Scald the milk, add the crumbs and stand for 10–15 minutes until soft. Beat the eggs and sugar together and add to the milk with the vanilla. Grease a 5 cup pudding basin (a charlotte mould makes a pretty shape) with butter and line the base with paper. Sprinkle basin with a little caster sugar. Pour in the milk mixture, cover with greaseproof paper and stand in a baking tray of hot water. Bake in a moderately slow oven (160°C/325°F) for 45 minutes or until firm to the touch.

Leave to stand for a few minutes and carefully unmould on to a hot serving dish. Remove ring of greaseproof paper and serve hot with Apricot Sauce. *Serves 6*

Gooseberry Pie

••

When the aroma of a freshly baked fruit pie wafts from the kitchen, nostalgic memories flood back of scratches after an afternoon blackberry picking, stained mulberry hands and face, the taste of a crisp, juicy apple or tart-sweet gooseberries, fresh or for most of us, frozen and just as good. A buttery, flaky crust tops the fruit filling, making this one of the most favoured of all hot desserts.

Pastry
1½ cups flour
pinch of salt
125 g (4 oz) butter
1 tablespoon caster sugar
1 egg yolk
1 tablespoon water

Filling
1 kg (2 lb) frozen gooseberries
grated rind of 1 orange
1 tablespoon flour
grated nutmeg
sugar

To make the pastry: Sift the flour and salt into a bowl. Add the butter to the flour and cut through with a knife into small pieces. Rub into the flour with fingertips until the mixture resembles fine breadcrumbs. Add the sugar. Make a well in the centre, add the egg yolk mixed with the water and combine quickly with a round-bladed knife. Press together with fingers to form a dough. Turn on to a floured board and knead until smooth. Roll into a ball and wrap in greaseproof paper. Chill for 30 minutes.

To prepare the filling: Combine the gooseberries with the orange rind, flour, nutmeg and sugar to taste. Use plenty of sugar as gooseberries can be very tart. Fill a 4 cup pie dish.

Roll out the pastry. Cut off a 1 cm (½ inch) strip and press around the rim of the pie dish. Brush with a little water. Lift the remaining pastry using a rolling pin and lay over the dish. Trim away excess pastry with a sharp knife. Seal pastry edges together with the back of a knife and crimp edges. Decorate with pastry scraps if liked. Brush pastry with cold water, sprinkle with caster sugar and bake in a moderately hot oven (190°C/375°F) for 30 minutes. If pastry begins to colour too much, cover pie with a double thickness of greaseproof paper. Serve hot with custard or cream. *Serves 4–6*

Yogurt Cream Cheese

•

Arabs have been making a beautiful soft creamy cheese called Labna for centuries. It is excellent with fruits, fruit pastes (quince, guava); it can be spooned over tomatoes or combined with herbs and used to stuff tomatoes. This recipe is rather like Labna and is truly delicious.

2 cups natural yogurt
1 cup cream

In a bowl combine the yogurt and cream. Pour the mixture into a sieve lined with a double thickness of dampened cheesecloth (or a double layer of Chux cloth) and set over a bowl. Let the mixture drain for 8 hours or until the whey has drained off and the curds are firm. *Makes about 1½ cups*

Ways to use it

★ Halve a small ripe melon and remove the seeds. Fill with a few spoons of yogurt cream cheese and sprinkle with a little brown sugar.

★ Serve the melon and yogurt cream cheese without the sugar. Curl a few slices of Parma ham or prosciutto and serve as a first course.

★ Mound about ½ cup of the cheese on a dessert plate, mask with sweetened cream and surround with any fresh summer fruit, sliced or halved stewed apricots, plums or peaches.

★ Serve a bowl of yogurt cream cheese with a square of guava or quince cheese (see recipe, page 342).

★ Offer a little black pumpernickel bread or Scottish or Irish oatcakes. Serve in place of a cheese board.

Figs with Yogurt Cheese

● ●

There's a 'new wave' feeling about this dessert – the combination of figs and soft yogurt cream cheese is lovely.

250 g (8 oz) dried figs
1 cup water
2 teaspoons brown sugar
2.5 cm (1 inch) piece cinnamon stick
1 thin slice lemon
1 quantity yogurt cream cheese (see page 279)

Decoration

1 orange
½ cup water
1 tablespoon sugar

Soak the figs in water for 2 hours. Transfer the figs and water to a saucepan and add the brown sugar, cinnamon and lemon. Bring to a boil and simmer, covered, for 20 minutes. Discard the cinnamon and lemon and chill the figs in the syrup.

With a swivel-bladed potato peeler remove thin strips of orange rind and cut into long julienne threads. Place in a saucepan with the water and bring to the boil. Add the sugar and cook gently for 2–3 minutes. Drain and pat dry with absorbent paper. Sprinkle over the figs and serve with yogurt cream cheese. *Serves 4*

Ginger Cheese Mould

● ●

There are times when you can't decide between a dessert or a cheese board for dinner. Why not combine the two? This is a delicious combination and if you haven't stocked up on quince cheese (page 342) you can buy it at good Italian delicatessens.

1 tablespoon gelatine
¼ cup cold water
160 g (6 oz) Philadelphia cream cheese
1 cup cream
2 tablespoons preserved ginger, finely chopped
125 g (4 oz) quince or guava cheese, to serve

In a bowl sprinkle the gelatine over the water and stand for 5 minutes. Dissolve over hot water. Soften the cream cheese by mashing with a spoonful of the cream. Mix the softened cheese with the ginger and gelatine and cool.

Whip the cream and fold into the cheese mixture. Pour into a 4 cup mould (a small deep loaf tin is ideal, rinsed out in cold water) and chill.

Dip the mould in hot water and unmould on to a chilled platter. Surround with squares or triangles of guava or quince cheese. *Serves 4*

Persian Oranges

● ●

6 oranges
½ cup raisins
2 tablespoons brandy
1 honeydew melon
shredded rind of 2 oranges
sherry

Peel the oranges and cut segments free of membranes. Soak raisins in brandy. Halve and seed the melon and scoop out small balls of the melon flesh. Combine the orange segments, brandied raisins, melon balls and orange rind, cover and chill in the refrigerator.

Arrange fruit in six bowls, spoon a little sherry over each and serve with sprays of mint or small garden leaves. *Serves 6*

Lime Buttermilk Sorbet

● ●

1 packet lime jelly
½ cup sugar
1 cup boiling water
1 cup buttermilk
1 teaspoon grated lemon rind
3 tablespoons lemon juice
1 egg white

Combine the jelly and sugar in a mixing bowl. Pour on the boiling water and stir until dissolved. Allow to cool. Add the buttermilk, lemon rind and juice. Turn into a 4 cup freezer tray and freeze until firm. Break into chunks and beat with an electric mixer until smooth. Whisk the egg white until stiff peaks form, then fold into the buttermilk mixture. Return to freezer tray and freeze until firm. *Serves 4*

Orange and Apple Cream

●

A simple dessert that is popular with weight watchers.

1 orange
2 large apples
4 cups natural yogurt

Wash and dry the orange and apples. Place the yogurt in a mixing bowl and grate the rind of the orange over it. Squeeze the orange and add the juice to the yogurt. Grate the unpeeled apples and fold into the mixture. Combine well and chill. *Serves 4*

Right: Apricot Bavarian Cream is served with an apricot jam, brandy and almond sauce (page 274).

Above: Grapes are baked in almond custard for French Grape Tart (page 291). When cherries are in season they can be cooked in the same way.

Right: Steamed Pineapple Pudding (page 289) is most decorative, with pineapple and cherries in a butterscotch glaze.

Buttermilk Mould

• •

1 teaspoon gelatine
¼ cup water
3 cups buttermilk
1 cup orange juice
2 tablespoons lemon juice
2 tablespoons honey
2 egg whites

Sprinkle the gelatine over the water and stand for 5 minutes or until spongy. Dissolve the gelatine over boiling water. Place the buttermilk, orange and lemon juices in a bowl and add the gelatine. Chill until beginning to set, when it will resemble the consistency of unbeaten egg white. Beat in the honey until the mixture is foamy. Stiffly beat the egg whites and fold into the buttermilk mixture. Spoon into a wetted 5 cup mould and chill until firm. To serve, unmould and decorate with orange segments or fruit in season. *Serves 6*

Pere Ripieni

(Stuffed pears)

• • •

*Pere Ripieni are not only good to eat but, with the Italian flair for design, take advantage of the lovely shape of pears to make a dessert that looks like a still life.
You may buy the macaroons for the stuffing, but your own homemade ones will be better. When pears are out of season, fresh peaches prepared in the same way make a luscious dessert.*

6 small or 3 large pears
½ cup dry white wine
2 tablespoons brown sugar
Stuffing
6 small Macaroons (see page 297)
1 egg yolk
grated rind of 1 orange
1–2 teaspoons dry sherry
To serve
1 cup sour cream
1–2 tablespoons brown sugar

First make the stuffing: Crush the macaroons. Beat the egg yolk slightly and mix with the crumbs, orange rind and sufficient sherry to make a firm paste.

Peel the pears but do not remove the stems. Halve carefully, splitting the stems. Remove the cores with a teaspoon and stuff the cavities with the macaroon mixture. Place the pears in a

Left: Apple Snow and Strawberry Snow (page 275) are easy-to-make desserts.

baking pan. Mix the wine and brown sugar and drizzle over the pears. Cover and poach in a slow oven (150°C/300°F) until the pears are soft, spooning the wine over once or twice. Time will vary with the size and type of pear, test with a toothpick in the thickest part.

The pears can be served warm or chilled. Pass a bowl of sour cream mixed with brown sugar to taste. Serve one half if the pears are large, two halves if they are small. *Serves 6*

Orange Chiffon

• •

Serve this dessert, after a rich meal.

1 tablespoon gelatine
¾ cup fresh orange juice
4 eggs, separated
2 tablespoons caster sugar
1 tablespoon lemon juice
½ teaspoon salt
1 tablespoon grated orange rind

Sprinkle the gelatine over ¼ cup of the orange juice and stand for 5 minutes to sponge. Beat the egg yolks, caster sugar, remaining juice and salt together. Place in a double saucepan and cook, stirring, until thick enough to coat the back of the spoon. Add the orange rind and softened gelatine and stir until the gelatine has dissolved. Cool.

When the mixture begins to thicken slightly, beat the egg whites until stiff and fold in carefully. Spoon into a glass bowl or individual serving dishes and chill. *Serves 4–6*

Passionfruit Flummery

• •

1 tablespoon gelatine
½ cup cold water
2 tablespoons flour
¼ cup sugar
¼ cup orange juice
1 tablespoon lemon juice
1 cup hot water
½ cup passionfruit pulp

Sprinkle the gelatine over the cold water. Combine the flour and sugar in a saucepan and add enough orange juice to blend to a smooth paste.

Add the remaining orange juice, lemon juice and hot water. Bring to the boil, stirring until the mixture thickens. Add the soaked gelatine, stir until it has dissolved. Cool, then transfer to a large bowl and chill until starting to set. Beat well until very thick and at least double in volume. Add the passionfruit pulp and beat well again. Turn into a glass bowl and chill. *Serves 4–6*

Mango Sorbet

••

A cool fruit sorbet which may be served as a dessert or to refresh the palate in between rich courses.

1 × 625 g (20 oz) can mangoes
1 teaspoon gelatine
juice of ½ a lemon
2 teaspoons rum
1 egg white

Place 3 tablespoons of mango syrup in a small saucepan, sprinkle over the gelatine and allow to sponge. Sieve the fruit with the remaining syrup to make a purée. Dissolve the gelatine over a low heat and stir into the purée with the lemon juice and rum.

Turn the freezer control to maximum. Place sorbet in an ice cream tray, cover with foil and freeze until mushy. Turn sorbet into a bowl and beat with a rotary beater until smooth but not melted. Fold in the stiffly beaten egg white. Return the freezer control to normal and freeze the sorbet until firm.

Allow the sorbet to stand at room temperature for a few minutes before serving. *Serves 4–6*

Fresh Peach and Plum Compote

•••

The perfume of fresh peaches and plums fills many a room during the summer months. When the first white peaches come into season, serve them simply sliced in wine with a little light sour cream. The yellow peaches and wonderful red plums that follow may be poached, not really cooked, in a syrup and served with a rich vanilla custard and delicious French fried bread – Pain Perdu.

1 cup sugar
1 orange
½ vanilla pod
2 cups water
3 choice dessert plums
3 choice dessert peaches

To serve

Pain Perdu (see right)
Crème à la Vanille (see right)

Dissolve the sugar in the water with the vanilla pod and thinly peeled orange rind over a low heat. When the sugar has dissolved, bring to the boil and simmer for a few minutes. Pour boiling water over the fruit and allow to stand for 3 minutes, drain, slip off the skins and place the fruit in the syrup. Poach gently for about 10 minutes, spooning the liquid over the fruit and carefully turning the fruit over in the syrup, using two spoons. Chill. Remove fruit to a serving bowl, reduce syrup a little over a moderate heat and pour the strained syrup over the fruit. Serve with Pain Perdu and a jug of Crème à la Vanille. Offer guests a choice of a peach or a plum. *Serves 6*

Pain Perdu

This is the sweet fried bread loved by the French. It is good on its own or as an accompaniment to fruit compotes.

6 thick slices of bread (toast bread)
½ cup milk
½ cup cream
2 tablespoons sugar
2 eggs
1 egg yolk
½ teaspoon vanilla
125 g (4 oz) Clarified Butter (see page 346)
2 tablespoons caster sugar
½ teaspoon cinnamon

Remove the crusts from the bread and cut each slice into four triangles. Combine the milk, cream, sugar, eggs and vanilla in a shallow dish. Soak the triangles for 2 minutes. Melt the butter and fry a few triangles at a time for about 2–3 minutes on each side, or until golden brown. Transfer to a heated plate and sprinkle with the combined sugar and cinnamon. Serve with Fresh Peach and Plum Compote, or by itself. *Makes 24 triangles*

Crème à la Vanille

This rich custard is known also as Crème à Anglaise; many a French cook considers it the only serious sauce to come out of England! You don't have to be French or English to appreciate it.

1¼ cups milk
vanilla pod
2 large or 3 small egg yolks
1 teaspoon arrowroot
1½ tablespoons sugar

Scald the milk with the vanilla pod, cover and leave to infuse for 2–3 minutes. Cream the egg yolks with the arrowroot and sugar until thick and light, then pour over the flavoured milk. Return to the saucepan and stir continuously over a gentle heat until the mixture coats the back of a spoon. Strain into a jug and serve. Serve with Fresh Peach and Plum Compote or as an accompaniment to many desserts. *Makes 1¼ cups*

Frozen Strawberry Mousse

• • •

*For many, the ultimate in a frozen dessert is homemade
strawberry ice cream. Now that ice cream
churns come electrically operated or, better still, the newer
compact sorbetières, it is something all devotees
can make for themselves. Failing these devices, use the
freezing compartment of a refrigerator.*

500 g (1 lb) strawberries (2 punnets)
1 cup milk
1 piece vanilla pod or 1 teaspoon vanilla
3 egg yolks
1 cup sugar
1 cup cream

Wipe, hull and slice the strawberries. Push them through a fine
sieve into a bowl or purée in a blender or food processor. Cover
and chill. Scald the milk with the vanilla pod.

In a bowl, beat the egg yolks and sugar together using an
electric mixer at high speed until the mixture forms a ribbon
when the beater is lifted. The consistency should be thick,
lemony and mousse-like. If beating the mixture using a hand
whisk, set the egg yolks and sugar in a bowl and place over a
pan of boiling water. Add the warm scalded milk (remove the
vanilla pod) in a steady stream, whisking. Place the bowl over
boiling water and cook, beating until the custard thickens and
lightly coats the back of a spoon.

If your electric mixer is not removable, beat in the bowl until
milk is added, remove bowl, place over a saucepan of boiling
water, stirring until it thickens and lightly coats the spoon.

Strain the custard into a large bowl and set over a bowl of ice
and stir until very cold. Add the strawberry purée and cream to
the custard and whip the mixture over the ice until it is thick
and begins to hold its shape. Follow one of the freezing
methods given below. *Serves 8–10*

To Freeze in Ice Cream Maker Transfer the mixture to the can
of an ice cream churn, put in the dasher, and lower the can,
covered, into the churn. Pack the churn with alternating layers
of cracked ice and rock salt, using about ½ cup rock salt for each
4 cups of cracked ice. Churn the mixture for 15 minutes, or until
the mixture is frozen. Remove the can and wipe it carefully to
remove the salt. Remove the dasher, scraping the ice cream
clinging to it back into the can. Press the ice cream down, and
recover the can. Put the can in the freezer compartment of the
refrigerator. Alternatively, pour off the salt water in the ice
cream churn, return the can and repack it with alternating
layers of ice and salt until serving time.

To Freeze in Refrigerator Turn freezer to lowest point.
Transfer mixture to two refrigerator trays, cover with wax
paper or foil, and freeze. When the mixture is set almost
through remove to a bowl, give a light whip or beat, return to
trays, cover and freeze. When firm return the freezer to normal
setting. Some freezers do not have a control, so select the
coldest part for freezing the ice cream.

To Freeze using a Sorbetière Small electric sorbetières are now
on the market and these are perfect for small quantities of
sorbet, granita or ice cream. The ice is put in the trays on the
flat metal base of the freezing compartment, it plugs into an
electric outlet and merrily paddles away until the ice firms.
These sorbetières are the simplest and best answer to small
quantities of frozen ices and creams.

Note: Once frozen ice cream should be held for a day when it
ripens into full flavour.

Petits Pots de Crème

• •

*All good cooks have succumbed to the lure of the specialty
cook shops. Like other enthusiasts, I have quite a
range of little ceramic pots with and without lids, for there
are so many wonderful, rich custard creams and
mousse recipes which are just right for these tiny pots.
Here is a recipe that can be made in one or all three
flavours, vanilla, coffee and chocolate.*

2½ cups milk
vanilla pod or vanilla
1 tablespoon caster sugar
4 egg yolks
1 egg
instant coffee powder
30–45 g (1–1½ oz) chocolate

Scald the milk with the vanilla pod and sugar. Remove the pod
and pour the milk on to the combined egg yolks and egg. Add
vanilla if no vanilla pod is available. Strain and divide into
three equal parts. Flavour one with the coffee dissolved in a
little water, one with the chocolate melted on a plate over warm
water and leave the third plain. Pour carefully into pots, stand
these in a shallow pan or tin filled with boiling water. Cover
with a lid or if the pots themselves have lids put them on. Lift
carefully into a moderate oven (180°C/350°F) and leave to set.
The time will vary from 12–20 minutes, according to the
thickness of the pots and the oven. Lift out the pan, lift lids
quickly so that no water falls into the creams. Remove and cool.
Serve with a crisp dessert biscuit. *Serves 6*

Ricotta Siciliana

•

This is a ricotta cheese 'pudding'. It is the same
filling that is put in between layers of sponge cake to become
Cassata alla Siciliana, but is often eaten, as here,
with a crisp biscuit.

375 g (12 oz) ricotta cheese
125 g (4 oz) milk chocolate, grated
½ cup finely chopped walnuts
3 tablespoons cream
3 tablespoons chopped candied fruit (optional)

Cream the ricotta, add the chocolate and nuts and blend
thoroughly. Add enough cream to make a smooth consistency.
If liked, add the chopped candied fruit (citrus peel is delicious).

Spoon into six wine or dessert glasses and serve with a
crisp biscuit like amaretti, cigarettes russe or boudoir biscuits.
Serves 6

Rice Romanov

• • •

Rich creamy rice is a reminder of the great period of haute
cuisine when Prince Romanov inspired chefs to
reach for the ultimate. Without the fresh strawberry sauce
this dish would not be entitled to its princely name.

½ cup short-grain rice
3½ cups milk
salt
2 cups cream
3 tablespoons Kirsch, Grand Marnier or Cognac
3 tablespoons sugar
½ cup flaked almonds
24 macaroons, soaked in Kirsch, Grand Marnier
or Cognac

Strawberry Sauce

2 cups strawberries, fresh or defrosted frozen
½ cup sugar
½ cup water
2 teaspoons arrowroot
Kirsch, Grand Marnier or Cognac

Wash rice well and soak in water to cover for 30 minutes, drain
well. In a heavy saucepan cook the rice in the milk with a pinch
of salt, partly covered, for 30 minutes or until the rice is very
tender; do not stir. Set aside to cool.

Whip the cream until stiff and flavour with the liqueur and
sugar. Fold in the almonds. Mix the cream thoroughly but
lightly into the rice.

Place one-third of the rice cream in an attractive serving
bowl. Arrange half the macaroons on top. Add another third of
the rice cream, then the remaining macaroons. Finish with rice
cream.

To make Strawberry Sauce: Mash the strawberries or purée in
a blender or food processor. For a finer finish, push the pulp
through a nylon mesh sieve.

Combine the sugar and water in a saucepan and bring to the
boil. Reduce the heat and simmer gently for 5 minutes.
Combine the sugar syrup with the sieved strawberries. Slake
the arrowroot with a little water, add to the strawberries and
bring to the boil. Flavour with the liqueur and chill until ready
to serve.

Chill the dessert for several hours. Decorate, if liked, with a
few additional strawberries and whipped cream. Serve with
strawberry sauce. *Serves 6*

Steamed Pineapple Pudding

••

Pineapple upside-down cake is a great favourite. Pineapple sitting in a butterscotch glaze not only looks good but is a great tasting duo. The same trick works well with a steamed pudding – if you own a 4 cup charlotte mould, steam it in that.

3 canned pineapple slices
6 glacé cherries

Butterscotch

75 g (2½ oz) butter
½ cup firmly packed brown sugar

Pudding

1 cup self-raising flour
pinch of salt
90 g (3 oz) butter
½ cup caster sugar
1 teaspoon vanilla
2 eggs
4 tablespoons milk

Grease a 4 cup pudding basin or charlotte mould. Slice the pineapple through to make six circles.

To make the Butterscotch: Cream the butter and sugar together and spread on the bottom and sides of the basin. Arrange the pineapple circles in the dish and decorate with the cherries.

To make the Pudding: Sift the flour and salt. Beat the butter until creamy and then add the sugar and vanilla and beat until light and fluffy. Beat in the eggs one at a time and then fold in the milk alternately with the flour, in two batches. Spoon into the basin.

Cover the basin with two thicknesses of pleated greaseproof paper (to allow for rising), tie firmly with string and place in a large saucepan of boiling water. Cover the pan tightly and steam for 1½ hours, topping up with boiling water when necessary. Serve with cream or custard sauce. *Serves 6*

Pastry in a Food Processor

•

The food processor makes tender light pastry in a moment and as sales of this magical appliance are soaring, it makes sense to include a recipe for Pâte Brisée (a flan pastry) using the special technique.

2 cups flour
125 g (4 oz) frozen butter, cut into
1 tablespoon pieces
¼ teaspoon salt
2 whole eggs
1 tablespoon lemon juice

With the double edged steel blade in place, put the flour, butter and salt into the bowl of the food processor. Process, turning on and off rapidly, until the butter is cut into the flour and very small granules are formed, about 10 seconds. Add the eggs and lemon juice. Continue processing until a ball of dough forms on the blades. If dough seems too soft, sprinkle with 1 to 2 tablespoons flour and process until all is combined, about 6 seconds.

Refrigerate and use for any recipe calling for Pâte Brisée.
Makes two 20 or 23 cm (8 or 9 inch) pastry shells

French Flan Pastry

••

Flan pastry may be made one to two days before required. If it is more convenient, a whole egg, rather than yolks only, can be used – 1 small egg is approximately 2 yolks.
No other liquid is usually added in making flan pastry, this is why it holds its shape and does not shrink during cooking. Use for sweet flan cases, fruit tartlet moulds or petits fours.

This quantity of pastry is sufficient for an 18 or 20 cm (7 or 8 inch) flan ring or 18 tartlet cases

1 cup plain flour
60 g (2 oz) softened butter
⅓ cup caster sugar
2 egg yolks
few drops vanilla or a little grated lemon rind

This quantity of pastry is sufficient for a 23 or 25 cm (9 or 10 inch) flan ring or 24 tartlet cases

1½ cups plain flour
90 g (3 oz) softened butter
½ cup caster sugar
2 egg yolks
few drops vanilla or a little grated lemon rind
1 tablespoon iced water (optional)

Sift the flour on to a pastry board or marble slab and make a well in the centre. Place the remaining ingredients in the well, except the water. Work the butter, sugar and egg yolks together with the fingertips of one hand. When blended, gradually mix in the flour using a spatula to draw it in, adding iced water if needed.

When all the flour is incorporated, work the mixture to a paste by pressing it out on the board with the heel of your hand.

As soon as the mixture binds together, form into a ball, wrap in paper and chill for at least 30 minutes.

Roll the pastry out thinly on a lightly floured surface and ease into the flan ring or tartlet cases without stretching the pastry. Trim off surplus pastry. Chill. Prick base with a fork. If a baked flan case is needed, place a sheet of greaseproof paper in the pastry case, scatter in a few dried beans and bake in a moderately hot oven (190°C/375°F). A large flan will take 12–15 minutes, remove beans for last 5 minutes; individual tartlets about 10 minutes.

French Apple Tart

••

The art of pastry making – and especially for fruit tarts – never went out of fashion in France. Young girls are taught to make superb fruit tarts with the same seriousness as they are taught etiquette or Latin. Certainly there is no relationship between the soggy crusted apple pies sometimes seen and the crisp fine crust filled with glistening apple slices of a French apple tart.

1 kg (2 lb) Granny Smith apples
90 g (3 oz) butter
2 tablespoons sugar
1 quantity French Flan Pastry for 23 cm (9 inch)
flan case (see left)
caster sugar

Apricot Glaze

¾ cup apricot jam
1 tablespoon water
1 teaspoon lemon juice

Peel the apples, core and cut into quarters, then thick slices. Cook the apple slices with the butter and sugar for about 5 minutes over a low heat.

Roll out the pastry and use to line a 23 cm (9 inch) flan ring standing on a baking sheet. Trim the top and fill with the apple slices, reserving the best for the top. Arrange reserved apple slices on top in overlapping circles until the apples underneath are completely covered. Brush top with a little of the butter in which the apples were cooked and then sprinkle with caster sugar.

Bake in a moderately hot oven (190°C/375°F) for 20–25 minutes or until the edges are tinged a deep golden brown.

Remove from oven and while still warm, brush with the Apricot Glaze.

To make the Apricot Glaze: Heat the jam and water, stirring until boiling. Cook until thick enough to coat the spoon lightly and the last drops are sticky when poured from the spoon. Add the lemon juice and press through a sieve. Use warm. Any unused glaze may be stored in a screwtop jar, warm again before using.

Serve warm with vanilla ice cream or whipped cream. This tart can also be served cold, but I think it's twice as nice when warm. *Serves 6*

French Grape Tart

••

Throughout France the most delectable fruit flans are made with fresh fruits and served warm from the oven. Nothing could be better. Stone fruits lend themselves particularly to a soft custard mixture with ground almonds. It may take a little time to pip the grapes or small stone fruit like cherries but it is well worth the time spent.

1 quantity French Flan Pastry for 25 cm
(10 inch) flan case (see opposite page)
500 g (1 lb) white grapes
250 g (8 oz) black grapes
2 eggs
½ cup caster sugar
4 tablespoons ground almonds
2 tablespoons sour cream

Roll out the pastry on a lightly floured board and use to line a 25 cm (10 inch) flan tin. Chill the pastry shell while preparing the filling.

Wash the grapes and drain well. Remove the pips with the pointed end of a knife or a new, clean hairpin.

Place the eggs and sugar in a mixing bowl and beat until thick and mousse-like. Add 3 tablespoons of the ground almonds and the sour cream. Combine well.

Sprinkle remaining tablespoon of ground almonds in the prepared pastry shell. Arrange the grapes on top of the almonds. Spoon over the custard mixture. Bake in a hot oven (200°C/400°F) for 10 minutes. Reduce heat to moderate (180°C/350°F) and bake for a further 30–35 minutes. Serve warm. *Serves 8*

Note: During cooking the grapes become very juicy and therefore the tart filling does not set as firmly as other tarts with an egg custard type filling.

Variation

French Cherry Tart Make as for French Grape Tart above. Substitute 750 g (1½ lb) cherries for the grapes. The cherries should be stoned. Use a cherry or olive stoner (most specialty kitchen departments stock these) or use a new, clean hairpin.

Strawberry Tart

• • •

French style fruit tarts that glisten like jewels and hold a king's ransom in promise are irresistible. They make a most elegant dessert for those who enjoy crisp, light, golden pastry and the fragrance of fresh fruit.

250 g (8 oz) puff pastry
1 egg white, slightly beaten
1 large punnet strawberries, hulled
½ cup cream, whipped
2 teaspoons sugar
2 teaspoons Kirsch
icing sugar
½ cup redcurrant jelly
1 teaspoon boiling water

Roll out the puff pastry on a lightly floured marble slab or board to 5 mm to 1.5 cm (¼ to ½ inch) thick and cut it into an oblong 25 × 20 cm (10 × 8 inch). With a floured sharp knife cut the pastry in half lengthwise. Fold one piece in half again, lengthwise. Cut out a strip from the folded side 20 × 2.5 cm (8 × 1 inch) wide, leaving a three-sided frame 2.5 cm (1 inch) wide all round. Discard the cut-out strip and use for other pastries.

Roll out the other unfolded half of the dough a little longer than the frame and about 13 cm (5 inch) wide. Lay this piece on a baking sheet, moistened with water. Brush the top edges with the beaten egg white. Carefully lay the unfolded frame on the base, and trim the edges of the two layers evenly. With the back of a knife, mark the border of the tart shell all around in a zigzag pattern. Prick the centre well with a fork dipped in flour. Chill the shell for 30 minutes.

Line the shell with wax paper and fill it with rice. Bake in a moderately hot oven (190°C/375°F) for 35–40 minutes or until it is golden brown. Cool. Remove the rice and paper.

Spread the bottom of the tart shell with a layer of whipped cream flavoured with the 2 teaspoons sugar and Kirsch. Sprinkle edges with a sifting of icing sugar. Arrange rows of perfect whole strawberries on the cream. Glaze with redcurrant jelly, melted and thinned with 1 teaspoon of boiling water.
Serves 6

Apple Pie with Cheddar Crust

• •

Apples and Cheddar are a twosome that enjoy wide acceptance – a wedge of cheese with apple pie is a natural. This combination is taken one step further with a delicious cheese pastry for an apple pie.

Pastry
155 g (5 oz) butter
1¼ cups flour
pinch of salt
155 g (5 oz) Cheddar cheese, grated
approximately ½ egg yolk

Filling
6 Granny Smith apples
3 tablespoons brown sugar
½ teaspoon cinnamon
pinch nutmeg
1 tablespoon cornflour
30 g (1 oz) unsalted butter
lemon juice

To make the Pastry: Rub the butter into the sifted flour and salt. Toss in the grated Cheddar and add enough egg yolk to bind the pastry. Wrap in greaseproof paper and chill overnight.
To make the Filling: Peel, core and slice apples thinly and toss with a mixture of the sugar, cinnamon, nutmeg and cornflour.

Roll out two-thirds of the pastry and use to line a 20 cm (8 inch) tart tin. Fill with layers of apples dotted with knobs of unsalted butter and a squeeze of lemon juice. Roll the remaining pastry to cover the pie or cover with a lattice crust binding the edges with a strip of pastry. Press the edges together in flutes. Bake in a hot oven (200°C/400°F) for 10 minutes then reduce heat to moderately hot (190°C/375°F) and continue cooking for 35 minutes. Best served warm, with or without whipped cream.
Serves 6

Right: If you like to ice your Christmas cake, it can be given a pretty 'snow' effect and bright trimmings can be added (page 308).

Bake Plum Cake (page 303) in a fluted tin for a pretty effect. Serve with tea or coffee or with cream for dessert.

Port Wine Jelly

•

Especially for men! Port wine and redcurrant jelly make this a sophisticated jelly ... not really the thing for children.

2 envelopes (20 g) gelatine
1½ cups water
1–2 tablespoons sugar
2 tablespoons redcurrant jelly
2½ cups port wine
few drops red food colouring (optional)
whipped cream to serve

Sprinkle the gelatine over the water placed in a saucepan. Allow to soak for 2 minutes. Add the sugar and redcurrant jelly. Stir over a gentle heat until dissolved then add the port and a few drops of red food colouring. Strain through muslin. Pour into a serving bowl and chill until set. Decorate with whipped cream. *Serves 6–8*

Note: This jelly may be served in old-fashioned custard cups; small wine glasses would also be suitable.

Port Wine Jelly Mould

•

Make Port Wine Jelly as above but increase gelatine quantity by 2 teaspoons. Using a 4 cup wetted mould or ring tin, pour the jelly in and allow to set in the refrigerator.

If liked, whole hulled and washed strawberries may be set in the jelly.

Unmould and serve with whipped cream. *Serves 8*

Strawberries Romanov

• •

Nothing compares with the flavour or fragrance of fresh strawberries except perhaps the combination of strawberries and the incomparable zest of oranges. Here's the best recipe I know for Strawberries Romanov ... a dish fit for any prince.

8 lumps loaf sugar
2 oranges
2 punnets strawberries
6 tablespoons Curaçao

Cream Chantilly

1¼ cups cream, chilled
sugar to taste
vanilla to taste

Rub lumps of sugar over the skins of oranges until they are well saturated with the flavour of the fruit. Crush the sugar. Wash and hull the strawberries. Macerate in Curaçao and sugar in a covered container in the refrigerator until serving time. Spoon into serving bowl or individual dessert dishes in a pyramid shape.

To make the Cream Chantilly: Whip the chilled cream with sugar to taste until firm. Fold in the vanilla. Put the Cream Chantilly into a piping bag with a rose or star tube and decorate the strawberries with rosettes of cream. Serve immediately. *Serves 4–6*

Cherry Quiche

• •

The French province of Lorraine produces the savoury Quiche Lorraine, known the world over. The same technique of covering the filling ingredients with a rich custard makes a sumptuous fruit quiche which is quite different from the classic French or English fruit tarts. Use fresh or canned cherries, or thinly sliced apple for a change.

1 quantity French Flan pastry for 23–25 cm
(9–10 inch) flan ring (see page 290)
1 kg (2 lb) cherries
sugar to taste
3 eggs
2½ cups cream or milk
30 g (1 oz) butter

Line a 25 cm (10 inch) flan ring with the pastry. Stone the cherries and place in a layer over the pastry case. Sprinkle the cherries with sugar and place in a hot oven (220°C/425°F) for 10 minutes. Beat the eggs with the cream or milk and add up to ¼ cup sugar, the mixture should taste sweet. Pour the egg mixture over the cherries in the partially baked pastry case and dot with the butter. Lower oven heat to moderate (180°C/350°F) for 30 minutes or until the custard is set. *Serves 6–8*

Variations

The quiche is much finer if made with cream, but milk or a mixture of cream and milk can be used.

For a 23 cm (9 inch) quiche, use the same quantity of pastry but reduce the quantity of cream to 2 cups.

Apple Quiche Make as for Cherry Quiche but substitute 500 g (1 lb) peeled, cored and thinly sliced apples for the cherries.

Decorating Small Desserts

Petits Pots de Crème, Apricot Orange Mousse and other such desserts are decorative enough, in their dear little pots or other pretty containers, to serve as is – but if you do want to gild the lily, pipe on a swirl of whipped cream with a 1 cm (½ inch) star pipe and top with one of the following:

★ Chocolate Caraque (below)
★ Chocolate Curls (below)
★ Sugared Violets (see The Duchess's Christmas Trifle, page 277)
★ Slivered almonds, toasted until golden in a moderate oven (180°C/350°F) for about 10 minutes
★ A sprinkle of nutmeg or cinnamon
★ Julienne strips of orange rind (see Figs with Yogurt Cheese, page 280)
★ One perfect strawberry, unhulled

Serve with bought or homemade dessert biscuits such as Cigarettes Russes, Boudoirs, Delicate French Fingers (page 319) or Almond Fans (page 318).

Chocolate Caraque

This is the classic chocolate decoration for cakes and many desserts. It takes practice and skill, but for those who have a feeling for chocolate it is worth the effort.

Shred or grate 90 g (3 oz) good dark chocolate and melt it on a plate over a pan of hot water. Do not allow the plate to get too hot and work the chocolate continually with a palette knife. Spread the melted chocolate thinly on a marble slab. When just on the point of setting, curl it off with a thin knife.

Caraque will store in the refrigerator (in hot climates) until required. Store covered for any length of time.

Chocolate Curls

The answer when you want a pretty chocolate decoration but have neither the skill nor time to make proper caraque.

Using a swivel-bladed vegetable peeler and a large block of milk chocolate (not cold from the refrigerator but at room temperature) proceed to cut little curls of chocolate from the edge of the chocolate block. Store as for caraque.

Choux Pastry

•

Choux pastry makes cream puffs, éclairs and profiteroles, either dessert-sized or very tiny ones to garnish soup. The secret of making light, crisp shells that never collapse is to place the shaped pastry into a hot oven so that it puffs quickly, then turn the heat down so that the puffs can bake without overbrowning until they are thoroughly dry. A puff that is brown outside but moist inside will collapse as it cools. Lay a piece of paper or foil over the puffs toward the end of cooking time, if necessary, to keep them from browning too much. A well-cooked puff is golden brown and feels light in the hand. The shells must be completely cooled before they are filled.

1 cup water
125 g (4 oz) butter
½ teaspoon salt
1 teaspoon sugar
1 cup flour
4 × 55 g eggs

Place the water, butter, salt and sugar into a small saucepan and bring slowly to the boil, the butter must be completely melted when boiling point is reached. Sift flour on to a piece of greaseproof paper, and as soon as the mixture in the saucepan boils, tip in the flour all at once. Beat vigorously over a low heat with a wooden spatula until the ingredients are thoroughly combined and the mixture comes away from the sides of the pan.

Remove from the heat, turn the mixture into a bowl and cool a little. Beat in the eggs one at a time, beating each until completely incorporated before adding the next.

Shape as directed in the recipe. Bake at 220°C (425°F) for 12 minutes then reduce the heat to 180°C (350°F) and bake until golden brown and light in the hand, a further 15–25 minutes depending on size.

Macaroons

••

This recipe makes more macaroons than you will want for
Pere Ripieni (see page 285) but macaroons keep
well in an airtight container. This is the best macaroon to use
in The Duchess's Christmas Trifle (see page 277).

125 g (4 oz) almonds
1 cup caster sugar
30 g (1 oz) granulated sugar
15 g (½ oz) rice flour
2 large or 3 small egg whites
½ teaspoon vanilla

Blanch the almonds: Place in a bowl and cover with boiling
water. Leave for 1 minute then drain and rinse under cold
water. The skins will slip off easily. Pulverize the nuts in a nut
mill, blender or food processor fitted with the double edged
steel blade. Mix the sugars together and combine with the
almonds and rice flour in a mixing bowl. Add the egg whites
and vanilla and beat together with a wooden spoon for about 5
minutes. Scrape down the sides of the bowl and leave to stand
for 5 minutes. Cut 8 cm (3 inch) squares of greaseproof paper
and arrange on a greased baking sheet. Grease again. Beat the
almond mixture for a further 5 minutes until thick and white.

Using a piping bag fitted with a 1 cm (½ inch) tube, pipe
rounds on to the paper. Alternatively, spoon on from a
teaspoon. Bake in a moderate oven (180°C/350°F) for 20 to 30
minutes or until very pale brown. Allow to cool and remove the
paper. If the paper sticks, dampen it slightly underneath and it
will come off.

Tiny Éclairs

• • •

1 qty Choux Pastry (see left)
Chocolate Icing (see recipe below)

Filling

½ cup cream
2 teaspoons caster sugar

To shape pastry: Lightly grease a baking tray. Mark the tray
with two sets of parallel lines, spaced a little finger's length
apart (use the point of a skewer for this). Place the paste into a
piping bag fitted with a plain 1 cm (½ inch) tube and pipe strips
between the lines about 4 cm (1½ inch) apart. Bake the éclairs
in a hot oven (220°C/425°F) for 12 minutes. Reduce the
temperature to moderate (180°C/350°F) and bake for a further
10 to 15 minutes or until the éclairs are golden brown and feel
light in the hand.

Slit each along the side as soon as they are removed from the
oven, then cool completely. Make the icing (see below).

Hold each éclair by the base, dip the top into chocolate icing
and put aside, not touching any other, to set.

·Shortly before serving, whip the cream with the sugar and
fill each éclair by piping or spooning cream through the slit
side. *Makes approximately 20*

Chocolate Icing

•

90 g (3 oz) dark chocolate
1 tablespoon coffee or rum
30 g (1 oz) soft butter

Melt the chocolate with the coffee or rum over hot water,
stirring until they form a smooth cream. Remove from heat and
beat in the butter a little at a time. Keep warm over hot water,
adding a little warm water if needed to maintain a dipping
consistency.

A SLICE OF CAKE AND A BARREL OF BISCUITS

Cakes and biscuits are the most sociable of foods. In Scandinavia and European countries, where the coffee pot murmurs 'welcome', the aromas of spice and yeast are forever present. In Scotland, England and far-away Australia, indeed, wherever the British have travelled they have taken their teapots and precious recipes for that gentle ceremony – afternoon tea. A tea party gives the cook the opportunity to show her skills at baking, surely first among the fine arts of the kitchen.

There's something about homemade cakes and biscuits that just can't be duplicated. Their freshness, good natural ingredients, and the love and care that go into their making combine to give them this special quality. A good recipe is essential, for this is one branch of cookery where indiscriminate inspiration is often disastrous. The balance of ingredients is critical, perhaps our grandmothers didn't use a recipe but they had a sure eye and an experienced hand and until you have both, don't experiment. Follow a recipe carefully and you'll soon be turning out lovely treats like the best of them.

Fortunately for those aspiring to be good at baking there are wonderful recipes created by skilled pastry cooks not lacking in ingenuity and inventiveness. There are endless variations of basic doughs, intriguing combinations of flavours and completely new techniques. There are butter cakes, nut tortes, sponges, meringues, fruit cakes, tea cakes, cakes that take time and skill and others that are made literally in a minute, like Spanish Tea Cake.

There is a goodly selection of biscuits – chewy, crispy, crunchy with nuts, sweet with sugar and spice, savoury with cheese; slices, bars, rolled or cut into dainty shapes.

Whether it's a magnificent spread for a tea party, a quiet cup of coffee with a friend or a luscious dessert cake for a dinner, there's something just right that can come out of your kitchen – join the club and become one of the elite band of good bakers.

Almond Macaroon Cake

• • •

This should be kept for at least 1 week before cutting. It has an interesting appearance, with an almond macaroon topping on a rich fruit cake. It has more angelica than usual, giving it a deliciously different flavour. A cake tin, larger than the cake, is used as a cover during baking to prevent the topping from burning.

125 g (4 oz) angelica
¾ cup currants
1 cup sultanas
125 g (4 oz) butter, softened
½ cup caster sugar
2 eggs
1 egg yolk
½ cup ground almonds
1⅓ cups plain flour
pinch of salt
3 tablespoons milk

Macaroon Topping

1 egg white
½ cup caster sugar
¾ cup ground almonds
few drops almond essence
30 g (1 oz) flaked almonds

Wash the sugar from the angelica and chop finely. Wash the currants and sultanas, drain, and spread with the angelica on a baking sheet lined with a kitchen towel. Place in a slow oven (150°C/300°F) for about 15 minutes until fruits are quite dry.

Grease a 20 cm (8 inch) round cake tin and line with a double thickness of greased greaseproof paper. Set oven to (180°C/350°F).

Cream the softened butter and gradually beat in the sugar. The mixture should be light and fluffy. Beat the eggs and yolk lightly and gradually add to creamed mixture, beating well after each addition to prevent the mixture curdling. If mixture begins to curdle beat in half of the ground almonds. When eggs are completely beaten in, stir in the ground almonds.

Sift the flour with the salt. With a large metal spoon fold the flour into the cake mixture in 3 parts alternately with the milk. Lastly fold in the fruits. Turn into prepared cake tin.

Make the Macaroon Topping: Beat the egg white until stiff and gently fold in the sugar, ground almonds and almond essence. The mixture should be of spreading consistency. If too stiff, gently stir in a little extra egg white. Spread over the top of cake and sprinkle with the flaked almonds.

Place an inverted cake tin to fit over the cake and bake in a moderate oven for 2½ hours. Failing a tin that fits on the top, use a double thickness of foil crimped to sit on top of the cake in tin, leaving room for mixture to rise. Remove cover for last 30 minutes of cooking to enable topping to become light golden. Cool on a wire rack and leave for at least 1 week before cutting. *Makes one 20 cm (8 inch) cake*

Almond Torte

• • •

This is among the classics of light, delicate, yet totally delicious tortes. A thick mousse of eggs, sugar, semolina and ground almonds is folded into a meringue, then baked. Fill and decorate it with whipped cream and any seasonal fresh fruit such as strawberries or plums, and add a fruit sauce of strawberries or plums. Serve it with coffee or as a dessert.

3 eggs, separated
½ cup caster sugar
grated rind and juice of 1 lemon
⅓ cup fine semolina
1 tablespoon ground almonds
1½ cups cream, whipped
2–3 plums or 12 strawberries
Strawberry or Plum Sauce (see below)

Grease a 20 cm (8 inch) cake tin and line it with greased greaseproof paper. Dust the tin lightly with a little caster sugar, then flour. Preheat the oven to moderate (180°C/350°F).

Beat the egg yolks, sugar, lemon rind and juice together until thick and mousse-like. Fold in the semolina and ground almonds. Beat the egg whites until stiff and, using a large metal spoon, fold into the almond mixture. Turn into the prepared tin and bake in a moderate oven for 30–40 minutes or until the torte shrinks away from the sides of the tin. Remove from the oven and leave in the tin for a few minutes before turning out on to a wire rack to cool.

Using a large bread or cake knife with a serrated edge split the cake in two. Fill with half of the whipped cream.

Slice the plums or strawberries, reserving some perfect slices or whole strawberries for decoration, and place on the cream. Spoon over three-quarters of the remaining cream. Replace top gently. Dust with icing sugar. Fill a pastry bag fitted with a star or rose pipe with the remaining cream and pipe rosettes on top, then decorate with reserved fruit. Serve with fruit sauce. *Makes one 20 cm (8 inch) cake*

Strawberry Sauce

250 g (8 oz) punnet of strawberries
2 tablespoons caster sugar
grated rind and juice of 1 orange
2 teaspoons arrowroot

Wash and hull the strawberries. Mash with a fork and push through a sieve. Mix with the sugar, orange rind and juice. Alternatively, purée in a blender with the sugar, orange rind and juice. Place in a saucepan and heat gently. Mix the arrowroot with a little cold water, add to the strawberry purée and bring to the boil, stirring for a few seconds. Allow to cool. Serve with Almond Torte. *Continued over page*

Plum Sauce

Make with blood plums if possible.

250 g (8 oz) plums
⅔ cup sugar
1¼ cups water
2–3 teaspoons arrowroot

Wash plums, halve and remove the stones. Dissolve the sugar in the water over a low heat. Add the plums and poach gently until tender. Remove from the heat and rub through a fine sieve.

Return to the saucepan, and add the arrowroot that has been mixed to a smooth paste with a little cold water. Bring to the boil, stirring until the sauce thickens slightly. Allow to cool. Serve with Almond Torte.

Butter Cake

A butter cake is excellent to have as a standby – whether for hungry children or unexpected guests.
By adding different flavouring ingredients to the basic cake mixture it can become up to six different cakes.
The cake can be served either dusted with icing sugar or iced with an appropriate flavoured icing or butter cream. Cut into generous wedges and it is the ideal accompaniment to a cup of tea.

Basic Butter Cake

••

Not one cake, but half a dozen or more. This mixture makes a moist, light cake that's excellent plain and also turns easily into a good standby orange, sultana, spice, seed or chocolate cake. Bake it in one deep round or square tin, in two sandwich tins, or small bar tins. Double the quantity and bake it in a bundt tin for a glamorous continental look, or add a little extra milk and make cup cakes.

125 g (4 oz) butter
¾ cup caster sugar
1 teaspoon vanilla
2 eggs
2 cups self-raising flour
pinch of salt
½ cup milk

Grease a 20 cm (8 inch) deep round or square cake tin. Line the base with greaseproof paper cut to fit, and grease again.

Cream the butter and sugar, add the vanilla and beat until pale and fluffy. Beat the eggs slightly and gradually beat into the butter and sugar mixture. If using an electric mixer, add the eggs one at a time and beat well after each addition.

Sift the flour and salt 3 times, then fold into the creamed mixture in several batches alternately with the milk, beginning and ending with flour. Pour into the prepared tin and bake in a preheated moderate oven (180°C/350°F) for 45 to 50 minutes or until a fine skewer, inserted into the centre, comes out clean. Turn out on to a wire rack, then invert immediately on to another wire rack so as not to mark the top.

Note: If baking the mixture in two 20 cm (8 inch) sandwich tins or in two 25 × 8 cm (10 × 3 inch) bar tins, it will take 25 to 30 minutes cooking time. A double quantity in a bundt tin will take about 1 hour.

Variations

Orange Cake Omit the vanilla and add the grated rind of 1 orange when creaming the butter and sugar. Ice with orange butter icing if liked.
Sultana Cake Add 1 teaspoon mixed spice when sifting the flour and salt and fold 1 cup sultanas into the finished mixture.
Seed Cake Add 1 tablespoon caraway seeds to the sifted flour and salt and sprinkle 1 tablespoon seeds on top before baking.
Spice Cake Sift 1 teaspoon mixed spice with the flour and salt. Fold 125 g (4 oz) chopped dates or walnuts into the finished mixture. Ice with thin lemon icing if liked.
Chocolate Cake Dissolve 60 g (2 oz) unsweetened chocolate in a little of the milk, warmed, then mix with the remaining milk. Ice with chocolate butter icing if liked.
Cup Cakes Make the Basic Butter Cake mixture, increasing milk to ⅔ cup. Spoon mixture into patty tins or cases. For smooth-topped cup cakes to be iced, bake in a moderately hot oven (190°C/375°F) for about 15 minutes.

For Butterfly Cakes: bake cup cakes in a hot oven (200°C/400°F) in the hottest part of the oven for about 10 minutes – this gives peaked tops. When cool, cut a circle from the top of each cake and fill with a spoonful of sweetened, whipped cream. Cut the circle in two and place on top in butterfly-wing fashion. Dust with icing sugar.

Icings

Orange Butter Icing Cream 15 g (½ oz) butter with 2 teaspoons grated orange rind. Stir in 2 teaspoons orange juice and gradually beat in 1 cup sifted icing sugar. Spread on the cooled cake with a round-ended knife.
Thin Lemon Icing Sift 1 cup icing sugar and mix with 1 tablespoon lemon juice, plus a little water if necessary to give the consistency of thin cream. Warm slightly over low heat. Pour over the warm or cooled cake.
Chocolate Butter Icing Melt 30 g (1 oz) chocolate over hot water. Cream the melted chocolate with 15 g (½ oz) butter and gradually beat in 1 cup sifted icing sugar. Spread on the cooled cake with a round-ended knife.

Beer and Date Cake

••

Beer gives this beautiful cake an intriguing taste and moist texture.

1 cup butter
2 cups brown sugar, firmly packed
2 eggs
1 cup chopped walnuts
1 cup chopped dates
3 cups plain flour
½ teaspoon salt
2 teaspoons bicarbonate of soda
1 teaspoon cinnamon
½ teaspoon mixed spice
½ teaspoon ground cloves
2 cups beer

Cream the butter and sugar together until light and fluffy. Add the eggs one at a time, beating well after each addition. Stir in the nuts and dates. Sift the flour, salt, soda and spices together. Fold in the flour alternately with the beer, beginning and ending with the flour.

Spoon into a greased 10 cup bundt or gugelhupf tin and bake in a moderate oven (180°C/350°F) for 1 to 1¼ hours or until a fine skewer inserted in the centre comes out clean. Turn cake on to a wire rack and cool. *Makes one cake*

Buttermilk Cake

•

Buttermilk cake requires no long creaming of butter, sugar, or beating of eggs (there are none). It is as easy to make as a packet cake mix – the excellent flavour and moistness is the difference.

2½ cups plain flour
1½ cups caster sugar
1½ teaspoons bicarbonate of soda
1 teaspoon baking powder
¼ teaspoon salt
1 teaspoon cinnamon
½ teaspoon ground cloves
½ cup melted butter
1½ cups buttermilk

Set oven temperature at moderate (180°C/350°F). Grease a 23 cm (9 inch) deep ring tin or fluted gugelhupf or bundt tin and dust with sugar.

Sift the flour with the dry ingredients into a bowl. Make a well in the centre. Place melted butter and buttermilk in the centre and stir the liquid, gradually taking in the flour, mixing until the batter is well combined and smooth. Pour into the prepared tin and bake in a moderate oven for 1 hour or until a fine skewer inserted comes out clean. Turn cake out on to a wire rack and leave to cool. *Makes one 23 cm (9 inch) cake*

Bishop's Cake

•

An old English fruit cake that got its name from the stained glass window appearance of each slice. It is sometimes known as American Christmas Cake and is more of a fruit and nut slab than a cake. This cake should be stored in the refrigerator, wrapped in foil and, being so rich and sweet, only a thin slice is necessary. It may be cut in finger blocks and is often served with sherry.

500 g (1 lb) shelled Brazil nuts
12 pitted dates
1 cup glacé cherries, red and green mixed
¾ cup plain flour
½ teaspoon baking powder
½ teaspoon salt
¾ cup caster sugar
3 eggs
1 teaspoon vanilla

Grease a 21 × 11 cm (8½ × 4½ inch) loaf tin and line the base and sides with greased greaseproof paper. Set oven temperature to slow (150°C/300°F).

Put the whole Brazil nuts, whole dates and whole glacé cherries into a large mixing bowl. Sift the dry ingredients over the fruit and nut mixture and mix thoroughly. Beat the eggs until frothy and pour over the fruit mixture with the vanilla. Stir well and spoon into the prepared tin. Bake in a slow oven for approximately 1¾ hours. Remove from tin, peel away paper and cool completely.

When cold, wrap in foil and store in the refrigerator. *Makes one 21 × 11 cm (8½ × 4½ inch) loaf cake*

Cherry Cake

••

This rich cherry cake has good keeping qualities. The mixture is slightly stiffer than a plain butter cake, to prevent the cherries sinking to the bottom.

½ cup glacé cherries
185 g (6 oz) butter or margarine
¾ cup caster sugar
1 teaspoon vanilla
2 eggs
1 cup plain flour
1 cup self-raising flour
pinch of salt
¼–⅓ cup milk

Brush a 20 cm (8 inch) fancy loaf tin with melted butter and dust lightly with flour. Set oven temperature at moderate (180°C/350°F). Halve the cherries, wash to remove all syrup and dry

completely. (The syrup in the middle of the cherries can be one of the causes of sinking.)

Cream the butter or margarine until soft and creamy, gradually add the sugar and vanilla and beat until light and fluffy. Beat the eggs lightly and add to the creamed mixture gradually. Sift both flours with the salt. Sprinkle the cherries with 2 tablespoons of the sifted flour. With a large metal spoon fold the remaining sifted flour into the creamed mixture alternately with the milk. Use just enough to make a stiff batter. Lastly, fold in the cherries and pour into the prepared tin.

Bake in a moderate oven for about 1¼ hours. To prevent the cake splitting and cracking on top, cover with two or three folds of greaseproof paper for the first 30 minutes of baking. Cool on a wire rack. *Makes one 20 cm (8 inch) loaf cake*

Black Forest Cherry Torte

• • •

Here is a recipe for one version, and there are many, of the most famous cake of all. Rich chocolate layers soaked with Kirsch are filled with cream and sour cherries; the cherries must be sour for the right contrast of flavours. A generous topping of whipped cream and chocolate curls – that's what this specialty from the Black Forest is all about.

275 g (9 oz) good chocolate
1 jar German sour cherries
3 tablespoons Kirsch
1 × 23 cm (9 inch) Chocolate Cake (see right)
2 cups cream
a few Maraschino cherries on stems (optional)

Make caraque with the chocolate (see page 295) or shave the block into thin curls (see page 295), chill. Drain the syrup from the cherries and mix the syrup with the Kirsch. Halve the cherries, leaving a few whole for decoration.

Cut the chocolate cake in two and prick the bottom layer with the tines of a fork or use a skewer. Place the bottom layer on a serving plate and soak it with half the cherry juice. Whip the cream until it just holds its shape and pile about one-third of the cream over the bottom layer. Spoon over half the cherries. Position the top layer, prick and pour the remaining cherry juice over, then press the layers together and spoon on the remaining cherry halves. Mask the cake with the remaining cream, piling most of the cream on top of the cake. Press chocolate caraque or curls around the sides of the cake and a few of the best over the top. Finish off with whole cherries or a few Maraschino cherries on stems, if liked. Chill for 1–2 hours. *Serves 10–12*

Chocolate Cake

••

This makes a perfect base for Black Forest Torte or is good by itself – either plain with Chocolate Icing, or a filling of whipped cream.

4 eggs
¾ cup caster sugar
¾ cup self-raising flour
1 teaspoon vanilla
grated rind of ½ lemon
45 g (1½ oz) butter, melted and cooled
90 g (3 oz) dark cooking chocolate
1 tablespoon water or coffee

Grease a 23 cm (9 inch) springform tin and line the base with greased greaseproof paper. Dust lightly with flour. Set oven temperature to moderate (180°C/350°F). Melt the chocolate with the water or coffee over a low heat.

Beat the eggs with the sugar until very light and fluffy. Sift in the flour and, using a large metal spoon, fold carefully into the egg mixture with the vanilla, lemon rind, melted butter and chocolate.

Turn into the prepared tin and bake in a moderate oven for 1 hour. Cool with the spring released. *Makes one 23 cm (9 inch) cake*

Plum Cake

••

This easy-to-make cake is delicious with tea or coffee, or may be served with cream or custard as dessert after a light main course.

8 fresh plums
60 g (2 oz) butter
⅓ cup sugar
1 egg
1 cup self-raising flour
¼ cup milk
cinnamon and sugar

Grease a 23 cm (9 inch) springform tin or a fluted, loose-based tin. Set the oven temperature to moderate (180°C/350°F). Wash, halve and stone the plums.

Cream the butter and sugar and add the lightly beaten egg, beat well. Sift the flour and add half to the mixture. Beat to combine. Add the milk and remaining flour alternately (this will make a thick mixture). Spread the mixture over the base of the prepared tin. Place the prepared plums, cut-side down, on the cake batter. Bake in a moderate oven for 1 hour. While still warm, sprinkle with cinnamon and sugar. *Makes one 23 cm (9 inch) cake*

Variations

Other fruits in season may be used instead of plums. Peaches or pears would be lovely, or you might like to try apples.
Apple Cake Prepare the cake batter as above and top with 3 medium apples. Peel and quarter the apples then remove the core. Cut the quartered apples into thin slices, but not all the way through, they should open like a fan. Put the apples as you prepare them in a bowl, and squeeze over the juice of a lemon. Place the apples, core side down, on the cake and finish as above.

Dutch Apple Cake

••

When you're out of doors, there's something comforting about a cake smelling warmly of apples and cinnamon ... essence of childhood memories. This is a wonderful cake to take on a picnic or for afternoon tea in the garden.

2 cups self-raising flour
½ teaspoon salt
1 tablespoon sugar
125 g (4 oz) butter
½ cup milk
2 medium Granny Smith apples

Topping
30 g (1 oz) butter, melted
1 teaspoon cinnamon
2 tablespoons sugar

Grease a 20 cm (8 inch) round cake tin and line the base with greaseproof paper.

Sift the flour, salt and sugar together, and rub the butter in with fingertips. Make a well in the centre and add the milk in a steady stream, stirring with a fork and incorporating the flour.

Place the mixture in the prepared tin and pat out level, making sure that it is pushed well into the edges and against the sides.

Peel and core the apples and cut into thin wedge-shaped slices. Arrange in a circular pattern to cover the top of the cake, pressing thin edges into the dough. Brush with melted butter, sprinkle with cinnamon and sugar, and bake in a moderate oven (180°C/350°F) for 40 minutes. This cake is best served warm, cut in wedges and buttered. *Makes one 20 cm (8 inch) cake*

Apple Tea Cake

••

This light and tender tea cake is topped with thin slices of apple and when baked is made extra fragrant with a spiced butter glaze. It is a lovely cake served warm with tea or coffee.

1 egg, separated
½ cup sugar
½ cup milk
½ teaspoon vanilla
1 cup self-raising flour
30 g (1 oz) butter, melted
1 small apple
extra butter for brushing
½ teaspoon cinnamon
1 tablespoon sugar

Grease an 18 cm (7 inch) sandwich tin. Preheat oven to moderately hot (190°C/375°F).

Beat the egg white stiffly and add the egg yolk. Gradually beat in the sugar, beating between additions. Mix the milk and vanilla and add a little at a time. Gently stir in the sifted flour and melted butter. Pour into the prepared tin.

Peel, halve and core the apple then cut in thin slices. Arrange the apple slices over the tea cake and bake in a moderately hot oven for 20 to 25 minutes. While hot, brush with some extra melted butter and sprinkle with the sugar and cinnamon mixed together. Serve warm or cold with butter. *Makes one 18 cm (7 inch) cake*

Cherry Nut Pound Cake

••

Glacé cherries can be used in place of Maraschino in this American pound cake. A cherry liqueur, slightly diluted, or even milk can be used instead of the Maraschino syrup. The cherries are chopped, giving the cake a pink tint and, with the addition of walnuts, a great flavour.

250 g (8 oz) butter or margarine, softened
1 cup sugar
1 tablespoon Maraschino cherry syrup
5 eggs, separated
¾ cup chopped walnuts
½ cup chopped Maraschino cherries
2 cups plain flour
1 teaspoon baking powder
½ teaspoon salt

Line a 20 cm (8 inch) square cake tin with greased brown paper. Set oven temperature to moderate (180°C/350°F).

Cream the butter or margarine and gradually add the sugar, beating until light. Add the cherry syrup. Beat the egg yolks until thick and lemon-coloured and add to the creamed mixture with the nuts and cherries. Add the sifted dry ingredients and, using a large metal spoon, blend in thoroughly. Beat the egg whites until stiff but not dry and fold in.

Bake in a moderate oven for approximately 1 hour 10 minutes or until a skewer inserted comes out clean. (If cake becomes too brown on top, cover with a sheet of kitchen paper during the last 10 minutes of baking.) Turn out on a wire rack and peel off the paper. *Makes one 20 cm (8 inch) cake*

Genoa Cake

••

*The distinctive feature of this fruit cake is the fresh
flavour of lemon combined with the fruitiness of currants,
sultanas, raisins and peel. It is moist and a
good keeper.*

250 g (8 oz) butter or margarine
1 cup caster sugar
grated rind and juice of 1 lemon
6 eggs
2½ cups plain flour
2 cups currants
1½ cups sultanas
½ cup raisins
¼ cup mixed peel
a few flaked almonds

Line a 20 cm (8 inch) square cake tin with two sheets of greased
greaseproof paper. Wrap a double strip of paper around the
outside of the tin (to stop the cake from browning too quickly)
and secure with string or a paper clip. Set oven temperature to
moderate (180°C/350°F).

Cream the butter and sugar thoroughly with the lemon rind.
Beat the eggs and gradually add half to the creamed mixture.
Sift flour and with a large metal spoon or spatula fold in
alternately with the remaining beaten eggs. Add the lemon
juice, currants, sultanas, raisins and peel. Turn into the
prepared tin and sprinkle the top with flaked almonds. Bake in
a moderate oven for 2½ hours or until a skewer inserted comes
out clean. *Makes one 20 cm (8 inch) cake*

Honey Chocolate Cake

••

*This is such a useful basic recipe, a light chocolate,
well-flavoured cake . . . honey, rum and sherry are behind
the elusive flavour.*

185 g (6 oz) butter
1 cup lightly packed brown sugar
⅓ cup honey
2 eggs
3 teaspoons rum
½ teaspoon vanilla
2 tablespoons cocoa
1¾ cups self-raising flour
pinch of salt
½ cup sweet sherry
¾ cup cream, whipped
few drops almond essence
icing sugar

Grease and line a 23 cm (9 inch) round cake tin. Set oven
temperature to moderate (180°C/350°F).

Cream the butter, brown sugar and honey until light and
fluffy. Beat in the eggs one at a time, add rum and vanilla. Sift
cocoa, flour and salt together three times. Fold into the butter
mixture alternately with the sherry. Spoon into the prepared
tin and bake in a moderate oven for 45 minutes or until cooked
when tested with a skewer. Cool in tin for 5 minutes, then turn
out on to a rack to cool.

When cold, split cake in two and fill with the whipped
cream, flavoured with a few drops of almond essence. Dust top
with icing sugar or spread with your favourite chocolate icing.
Makes one 23 cm (9 inch) cake

Orange Cake

••

*A basic butter cake flavoured with orange rind and juice, this
has a fine texture and keeps well. Serve it plain,
dusted with caster sugar, or iced with orange frosting and
decorated with finely shredded, blanched
orange rind.*

250 g (8 oz) softened butter
grated rind and juice of 1 large orange
1 cup caster sugar
4 large eggs
2 cups self-raising flour
pinch of salt

Grease and lightly flour a 20 cm (8 inch) loaf tin and line the
base with greased greaseproof paper. Set oven temperature to
moderate (180°C/350°F).

Cream the butter with the orange rind until very smooth.
Gradually add the sugar, beating well between each addition
until it is thoroughly incorporated and the mixture is light and
fluffy. Beat the eggs until blended and gradually add to the
butter and sugar mixture, beating thoroughly to prevent
curdling. Sift flour with salt; using a metal spoon fold in flour
alternately with the orange juice.

Turn mixture into prepared tin and bake in a moderate oven
for 45 minutes or until the cake is cooked when tested with a
skewer. Remove from tin and cool on a wire rack.

If liked, the cake can be iced with Orange Frosting: Cream
30 g (1 oz) butter with 1 tablespoon orange juice. Gradually add
2 cups sifted icing sugar, beating until smooth. Use to ice the
cake, smoothing with a round-edged knife. *Makes one 20 cm
(8 inch) cake*

Note: The orange cake can also be made in a greased 20 cm
(8 inch) loose bottomed cake tin with a fluted edge, or a fluted
bundt tin.

Honey Nut Roll

• •

30 g (1 oz) butter
½ cup honey
1 egg
1 cup plain flour
pinch of salt
1 teaspoon baking powder
¼ cup milk
½ cup chopped walnuts
½ cup sultanas

Grease a nut roll tin and set oven temperature to moderate (180°C/350°F).

Beat the butter and honey until light. Add the egg and beat in well. Sift flour, salt and baking powder together. Fold into creamed mixture alternately with milk, walnuts and sultanas. Spoon into prepared tin and bake in a moderate oven for 50–60 minutes or until a fine skewer inserted in the centre comes out clean. Serve warm or cold, sliced and spread with butter. *Makes one roll*

Prune and Apricot Upside-Down Cake

• •

A popular dessert cake when served with whipped cream or custard. The important thing about all upside-down cakes is that the base of the cake tin is covered with a butter and brown sugar mix to form a caramel, then this base should be **completely** *covered with fruit arranged in a decorative fashion. Thin rings of pineapple (split through horizontally if using canned) and glacé cherries are perhaps the best known decoration. This version is different.*

Fruit Glaze

30 g (1 oz) butter
4 tablespoons brown sugar
12 prunes, pitted
12 dried apricots
4 glacé cherries
8 blanched almonds

Cake

60 g (2 oz) butter
¼ cup sugar
few drops vanilla
1 egg
2½ tablespoons milk
1 cup self-raising flour
pinch of salt

Set oven temperature to moderate (180°C/350°F).
To make the Fruit Glaze: Melt the butter in an 18 cm (7 inch) square cake tin. Sprinkle evenly with the brown sugar and arrange the prunes, apricots, cherries and almonds on the glaze in an attractive pattern.
To make the Cake: Cream the butter, gradually add the sugar and beat until light and fluffy. Add the vanilla, beat egg lightly and gradually add to the creamed mixture. Sift flour with salt and fold in alternately with milk. Spoon cake mixture carefully over fruit, taking care not to disturb the arrangement.

Bake in a moderate oven for 25 minutes. Turn out, leaving the fruit side up. For a dessert, serve warm with cream; cool if serving as a cake. *Makes one 18 cm (7 inch) cake*

Lemon Tea Ring

• •

One of the best lemon cakes I know, very moist with a true sharp-sweet lemon flavour. It's the lemon juice added after *baking that does it.*

1½ cups plain flour
1 cup sugar
1 teaspoon baking powder
¼ teaspoon salt
125 g (4 oz) butter or margarine
2 eggs, beaten
½ cup milk
grated rind of 1 lemon
½ cup chopped walnuts

To pour over

juice of 1 lemon
¼ cup sugar

Grease a 20 cm (8 inch) ring tin or a 23 × 13 × 8 cm (9 × 5 × 3 inch) loaf tin. Line the base with greaseproof paper and grease again.

Sift the flour, sugar, baking powder and salt together into a bowl. Rub in the butter or margarine with fingertips. Mix the beaten eggs and milk together and stir in, then fold in the lemon rind and walnuts.

Pour mixture into prepared tin and bake in a moderate oven (180°C/350°F) until firm to the touch and a straw or fine skewer inserted into the centre comes out clean – about 50 minutes for a ring, 1 hour and 20 minutes for a loaf.

Mix the lemon juice and sugar together and, when the cake is cooked, pour over the top. Allow to cool in the pan. *Makes one ring or loaf cake.*

Finnish Sour Cream Cake

•

Sour cream gives cakes a rich flavour and moistness that makes them keep well. This delicious Finnish cake has a spicy taste and the quantity here makes two cakes, one to freeze and one to eat, or one large spectacular cake in a fluted gugelhupf or bundt tin.

2 eggs, beaten
2 cups sour cream
2 cups caster sugar
2–3 drops almond essence
3 cups plain flour
1 teaspoon bicarbonate of soda
½ teaspoon salt
½ teaspoon cinnamon
½ teaspoon ground cardamom

Set oven temperature to moderate (180°C/350°F). Grease two 20 cm (8 inch) deep ring tins, plain or fluted, and dust lightly with sugar. If liked, one large 23 cm (9 inch) gugelhupf or bundt fluted cake tin may be used.

Combine the eggs, sour cream, sugar and almond essence. Sift flour with remaining ingredients and add gradually to the egg mixture, beating until the batter is smooth and well combined. Pour into the prepared tins and bake in a moderate oven for 1 hour (1 hour 15 minutes if a large tin is used). Leave for 10 minutes before turning out. Cool on a wire rack; serve dusted with icing sugar. *Makes two 20 cm (8 inch) cakes or one 23 cm (9 inch) cake*

Sour Cream Waffles

••

Most homes have boasted a waffle iron at one time or another, for waffles appeal to all ages. This Norwegian recipe makes 12 whole generous waffles; light and tender with a delicious spiced flavour they make a great 'fun' base for fruits, jam, honey, syrup and cream.

5 eggs
½ cup caster sugar
1 cup flour
1 teaspoon baking powder
1 teaspoon bicarbonate of soda
1 teaspoon ground cardamom or ginger
1 cup sour cream
60 g (2 oz) unsalted butter

Beat the eggs and sugar together for 5 to 10 minutes, with an electric beater or by hand with a wire whisk, until the mixture falls back into the bowl in a ribbon when the beater is lifted out. Sift together the dry ingredients. Using a large metal spoon fold in half the sifted flour, then the sour cream and the remaining flour. Melt the butter and stir in lightly. Set aside for 10 minutes before using, then put into a large jug.

To Cook the Waffles: Heat the waffle iron until the indicator shows it is ready to use. If the iron is not an electric one, heat until a splash of water sizzles dry. If the waffle iron has been well seasoned, or has a non-stick coating, butter will not be necessary. If uncertain, brush with butter.

Cover the surface of the hot iron two-thirds full with mixture. Close the lid and wait about 3 minutes, turn after 2 minutes if using a non-electric one. When the waffle is ready all the steam will have stopped emerging from the sides. If you try to lift the top of the iron and it shows resistance, the waffle is probably not quite done. Cook about 1 minute more and try again.

Serve with golden or maple syrup or honey or a square of butter. Waffles are delicious with stewed or fresh fruit and cream. Americans enjoy them with crisp bacon rashers and maple syrup. A good berry jam and sour cream is favoured by many Scandinavians. *Makes 12 large waffles*

Spanish Tea Cake

•

When I was first offered this teacake with a glass of Spanish sherry, it seemed just right. Made with Spanish olive oil or a polyunsaturated oil, it is a cake you can prepare easily by hand or with an electric mixer (don't overbeat). It is a breeze, of course, to make in a food processor.

2 cups self-raising flour
1 cup sugar
1–2 teaspoons aniseed or caraway seeds
3 eggs, well beaten
½ cup milk
1 cup olive oil

Set oven temperature to moderate (180°C/350°F). Grease a 20 to 23 cm (8 to 9 inch) plain or fluted round cake tin and line the base with greased greaseproof paper.

Sift the flour into a large bowl. Stir in the sugar and seeds. Gradually beat in the eggs, milk and olive oil, beating until well combined. Pour into prepared tin and bake in a moderate oven for 1½ hours or until a fine skewer inserted in the centre comes out clean. *Makes one 20 or 23 cm (8 or 9 inch) cake*

To Make In a Food Processor: Have all ingredients measured and assembled nearby (the mixing takes literally 1 minute). Place flour and sugar in the bowl fitted with the double edged steel blade, combine. Add the eggs, milk, olive oil, and lastly the seeds. Then bake as above.

Rich Christmas Cake

• • •

The rich spicy fruit cake of England, made several months before Christmas so that it will age gracefully, ripening into a truly festive cake, symbolises the spirit and promise of a full and happy Christmas Day with more to come.

Fruit

250 g (8 oz) raisins
250 g (8 oz) sultanas
250 g (8 oz) currants
185 g (6 oz) mixed peel, finely chopped
60 g (2 oz) glacé cherries, diced
60 g (2 oz) glacé apricots, diced
2 slices glacé pineapple, diced
6 tablespoons brandy or rum
3 tablespoons sherry

Cake Mixture

250 g (8 oz) butter
1⅓ cups brown sugar
grated rind of 1 lemon
2 tablespoons marmalade
5 eggs
2½ cups plain flour
1 teaspoon mixed spice
1 teaspoon cinnamon
¼ teaspoon salt
125 g (4 oz) blanched almonds, chopped
extra almonds (optional)
extra brandy

Prepare Fruit Overnight: Chop the raisins. Put into a bowl with the remaining fruit. Sprinkle with brandy or rum and sherry. Leave overnight.

Next day, first line the tin then make the cake. Use a 20 cm (8 inch) round or square deep tin.

To Line the Tin: For a round tin, grease the tin. Cut a folded strip (double thickness) of greaseproof or kitchen paper 8 cm (3 inch) higher than the cake tin and long enough to go round the tin with a small overlap. Fold over a 1 cm (½ inch) hem, nick the hem with a pair of scissors at 2.5 cm (1 inch) intervals, and fit this strip into the tin, making sure the hem lies flat on the tin. Cut two circles of paper to fit the base of the tin. Place the circles of paper into the tin giving a neat finish to the tin, then brush with melted butter.

For a square tin, follow the same technique as for a round tin, making sure corners are squared, and naturally the paper for the bottom is cut to fit the tin.

To Make the Cake: Beat the butter and brown sugar with the lemon rind until light and creamy. Add the marmalade. Beat well. Add the eggs one at a time, beating well after each addition. Add 1 tablespoon flour with the last egg.

Sift together the flour, mixed spice, cinnamon and salt and stir into creamed mixture alternately with the fruit and almonds.

Spoon mixture into a prepared 20 cm (8 inch) round or square tin. If not icing the cake with almond paste and royal icing, decorate with almonds arranged in a pattern on top. Bake in a slow oven (150°C/300°F) for about 4 hours or until cooked. Remove from the oven and immediately sprinkle with about 1 tablespoon extra brandy. Remove cake from tin, leaving paper on cake. Wrap in a tea-towel and leave until cool. Store in an airtight tin. *Makes one 20 cm (8 inch) cake*

Decorating the Christmas Cake

Some people prefer a Christmas cake decorated with blanched almonds. Others like the festive look of an iced cake. Icing a cake takes 3 days – not literally, mind you – but the almond paste does take 48 hours to set. A few Christmas decorations, fir trees, Santa Claus, or an appropriate greeting may be used to give a dash of colour.

Almond Paste

185 g (6 oz) ground almonds
½ cup caster sugar
⅓ cup icing sugar
1 teaspoon lemon juice
1 egg yolk
½ teaspoon almond essence

Glaze

3 tablespoons apricot jam
1½ tablespoons water
½ teaspoon lemon juice

Royal Icing

500 g (1 lb) pure icing sugar
2 egg whites
1–2 teaspoons lemon juice

To make the Almond Paste: Stir together the ground almonds, caster sugar and icing sugar. Add the lemon juice, egg yolk and almond essence. Mix to a fairly stiff paste and knead lightly until smooth.

To make the Glaze: Bring the apricot jam and water to the boil. Boil for 4 minutes. Strain, add lemon juice and place back on the heat once more. Boil until glaze is thick enough to coat a wooden spoon.

Brush hot glaze evenly over top of cake.

Roll out the almond paste into a circle about 1 cm (½ inch) thick to fit top of cake. Place on cake and gently press with the edge of a rolling pin. Leave for at least 48 hours before icing.

To make the Royal Icing: Sieve the icing sugar. Whisk the egg whites to a light froth, add the icing sugar, a spoonful at a time, beating well. Stir in the lemon juice and continue beating until the icing will stand in soft peaks. Spread icing evenly over the top and sides of the cake. Rough up the icing over the edge of the cake to resemble snow. Allow at least 1 day for the icing to set.

Note: Some people may prefer to ice the top of the cake only and tie a ribbon or put a paper frill around it. If so, make half the quantity only of royal icing. A little royal icing may be set aside, coloured, and used to inscribe Merry Christmas on the cake.

Spiced Honey Cake

••

The honey and sour cream in this continental cake make it a good 'keeping' cake.

2 cups plain flour
1 teaspoon ground cinnamon
½ teaspoon grated nutmeg
½ teaspoon cream of tartar
½ teaspoon bicarbonate of soda
1 teaspoon ground cardamom
pinch of salt
185 g (6 oz) butter
2 tablespoons brown sugar
1 tablespoon sugar
3 small eggs
1 cup honey
½ cup sour cream
almonds to decorate

Line a 23 cm (9 inch) square deep cake tin with greased greaseproof paper. Set oven temperature to moderate (180°C/350°F).

Sift the flour with the cinnamon, nutmeg, cream of tartar, bicarbonate of soda, ground cardamom and salt. Melt butter and stir in the sugars.

In a large bowl beat the eggs until they are very fluffy, and add the honey and sour cream gradually. Add the butter mixture, stirring briskly. Gradually stir in the sifted dry ingredients. Pour batter into prepared tin and bake in a moderate oven for 1 hour or until cake is cooked when tested with a skewer.

After 20 minutes of baking, take cake out and decorate with almonds, then continue baking for remaining time.

Turn cake out on to a wire rack to cool, then put in an airtight container to ripen for at least 2 days before cutting. This cake keeps for weeks. *Makes one 23 cm (9 inch) cake*

PERFECT SPONGES

Like happiness, the perfect sponge is different things to different people. Some sponge-fanciers dote on a fine, super-light cake that is the ideal partner to plenty of cream and fruit or other luscious things; others like a sponge to be moist and golden, needing only a dusting of icing sugar and a good cup of tea alongside; Americans love their snow-white Angel Cake which is 'hung' from a special pan (hard to get outside the U.S.A.); Victoria Sponge which keeps so well is the specialty of many a British cook; then there are Swiss Rolls and Sponge Sandwiches, the star of Australian afternoon teas, with jam or our superb fresh fruits.

Cooks who possess 'a good hand' with sponges say that they're the easiest of cakes, some others approach sponges with trepidation. I think that the secret of success is to have everything organised – tins prepared, oven heating with shelves in the right position, beaters, bowls and all implements at hand (check through the recipe carefully) and ingredients measured, with dry ingredients sifted and eggs separated if this is called for.

Basic Sponge Sandwich

••

Sponge Sandwich is a truly Australian cake. It makes me think of those glorious and sinfully fattening afternoon teas that are served at country gatherings in Australia. How I look forward to one of these! Some of the 'ordinary housewives' who contribute are absolute geniuses at their specialties. I always hope that there will be a Sponge Sandwich, so fresh and light in flavour and texture, with cream and jam or one of the marvellous fresh sharp-sweet fruits – strawberries, passionfruit or kiwi fruit.

1½ cups self-raising flour
pinch of salt
4 tablespoons water
1 teaspoon butter
4 eggs
1 cup caster sugar

Filling and Topping

strawberry or raspberry jam
whipped cream (optional)
icing sugar
or whipped cream and fresh fruit

Brush two 20 cm (8 inch) sandwich tins with melted butter. Line bases with greaseproof paper cut to fit, brush again with butter and dust with sifted flour. Set oven temperature to 190°C(375°F).

Sift flour and salt together twice and return to sifter. Heat water with butter until the butter melts and set aside. Separate the eggs and beat the whites until they stand in soft peaks. Gradually add the sugar, beating until the mixture is very thick. Add the egg yolks all at once and beat only until incorporated.

Sift flour over the top of the egg mixture and fold through. Pour the water and butter mixture around the edge of the bowl and fold in. Pour into the prepared tins and bake for 20–25 minutes or until the cake springs back when touched in the centre. Turn out on to a wire rack to cool. When cold join together with jam or jam and whipped cream and dust with icing sugar. Alternatively, join and top with whipped cream and sliced or whole fresh fruit, or passionfruit pulp spooned over the whipped cream. *Makes one 20 cm (8 inch) sponge sandwich*

Variations

18 cm (7 inch) Sponge Sandwich: Follow recipe for Basic Sponge Sandwich using 3 eggs, ¾ cup caster sugar, 1 cup self-raising flour, pinch of salt, 1 teaspoon butter and 3 tablespoons water. Make as above and pour into two prepared 18 cm (7 inch) sandwich tins. Bake for about 20 minutes.

23 cm (9 inch) Sponge Sandwich: Follow recipe for Basic Sponge Sandwich using 5 eggs, 1¼ cups caster sugar, 1¾ cups self-raising flour, pinch of salt, 1½ teaspoons butter and 5 tablespoons water. Pour into two prepared 23 cm (9 inch) sandwich tins. Bake for about 30 minutes.

Right: Prune and Apricot Upside Down Cake (page 306) and Fruit and Date Squares (page 320).

Above: Cakes for keeping include Spiced Honey (page 309); Almond Macaroon (page 299); Cherry (page 302); Cherry Nut Pound (page 304) and a fruity Genoa (page 305).

Right: Beer adds intriguing flavour to moist, spicy Beer and Date Cake (page 301).

Spiced Blowaway Sponge

• • •

The Blowaway Sponge is as light as a puff of air. It owes this extra lightness to the cornflour in the mixture, but it should be eaten on the day it is made. Its very delicacy makes it a cake that will dry out on being kept. Any Lemon Curd not used for sandwiching the cakes can be used for little pastry cases.

½ cup maize cornflour
3 tablespoons plain flour
1 teaspoon baking powder
2 teaspoons ground ginger
1 teaspoon mixed spice
2 teaspoons cocoa
4 eggs
¾ cup caster sugar
2 tablespoons hot water
2 teaspoons lemon juice

Lemon Curd

250 g (8 oz) sugar
125 g (4 oz) butter
grated rind and juice 2 large lemons
3 eggs, well beaten

Lemon Icing

1 cup icing sugar
nut of butter
1 tablespoon lemon juice
few drops yellow food colouring

First make the Lemon Curd: Put the sugar, butter, lemon rind and juice, and eggs in a large enamel saucepan. Stir gently over a low heat until the mixture is thick. Great care must be taken not to let the mixture boil or it will curdle. Pour into a clean dry pot.

Brush two 20 cm (8 inch) sandwich tins with melted butter. Line bases with greaseproof paper cut to fit, brush again with butter and dust with sifted flour. Set oven to 190°C (375°F). Sift the cornflour, plain flour, baking powder, cocoa, ginger and mixed spice twice and return to the sifter. Separate the eggs and beat the whites until they stand in stiff peaks. Add the sugar gradually, beating until the whites stand thick and are glossy. Add the egg yolks all at once and beat only until mixed. Sift the dry ingredients over the egg mixture and fold in with a large metal spoon or rubber scraper, then pour the hot water and lemon juice around the edges of the bowl and fold in. Pour into the prepared tins and bake for 20 minutes or until the centre springs back when touched with a finger. Turn out and cool on wire racks. Sandwich the cooled sponges with Lemon Curd and frost with Lemon Icing (see above right). *Makes one 20 cm (8 inch) sponge sandwich*

Left: Black Forest Cherry Torte (page 302) is decorated with cream, sour cherries and chocolate.

To make the Lemon Icing: Sift the icing sugar into a bowl. Make a well in the centre and add the lemon juice and butter. Place over a pan of boiling water and stir until shiny. Add a few drops of lemon colour and while warm pour at once on to the cake and, using a spatula, spread with bold sweeping strokes. At this stage the icing sets quickly.

Victoria Sponge Sandwich

• •

Victoria Sponge with its high butter content is the one to make if you want a sponge that will keep. Any that is left over makes a good base for trifle.

250 g (8 oz) butter
few drops vanilla
1 cup caster sugar
4 eggs
2 cups self-raising flour
pinch of salt

Filling and Topping

strawberry jam
caster sugar

Brush two 20 cm (8 inch) sandwich tins with melted butter. Line bases with greaseproof paper cut to fit, brush again with butter and dust with flour. Set oven temperature to 190°C (375°F).

Cream the butter and vanilla, and gradually add the sugar, beating until light and fluffy. Beat the eggs lightly and add gradually to the butter mixture, continuing to beat well. Sift the flour and salt together over the surface and fold in with a large metal spoon or rubber scraper. Divide mixture evenly between prepared tins and spread level with a spatula, making a slight depression in the centre so the cakes will rise evenly.

Bake for 30 minutes or until the centre springs back when touched with a finger. Turn out on to a wire rack and, when cool, join with strawberry jam and dust the top with caster sugar. *Makes one 20 cm (8 inch) sponge sandwich*
Note: A Victoria Sponge may also be made in a 20 cm (8 inch) deep cake tin or a 20 cm (8 inch) loose-based tin with a fluted edge. Use the same mixture but bake for about 45 minutes. Cool and dust with caster sugar.

Strawberry Sponge Gateau

••

This is a true sponge recipe, where the lightness of the cake depends entirely on the air beaten into the eggs which are whisked together for a long time. If you don't have an electric mixer, use a rotary beater and stand the bowl over a pan of gently simmering water.

¾ cup plain flour
½ teaspoon cinnamon
good pinch of salt
3 eggs
½ cup caster sugar
finely grated rind of ½ lemon

Filling and Topping

½ cup cream
2 tablespoons strawberry jam
icing sugar

Brush a 20 cm (8 inch) moule à manqué (French style pan with sloping sides) or sandwich tin with melted butter. Line the base with greaseproof paper cut to fit, brush again with butter and dust with sifted flour. Set oven temperature to 180°C (350°F).

Sift the flour, cinnamon and salt together twice and return to the sifter. Beat the eggs, using the high speed of an electric mixer for 5 minutes until very thick and pale. Gradually add the sugar, beating all the time. Sift dry ingredients over the top. Add lemon rind and fold into the egg mixture with a large metal spoon or rubber scraper.

As soon as the flour is incorporated into the egg mixture, pour into the prepared tin. Give the tin a gentle shake to distribute the mixture evenly and bake for 30–35 minutes or until the cake springs back when lightly touched with a finger. Allow to stand for 1 minute before turning out on a wire rack to cool.

Whip the cream and gently fold in the jam. Split the cooled cake and join with the cream mixture.

For a decorative effect, place a few ivy or other good-shaped leaves on top and sift icing sugar over surface of cake. Remove the leaves and you have a pretty pattern on top. *Makes one 20 cm (8 inch) cake*

Swiss Roll

•••

Swiss roll tins come in varying sizes and each requires a different amount of mixture. Here I give the quantity of mixture for the size which is currently on the market, and the amount for larger tins follows.

1 cup self-raising flour
pinch of salt
2 eggs, separated
½ cup caster sugar
3 tablespoons hot water

Filling and Coating

raspberry or strawberry jam, warmed, or Lemon Curd
(see page 315)
sugar

Brush a 25 × 30 cm (10 × 12 inch) Swiss roll tin with melted butter and line with a sheet of greaseproof paper, large enough to fit in and come 2.5 cm (1 inch) up the sides. With scissors make diagonal cuts in each corner, then turn the corners so that the paper fits neatly into the tin. Brush paper with melted butter. Set oven temperature to 190°C (375°F).

Sift the flour and salt twice and return to the sifter. Beat the egg whites until they form soft peaks and gradually add the sifted sugar, beating all the time until the mixture is thick and glossy. Add the egg yolks all at once and beat only until mixed through. Sift the flour mixture over the top and fold through the egg mixture with a large metal spoon or rubber scraper. Pour the water around the sides of the bowl and fold in.

Pour the mixture into the prepared tin and gently push with a scraper to fill the corners. Bake for 12–15 minutes or until the centre springs back when lightly touched with a finger.

Have ready a sheet of greaseproof paper or a tea-towel liberally sprinkled with sugar, and a serrated knife and the warm jam nearby. As soon as the cake is removed from the oven, turn over on to the paper, immediately peel off the lining paper from the base of the cake, then trim off the crusts. Roll quickly in the paper, count 3, then unroll, spread with warm jam and roll again, this time without the paper. Leave to cool.

For a cream-filled Swiss Roll, let the sponge cool completely. Carefully unroll the cooled sponge and spread with whipped cream. Carefully re-roll.

Note: When first rolling a Swiss Roll, take care not to roll tightly as this will cause the sponge to compress and result in a doughy texture.

Larger Swiss Rolls

For a 25 × 35 cm (10 × 14 inch) Swiss roll tin use 1½ cups self-raising flour, pinch of salt, 4 tablespoons hot water, ¾ cup sugar and 3 eggs. Cooking time will be the same. For a 26 × 39 cm (10½ × 15½ inch) Swiss roll tin, double all ingredients. Cooking time will be the same.

A BARREL OF BISCUITS

The welcome of freshly-baked homemade biscuits is something to be remembered. Flatter your family and friends by always having a barrel of biscuits on hand – there's no better way to greet unexpected callers or hungry children.

Basic Drop Cookies

••

This is the kind of recipe good cooks learn to make at the drop of a hat

1¾ cups plain flour
2 teaspoons baking powder
pinch of salt
125 g (4 oz) butter or margarine
½ cup caster sugar
1½ teaspoons vanilla
2 tablespoons honey
1 egg
2 tablespoons milk

Sift the flour, baking powder and salt. Cream the butter or margarine, sugar and vanilla. Add the honey and egg and beat well. Blend in the sifted dry ingredients, a little at a time, alternating with the milk. Drop from a teaspoon on to greased baking trays and bake in a hot oven (200°C/400°F) for 10 minutes or until golden. *Makes about 3 dozen*

Variations

Cherry Winks Drop teaspoonsful of the mixture into lightly crushed cornflakes. Place on greased trays and press a halved glacé cherry in the centre of each. Bake as above.

Mocha Drops Blend ½ teaspoon coffee essence with the milk before adding to the creamed mixture with the flour. Stir-in 2 packets choc-bits and bake as described above.

Chocolate Drop Cookies Add 60 g (2 oz) cooking chocolate, melted and cooled, to the butter and egg mixture. Bake as described above.

Fruit Drop Cookies Add ½ cup raisins, sultanas or chopped dates to the mixture. Bake as described above.

Orange Drop Cookies Substitute orange juice for the milk and 2 teaspoons grated orange rind for the vanilla. When the biscuits have cooled, frost tops with orange icing made by mixing 1 cup sifted icing sugar with 1 tablespoon hot orange juice. Decorate with finely chopped mixed peel.

Almond Fans

••

*A crisp and dainty biscuit for after-dinner coffee or one
to serve with a creamy dessert or mousse.*

1½ cups plain flour
½ cup ground almonds
⅓ cup sugar
125 g (4 oz) butter, softened
½ teaspoon salt
2 egg yolks, slightly beaten
1 teaspoon lemon juice

To glaze and finish

1 egg, beaten
icing sugar

In a mixing bowl, combine the flour, almonds, sugar, butter
and salt. Add the egg yolks and lemon juice. Knead until the
dough forms a ball, then chill for 2 hours. Roll out thinly and
cut into circles 10 cm (4 inch) in diameter. Press a scallop design
around the edge with a teaspoon and cut each circle into four
wedges. Brush with the beaten egg to glaze and sprinkle with
icing sugar. Bake on greased and floured baking sheets in a
moderately hot oven (190°C/375°F) for 10–15 minutes or until
golden. *Makes about 5 dozen*

Apricot Hearts

••

*Apricot hearts are dainty little cheese pastry
biscuits filled with apricot jam. Serve them at a kitchen tea or
on St. Valentine's Day.*

1 cup plain flour
pinch of salt
125 g (4 oz) butter
125 g (4 oz) cream cheese
apricot jam
beaten egg
sugar

Sift the flour and salt into a bowl. Rub in the butter and cream
cheese until the mixture is well blended. Roll into a ball, wrap
in greaseproof paper and chill in the refrigerator for at least 1
hour.

Roll out the pastry very thinly and cut into heart shapes.
Place half on baking trays and in the centre put a little apricot
jam. Brush the edges with beaten egg, cover with the second
pastry heart and seal the edges by pressing down lightly with a
fork. Brush the top with beaten egg and sprinkle with some
sugar. Bake in hot oven (200°C/400°F) for 12–15 minutes or until
golden. Cool on a wire rack. *Makes about 2 dozen*

Redcurrant Crescents Make pastry as for Apricot Hearts but
cut into circles. Put a little redcurrant jelly on one side of each
circle, brush edges with beaten egg and fold over. Seal edges
by pressing down with fork. Bake as above.

Cardamom Spice Balls

••

*Scandinavian cooks use cardamom as the English use
nutmeg . . . take your choice.*

2 cups plain flour
1 teaspoon baking powder
¼ teaspoon salt
1 teaspoon powdered cardamom or nutmeg
125 g (4 oz) butter
½ cup sugar
1 egg
¼ cup cream
walnuts or hazelnuts for decoration

To glaze and finish

1 egg, beaten
icing sugar

Sift the flour, salt, baking powder and cardamom or nutmeg.
Cream the butter and sugar, add the egg and beat well. Add the
cream and sifted dry ingredients and mix to form a stiff dough.
Chill for 30 minutes before shaping into small balls, about
2.5 cm (1 inch) in diameter or less.

Arrange on greased baking trays and decorate with the nuts.
Brush with beaten egg glaze and bake in a moderately hot oven
(190°C/375°F) for 10–15 minutes or until golden; sprinkle with
icing sugar if liked. *Makes about 40*

Variation

Ginger Spice Balls Add ½ teaspoon ground ginger to the dry
ingredients and place a piece of preserved ginger in centre of
each ball before baking.
Cardamon Spice Crescents The balls may also be moulded
into crescent shapes for variety, and dusted with icing sugar.

Danish Cookies

•

*No butter, but cream gives these roll-out cookies
flavour and texture.*

2 cups plain flour
1 teaspoon baking powder
¼ teaspoon salt
⅔ cup sugar
1 egg, beaten
½ cup cream

Sift the flour, baking powder, salt and sugar together. Add the beaten egg to the cream. Slowly add the egg mixture to the dry ingredients and blend thoroughly. Chill.

Roll the dough out thinly on a floured board. Using various shapes, cut out cookies and place on greased trays. Bake in a moderate oven (180°C/350°F) for 12–15 minutes. Remove from trays and cool on a wire rack. If liked, the cookies can be iced as below. *Makes at least 24 cookies*

Iced Danish Cookies Sift 1 cup icing sugar and blend with 1 tablespoon hot water and a few drops of vanilla or lemon juice to taste. Tint with colouring if liked. Ice the biscuits and decorate with whole nuts, halved glacé cherries, choc-bits or chocolate sprinkles.

Delicate French Fingers

••

Strips of pastry that bake into a light, flaky biscuit are perfect to serve with a dessert or, when sandwiched together with butter cream, stand on their own on a tea or coffee tray.

Pastry
2½ cups plain flour
250 g (8 oz) butter
1 tablespoon vinegar
⅓ cup water
⅔ cup sugar

Filling
185 g (6 oz) butter
½ cup sifted pure icing sugar
1 egg yolk
1 teaspoon vanilla

To Make the Pastry: Sift the flour into a bowl and cut in the butter with two knives or a pastry blender until the mixture resembles coarse breadcrumbs. Add the vinegar to the water and sprinkle over the dry mixture, 1 tablespoon at a time, while tossing with a fork. Continue to add the water mixture until the dough is just moist enough to hold together. Divide dough into 2 balls and chill for 20 minutes.

On a lightly floured surface roll out the dough to 3 mm (⅛ inch) thickness. Cut into oblong shapes 5 × 2.5 cm (2 × 1 inch). Place the sugar on greaseproof paper and press each biscuit shape on lightly so the sugar clings to it. Transfer, sugar side up, to ungreased baking trays and bake in a very hot oven (230°C/450°F) for 8–10 minutes, or until the top begins to caramelize. Roll and cook the remaining dough in the same way. Cool on wire racks.

To Make the Filling: Cream the butter until light. Add the sifted icing sugar, then beat in the egg yolk and vanilla. Beat until light, smooth and creamy.

Before serving, sandwich pairs of biscuits with the filling. *Makes 24 pairs*

Dutch Spice Cookies

••

Early Dutch traders brought valuable cargoes of spices back from the New World; they were a luxury and kept for special occasions. A spiced biscuit, called Speculaas, sometimes in the shape of men, women, stars or even in the shape of St. Nicholas himself, was a highlight of the St. Nicholas Eve festival. Today the availability of freshly ground spices makes these wonderful little biscuits an everyday possibility, yet still special enough for Christmas giving.

3 cups plain flour
4 teaspoons baking powder
1 tablespoon cinnamon
1 teaspoon each ground cloves and nutmeg
½ teaspoon each ground aniseed, salt and ground ginger or white pepper
250 g (8 oz) butter
1½ cups brown sugar
1 egg white, lightly beaten
125 g (4 oz) slivered blanched almonds, for decoration

Sift together the flour, baking powder, cinnamon, cloves, nutmeg, aniseed, salt and ginger or pepper. Beat the butter until creamy and add the brown sugar gradually, beating until the mixture is light and fluffy.

Gradually add the flour mixture, stirring until well combined and then form the dough into a ball. Knead the dough on a board sprinkled with about ¼ cup of sifted flour. Divide the dough in two and roll out one portion of dough into a rectangle 3 mm (⅛ inch) thick. With a sharp knife cut the dough into rectangles 6 × 3 cm (2½ × 1½ inch) or using a cutter cut heart or star shapes. Place on a buttered baking tray, brush with the lightly beaten egg white and decorate with the slivered almonds. Bake in a moderately hot oven (190°C/375°F) for 12 minutes or until brown and firm. Repeat with the remaining dough.

Cool on a wire rack and store in an airtight tin. *Makes about 4 dozen*

Fruit Squares

•

For those who dote on dried fruits of any kind, who make their own fruit mince or buy a commercial one, like dates or plump raisins – try this rich crumbly slice that can be filled with your favourite dried fruit.

1 cup firmly packed brown sugar
1½ cups rolled oats
1½ cups plain flour
½ teaspoon salt
185 g (6 oz) butter
2 cups fruit mince
1 egg, beaten

Combine the brown sugar, rolled oats, flour and salt, mix well. Rub in the butter until the mixture resembles the consistency of coarse crumbs. Spread half the mixture into a 28 × 18 cm (11 × 7 inch) slab cake tin. Cover with fruit mince. Spread the remaining crumb mixture over the fruit mince and gently brush with the beaten egg. Bake in a hot oven (200°C/400°F) for 20–25 minutes. When cool, cut into squares, bars or diamond shapes. *Cuts into approximately 20 bars*

Variations

Date Filling Combine 1½ cups sliced dates, ⅔ cup water, ¾ cup sugar and 2 tablespoons lemon juice in a pan. Cook over gentle heat until thick, about 5 minutes, and cool thoroughly before spreading.
Raisin Filling Blend 1 tablespoon arrowroot with 3 tablespoons water. Place 1½ cups raisins, 4 tablespoons brown sugar, 3 tablespoons each orange and lemon juice, 1 teaspoon each grated orange and lemon rind into a saucepan and bring to the boil. Stir in the blended arrowroot and cook until the mixture boils and thickens. Cool before using.

Ginger Crisps

•

Children love to make these simple drop cookies. Flavoured with chopped ginger and crunchy with cornflakes they are quick to make and quick to disappear too.

125 g (4 oz) butter
¾ cup sugar
1 egg
1 cup self-raising flour, sifted
½ cup crystallised ginger, finely chopped
½ cup cornflakes
extra cornflakes
glacé cherries

Cream the butter and sugar, add the egg and beat well. Stir in the sifted flour, ginger and ½ cup of cornflakes. Drop from a teaspoon into the extra cornflakes and toss lightly. Place on prepared trays and decorate each with half a glacé cherry. Bake in a moderate oven (180°C/350°F) for 10–15 minutes. *Makes about 36*

Ischl Biscuits

• • •

These delicious, chocolate covered hazelnut biscuits were a favourite treat of the Emperor Franz Joseph of Austria. They are named after his holiday home in the Austrian Alps.

185 g (6 oz) butter
¾ cup icing sugar, sifted
1 teaspoon grated lemon rind
2 teaspoons lemon juice
90 g (3 oz) ground hazelnuts
1¾ cups plain flour
¼ teaspoon cinnamon
185 g (6 oz) dark chocolate
3 teaspoons butter
strawberry jam

Cream the butter until light and add the sugar gradually, beating in well. Add the lemon rind and juice and stir in the ground hazelnuts. Sift the flour and cinnamon together. Fold into the butter mixture in thirds, blending well. Chill for 30 minutes.

Roll out the dough fairly thinly on a lightly floured board, then cut into rounds with a floured biscuit cutter. Place biscuits 2.5 cm (1 inch) apart on greased baking trays. Bake in a moderate oven (180°C/350°F) for 15–20 minutes. Remove to racks and cool. Store in an airtight tin until required.

Melt the chocolate over simmering water in the top of a double boiler, add the butter, cool. When chocolate is of a spreadable consistency, spread a thin covering of chocolate over half the biscuits. Allow to set. Spread remaining biscuits with strawberry jam. Place chocolate covered biscuits on top and sandwich together. *Makes 24*

Lemon Shortbread Biscuits

•

Biscuits with a fresh lemon, buttery flavour – these are perfect with a cup of tea or coffee.

250 g (8 oz) butter
grated rind of 1 lemon
1 cup icing sugar, sifted
2 cups plain flour, sifted

Beat the butter and lemon rind until creamy. Add the icing sugar and beat well. With a metal spoon stir in the sifted flour.

Take level teaspoons of the mixture and roll lightly into balls. Place on ungreased baking trays and press down well with a fork which has been dipped in cold water to prevent sticking.

Bake in a moderate oven (180°C/350°F) for 10–12 minutes or until slightly coloured. Cool and store in an airtight tin. *Makes about 4 dozen*

Powder Puffs

••

When the vicar was due to call, these crisp little sponge cakes were taken out of their airtight tins. They were filled with whipped cream and in one hour they had risen into light and tender puffs – then a dusting of icing sugar and they earned their name – Powder Puffs.
Don't wait for the vicar to call!

2 eggs
½ cup caster sugar
3 tablespoons flour
3 tablespoons cornflour
1 teaspoon baking powder
To serve
¾ cup cream, whipped
icing sugar

Beat the eggs and gradually add the sugar, beating until light and creamy (the consistency of half-whipped cream). Sift the flour, cornflour and baking powder together and lightly fold into the egg mixture. Spoon into a piping bag fitted with a 1 cm (½ inch) tube. Pipe small rounds on to greased trays, or use a teaspoon to make small drops. Bake in a hot oven (220°C/425°F) for 6 minutes. Lift carefully on to a wire rack and cool.

These can be made days in advance and stored in an airtight container until required.

Join together with the whipped cream sweetened to taste, place in a cake tin, cover and in one hour they will puff up into light little cakes. Dust with icing sugar to serve. *Makes 48 powder puffs*

Sour Cream Cookies

••

Sour cream is becoming a staple in the refrigerator because of its versatility. Here it adds subtle flavour to a Scandinavian-type biscuit.

125 g (4 oz) butter
1 cup firmly packed brown sugar
1 egg, beaten
½ cup raisins
2 cups plain flour
½ teaspoon bicarbonate of soda
½ teaspoon salt
2 teaspoons baking powder
½ teaspoon nutmeg
½ cup sour cream
½ cup roughly chopped walnuts

Cream the butter and sugar and add the egg and raisins. Sift the flour, soda, salt, baking powder and nutmeg and add alternately to the raisin mixture with the sour cream. Stir in the walnuts. Drop teaspoonsful of the mixture on to greased baking trays and bake in a hot oven (200°C/400°F) for 12–15 minutes. *Makes approximately 36*

Virginiennes

••

For those who like a soft, cake-like biscuit with good chocolate flavour, and also enjoy a dash of rum, these biscuits are for you! This makes about 9 dozen biscuits, but they keep well.

250 g (8 oz) plus 2 teaspoons, butter
1 teaspoon vanilla
2 cups brown sugar
2 eggs, lightly beaten
¾ cup milk
¼ cup rum
3 cups plain flour
½ teaspoon salt
¾ teaspoon bicarbonate of soda
90 g (3 oz) chocolate
1 cup chopped blanched almonds

Cream the 250 g (8 oz) of butter with the vanilla until light and lemon-coloured. Add the brown sugar, beating well. Beat in the eggs, one at a time and set the mixture aside.

Combine the milk and rum. Sift the flour, salt and soda. Using a metal spoon add the milk and flour alternately to the butter-egg mixture, stirring after each addition. Chop the chocolate, place in a bowl with the remaining 2 teaspoons of butter and melt over a saucepan of hot water. Add to the flour mixture with the chopped almonds, mixing in well.

Drop teaspoonsful of the mixture on to greased baking trays and bake the cookies in a moderate oven (180°C/350°F) for about 10–12 minutes. When cool, store in an airtight container. *Makes about 9 dozen*

REFRIGERATOR BISCUITS

The idea of refrigerator biscuits is that they can be made when time permits, wrapped in wax paper or foil and stored in the refrigerator or freezer until wanted. When needed, slice from the roll and bake as directed, then you may replace the remaining dough in the refrigerator for later use. The dough will keep for up to 3 weeks in the refrigerator or 3 months in the freezer. Some cheese doughs should be used within one week.

Here are recipes for both sweet and savoury refrigerator biscuits.

Butterscotch Crisps

••

125 g (4 oz) butter or margarine
1 teaspoon vanilla
⅓ cup sugar
⅓ cup firmly packed brown sugar
1 egg, lightly beaten
1⅓ cups plain flour
¾ teaspoon baking powder
⅓ cup chopped walnuts

Cream the butter, vanilla and sugars together well, until light and fluffy. Add the egg and beat well. Sift the flour and baking powder and work into the butter mixture, add the walnuts. Shape the dough into a long roll about 4 cm (1½ inch) in diameter. Wrap in plastic wrap or foil and chill thoroughly.

When ready to bake, slice thinly as many crisps as are needed from the dough roll. Bake on ungreased baking trays in a moderate oven (180°C/350°F) for 10 minutes or until lightly coloured. Remove and cool on a wire rack. Serve with tea or coffee or store in airtight tins. *Makes about 5 dozen*

Heidesand Biscuits

••

A German recipe made with 'brown' butter and more vanilla than usual – the result is a super flavour and crunch.

155 g (5 oz) butter
½ cup caster sugar
½ packet vanillin or 1½ teaspoons vanilla
2 tablespoons milk
1⅔ cups plain flour
½ teaspoon baking powder

Heat the butter gently until dark brown, then cool. When cold, beat the butter and gradually add the sugar, vanillin flavouring or vanilla and milk. Continue to beat until the mixture is creamy white. Sift the flour and baking powder together. Turn the butter mixture on to a floured board and work in the flour.

Shape the dough into a roll about 3 cm (1¼ inch) in diameter. Chill the dough, wrapped in plastic wrap or foil, until a little firmer and easier to slice. Cut into 6 mm (¼ inch) thick slices and place on greased baking trays. Bake in a moderately hot oven (190°C/375°F) for about 10–15 minutes or until a pale, sandy colour. Remove from baking trays and cool on wire racks. *Makes about 3 dozen*
Note: Packets of vanillin flavouring are available from delicatessens and some supermarkets.

Right: From rear clockwise: Orange Cake (page 305); Ginger Crisps (page 320) and Sour Cream Waffles (page 307).

Right: Assembling the ingredients for Rich Christmas Cake (page 308).

Below: Almond Torte (page 299) is very special. It is filled and topped with cream and plums and served with Plum Sauce.

Cheese Discs

••

With rolls of this unbaked dough in the refrigerator or freezer there is always something fresh, crisp and hot to serve guests with a sherry or with drinks before a meal. This mixture keeps well in the refrigerator for 1 week ready to be baked or can be kept in the freezer baked or unbaked.

250 g (8 oz) Cheddar cheese
125 g (4 oz) butter
½ teaspoon salt
pinch cayenne pepper or ¼ teaspoon
seasoned pepper
1½ cups flour, sifted

Grate the cheese. Cream the cheese, butter, salt and pepper together. Add the sifted flour and blend well. This may be done in a food processor fitted with the double edged steel blade.

Form the mixture into three rolls, about 2.5 cm (1 inch) in diameter and wrap in plastic wrap or foil. Chill for 2 hours in the refrigerator.

Slice the roll into thin wafers, bake in a moderate oven (180°C/350°F) for 10 minutes or until pale golden. Watch carefully during the last few minutes and take care not to overcook. Like all cheese biscuits they go bitter once they overcook. Serve hot or cold. *Makes approximately 6 dozen*

Cheese Straws

••

90 g (3 oz) butter
90 g (3 oz) Cheddar cheese, finely grated
1 tablespoon grated Parmesan cheese
¾ cup plain flour
½ teaspoon paprika
pinch cayenne pepper
½ teaspoon salt
beaten egg for glazing

Cream the butter and cheeses. Sift the flour, paprika, cayenne pepper and salt and add to the creamed mixture. Mix well, wrap in plastic wrap or foil and chill the dough for at least 1 hour.

Roll out the dough on a lightly floured board or between sheets of plastic, to 6 mm (¼ inch) thickness. Cut into 10 cm (4 inch) lengths, then into 6 mm (¼ inch) wide strips. Put on baking trays, brush with egg glaze and bake in a moderate oven (180°C/350°F) for 8–10 minutes. Cool and store in airtight tins. *Makes approximately 60 straws*

Left: Many different breads can be made from Basic Sweet Rich Dough. See the recipes starting on page 329.

Sesame Cheese Biscuits

••

Crisp, delicate and full of the flavours that go so well with pre-dinner drinks. Keep a roll of unbaked dough in the freezer for emergencies, slice and bake when needed.

125 g (4 oz) finely grated Cheddar cheese
185 g (6 oz) butter
1½ cups plain flour
1 teaspoon paprika
¼ teaspoon pepper
1 teaspoon salt
2 tablespoons toasted sesame seeds

Cream cheese and butter until soft. Sift the flour, paprika, pepper and salt. Stir the flour into the creamed mixture with the toasted sesame seeds. Mix well and form into a roll, 4 cm (1½ inch) in diameter. Wrap in plastic wrap or foil and refrigerate for 1 hour. Cut into thin discs and bake on ungreased baking trays in a moderate oven (180°C/350°F) for 10–12 minutes. *Makes approximately 100 biscuits*

Variations

Using a Biscuit Press The mixture may be put into a biscuit press fitted with a fancy nozzle. Press the mixture on to ungreased baking trays and bake in a moderate oven (180°C/350°F) for 12–15 minutes.

Sesame Cheese Straws The mixture can be rolled out and cut into straws 8 cm × 6 mm (3 × ¼ inch). Bake in a moderate oven (180°C/350°F) for 10 minutes.

OUR DAILY BREAD

Breadmaking *was* becoming a forgotten art, but the tide has turned. Those who enjoy their daily bread have been carrying out a quiet revolution – mostly against the monotony of bread that has a sameness about it and has been all too readily available. True, many bakeries have now realised there is a market for good and varied breads, but it's too late. Many good cooks have discovered that with just a little practice they can make very good bread – what an achievement! What's more, cooking with yeast is an interesting and enjoyable occupation.

The Easter and Christmas breads bring another challenge. Stollen, rich with fruit and nuts and a snowy drift of icing sugar; plump spicy buns with their simple cross decoration; braids and plaits in which nestles an Easter egg . . . carrying their symbolic meanings, all play an esteemed role in ethnic celebrations in many lands.

Spice, citrus fruits and nuts assert their subtle flavours in breads that are shaped, woven or cast into rounds, cylinders or rings. For me, baking these many and varied breads is one of the great joys of Easter and Christmas.

There's been a revival in making many of the quick tea time treats like scones, pikelets and nut loaves, and while the days of elaborate and perfect tea parties may never return (Buckingham Palace now calls in caterers for the Royal garden parties – so I'm told), people are turning their hands to a quickly mixed cake or bread to enjoy over a cup of tea with friends. The electric mixers, blenders and finally food processors have undoubtedly attracted many erstwhile cooks back into the kitchen. Whatever the reason, the wonderful aromas of sugar and spice and natural grains baking in the kitchen make a home a very special place.

Basic Sweet Rich Dough

• • •

From this basic dough, you can make many different breads of all shapes and sizes – loaves, rolls and twists. Spices, fruits, cherries and nuts can also be added to give variety. Brush with melted butter and sprinkle with cinnamon and sugar before baking, or bake and cool and then drizzle over some glacé icing.

4½ cups plain flour
large pinch of salt
¼–1 cup milk
125 g (4 oz) butter
30 g (1 oz) compressed yeast
½ cup caster sugar
2 eggs, beaten

Sift the flour with salt into a large bowl. Heat ¼ cup of milk to lukewarm, add the butter and allow to melt, then add to the yeast and stir until dissolved. Mix in the sugar and beaten eggs. Make a well in the flour, pour in the milk mixture and stir until smooth, first with a wooden spoon and then with the hand. Add more warm milk if necessary to make a soft dough. When the dough comes away cleanly from the sides of the bowl, turn on to a floured surface and knead until smooth and elastic. Add a little more flour if the dough is too soft to knead.

Place dough in a greased bowl, turning dough over in bowl so that it is lightly greased all over. Cover with a damp cloth and leave to rise in a warm place for 45–50 minutes or until doubled in bulk. Punch down dough, pull sides to centre, turn over then cover and allow to rise again for 30 minutes before shaping and baking.

Ways to use the Basic Sweet Rich Dough

Sugarplum Ring Use half the quantity of Basic Sweet Rich Dough. Leave to rise in a warm place until doubled in bulk, about 1¼–1½ hours. Pinch off bits of the dough and form into balls about 2·5 cm (1 inch) in diameter. Knead balls lightly on a floured board. Roll the balls of dough in melted butter, then in brown sugar and cinnamon (which have been mixed together) and place in a 20 cm (8 inch) ring tin. Leave a little space between each to allow for rising. Cover with a floured, damp cloth and allow to stand in a warm place until almost doubled in bulk. Sprinkle over chopped walnuts or almonds. Bake in a moderate oven (180°C/350°F) for 30–35 minutes.

Cloverleaf Rolls Use half the quantity of Basic Sweet Rich Dough. Leave to rise in a warm place, until doubled in bulk. Shape risen dough into small walnut-sized balls. Grease muffin or patty tins and put three balls of dough in each, cover and let rise in a warm place until doubled in bulk, about 30–45 minutes. Brush rolls with milk or beaten egg and bake in a hot oven (200°C/400°F) for about 15 minutes. *Makes 12–18 rolls*

Crescents Use half the quantity of Basic Rich Sweet Dough. Leave to rise in a warm place until double in bulk. Roll dough out to the size of a dinner plate. Spread with soft butter, sprinkle with poppy seeds or sesame seeds. Cut into 8 wedges, roll up each wedge from the widest edge towards the point. Stretch the dough gently and shape into a crescent.

Place the crescents well apart on a greased baking tray. Cover with a cloth and allow to rise in a warm place until the rolls double in size. Brush with a little beaten egg or milk and sprinkle over a few poppy seeds or sesame seeds. Bake in a very hot oven (230°C/450°F) for 10–15 minutes or until the rolls are golden. *Makes 8 crescents*

Glacé Icing Sift 1 cup icing sugar into a small bowl and stir in 1 tablespoon hot milk – enough to make a runny icing consistency. Add more milk if necessary. Drizzle over yeast cakes while still warm. Use sparingly as thick glacé icing is unattractive.

Note: This icing may be coloured by adding a few drops of food colouring.

Cardamom Braid

• • •

½ quantity Basic Sweet Rich Dough (see left)
1–2 teaspoons ground cardamom
1 egg
2 teaspoons milk
caster sugar

Make up Basic Sweet Rich Dough as directed, adding ground cardamom to the flour before sifting. Leave in a warm place until doubled in bulk.

Turn on to a floured surface and knead lightly. Divide into three equal portions and shape each piece into a rope about 1 cm (½ inch) in diameter. Line ropes up together on a greased baking tray and, starting from the middle, plait loosely towards the ends, taking care not to stretch the dough. Seal ends by pinching well together. Cover and leave in a warm place to rise until doubled in bulk. Set oven temperature to moderate (180°C/350°F).

Beat the egg and milk and brush over the braid. Sprinkle generously with caster sugar and bake in a moderate oven for 30–35 minutes, or until brown. Remove to a wire rack and loosely cover with a tea-towel. Cool before slicing.

Note: This quantity makes one large braid. If desired, it can be made into two smaller braids.

Italian Easter Bread

• • •

*It's an old Italian custom to bake eggs in a nest of sweet
dough. Use raw eggs, either natural white or
brown, or colour them with Easter egg dye obtainable from
many Greek delicatessens.*

1 quantity Basic Sweet Rich Dough (see page 329)
½ cup finely chopped mixed peel
¼ cup chopped almonds
½ teaspoon aniseed (optional)
5 raw eggs in shells
Glacé Icing (page 329)
chopped nuts or fruit jellies to decorate

Prepare Basic Sweet Rich Dough and leave in a warm place to
rise. After second rising, turn on to a floured surface.

Combine the peel, almonds and aniseed, if using, and
knead into the dough. Divide the dough in half and roll each
half into a long rope about 60 cm (24 inch) long. Twist ropes
loosely together and shape into a ring on a large greased baking
tray. Arrange the unshelled eggs in the hollows evenly
around the ring. Cover and leave in a warm place to rise, about
30–40 minutes. Set oven temperature to moderately hot
(190°C/375°F).

Bake the bread in a moderately hot oven for 30–35 minutes.
Remove to a wire rack to cool. When cool, spread with the glacé
icing, tinted pale pink, leaving the eggs uncovered. Decorate
with chopped nuts or brightly coloured fruit jellies.

Greek Feast Bread

• • •

*This subtly lemon-flavoured loaf, with its
three-in-one design, represents the Holy Trinity. It is
decorated with cherries and almonds.*

1 quantity Basic Sweet Rich Dough (see page 329)
1 tablespoon grated lemon rind
1 cup sultanas
icing
glacé cherries and whole almonds to decorate

Prepare Basic Sweet Rich Dough, adding the lemon rind and
sultanas with the yeast mixture. Cover dough and leave in a
warm place to rise until doubled in bulk, then punch down and
leave to rise again. After the second rising, turn on to a floured
surface and knead lightly, divide into three. Roll each portion
into a ball. Place on a large greased baking tray in a clover leaf
pattern, 1.5–2.5 cm (½–1 inch) apart. Cover and leave in a
warm place to rise again until doubled, about 30 minutes. Set
oven temperature to moderately hot (190°C/375°F).

Bake bread in a moderately hot oven for about 30 minutes
until lightly browned and bread is cooked when tested with a
fine skewer. Remove to a wire rack and cover loosely with a tea-

towel. Ice when cool, and decorate with cherries and almonds.

This quantity makes one very large bread. If your baking tray
is small, use only two-thirds to make the three balls of dough
for the bread and use the remaining dough for small rolls. If
desired, the rolls can be made in the shape of nests and a whole
raw egg in the shell placed on top of each before rising, to be
baked with the rolls as in the Italian Easter Bread.

Icing: Mix ½ cup sifted icing sugar with 1–2 tablespoons
boiling water to make a smooth paste of a running consistency.
Tint pale pink with red food colouring if desired. Spread over
breads. For a thinner icing, add a squeeze of orange or lemon
juice and brush icing over the bread while still warm.

Hot Cross Buns

• • •

*This is my favourite recipe for Hot Cross Buns
and one that always works. Its nice balance of fruit and
spices gives these Easter buns their fragrant
aroma when they're hot from the oven.*

4 cups plain flour
1 teaspoon mixed spice
½ teaspoon cinnamon
1 teaspoon salt
60 g (2 oz) butter
¼ cup currants or sultanas
¼ cup chopped mixed peel
30 g (1 oz) compressed yeast
½ cup caster sugar
½ cup lukewarm water
½ cup lukewarm milk
1 egg, lightly beaten

Paste for Cross

4 tablespoons self-raising flour
2 tablespoons cold water

Glaze

¼ teaspoon gelatine
2 tablespoons water
1 tablespoon sugar

Sift the flour, mixed spice, cinnamon and salt into a bowl. Rub
in the softened butter, then stir in the currants or sultanas and
peel. Make a well in the centre. Cream the yeast with the sugar,
and add a little warm water to dissolve the yeast completely.
Blend the remaining water and milk with the yeast and add
with the beaten egg to the flour. Mix to form a soft dough. Turn
on to a lightly floured surface and knead until smooth and
elastic. Shape into a ball, place in a clean, greased bowl and
turn over so that the top of the dough is greased. Cover and
leave to rise in a warm place until doubled in bulk, about 1¼–
1½ hours.

Turn the risen dough on to a lightly floured surface and
gently press out to 1 cm (½ inch) thickness. Divide dough into

330

16 pieces and shape each into a small ball. Place buns on a greased baking tray at least 2.5 cm (1 inch) apart, or arrange in greased round cake tins. Cover and leave to rise in a warm place for a further 20–30 minutes.

To Make the Paste for the Cross: Combine the flour and water and beat to a smooth paste. Fill into a greaseproof paper funnel or small piping bag. Using a sharp knife, make a slight indentation in the shape of a cross on the top of each bun just before baking and pipe prepared paste into the cross.

Bake the buns in a hot oven (200°C/400°F) for about 15 minutes. Remove from oven and brush with Glaze while still hot. Stand the buns in a warm place, like the opened door of a turned-off oven. This helps to set the glaze. *Makes 16 buns*

To Make the Glaze: Sprinkle gelatine over the water in a small saucepan. When softened, dissolve over a low heat. Add the sugar and stir until dissolved. Remove from heat and brush while warm over the hot buns.

To Make an Icing Cross: If liked, omit the paste cross and decorate with a sweet cross. Mix 1 cup sifted icing sugar with enough hot milk to make a firm consistency, about 2 teaspoons. Fill into an icing bag fitted with a plain tube and pipe crosses on warm buns.

Stollen

• • •

This German bread is rich with butter, eggs, almonds and rum-macerated fruits. It improves with keeping as the fruits help to moisten the dry dough. Once it becomes too dry, it is almost as good cut into slices and toasted back to freshness. The custom of the German frau is to bake two stollens – one for herself and family and one for her neighbour.

Fruit

2 strips of angelica
1/3 cup raisins
1/3 cup currants
1/3 cup glacé cherries, halved
2/3 cup chopped peel
1/3 cup rum
1/2 cup blanched slivered almonds

Yeast Dough

4 cups plain flour
large pinch of salt
1/4 cup warm milk
30 g (1 oz) compressed yeast
125 g (4 oz) butter
1/2 cup caster sugar
2 eggs, lightly beaten

To Finish

melted butter
icing sugar

To prepare the Fruit: Cut strips of angelica into 1 cm (1/2 inch) dice. Place with the remaining fruit in a bowl and pour over the rum. Toss well and allow to stand for 2 hours, preferably overnight. Drain and dry the fruit well on kitchen paper before adding to the yeast dough with the almonds.

To make the Yeast Dough: Sift the flour with salt into a bowl. Place lukewarm milk in a bowl, add the yeast and butter and stir until yeast is dissolved and then mix in sugar and eggs.

Make a well in the centre of the flour, pour in the yeast mixture and mix until smooth, commencing with a wooden spoon and then finishing off with the hand. When dough leaves sides of the bowl, turn on to a lightly floured board and knead until smooth and elastic – this may take 10–15 minutes.

Place dough into a clean greased bowl, cover with a damp cloth and place in a warm spot until doubled in quantity – approximately 50 minutes to 1 hour.

Knock down dough and shape into a square. Spoon the rum-soaked fruits, which have been well dried and tossed in a little flour, together with the almonds, into the middle of the square. Fold dough over the fruits. Knead fruits lightly into the dough. Place into a greased bowl, cover and leave in a warm place to rise for 30–45 minutes.

Punch dough down and turn on to a floured board. Roll out into an oblong 38 × 23 cm (15 × 9 inch). Fold into three lengthwise, overlapping the centre with each edge by about 2.5 cm (1 inch). Press edges gently to keep in place. Lightly flour hands, taper ends slightly and pat sides to mound stollen in the centre.

The finished loaf should be about 8 cm (3 inch) wide. Place on a greased baking tray, brush with a little melted butter and stand in a warm place for about 1 hour or until doubled in bulk.

Bake in a moderately hot oven (190°C/375°F) for about 45 minutes or until golden brown and crusty. Cool on a wire rack. Dust Stollen heavily with sifted icing sugar before slicing and buttering.

Tea Ring

• • •

½ quantity Basic Sweet Rich Dough (see page 329)
30 g (1 oz) softened butter
¼ cup caster sugar
⅓ cup raisins
2 teaspoons ground cinnamon

To decorate

Icing (see page 330)
walnut halves
glacé cherries
angelica

Turn the risen dough on to a floured surface and roll out to an oblong about 1 cm (½ inch) thick. Dot the surface with softened butter and sprinkle with the sugar, raisins and cinnamon. Roll dough up tightly, beginning at longer side, and seal by pinching edges well together. Curl dough into a ring, joining ends together well, and place on a greased baking tray. Using scissors or a sharp knife, snip the ring at 2.5 cm (1 inch) intervals around the outside edge, making each cut or snip two-thirds through the dough. Cover with a cloth and leave to prove for 15–20 minutes. Set oven temperature to moderately hot (190°C/375°F).

Bake in a moderately hot oven for about 25 minutes, until golden brown. Test if cooked by inserting a fine skewer; it should come out clean.

Make a thin icing and brush over the ring while still warm, then decorate with nuts, cherries and angelica.

INDIAN BREADS

A special treat in India, breads come in different shapes and sizes; some are baked in a tandoori clay oven, some on a hot griddle, and some are fried to a round golden puff. All are wholesome, being made with whole grain flour, and all are delicious.

Chapatis and Puris are two Indian unleavened breads you can make at home. The light texture of both is obtained by kneading the dough until elastic.

Indian breads are not usually served at the same time as rice. They are delicious with dry types of curry; simply break a piece off and use it to scoop up some of the curry. Skewered foods (not only Indian) are often served inside a folded Chapati and eaten like a hamburger.

Puris

• • •

Puri is a round, light and hollow, fried wheatmeal bread. The secret of making the Puris 'puff' depends on the oil being hot before you start frying. This can be done in a Chinese wok (frying pan); it is the closest thing to an Indian Karahi, a round pan used for frying. Break off a piece and use it to scoop up a quantity of curry or dhal. Wheatmeal flour and the roti flour used in Chapatis are available from large grocery stores and many health food shops. Wheatmeal flour is different from wholemeal flour, although this particular recipe may be made with wholemeal.

1½ cups plain wheatmeal flour
1 cup self-raising flour
1 teaspoon salt
1 teaspoon ghee or butter
1 cup warm water
oil for frying

Sift flours and salt. Rub in the ghee or butter, then add the warm water and mix to a stiff dough. Knead for several minutes. The dough should be smooth and elastic. Cover and leave for 15 minutes. The dough should spring back into shape when pressed with a fingertip.

Divide dough into 12 equal portions. Shape each portion into a ball and roll out fairly thinly on a lightly floured board.

Heat 2.5 cm (1 inch) of oil in a deep frying pan and when smoking hot fry each puri, separately and quickly. If oil does not cover puri, splash top with oil. Turn so that puri is well-fried on both sides.

When golden brown drain well on crumpled kitchen paper. Serve hot. *Makes 12 puris*

Chapatis

• • •

Serve Chapatis with curries. Break off a piece of bread and use it to scoop up the curry. In India this is an important part of a vegetarian meal, often served with a vegetable purée or Dhal.

2 cups fine wheatmeal or roti flour
1 teaspoon salt
1 tablespoon ghee or peanut oil
1 cup lukewarm water

Place flour in a bowl, reserving ½ cup. Add salt to the flour. Rub in ghee or add oil. Make a well in the centre and add the water all at once, mixing with one hand to form a dough. Knead dough for at least 10 minutes. Wrap in plastic and chill for at least 1 hour. It is preferable to chill dough overnight for a lighter Chapati.

Shape dough into 12 to 14 small balls about the size of a large walnut. Roll out each one on a lightly floured board, using reserved flour, to a round 13 cm (5 inch) in diameter. Heat a heavy frying pan until a drop of water will spit on the pan. Place Chapati in pan and press edge with a folded tea-towel to encourage bubbles to form and make the Chapati light. Cook for 1 minute and turn to cook the other side. Wrap each in a tea-towel as soon as it is cooked. Serve hot to accompany dry curries or vegetable dishes. *Makes 12 to 14 chapatis*

Poppadams

•

These lentil wafers are available in many varieties and are a popular addition to the curry table. Fry one at a time in a little hot oil for only a few seconds until pale gold. Drain on crumpled absorbent paper and serve immediately, or they can be stored in an airtight container until required. Heat in an oven bag in a moderate oven (180°C/350°F) before serving.

BREAD MAKING

Why do people make their own bread? Simply because they like it better than any they can buy. It's cheaper too, but that's incidental to the pleasure and interest of bread making. If your first attempts are not all that great, take heart, it is one branch of baking where practice makes perfect. Once you've made bread a few times, it becomes second nature and a job you look forward to. You have the choice of white, wholemeal, fine-textured or crunchy; it can be salt encrusted or coated with nutty grain.

Bake bread in tins or shape a cottage loaf – it's fun deciding what to bake and how to vary your loaves.

Household Bread

• • •

1.5 kg (3 lb) plain flour
1 tablespoon salt
30 g (1 oz) compressed yeast
1 teaspoon sugar
3¾ cups tepid water

Grease three 23 cm (9 inch) loaf or bread tins.

Sift flour with salt into a large warmed mixing bowl. Place yeast in a small bowl and sprinkle with the sugar. Stir gently until the yeast is liquid, then blend in a little of the tepid water

and allow it to sponge. Make a well in the centre of the flour and pour in the yeast mixture, mixed with the remaining water. With a wooden spoon stir in enough of the surrounding flour to make a thick batter and dust this thickly with some flour in the bowl. Cover with a damp cloth and leave in a warm place for 15 minutes to 'sponge', until the yeast breaks through.

Draw the remaining flour into the yeast mixture, using first the wooden spoon, then your hand. When the mixture is thoroughly incorporated turn on to a floured surface and knead well for about 10 minutes until smooth and elastic. Place in an oiled bowl, then turn the dough over so that the top is lightly oiled. Cover with a damp cloth and leave to rise in a warm place until doubled in bulk, about 1–1½ hours.

Turn dough on to a floured surface; cut into three pieces and shape into loaves, kneading lightly. Set each piece in the prepared loaf tin, cover again with a damp cloth and leave in a warm place to prove until the sides of the dough reach the top of the tin and the centre is well rounded, about 15 minutes.

Bake in a very hot oven (230°C/450°F) for 30–40 minutes. When done, the bread will shrink slightly from the sides of the tin and will sound hollow if the bottom is tapped after being turned out. Turn out and cool on a wire rack. *Makes 3 loaves*

Variations

★ For a fine wholemeal bread, follow the basic bread recipe using 1 kg (2 lb) wholemeal flour and 500 g (1 lb) plain white flour.

★ For a grainy wholemeal, use 750 g (1½ lb) wholemeal flour, 250 g (8 oz) wheatmeal (fine or medium, as you prefer), and 500 g (1 lb) plain white flour. Add an extra ½–1 cup of warm water for this combination as the wheatmeal absorbs a lot more liquid.

★ The basic dough can be formed into various shapes; try making a round loaf, or baking the bread straight on the baking tray without the use of tins. When baking three loaves on a baking tray, bake them together, giving them support in baking so that they rise without the tendency to spread. This recipe can also be made into rolls; just divide the mixture into small rounds and bake for 10–15 minutes.

★ The topping may be varied – for a crisp crust, brush with cold water and repeat several times during baking. For a golden shiny crust brush with a little beaten egg; for a cottage loaf dust the bread lightly with flour; for a rich crust brush with melted butter.

★ Coarse salt, poppy, sesame or caraway seeds, or coarse crushed wheat sprinkled over the bread before baking make good flavour changes.

Breakfast Rolls

• • •

Some of the best breakfast rolls are those made in Scotland, known locally as Baps or, in some parts, Butteries. In old recipes for these the dough is generally left to rise all night, involving kitchen activity late in the evening. It is kneaded, then left to rise, ready for shaping and proving, for freshly baked rolls to have at breakfast. Today the dough may be left to prove slowly overnight in the refrigerator.

4 cups plain flour
1 teaspoon salt
¾ cup water
½ cup milk
60 g (2 oz) butter
15 g (½ oz) compressed yeast
1 teaspoon sugar

Sift flour with salt into a large warmed bowl. Heat the water, milk and butter until the butter has melted without boiling. Cool to lukewarm.

Sprinkle yeast with sugar and leave a few minutes until the yeast has become liquid. Stir dissolved yeast into milk and butter mixture. Make a well in the centre of flour and pour in the liquid. Stir in a little of the flour from the side until it is the consistency of a thick batter. Cover with a folded cloth and place in a warm spot to sponge. When yeast mixture has doubled and bubbles have formed, mix in all the flour.

Turn on to a floured board and knead until the dough is smooth and elastic, about 5 minutes. Place in a clean, greased bowl and turn dough over so that the top surface is lightly greased. Cover with a cloth and leave in a warm place for about 2 hours or until well risen and doubled in bulk or leave in the refrigerator overnight. Knock down dough and turn on to a floured board. Knead lightly, divide dough into 12 pieces and shape each into a round ball. Place on to a greased baking tray, cover and allow to prove in a warm place for about 15 minutes. Bake in a hot oven (200°C/400°F) for 12–15 minutes or until a pale golden. Serve hot or cold with butter. *Makes 12 generous rolls*

Note: If refrigerating overnight, remove and warm slightly before final kneading and shaping into buns.

Scones

• •

A light quick hand is what is needed for scones; overmixing will toughen the dough.

2 cups self-raising flour
1 teaspoon salt
60 g (2 oz) butter
1 cup milk, soured with ½ teaspoon lemon juice

Set oven temperature to very hot (230°C/450°F). Lightly grease a baking tray.

Sift flour and salt into a bowl. Rub in the butter. Make a well in centre and add the milk in a steady, quick stream, quickly taking in the flour to the centre and adding more milk if necessary to make a soft dough. Form into a ball with your hand, then turn out and knead lightly on a floured board and roll out to 2 cm (¾ inch) thickness. Cut into rounds with a floured cutter. Place on prepared tray. Brush tops with a little milk and bake in a very hot oven for 10–15 minutes. Serve warm with butter or jam and cream. *Makes 12 scones*

Cheese Scone Loaf

• •

Many a countrywoman's answer to what to make when there's no fresh bread.

3 cups self-raising flour
1 teaspoon salt
¼ teaspoon cayenne pepper
60 g (2 oz) butter
125 g (4 oz) Cheddar cheese, grated
1 cup milk, soured with ½ teaspoon lemon juice

Grease a baking tray and set oven temperature to hot (200°C/400°F).

Sift flour, salt and cayenne pepper into a bowl. Rub in the butter. Reserve 2 tablespoons of grated cheese for the top and add remaining cheese to mixture. Make a well in the centre and mix in milk, adding more if necessary to make a soft dough. Knead lightly on a floured board. Place on prepared tray and pat out into a circle 2.5 cm (1 inch) thick. Mark top into eighths with a knife dipped in flour, cutting approximately half-way through the mixture. Brush top with milk and sprinkle with reserved cheese. Bake in a hot oven for 25–30 minutes. Serve warm or cooled, with butter. *Makes 8 wedges*

Right: Country baking has always been popular. From right rear clockwise: Cheese Scone Loaf (above); Gem Scones (page 337); Girdle Scones (Pikelets) (page 337); Honey Nut Roll (page 306) and Scones (above).

Gem Scones

• •

For these little 'gems' you need the special irons that have been part of Australia's cooking scene for generations. Country cooks treasure them, many are passed from mother to daughter. You can use small patty tins, heating them in the oven first.

30 g (1 oz) butter
2 tablespoons sugar
1 egg
pinch of salt
½ cup milk
1 cup self-raising flour

Heat gem irons in a hot oven (200°C/400°F). Cream the butter and sugar. Add the egg, salt and milk and combine with the creamed mixture. Sift flour and fold lightly into the mixture until blended. Have irons very hot and grease well. Spoon mixture in to three-quarters fill each 'cup'. Bake in a hot oven for 10–15 minutes. Serve warm with butter. *Makes 12 gem scones*

Girdle Scones (Pikelets)

• •

An old Scottish scone, formerly cooked on a round 'girdle' suspended over an open fire. This is still a popular, quick, tea-time specialty, made more conveniently over a modern hot plate. A heavy iron frying pan or electric frypan makes a good 'girdle'.

1 cup self-raising flour
½ teaspoon salt
¼ teaspoon bicarbonate of soda
1 tablespoon golden syrup or 2 tablespoons sugar
1 egg, beaten
½ cup milk soured with 1 teaspoon vinegar
(or ½ cup buttermilk)
1 teaspoon butter for greasing

Sift flour, salt and soda into a medium sized bowl. Make a well in the centre, add the golden syrup or sugar, egg and milk. Stir, gradually drawing in flour from the sides to make a smooth batter.

Drop by tablespoons on to a hot, lightly greased girdle or heavy frying pan. Turn over when bubbles appear on top and the bottom is golden brown, then cook the other side. If batter thickens, use a little more milk.

Left: Fruit bottling is a rewarding job, as favourite summer fruits can be enjoyed during the winter months (see page 343).

Cool on a clean tea-towel or napkin, keeping them wrapped until ready to serve. Serve warm or cold with butter, honey or jam. They will keep some time in a tin. They can be heated briefly in a warm oven or micro-wave oven or under a slow grill if preferred warm. *Makes about 16 scones*

Pizza Home Style

• • •

I came across the recipe for this Pizza bread base quite by chance, but friends quickly assured me it was the best they'd ever tasted. To make things easier I discovered I could make it in a breeze in the food processor, blending the flour and yeast and water, then adding the oil in a flowing stream; the kneading was done in short bursts for about 2 to 3 minutes.

Bread Base

30 g (1 oz) compressed yeast
1¼ cups warm water
4 cups flour
1 teaspoon salt
1 cup oil
olive oil for brushing

Topping

4 tomatoes
8 mushrooms
salt
seasoned pepper
8 slices Cheddar or Mozarella cheese
4 tablespoons grated Parmesan cheese

To make the Bread Base Soften the yeast in the warm water. Sift the flour and salt into a warm bowl, make a well in the middle and add the yeast mixture. Mix in with a wooden spoon and knead dough vigorously, adding oil as it becomes sticky. Continue kneading for 15 minutes, roll into a ball, cover and leave in a warm place until doubled in size.

Knock down the dough and divide into four, or two, depending on whether you want four individual pizzas or two to cut into wedges. Knead each into a round shape. Roll into circles about 6 mm (¼ inch) thick. Place on to greased baking sheets, cover and allow to rise in a warm place for about 15 minutes. Brush a little olive oil over each base.

To Make the Topping Peel and slice the tomatoes and slice the mushrooms. Arrange tomatoes over base, top with mushrooms, season well with salt and pepper, top with slices of cheese, then Parmesan. Drizzle a little more oil over.

Bake in a hot oven (200°C/400°F) for 18–20 minutes or until the crust is crispy golden around the edge. Serve immediately. These Pizzas may be taken on a picnic and are still good when warm – even cold! *Makes 4 individual pizzas or 2 larger ones*

V.I.P.'s

very important preserves and pickles

No cookery book would be complete without a few of the lovely preserves, jams, fruit cheeses, sweetmeats and pickles which enhance a kitchen cupboard and add a pleasant touch to many a meal.

Making preserves is a most satisfying occupation for everyone, not just the perogative of country folk. A new generation of city cooks is discovering that a few pots of jam or marmalade and pickled vegetables can be made from a small purchase from the local greengrocer. Today's homes don't usually boast a large larder, but a few carefully made jars of pickles or spiced fruit add great charm to meals – just make them in smaller quantities than the formidable Mrs Beeton suggested.

If you like giving presents that have a personal touch, also consider something from your own kitchen. Many of the recipes here would make delicious Christmas gifts, and of course are also suitable for fetes and other fund-raising occasions. Use your prettiest pots and jars, add a descriptive label and a bright ribbon, and your stall will be among the busiest – that's a promise!

Three Fruit Marmalade

● ●

Did you know Scotland was the first country to put Seville oranges on the gastronomic map when a Scot invented marmalade early in the 18th century? Ever since then, marmalade for his toast is what makes breakfast for any Englishman. Once you get the taste for its sweet tart flavour it seems the most natural way to start the day. When the Seville oranges first come in, use them for marmalade. They are not as sweet as other oranges, but the tart flavour and very bright orange skin gives Seville marmalade its distinctive taste and glorious, red-gold colour. Failing Sevilles, use any fresh new-season orange.

Citrus fruit varies in weight, so allow about 750 g (1½ lb) of fruit to 1.5 kg (3 lb) of sugar.

1 large lemon
1 large grapefruit
1 large orange

Peel the rind from the lemon and discard all the white pith; shred rind finely. Cut the lemon, grapefruit and orange into quarters or halves. Remove centre cores and slice fruit thinly. Save seeds and put in a small bowl. Cover with about ¼ cup water and let stand overnight. At the same time, measure the lemon rind, fruit and any juice. Put in a large bowl and for each cup of fruit add 3 cups of water. Cover and let stand overnight.
Next Day: Put the fruits, rind and water into a large saucepan. Strain the liquid from the seeds into the pan. Simmer gently, uncovered, for about 30 minutes or until the fruit is tender. Cool.

Measure, and for each cup of fruit mixture, allow ¾ cup sugar. Warm the sugar in a low oven. While the sugar is warming, bring the fruit mixture to the boil. Add the warmed sugar and stir gently until dissolved. Bring to a rolling boil and cook rapidly until set when tested (see below). Cool slightly (to prevent the fruit from rising in the jars) and stir once to distribute the fruit evenly.

Ladle into warm dry jars. Moisten clear preserve covers with a cloth dipped in vinegar and cover. Tie down when cool.
To test for setting point: Place a small teaspoon of jam on a saucer and wait 20 seconds, then run a finger through it. If it crinkles at the edges and stays in two separate portions the jam is right for bottling.

Plum Jam

••

Blood plums make a particularly good jam – rich and tart with a brilliant deep colour that enhances desserts, cakes and quick breads. The satsuma is also a good plum for jam, so make a few jars of each when in season.

1 kg (2 lb) blood plums or satsumas
1 kg (2 lb) sugar
butter
¼ cup water

Wash and halve the plums. Remove the stones, crack a few and remove the kernels. Warm sugar on a tray in a low oven. Rub over the base of a preserving pan or heavy saucepan with a little butter. Place the prepared fruit and water in the pan and cook slowly until tender, about 15–20 minutes. Add the warm sugar and heat until the sugar dissolves. Add the kernels. Bring to the boil rapidly and boil vigorously for approximately 20 minutes, until setting point is reached (see below).

At this stage, remove the pan from the heat immediately. Allow to cool a little. Pour into sterilized jars (that have been washed well and set in a warm oven to dry) and seal with cellophane circles and rubber bands. Alternatively, wait until the jam is cold and pour over melted paraffin, tilting the bottles to fill the crevices. Store in a dark, cool place.

To test for setting point: Dip a clean wooden spoon into the jam and hold horizontally in the hand. Hold for a few seconds until the jam on the edge is slightly cooled. At setting point, the jam runs to the centre of the edge and falls in a heavy jelly-like drop or flakes which break distinctly from the spoon.

Apricot Jam

(with Dried Fruit)

••

Apricot is one of the most useful of jams. As well as being a favourite for eating with bread, scones and teacakes it has many uses in finishing off and glazing cakes, biscuits and fruit tarts. The stone fruit season is all too short, but this really doesn't matter as jam made from the dried fruit is just as good – some say even better.

250 g (8 oz) dried apricots
2 lemons
4 cups water
4 cups sugar
6 blanched almonds

Cut each apricot in half. Halve the lemons and squeeze 3 tablespoons of the juice, reserve. Gather the lemon pips and tie in a muslin bag. Soak the apricots and lemon pips in the 4 cups of water for several hours. Put the apricots, pips and water into a saucepan and cook slowly until the fruit is soft and clear. Remove the pips. Warm the sugar in a low oven and add to the fruit with the strained lemon juice. Stir with a wooden spoon until the sugar is dissolved. Boil quickly until setting point is reached (see Plum Jam for spoon method or Three Fruit Marmalade for saucer method). Cool slightly and stir once to distribute the fruit evenly. Ladle into warm dry jars, including one or two almonds in each jar to represent the kernel. Moisten clear preserve covers with a cloth dipped in vinegar and cover, or cover with sterilized screw-on lids. Tie down when cool and label.

Bread and Butter Pickles

••

Try and get the tiny pickling cucumbers for the very best results – failing that use the youngest, freshest cucumbers you can get.

4 cups sliced unpeeled tiny cucumbers
1 large onion, sliced
1 tablespoon salt
1 cup cider vinegar
1 teaspoon celery seeds
1¼ cups sugar
1 teaspoon ground turmeric
1 cinnamon stick
1 teaspoon brown mustard seeds

Mix the cucumbers and onion together and sprinkle with the salt. Cover with ice cubes and cold water, leave 1 hour, then drain. Put the remaining ingredients in a large saucepan and stir over a low heat until the sugar dissolves. Add the cucumbers and onion. Bring to the boil and simmer for 30 minutes stirring occasionally. Pour the mixture into hot, sterilized jars, then seal and cool. Store in a cool place preferably in the refrigerator, where they will keep for several months. If you wish to keep them longer, they should be processed further in the following way. Place a wire rack in the bottom of a large pot, arrange the sealed jars of pickles on the rack, making sure they do not touch. Fill the pot with water so it comes at least 5 cm (2 inch) up the jars and cover with a lid. Bring to the boil and boil for 15 minutes. When cool enough to handle, remove jars from the water, cool, and test seal the next day.

To test seal: Remove clips and hold each jar up by the lid. If the lid holds the jar, the seal is airtight. If not, refrigerate and use within a few months. If the test seal is positive, pickles processed in this manner will keep for 1 year.

Zucchini Pickle

• •

*This delicious pickle goes well with cold pickled pork,
brawn or other cold meats.*

8–10 small zucchini
2 medium onions
¼ cup salt
2¼ cups white vinegar
1 cup sugar
1 teaspoon each celery and mustard seeds
1 teaspoon turmeric
½ teaspoon dry mustard

Wash, trim ends, and very thinly slice the unpeeled zucchini.
Cut the onions in half lengthwise. Cut in half again lengthwise
and in half again, if the onions are large. Onion will now break
apart into 'petals'. Put zucchini and onions into a bowl, cover
with water and add the salt. Allow to stand for 1 hour, then
drain.

Mix the remaining ingredients and bring to the boil. Pour
over the zucchini and onion, allow to stand for 1 hour. Bring
the mixture to the boil and cook for 3 minutes. Pack into 3
sterilised jars to within 1 cm (½ inch) of the top. Seal.
Note: The pickle can be stored, covered, and will keep for
several months in the refrigerator.

Spiced Pickled Onions

• •

*There's hardly a soul who doesn't love pickled
onions! Good ones are certainly 'more-ish' and add zest to
many casual meals.*

1 kg (2 lb) small white onions
⅓ cup salt
2 cups white vinegar
⅔ cup water
⅓ cup sugar
1 tablespoon pickling spice
1 red chilli (optional)
1 teaspoon salt

In a large bowl soak the onions in boiling water to cover for
15 minutes. Drain and peel. Return onions to bowl and soak in
water to cover with ⅓ cup of salt for 48 hours (cover bowl with
plastic wrap). Drain and rinse onions. In a large heavy
saucepan bring the vinegar, water, sugar, pickling spice, chilli
and 1 teaspoon of salt to the boil. Add onions and cook the
mixture for 5 minutes. Divide the onions between sterilized
preserving jars and add hot spiced vinegar to cover. Seal jars
with lids and let them stand in a cool place for at least 2 weeks.
Sealed, they will keep indefinitely.

Glacé Cumquats

• • •

*The cumquat tree is becoming quite commonplace in many
gardens and although brandied cumquats are
delicious there are some cheaper and still excellent ways
of using them. When I gather about 12–18 from the
tree, I like to make glacé cumquats.*

Using a fine skewer, pierce about eight times into the skin of
each cumquat. Place in a bowl, cover with water, leave
overnight, then drain. Put into pan with fresh water to cover,
bring to the boil and simmer until tender, about 30 minutes.
Drain and put in a heavy syrup to cover. Make the syrup using
500 g (1 lb) sugar to every 2½ cups water. Cook cumquats in the
syrup until clear and transparent. Put in a bowl and stand
overnight. Drain the syrup into a saucepan, add ¼ cup sugar,
bring to boil and pour over the cumquats. Leave for 48 hours.
Repeat this process once more, adding another ¼ cup sugar,
and leaving a further 48 hours. Lastly, drain from the syrup,
roll in coarse sugar and place on a wire cake rack to dry,
preferably in a very slow oven. Store in an airtight container in
a cool place. Serve in small confectionary paper cases or use to
flavour ice-cream or decorate creamy desserts. Glacé cumquats
are delicious with after dinner coffee!

Brandied Cumquats

• • •

*If you have a decorative cumquat tree, the thought of
Cumquat Liqueur is irresistible. It's easy to
make, but takes a few months' storage before it is ready to
drink, or be used to flavour desserts, drinks, custards
or ice cream. The cumquats may be eaten as a dessert with ice
cream or cream or served as a sweetmeat. They
may be dipped in chocolate to serve with coffee, and perhaps
the accompanying Cumquat Liqueur – a double
delight from your little tree.*

20 cumquats
500 g (1 lb) sugar
1 stick cinnamon
1 bottle brandy

Using a darning needle lightly prick the cumquats in several
places. Place in layers sprinkled with the sugar in a wide
mouthed jar, and allow to stand overnight until the sugar has
become impregnated with the oils and juice of the fruit.

The next day add the cinnamon stick and enough brandy to
fill the jar. Close with a lid, preferably a preserving jar with
clamp-on lid, and allow it to rest on its side, shaking it gently
every few days to distribute the sugar until it has completely
dissolved. Allow to lie undisturbed for at least 2 months. Strain
off the liquor, reserving the cumquats. The fruit is now very
strongly perfumed with brandy and may be served as a dessert

with ice cream, or dried well and rolled in sugar, or dipped in melted chocolate. Serve the liquor as Cumquat Liqueur.

To Dry Cumquats: Using the cumquats from the liquor, drain from all syrup on a wire cake cooler, place in a slow oven or in a warming oven to dry out. This may take several hours, or even half a day. Roll fruit in coarse sugar when half dried if liked. Serve in small paper (confectionary) containers as a sweetmeat. If liked, dip in melted chocolate to coat the fruit.

Brandied Cherries

• • •

Here today, gone tomorrow. Sad but true, cherries know such a short but sweet season. So put some by and enjoy them out of season.

1 cup sugar
1 cup water
1 strip lemon peel
1.5 kg (3 lb) dark cherries, stoned
brandy

Make a syrup with sugar, water and lemon peel. Bring slowly to the boil, stirring until the sugar has dissolved and then boil for 10 minutes. Add the cherries and cook gently for 5 minutes.

Pack into warm sterilized jars, half fill with brandy and top with syrup. Seal jars straight away. Store in a dark cool place for at least 1 month.

Variations

A few whole cloves, a piece of vanilla pod or a small cinnamon stick may be placed in the jar with the cherries.

Brandied Cherries in Wine Half fill a wine glass with some Brandied Cherries and some of their liquor. Fill up with chilled red wine. Serve with a crisp, macaroon-type biscuit.

Passionfruit Cheese

• •

Everyone knows lemon cheese. Passionfruit cheese is very similar – soft, creamy and delicious.

60 g (2 oz) butter
4 passionfruit
2 egg yolks
½ cup sugar

Melt butter in the top of a double boiler or in a bowl over a pan of gently simmering water. Add the passionfruit pulp, egg yolks and sugar. Using a wooden spoon stir over a gentle heat until the mixture has thickened. Allow to cool and pour into a clean jar. Seal with waxed paper or plastic wrap. Use as a filling for sponge cakes, pastry tarts and butterfly cakes or as a spread on bread.

Spiced Prunes

• •

This preserve can be made at any time, and can be eaten 24 hours after making. It is very good with cold pork, or warmed and served with roast fillet or ribs of beef.

500 g (1 lb) prunes
4 cups freshly brewed tea
1 lemon
2 cups red wine vinegar
1 cup sugar
1 teaspoon mixed pickling spice (tied in muslin)

Soak prunes overnight in the cooled tea. Next day drain and place in a pan with half the remaining soaking liquid. Cover and cook for 10–15 minutes or until the prunes are tender, then drain and reserve the cooking liquor. Thinly pare the rind from the lemon and put with the vinegar, sugar and spices in to a clean pan. Boil for 5 minutes, add 1¼ cups of the reserved cooking liquor and return to the boil. Remove spices and lemon rind and pour the liquid over the prunes. Put into warm, dry jars and cover at once.

Pickled Dried Figs

•

Pickled figs are good with cold meats such as pork, ham and roast mutton.

500 g (1 lb) dried figs
1¼ cups white wine vinegar
125 g (4 oz) sugar
2.5 cm (1 inch) stick cinnamon
4 cloves
3 allspice berries

Place figs in a pan, cover with cold water, bring to the boil and simmer for 15 minutes. Drain off water and add the vinegar, sugar and spices, which have been tied in a muslin bag, to the figs. Simmer for another 15 minutes, then remove the bag of spices and pour into hot sterilized jars. Seal immediately.

Quince Cheese

(Quince Paste)

• • •

One of the most delicious sweetmeats to have on hand is a thick cheese or paste made from the fruit of quince. This tart and astringent fruit with a very sweet smell is full of pectin which 'sets' the cooked fruit. If you own an electric slow-cooker the whole fruit may be cooked on a low temperature overnight, or cook it in an oven — aim for slow cooking to develop a rich amethyst colour.
Served as part of a cheese board, it is particularly good with fresh soft cheeses (see desserts, page 279 and 280), fresh goat's or sheep's or homemade cream cheese.

6 quinces
½ cup water
white sugar

Rub the quinces with a cloth to remove the down. Put them whole and unpeeled into a moderate oven (180°C/350°F) and cook until tender, about 3 hours; or quarter them (do not peel), remove seeds and steam them in the small amount of water. The quinces should become a deep amethyst colour and should be soft but not breaking up.

When they are cool enough to handle, slice them (without peeling) into a bowl, discarding the cores and any bruised or hard pieces. Put the sliced fruit through a food mill or sieve. Weigh the purée and add an equal weight of white sugar. Boil in a heavy pan, stirring nearly all the time until the cheese begins to candy and come away from the bottom as well as the sides of the pan. Use a long-handled wooden spoon for stirring. The boiling paste erupts and spits so take care.

Turn off the heat and continue stirring until the boiling has ceased. Fill shallow rectangular earthenware or tin dishes or one dish with the cheese, and leave to get quite cold. Next day put these moulds into the lowest possible oven until the cheese has dried out and is quite firm, about 3 to 4 hours, although it may take longer. On bright sunny days it may be left in the sun to dry out.

Turn out the slabs of paste and cut into portions you are likely to use at one time. Wrap them in greaseproof or plastic film or foil, and store in tins in a dry place.
Note: For the cheese board the quince cheese may be cut into small pieces. Guests help themselves as with the milk cheeses.

Variation

Quince Sweetmeats Prepare Quince Cheese and cut into squares or oblong shapes, or roll into walnut-size balls. Toss in caster sugar to coat and set in tiny paper cups or wrap in cellophane paper.

Serve with coffee and sweet fortified wine or simply offer as a sweetmeat at any time.

Marzipan Stuffed Prunes

• •

With a few small preserving jars on hand you have the beginnings of a truly individual gift from your kitchen — this delicious sweetmeat of prunes is first stuffed with marzipan then soaked in your favourite spirit or fortified wine. Serve 2 or 3 on small plates with some of the liquor and a small spoon, or use 1 or 2 to top ice cream. The remaining liquor may be used to flavour desserts or ice cream or simply drunk as a liqueur.

500 g (1 lb) dessert prunes
2 cups strong tea, freshly brewed
200 g packet good marzipan
brandy and port

Soak the prunes in the tea for several hours. Drain, make a slit in the prunes, and remove the stones.

Soften the marzipan with a little brandy or port or both if you like. Mould into small oval shapes and use to fill the prunes. Pack into two, 2 cup size sterilized jars. Fill jars with brandy or port or a combination of both. Cover and clamp on lids with rubbers to seal.

Store in a cool place for at least 2 weeks. The prunes will keep indefinitely.

FRUIT BOTTLING

The stone fruit season is all too short. It used to signal a busy time ahead for those intrepid souls who, like me, were bent on capturing the harvest. My family, young and old, were pressed into duty as case after case of peaches, apricots, plums and cherries were carefully packed then processed in gleaming jars. It was a frenzied time, to say the least.

Today I am content to put a few dozen bottles down. For this I find the oven method is most convenient. No special equipment or outsized pans are required, the whole operation can fit in between other jobs, yet it affords me the luxury of offering peaches or cherries out of season.

Bottled fruits retain their natural flavour, colour and texture and are ideal for serving chilled with their own syrup or in pies and tarts or in favourite dessert recipes. Included as fruit are tomatoes.

Successful fruit bottling depends on efficient sterilization – by this is meant that anything that will cause the fruit to ferment or turn mouldy must be killed by heat. This can be done in an oven. It is most important to have good preserving jars, and there is a wide choice. Take care of them, particularly when opening jars; don't probe them unduly with knives or sharp instruments, any chip will render the jars useless for later processing.

To Bottle Fruit in the Oven

The procedure of sterilizing bottled fruit in the oven is one of the simplest of all methods. The oven method is convenient when only small quantities of fruit are to be processed.

Choice of Fruit

All fruits are suitable for bottling but because of their short season stone and berry fruits are particular favourites.

Fruit should be prepared as for stewing. Apricots, plums and peaches are halved and the stones removed. To remove skins of peaches, plunge into boiling water, count to 10, then cool in iced water and the skins should slip off easily. Pears are peeled and halved, pineapples are trimmed and sliced. Berry fruits are washed lightly and drained, and so on. Tomatoes are left whole to be preserved in salted water, or softened tomatoes can be turned into tomato juice.

There are a few basic rules.
★ Preserve only choice and sound fruit.
★ Prepare small quantities at a time.
★ Ensure that jars and rubbers are sterile, wash in hot soapy water, rinse in boiling water.
★ Check all jars to be used, to make sure these are free from flaws.
★ Use only new rubber rings, not old ones.

Steps to Oven Bottling

1. Preheat oven to 120°C (240°F). Slow cooking of the fruit is required. If the fruit cooks too quickly it will burst, go pulpy and lose its shape.
2. Pack fruit prepared as described in Choice of Fruit above into the bottles. The fruit will shrink during cooking, so jars must be well filled.
3. Stand the bottles on an asbestos mat or baking sheet on a shelf in the lower half of the oven. Jars must not touch each other. Put on lids of jars, but not the rubber rings, and do not clip on.
4. Leave the fruit in the oven until it looks cooked, has shrunk and changed colour slightly. This normally takes 45 minutes to 1 hour. Pears and tomatoes need 1½ hours in the oven.
5. Prepare the syrup (see below) and when required, bring back to boiling point. Remove one bottle from the oven and stand on a double thickness of kitchen towel or tea-towel.
6. Have rubber rings soaking in water, place rubber ring on the lid of the jar. Add boiling syrup to fill the jar, until it just overflows. Clip jar tightly.
7. Allow jar to cool and repeat step 6 with the remaining jars. The procedure is the same for tomatoes except that salted water or tomato juice replaces the syrup.
8. The next day test the seal; remove or release the clip, hold jar by the lid, if the lid stays on your jars are airtight. If not, use the contents within a few days or reprocess.
Note: It is very important to perform the steps as quickly as possible, and with one jar only at a time.

Sugar Syrup

The syrup should be made while the fruit is heating in the oven. Half to three-quarters of a cup of syrup will be needed for each ½ litre (2 cup) jar. The strength of the syrup is largely a matter of personal taste, but a guide to quantities is:
Light Syrup: 1 cup sugar to 3 cups water
Medium Syrup: 2 cups sugar to 3 cups water
Heavy Syrup: 3 cups sugar to 3 cups water
Figs require a heavy syrup, while apples are better done in a light syrup, but for most fruits use a medium syrup.

Variations

Brandied Fruit: For special occasions, brandied fruit is really superb. Fill jars of fruit 3 parts full or more with syrup, top up with brandy, cover and clamp to seal.
Bottling in Water: Home-bottled fruit is excellent for diabetic people and dieters. Simply use boiling water instead of syrup. The best size to use are ½ litre jars. If desired, the fruit may be sweetened before serving with artificial sweeteners.

Rhubarb is considered particularly good for diabetics and dieters. Peaches, pears, apricots, pineapples, plums, figs and quinces are also very suitable for bottling in water.

THE FINAL TOUCH

It is an art and a pleasure to make good food; it is another to present it well. I am not about to urge you to turn out every meal with fancy touches, or indeed to present any food, ever, with that dreaded over-trimmed look – but the difference between food with flair and food that looks ordinary is, very often, a knowing final touch.

A few pointers to garnishing: one telling effect is better than garnish spotted here and there – lemon twists or overlapping slices marching down the centre of a fish, not spaced round the edges; parsley or watercress in a single generous bouquet, not dotted about in sprigs. There is a place for clever chefs' tricks when they're used in a bold and stylish way, like the tomato rose photographed on page 122, but in general, work with the beauty of natural shapes, colours and textures. Just as accessories should suit the style and mood of clothes, garnish should suit the style of the dish – roughly chopped parsley and chunky croûtons for a hearty peasant soup, but parsley as fine as moss and tiny croûtons for an elegant soup.

Purists insist that every garnish should be something you would eat with the dish, but I like to feel freer than that. A sense of fun is an asset, but avoid the ridiculous. Look at food with the eye of the artist – that's the key word to the final touch.

Here is a check list of ideas. We begin with the Big Two:

Parsley chopped, bunched or in sprigs. You will use chopped parsley more readily if you keep a supply at hand: chop a cupful or more at a time (the food processor is brilliant for this) and store in a screw-top jar in the refrigerator. Fried parsley is good with deep-fried foods: place well-dried sprigs in a frying basket or sieve and plunge into very hot oil for a few seconds. Remove while still green and crisp and drain on crumpled paper towels. Single leaves of flat Italian parsley, overlapped in a row, make a decorative finish for small food such as breast of chicken.

Lemons or limes slices, wedges, halves or the zest, grated or in julienne strips. Slices of lime on the larger slices of lemon give lovely colour. Twists add height to a dish: cut from edge to centre of a thin slice and twist the two sides of the slit in opposite directions to make a 'foot' so that the slice can stand up. Wedges of lemon or lime must have the centre rib removed so that they will squeeze without squirting, cut the rib off flat or in a little wedge. Sorbets, mousses and fish pâtés are glamorous in hollowed-out lemon shells. Oranges may be used in the above way. Remove *all* seeds from citrus garnishes.

Fruits and flowers plain or sugared strawberries, grapes, raspberries or redcurrants; sugared rose petals, violets, borage flowers, mint leaves (see page 277 for the way to sugar fruits or flowers); glacé fruits or crystallized peel. Use glacé cherries either whole or halved – to quote a Cordon Bleu teacher, 'quarters or pieces are tea-shoppey'. Bright red cherries with their stems are available in a Maraschino syrup. They look very festive on the right dish.

Nuts walnuts, hazelnuts, almonds, pine nuts, pistachios, pecans, cashews, peanuts – whole, flaked, slivered, chopped or toasted.

Herbs charming in sprays as well as chopped and sprinkled. A small bouquet of mixed herbs gives a rustic, wholesome air to a board or platter of cheeses, breads or meats.

Vegetables radish, the root ends nipped off and all leaves except one or two tiny ones removed; spring onions, celery or gherkins sliced across as usual or, more interestingly, shredded on the long diagonal into slivers; latticed strips of canned red pimiento; red or green capsicum rings or shreds; asparagus tips; capers; cherry tomatoes. A showy flourish for a buffet table is made by threading two metal skewers with decorative vegetables and spearing them, V-fashion, into a large 'piece' such as a cold bird. Place the smallest vegetables at the top next to the ring end and be creative with the lovely design and colour of radish, patty pan squash, mushrooms, Brussels sprouts, small tomatoes or whatever inspires you; end with a half lemon, orange or capsicum, these may be cut in vandyke (zigzag) pattern. Polish the vegetables by rubbing lightly with oiled palms, if you like.

Mayonnaise, Flavoured Butter swirl from a spoon or little dobs; piped rosettes or slices cut from a roll of chilled flavoured butter.

Leaves lettuce leaves including the pretty mignonette, cos, witloof or Belgian endive, curly endive and Chinese cabbage, are just the beginning; nasturtium, vine, strawberry, ivy, citrus and rose leaves all work well – give them sheen with the merest fingertip stroking of oil if you wish; feathery dill and fennel are naturals with fish and bay leaves look well on pâté; scented geranium leaves make delightful bases for cheese on a board.

Sprinkles grated cheese; sieved hard-boiled egg yolk; chopped parsley; chives and other herbs; coconut, toasted or plain; paprika; chopped nuts; sifted icing sugar; caster sugar. For a stylish effect, you may lay strips of paper across the dish before sprinkling so that the garnish will appear in bands.

Cream swirls or rosettes of whipped cream; a spoonful of sour cream mixed with brown sugar is perfect on fruit; a spoonful of sour cream, lightly salted, floated on soup; pouring cream swirled through soup in a marbled pattern.

Chocolate caraque or curls, see page 295.

Watercress classically used as a bouquet. Gather stems one at a time into one hand as if you were gathering primroses or violets, then pull the bottom of the bunch down so that the leafy tops are touching your hand, hold firmly and cut stems off as short as possible. Hold your hand where you want to place the garnish and open it, and the watercress will fall into a natural-looking clump. If preparing bouquets beforehand, secure with a rubber band and stand in a bowl of water until required, then it is a simple matter to take out a bouquet for garnish or salads.

Mushrooms whole, quartered or sliced. Whole caps may be fluted: use very firm, white, fresh caps and a very sharp, pointed small knife. Hold the cap in one hand and the knife against the centre of the mushroom in the other hand. Using the thumb of the knife hand as a pivot, rotate the cap towards you so that the mushroom 'cuts itself' in a slanting strip against the blade. Continue evenly all round. To quarter or slice, trim stem even with or a little beyond the cap and cut downwards to make umbrella shapes. Slices look pretty overlapped in a row.

Croûtons cubed, round or heart-shaped. Cut from bread a day or two old and fry in clarified butter or oil until golden brown. Drain on crumpled paper towels. For heart-shaped croûtons, remove the crust from a sandwich loaf and cut bread diagonally into triangular halves along the complete length. Cut a groove the length of the bread in the centre of the longest side of the triangle, then trim the corners to make a heart shape. Slice 6 mm (¼ inch) thick into croûtons.

Olives black or green, lightly oiled for gloss. Slices of pimiento-stuffed olives are colourful and can make a row of 'flowers' with parsley leaves.

WORDS YOU SHOULD KNOW

Not even the most experienced cooks are familiar with all the vocabulary of the kitchen. Many words are self-explanatory, like dust – to sprinkle lightly with sugar, flour etc.; others are not. We all know what a kiss is, but when it is used in a culinary sense it is a small bite-sized piece of candy or two small meringues or biscuits joined together, in a 'kiss' of course. Duchess not only denotes a grand lady, at the table it describes a purée of potato and egg yolk.

It's fun to play around with the language of the kitchen, it's not fun when you are making a dish and you don't know what a term means, or don't observe correctly any instruction. Here are a few words you should know.

Baste To spoon or brush melted butter, fat or other liquid over food as it cooks.

Beurre Manié (kneaded butter) Butter blended with flour and used to thicken sauces, casseroles etc. at the end of cooking. Place soft butter in a small bowl and mix in flour in the proportion of ¼ cup flour to 60 g (2 oz) butter. Place a small piece on the end of a whisk and beat it into the simmering liquid. It will thicken almost immediately. Add more beurre manié, small piece by small piece, in the same manner until the required consistency is reached. Many cooks keep a small covered jar of beurre manié in the refrigerator for emergencies.

Bind To hold together; egg holds raw minced meat together for a hamburger, meat loaf or terrine. The foods to be bound together should be combined with a light touch.

Blanch Literally 'to whiten', but used in cooking to mean:

1. To remove the skin of certain foods. Almonds, peaches, tomatoes and tongue are blanched by covering with boiling water for a given time then slipping the loosened skin off with the fingers. Hazelnuts and pistachios are blanched by roasting at 180°C (350°F) for 10 minutes then rubbing the skins off in a cloth.

2. To firm and whiten meats (sweetbreads, brains, rabbit, veal) or to remove undesirably strong flavour from meats or vegetables (bacon, onion). The food is placed into cold water to cover, brought to the boil and sometimes simmered for a given time, then drained and plunged into cold water before cooking.

3. To brighten the colour and partially cook vegetables, especially green ones, or to retard enzyme activity in fruits and vegetables before freezing. The food is plunged into rapidly boiling water for a given time, drained and then plunged into cold water ('refreshed') before further cooking or freezing.

Boiling, Simmering, Poaching It is important to understand the difference between these three stages of heating a liquid, and to use the one specified in a recipe. Foods that are boiled when they should be poached or simmered are likely to toughen or to fall apart, while White Chicken (page 141) *must* be plunged into rapidly boiling water so that it will be sealed immediately, it is then 'steeped' (see below).
Boiling: A liquid is boiling when bubbles rise vigorously to the surface; it is boiling rapidly when the surface is rolling and seething with bubbles.
Simmering: A liquid is simmering when the surface shudders and bubbles rise one at a time.
Poaching: A liquid is at poaching temperature when the surface shivers but no bubbles appear (in a clear liquid, bubbles can be seen on the bottom but they do not rise).

Bouquet Garni A bundle or 'faggot' of herbs and aromatics for flavouring soups, stocks and casseroles. The classic formula is 3 or 4 parsley stalks, 1 small bay leaf, 1 large sprig of thyme, 1 piece of celery about 8 cm (3 inch) long and 1 or 2 strips of leek, but the ingredients may be varied according to the requirements of the dish. The ingredients are made into a bundle with the herbs on the inside and tightly tied with white string, with a long enough 'tail' to tie to the handle of the pan for easy removal at the end of cooking. Unless otherwise instructed, if a bouquet garni is called for in any of the recipes in this book, the above ingredients should be used.

Butter and Oil Often specified for sautéed dishes or shallow frying. The butter, of course, contributes its own fine flavour while the oil, which has a higher smoking point, protects the butter so that the mixture can be heated to a higher temperature without burning. Most oils, like butter, have their own distinctive flavour; the exceptions are peanut and some polyunsaturated oils which are practically tasteless. Heat the pan first, then add the oil and heat and lastly add the butter. Unless otherwise instructed, use equal quantities of butter and oil.

Chine The backbone of an animal. A joint is chined by sawing through this bone, lengthwise, to make it easy for the cook to remove; or it may be left attached but chopped through at intervals so that the joint can be easily carved downward into chops or cutlets.

Clarified Butter Butter from which the milk solids have been removed. It can be heated further than ordinary butter without burning. It is sold as 'ghee' (its name in Indian cooking, where it is extensively used) or you can make it yourself. Cut butter into pieces and heat slowly. When it has melted, a milky residue will sink to the bottom and the clear yellow liquid above it is the clarified butter. Skim off carefully leaving the residue behind. This residue may be added to soups or sauces to enrich them.

Deglaze To simmer stock and/or wine in the pan after roasting or sautéing, having first spooned off the fat. The flavoursome brown bits from the pan are scraped and stirred into the liquid, which may then be used alone or as part of the sauce for the meat.

Degorge, Degorger To draw out bitter juices. Vegetables such as cucumber, eggplant and zucchini are sliced, salted lightly and allowed to stand, from 20 minutes to an hour or so, on a plate set at a slight tilt so that juices drain away. Wash excess salt off before proceeding with recipe.

Emulsion Emulsion sauces are those thickened by the emulsifying action of egg yolk which acts as a 'go-between' to hold together ingredients which are naturally incompatible – vinegar or lemon juice with oil or butter. These are the richest and smoothest of all sauces, whether cold (Mayonnaise) or warm (Hollandaise and Béarnaise).

Flour The single word 'flour' in a recipe always means plain (wheat) flour. Self-raising flour is always specified fully, as are cornflour and rice flour.

Fold, Stir, Beat, Whisk All methods of mixing, but each different in the action used and in its effect.

Fold: to blend ingredients or mixtures delicately together with a sharp-edged implement (a rubber or plastic spatula or better still a large metal folding spoon), using a gentle cutting and turning motion and leading with the edge.

Stir: to combine ingredients or keep a mixture moving with a circular or figure eight movement reaching right to the sides and bottom of the container.

Beat: to mix foods vigorously and thoroughly, using a spoon, fork, hand rotary beater, wire whisk or electric beater at low to medium speed. If using a hand implement, the action is a 'hitting' motion in one direction. Beating smooths foods and may also incorporate air.

Whisk, Whip: To incorporate air into an ingredient or mixture, using a fork, hand rotary beater, wire whisk or electric beater at medium to high speed. If using a hand implement, the action is a rapid, vertical, circular motion, keeping the whole mixture moving up and over and around by rotating the bowl or circulating the mixer. Whisking increases volume and makes the food light and puffy because of the air trapped in it.

Infuse To steep ingredients in a liquid in order to flavour it. Tea is one example, the milk for Bechamel sauce another. The flavouring ingredients are removed before the liquid is used.

Julienne Vegetables cut into fine match-stick shreds about 4 cm (1½ inch) long.

Liaison An ingredient or ingredients used to thicken a sauce, gravy, casserole or soup. The best known are roux (fat and flour cooked together), egg yolks, thick sweet or sour cream, yogurt, vegetable or fruit purées, cornflour and beurre manié (see far left).

Mace The lacy outer covering of the nutmeg. It is made up of frond-like tendrils; one tendril, left whole, is a blade. Mace is also available ground.

Nut of Butter A piece of butter the size of an unshelled hazelnut.

Parboil To half-cook food by boiling, before completing cooking by another method. Sausages are parboiled before barbecuing, potatoes and other root vegetables are parboiled before roasting.

Refresh To cool food rapidly by plunging it into cold water or holding under running cold water after cooking or blanching. The cold water bath arrests cooking, sets the colour of green vegetables and 'stiffens' delicate white meats.

Scald To heat a liquid to just under boiling point. To scald milk, heat until bubbles appear around the edge then remove from heat.

Season To improve the flavour of food by the addition of salt, pepper, herbs, spices or other flavourings. If a recipe simply says 'season' without further details, add salt and possibly pepper, according to taste. All seasonings should underline and enhance, not dominate the flavours of the food itself, the correct amount is usually best determined by tasting.

Seasoned Flour Plain flour seasoned with salt and pepper in the proportion of 1 teaspoon salt and ¼ teaspoon pepper to 1 cup of flour. Seasoned flour is used to coat food lightly before frying or as a preliminary to coating with egg and bread-crumbs. The food must be well dried first and the flouring must be done at the last minute as it becomes damp and sticky if allowed to stand.

Shallot See Spring Onion. A member of the lily family; onion, garlic, leek, chives and spring onion are among them. A true shallot grows like an onion, but instead of being one main bulb it is formed more like garlic, with fat cloves or sections which come away easily.

Spring Onion The names spring onion and shallots are used variously – and confusingly – from one area to another to denote different members of the onion family. A spring onion is, correctly, the variety with a small bulb and long green leaves. However, the one with no bulb formation and long green leaves is the one to use where spring onion is specified in this book. For some reason it is the choice of many shoppers and greengrocers, so we made it ours.

Steep To stand in a hot or cold liquid for a given time.

Sweat To cook slowly, without browning, in a little fat in a covered pan. This is often the first stage in making vegetable soups and some sauces and stews or casseroles.

Zest Essential oils are held in the zest or outer rind of citrus fruit. These oils have the concentrated flavour of the fruit and the thin highly coloured rind (no white pith please!) is an accommodating way of presenting it. Grated, or thinly peeled and cut into julienne strips, it adds great zest to many dishes.

INDEX

PDO 79-507